SLEEPY PRINCESS IN THE DEMON CASTLE

3

STORY & ART BY
KAGIJI KUMANOMATA

NIGHTS

27th Night: Sloth Generator

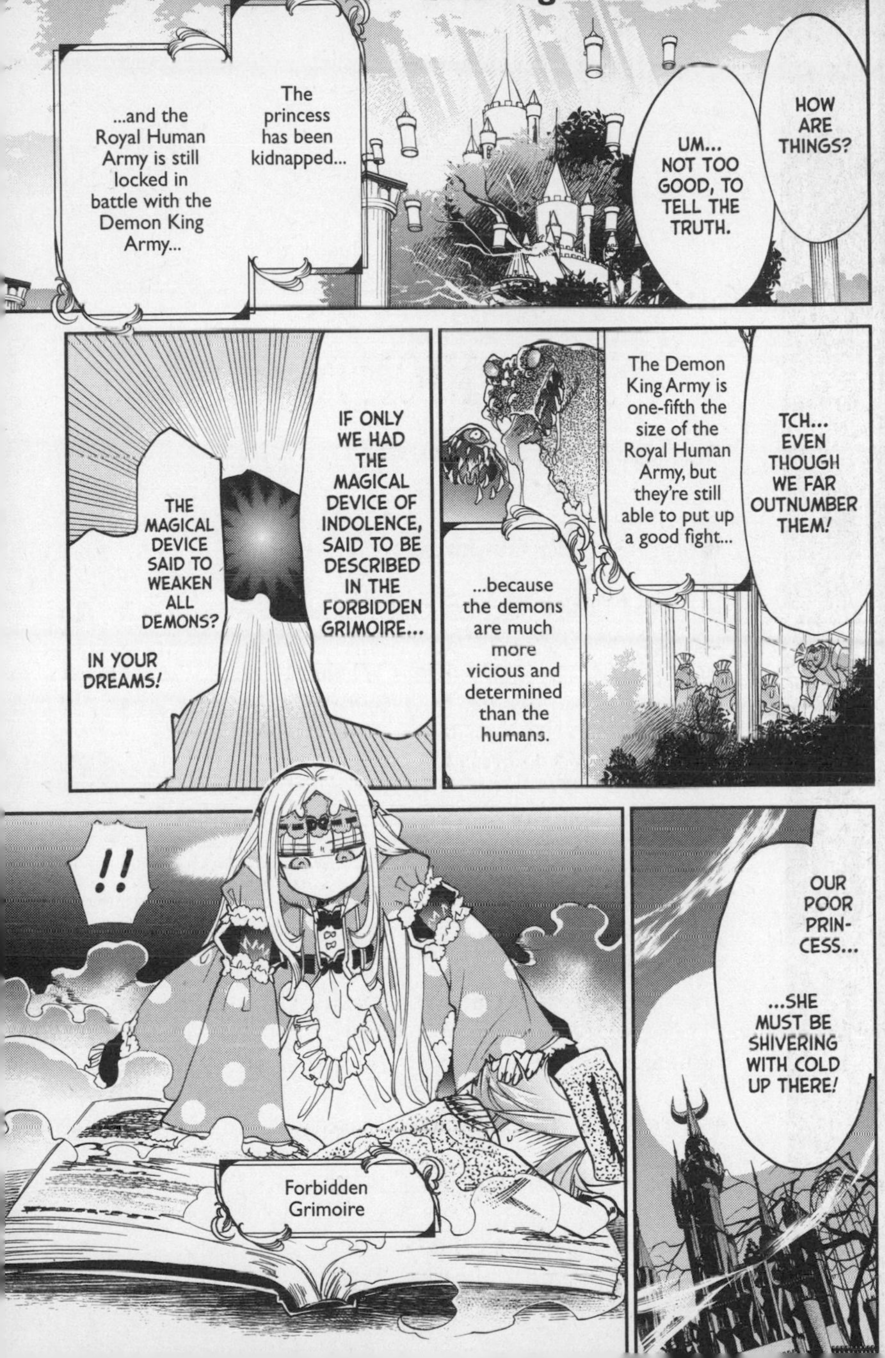
HOW ARE THINGS?
UM... NOT TOO GOOD, TO TELL THE TRUTH.
The princess has been kidnapped...
...and the Royal Human Army is still locked in battle with the Demon King Army...
TCH... EVEN THOUGH WE FAR OUTNUMBER THEM!
The Demon King Army is one-fifth the size of the Royal Human Army, but they're still able to put up a good fight...
...because the demons are much more vicious and determined than the humans.
IF ONLY WE HAD THE MAGICAL DEVICE OF INDOLENCE, SAID TO BE DESCRIBED IN THE FORBIDDEN GRIMOIRE...
THE MAGICAL DEVICE SAID TO WEAKEN ALL DEMONS?
IN YOUR DREAMS!
OUR POOR PRIN-CESS...
...SHE MUST BE SHIVERING WITH COLD UP THERE!
!!
Forbidden Grimoire

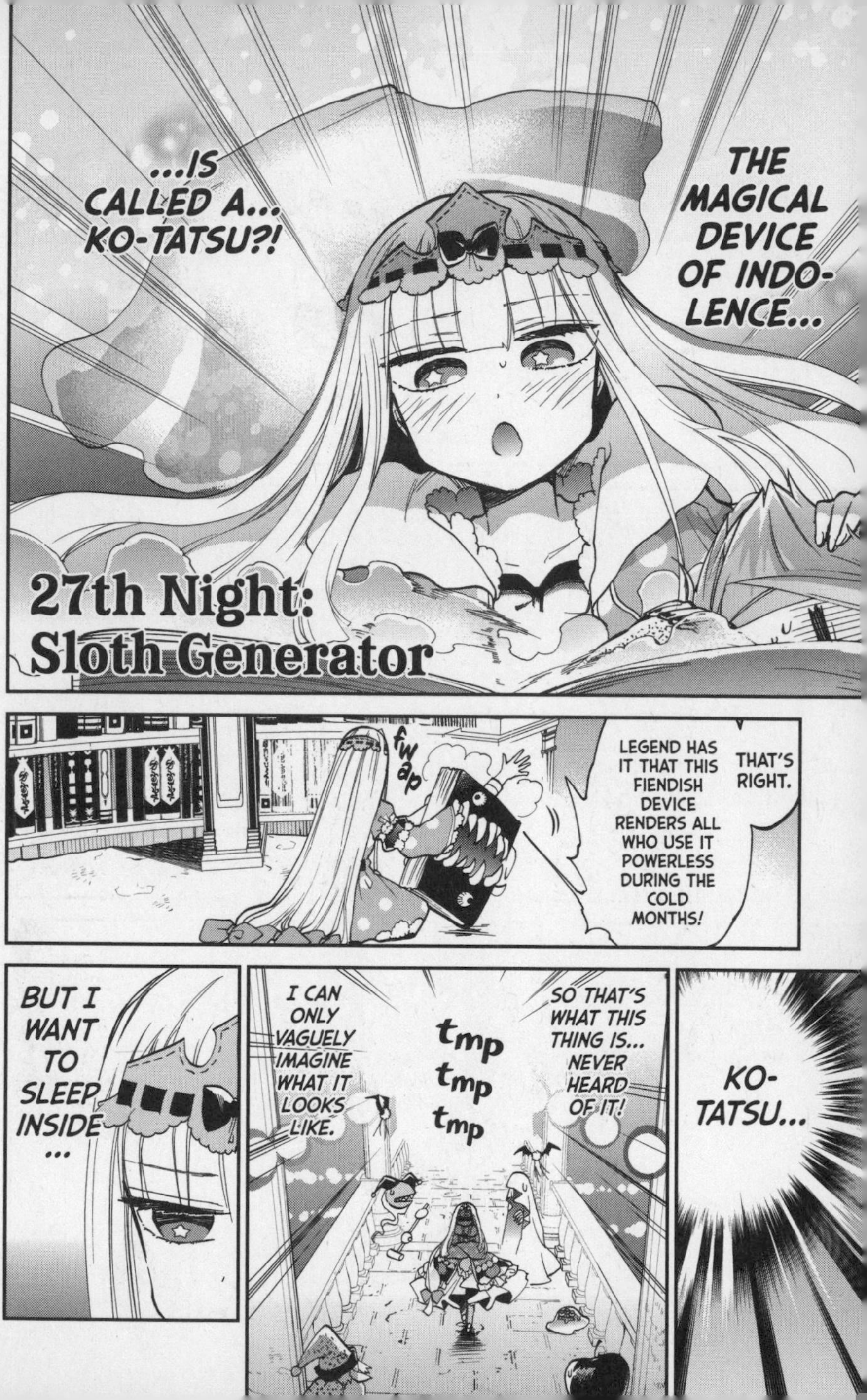
THE MAGICAL DEVICE OF INDO-LENCE...
...IS CALLED A... KO-TATSU?!
27th Night: Sloth Generator
THAT'S RIGHT.
LEGEND HAS IT THAT THIS FIENDISH DEVICE RENDERS ALL WHO USE IT POWERLESS DURING THE COLD MONTHS!
fwap
KO-TATSU...
SO THAT'S WHAT THIS THING IS... NEVER HEARD OF IT!
tmp tmp tmp
I CAN ONLY VAGUELY IMAGINE WHAT IT LOOKS LIKE.
BUT I WANT TO SLEEP INSIDE...

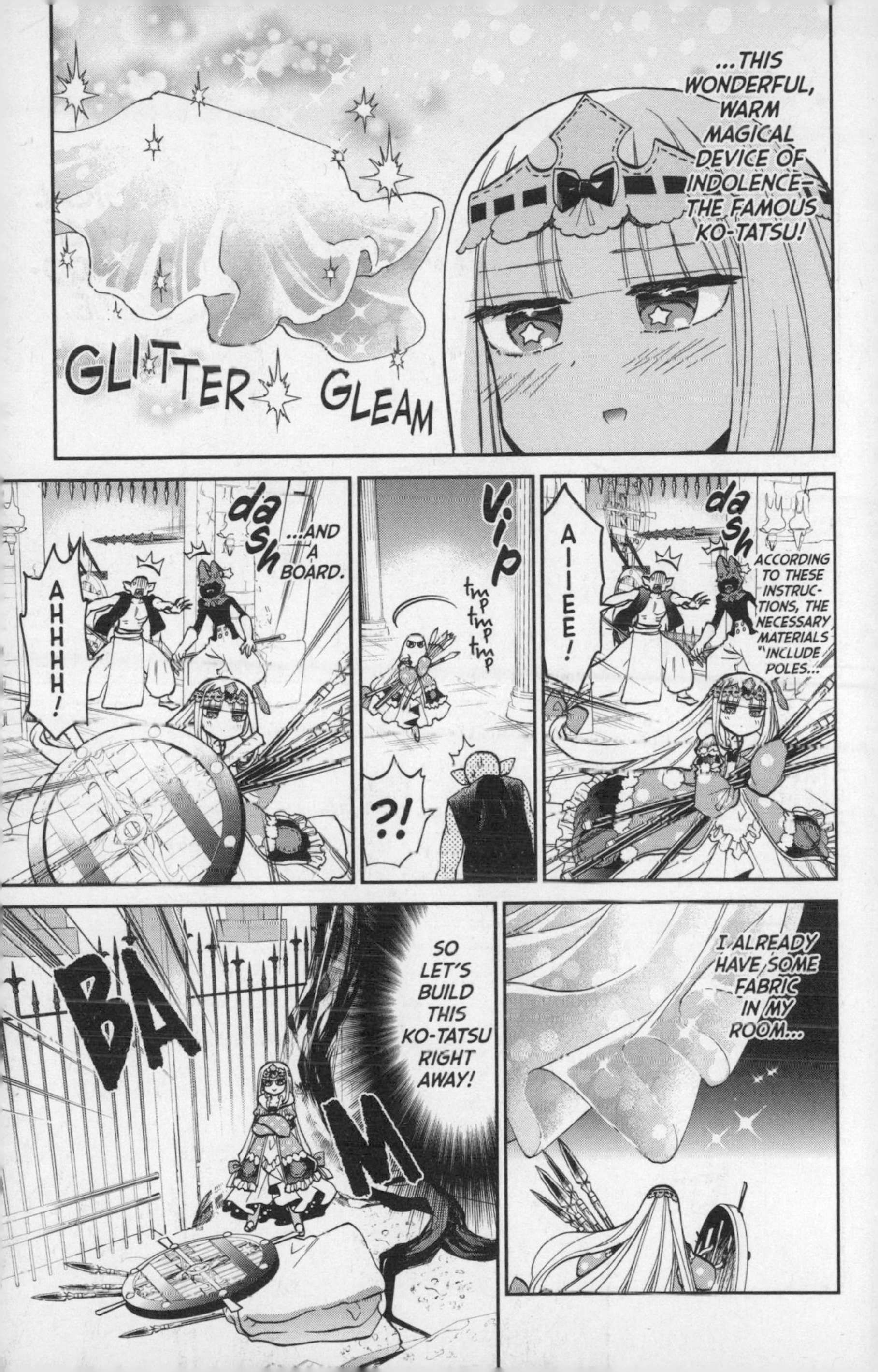
...THIS WONDERFUL, WARM MAGICAL DEVICE OF INDOLENCE—THE FAMOUS KO-TATSU!
GLITTER
GLEAM
dash
AIIEE!
ACCORDING TO THESE INSTRUCTIONS, THE NECESSARY MATERIALS INCLUDE POLES...
vip
tmp tmp tmp tmp
?!
dash
AHHHH!
...AND A BOARD.
I ALREADY HAVE SOME FABRIC IN MY ROOM...
SO LET'S BUILD THIS KO-TATSU RIGHT AWAY!
BAM

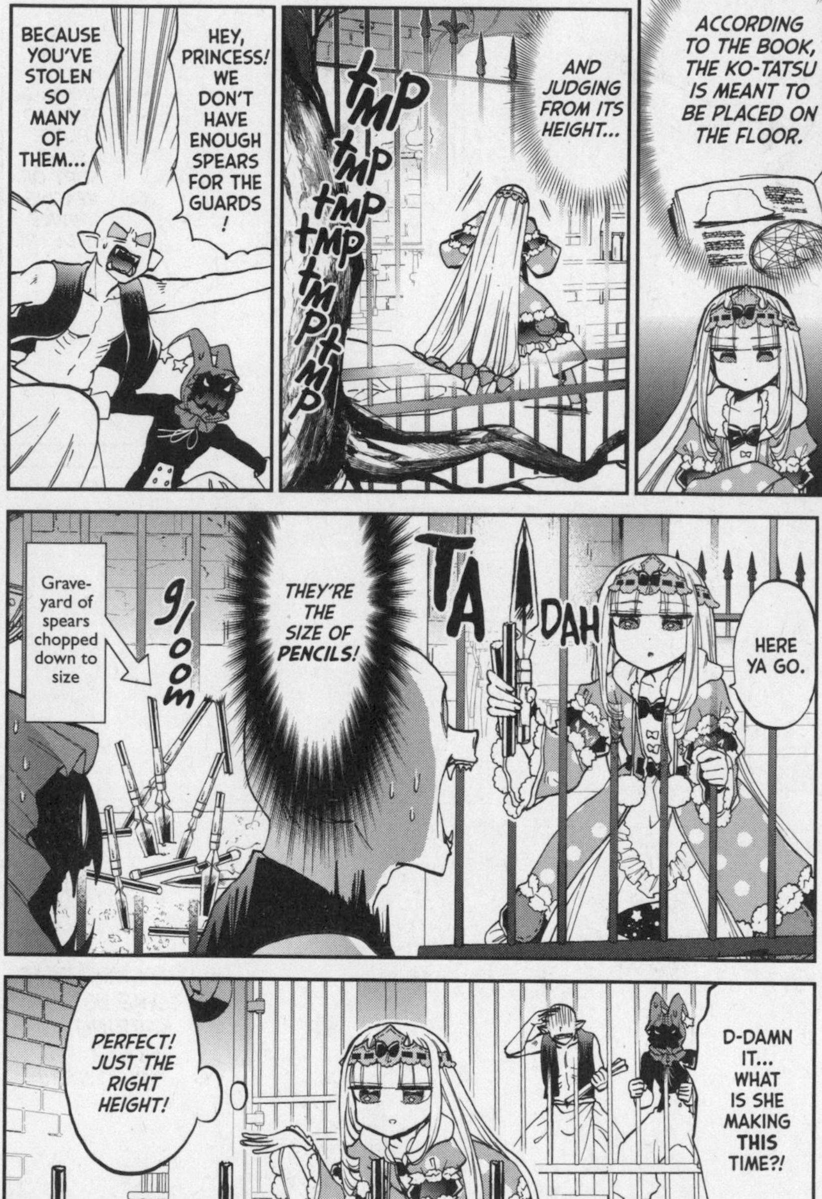
ACCORDING TO THE BOOK, THE KO-TATSU IS MEANT TO BE PLACED ON THE FLOOR.
AND JUDGING FROM ITS HEIGHT...
tmp tmp tmp tmp tmp tmp
HEY, PRINCESS! WE DON'T HAVE ENOUGH SPEARS FOR THE GUARDS!
BECAUSE YOU'VE STOLEN SO MANY OF THEM...
HERE YA GO.
TA DAH
THEY'RE THE SIZE OF PENCILS!
g/oom
Graveyard of spears chopped down to size
D-DAMN IT... WHAT IS SHE MAKING THIS TIME?!
PERFECT! JUST THE RIGHT HEIGHT!

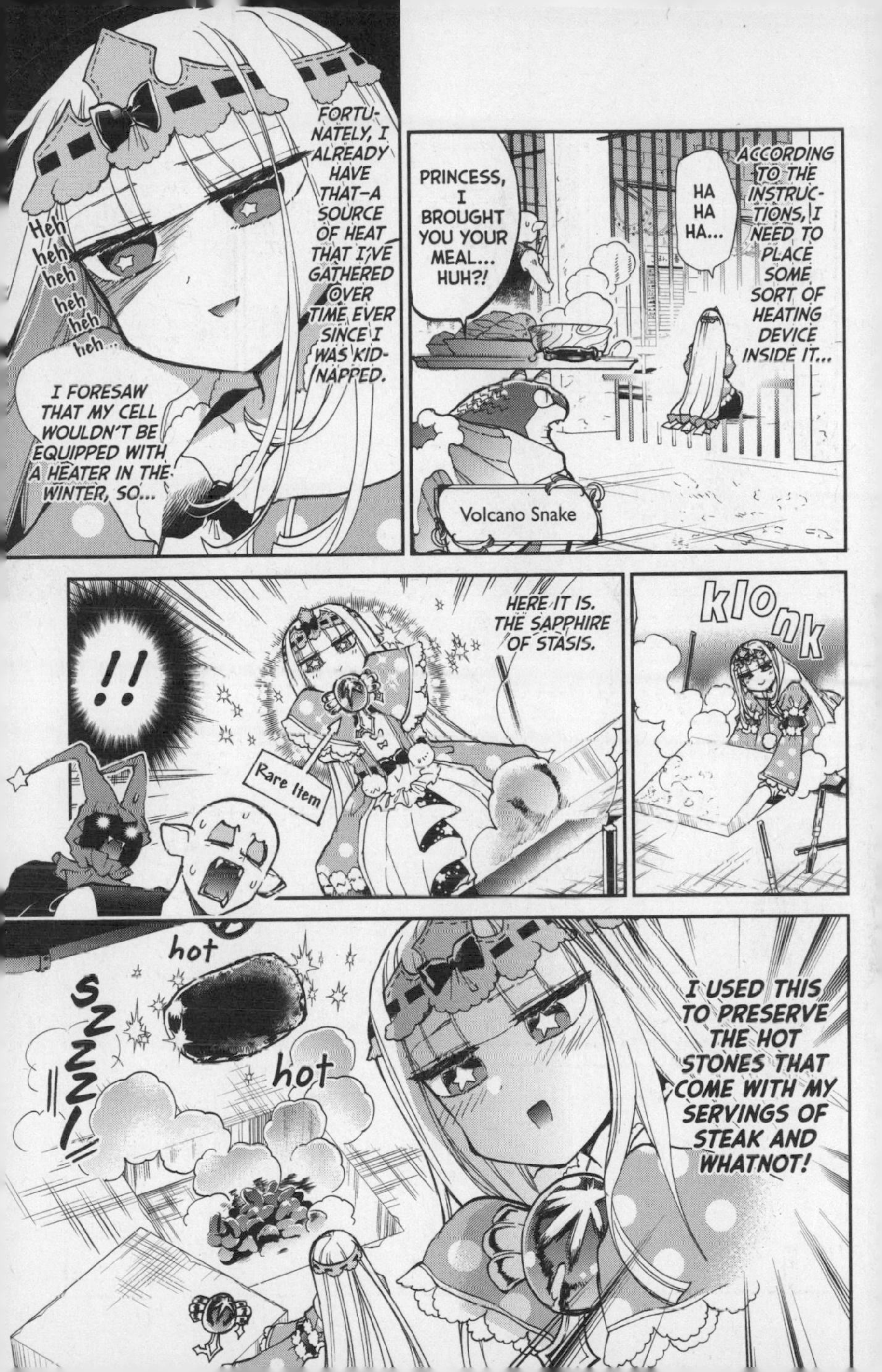
ACCORDING TO THE INSTRUCTIONS, I NEED TO PLACE SOME SORT OF HEATING DEVICE INSIDE IT...
HA HA HA...
PRINCESS, I BROUGHT YOU YOUR MEAL... HUH?!
Volcano Snake
FORTUNATELY, I ALREADY HAVE THAT—A SOURCE OF HEAT THAT I'VE GATHERED OVER TIME EVER SINCE I WAS KIDNAPPED.
Heh heh heh heh heh heh...
I FORESAW THAT MY CELL WOULDN'T BE EQUIPPED WITH A HEATER IN THE WINTER, SO...
klonk
HERE IT IS. THE SAPPHIRE OF STASIS.
!!
Rare Item
I USED THIS TO PRESERVE THE HOT STONES THAT COME WITH MY SERVINGS OF STEAK AND WHATNOT!
hot
hot
SZZZZ!

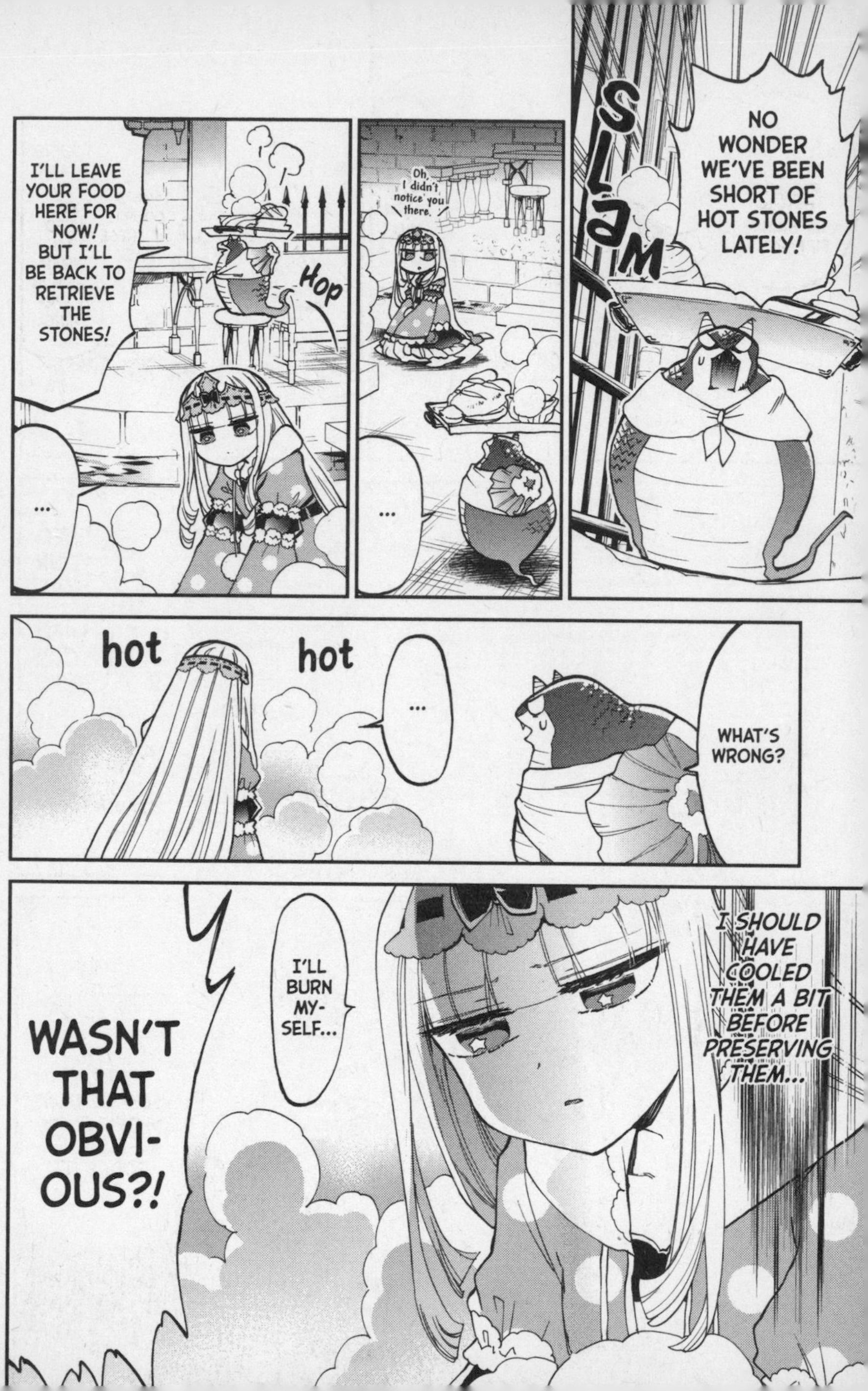
NO WONDER WE'VE BEEN SHORT OF HOT STONES LATELY!
SLAM
Oh, I didn't notice you there.
...
I'LL LEAVE YOUR FOOD HERE FOR NOW! BUT I'LL BE BACK TO RETRIEVE THE STONES!
Hop
...
WHAT'S WRONG?
...
hot
hot
I SHOULD HAVE COOLED THEM A BIT BEFORE PRESERVING THEM...
I'LL BURN MY-SELF...
WASN'T THAT OBVI-OUS?!

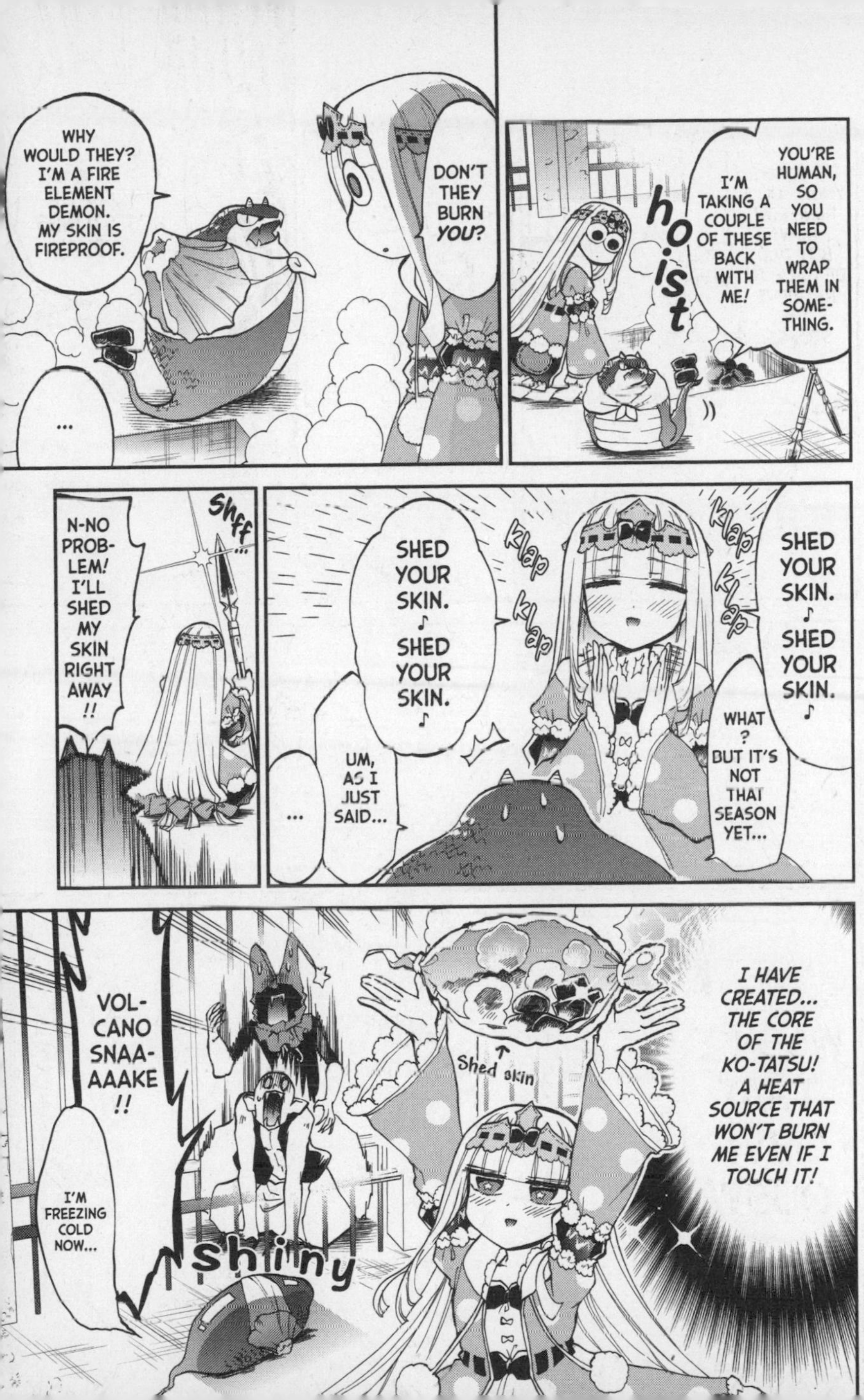
YOU'RE HUMAN, SO YOU NEED TO WRAP THEM IN SOME-THING.
I'M TAKING A COUPLE OF THESE BACK WITH ME!
hoist
DON'T THEY BURN *YOU*?
WHY WOULD THEY? I'M A FIRE ELEMENT DEMON. MY SKIN IS FIREPROOF.
...
SHED YOUR SKIN. ♪ SHED YOUR SKIN. ♪
klap klap
klap klap
SHED YOUR SKIN. ♪ SHED YOUR SKIN. ♪
WHAT? BUT IT'S NOT THAT SEASON YET...
UM, AS I JUST SAID...
...
Shff...
N-NO PROBLEM! I'LL SHED MY SKIN RIGHT AWAY!!
I HAVE CREATED... THE CORE OF THE KO-TATSU! A HEAT SOURCE THAT WON'T BURN ME EVEN IF I TOUCH IT!
Shed skin
VOLCANO SNAAAAAKE!!
Shiny
I'M FREEZING COLD NOW...

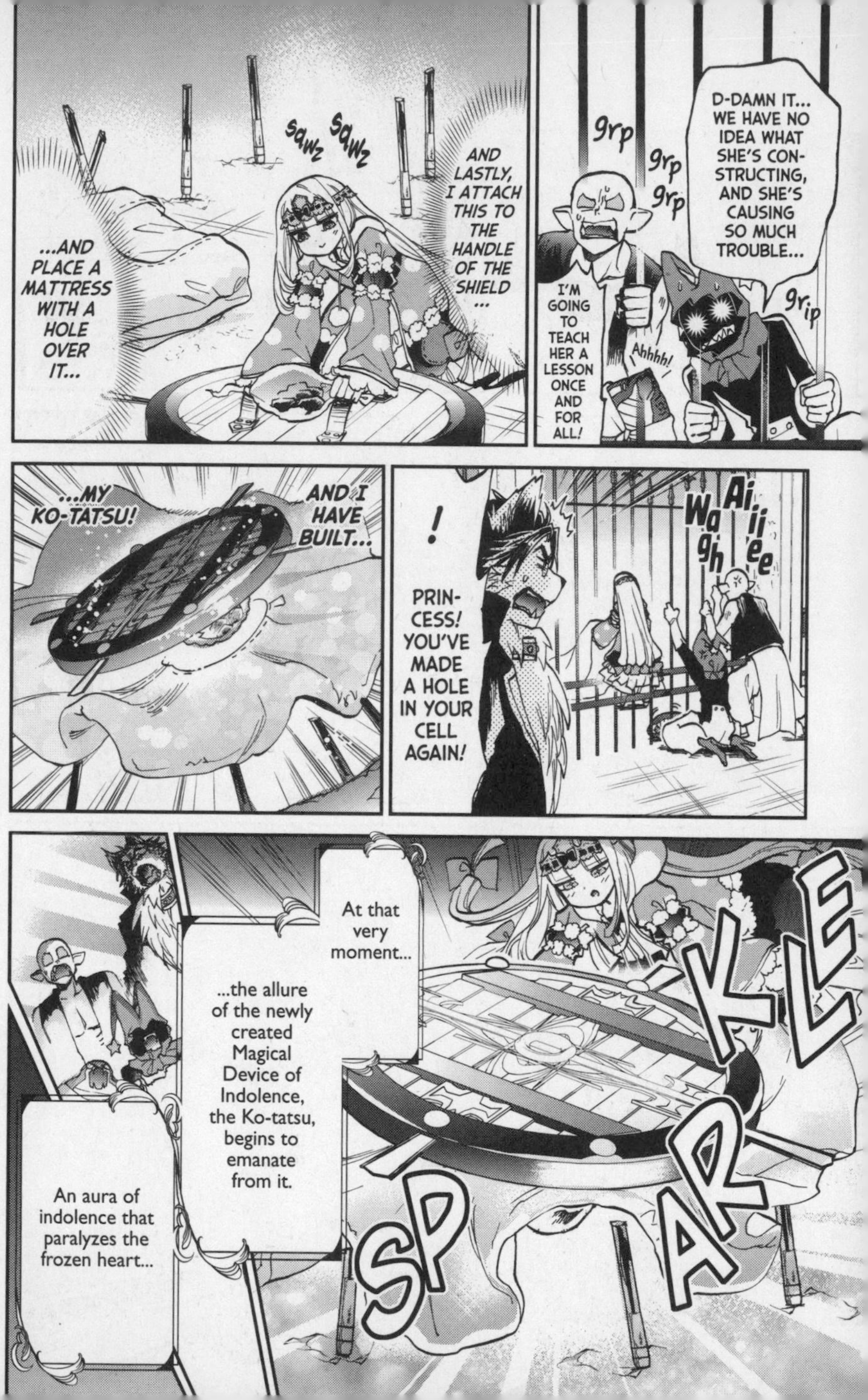
grp
grp
grp
D-DAMN IT... WE HAVE NO IDEA WHAT SHE'S CON-STRUCTING, AND SHE'S CAUSING SO MUCH TROUBLE...
grip
I'M GOING TO TEACH HER A LESSON ONCE AND FOR ALL!
Ahhhh!
sawz sawz
AND LASTLY, I ATTACH THIS TO THE HANDLE OF THE SHIELD...
...AND PLACE A MATTRESS WITH A HOLE OVER IT...
Aiiiee
Waagh
!
PRIN-CESS! YOU'VE MADE A HOLE IN YOUR CELL AGAIN!
AND I HAVE BUILT...
...MY KO-TATSU!
SPARKLE
At that very moment...
...the allure of the newly created Magical Device of Indolence, the Ko-tatsu, begins to emanate from it.
An aura of indolence that paralyzes the frozen heart...

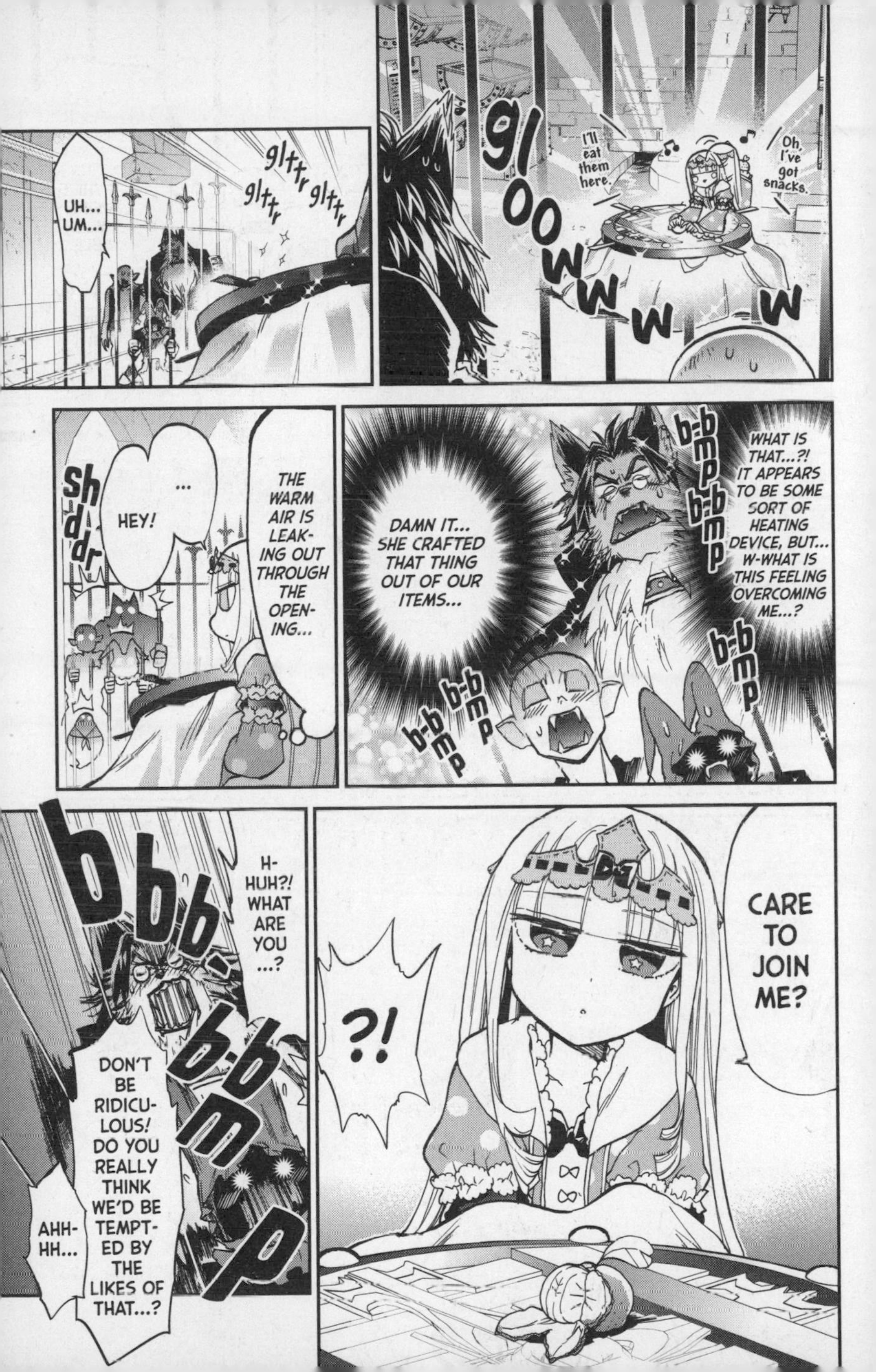
Oh, I've got snacks.
I'll eat them here.
glooowwwww
glttr glttr glttr
UH... UM...
WHAT IS THAT...?! IT APPEARS TO BE SOME SORT OF HEATING DEVICE, BUT... W-WHAT IS THIS FEELING OVERCOMING ME...?
b-bmp b-bmp
b-bmp
DAMN IT... SHE CRAFTED THAT THING OUT OF OUR ITEMS...
b-bmp b-bmp
THE WARM AIR IS LEAK-ING OUT THROUGH THE OPEN-ING...
...
HEY!
shddr
CARE TO JOIN ME?
?!
H-HUH?! WHAT ARE YOU ...?
bbb-bbmp
DON'T BE RIDICU-LOUS! DO YOU REALLY THINK WE'D BE TEMPT-ED BY THE LIKES OF THAT...?
AHH-HH...

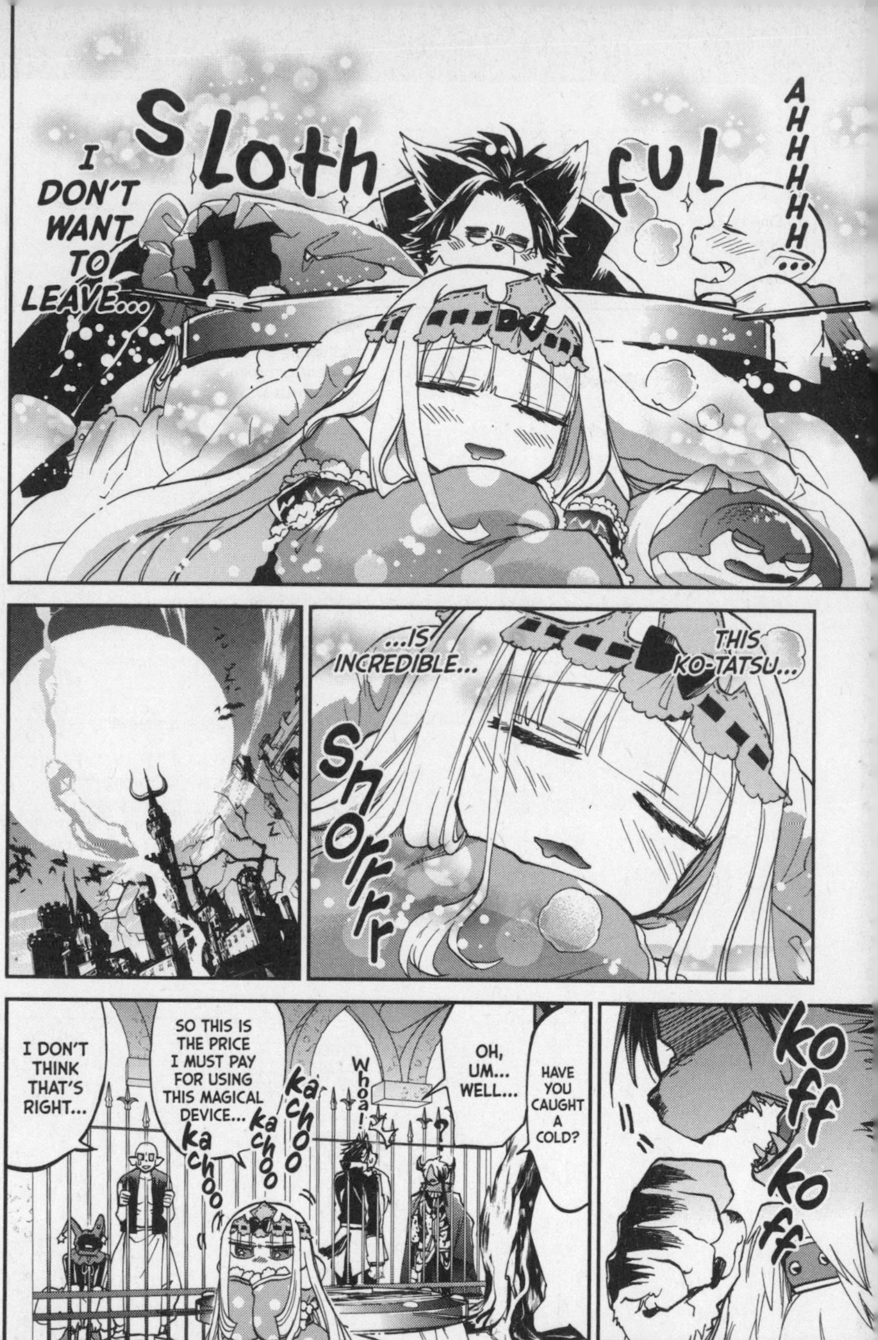
AHHHHHH...
Slothful
I DON'T WANT TO LEAVE...
THIS KO-TATSU...
...IS INCREDIBLE...
Snorrrr
koff
koff
koff
HAVE YOU CAUGHT A COLD?
OH, UM... WELL...
Whoa!
kachoo
kachoo
kachoo
SO THIS IS THE PRICE I MUST PAY FOR USING THIS MAGICAL DEVICE...
I DON'T THINK THAT'S RIGHT...

Magical Device of Indolence:
Ko-tatsu

One of the seven Magical Devices.

Laziness: ☆☆☆☆☆☆☆☆☆☆

You mustn't sleep in it: ☆☆☆☆☆☆

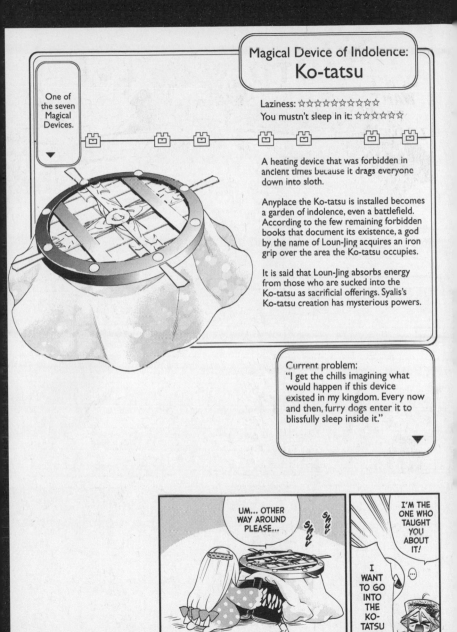

A heating device that was forbidden in ancient times because it drags everyone down into sloth.

Anyplace the Ko-tatsu is installed becomes a garden of indolence, even a battlefield. According to the few remaining forbidden books that document its existence, a god by the name of Loun-Jing acquires an iron grip over the area the Ko-tatsu occupies.

It is said that Loun-Jing absorbs energy from those who are sucked into the Ko-tatsu as sacrificial offerings. Syalis's Ko-tatsu creation has mysterious powers.

Current problem:
"I get the chills imagining what would happen if this device existed in my kingdom. Every now and then, furry dogs enter it to blissfully sleep inside it."

I'M THE ONE WHO TAUGHT YOU ABOUT IT!
I WANT TO GO INTO THE KO-TATSU TOO!
...
UM... OTHER WAY AROUND PLEASE...
SHUV SHUV

Would you like to change your class?
11 changes remaining

▶Yes

No ▼

Grave Keeper

"I'm going to slay 100 grave robbers."

▼

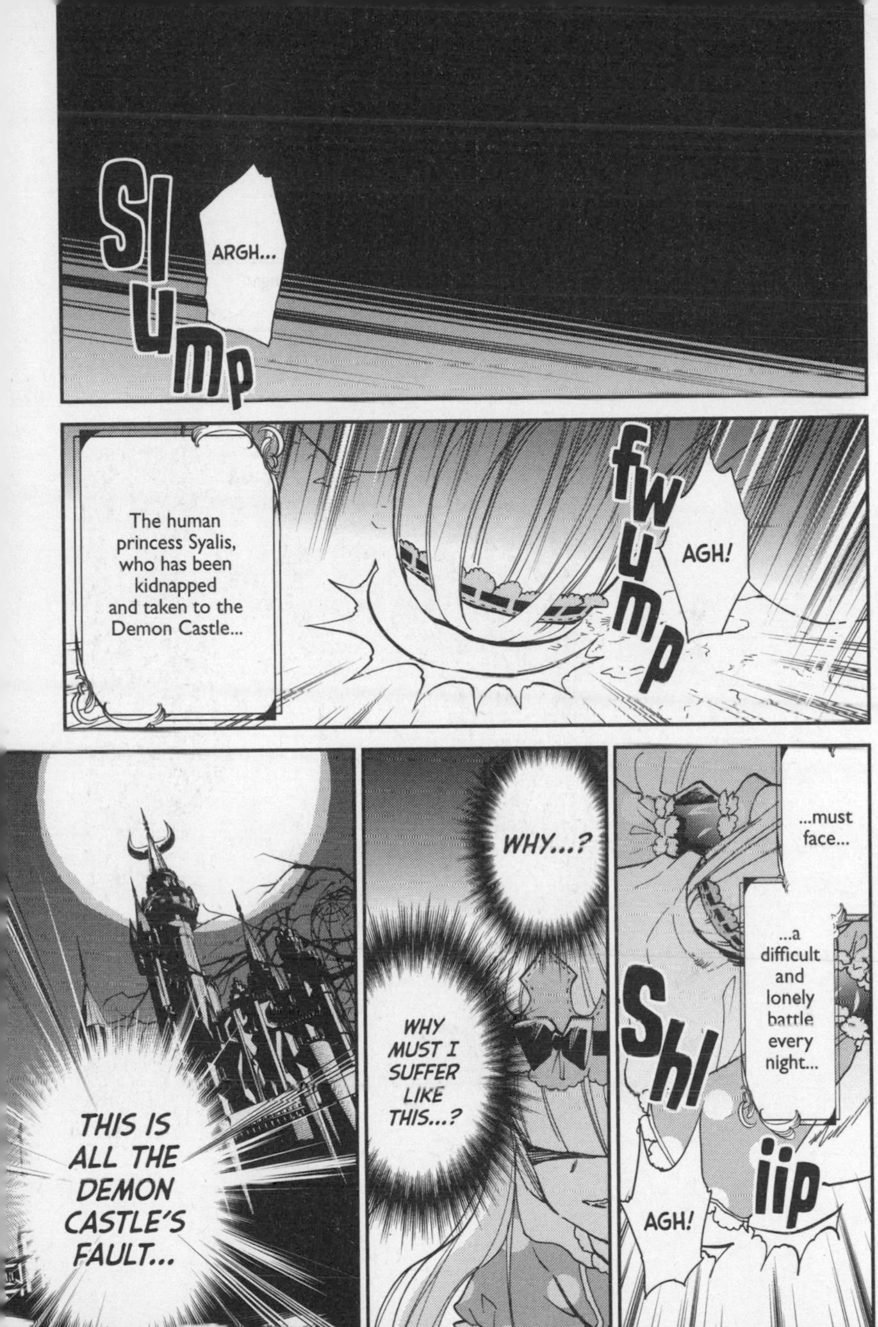
SLUMP
ARGH...
FWUMP
AGH!
The human princess Syalis, who has been kidnapped and taken to the Demon Castle...
...must face...
...a difficult and lonely battle every night...
SHLIIP
AGH!
WHY...?
WHY MUST I SUFFER LIKE THIS...?
THIS IS ALL THE DEMON CASTLE'S FAULT...

28th Night: Fluffy Comforter Taxi

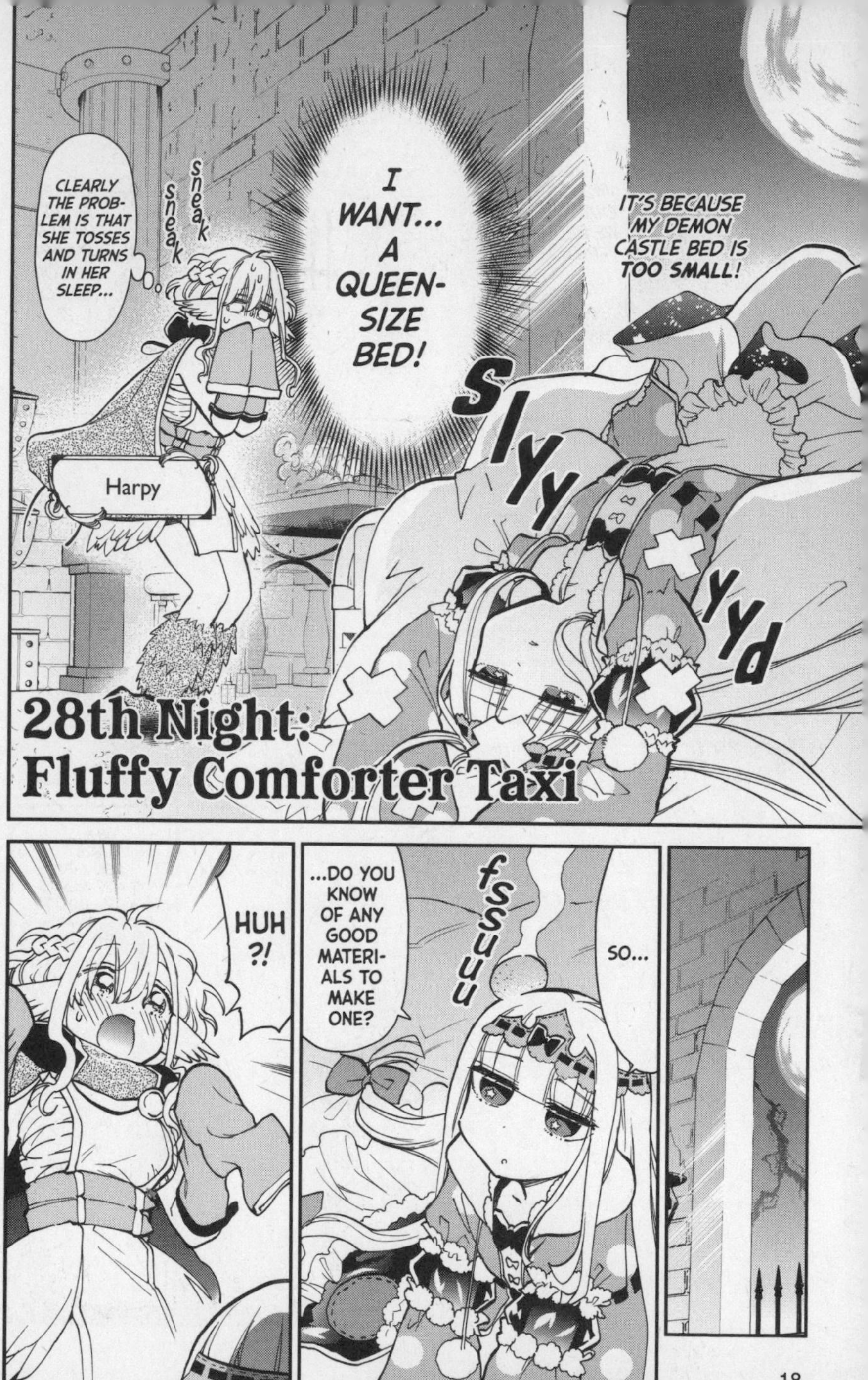
IT'S BECAUSE MY DEMON CASTLE BED IS TOO SMALL!
I WANT... A QUEEN-SIZE BED!
Slyyyyd
sneak sneak
CLEARLY THE PROB-LEM IS THAT SHE TOSSES AND TURNS IN HER SLEEP...
Harpy
28th Night: Fluffy Comforter Taxi
SO...
fssuuu
...DO YOU KNOW OF ANY GOOD MATERI-ALS TO MAKE ONE?
HUH ?!

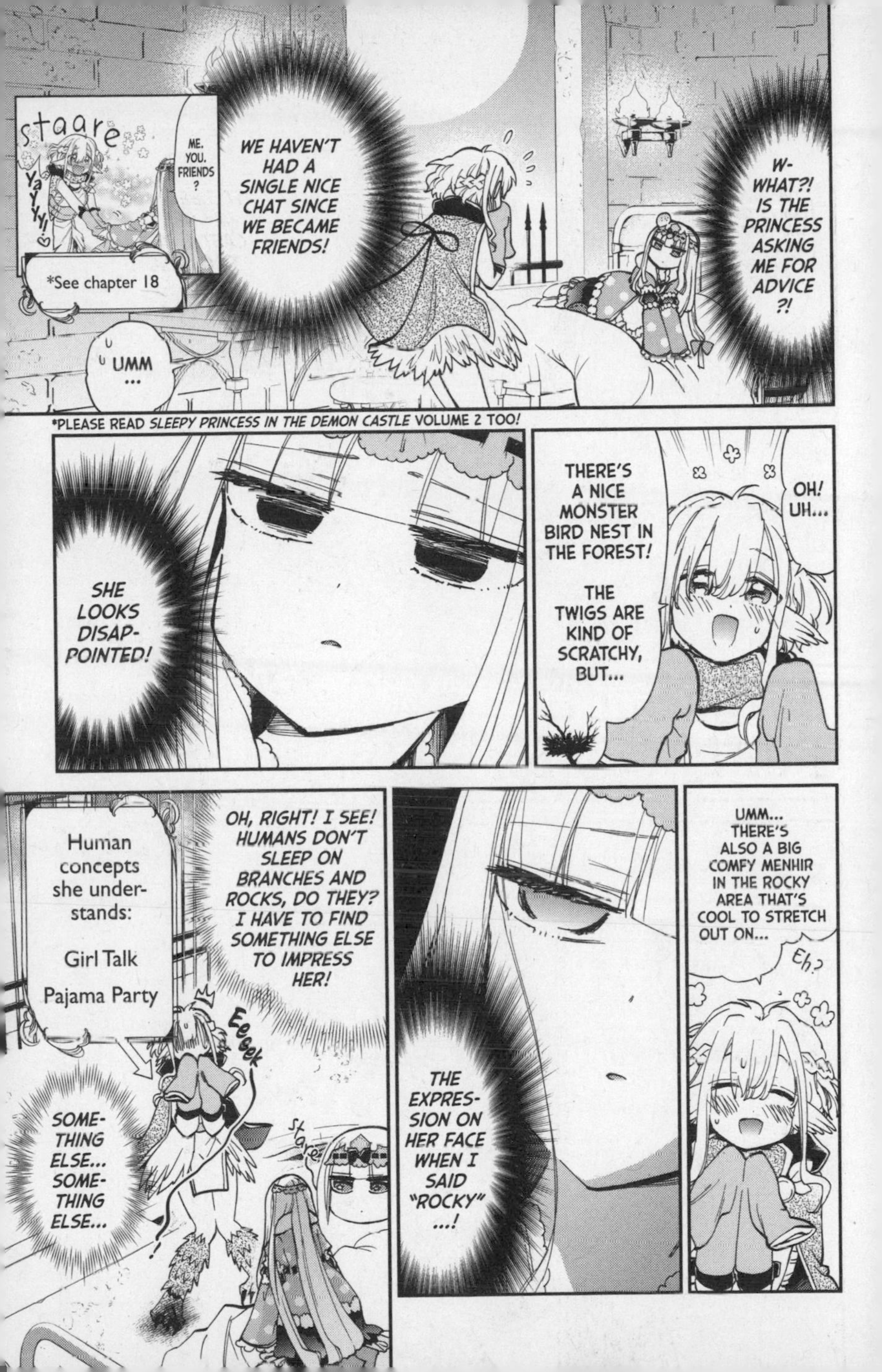
W-WHAT?! IS THE PRINCESS ASKING ME FOR ADVICE?!
WE HAVEN'T HAD A SINGLE NICE CHAT SINCE WE BECAME FRIENDS!
ME. YOU. FRIENDS?
staare
YaYYYY!
*See chapter 18
UMM...
*PLEASE READ SLEEPY PRINCESS IN THE DEMON CASTLE VOLUME 2 TOO!
OH! UH...
THERE'S A NICE MONSTER BIRD NEST IN THE FOREST!
THE TWIGS ARE KIND OF SCRATCHY, BUT...
SHE LOOKS DISAP-POINTED!
UMM... THERE'S ALSO A BIG COMFY MENHIR IN THE ROCKY AREA THAT'S COOL TO STRETCH OUT ON...
Eh?
THE EXPRES-SION ON HER FACE WHEN I SAID "ROCKY" ...!
OH, RIGHT! I SEE! HUMANS DON'T SLEEP ON BRANCHES AND ROCKS, DO THEY? I HAVE TO FIND SOMETHING ELSE TO IMPRESS HER!
Human concepts she under-stands:
Girl Talk
Pajama Party
Eeeek
stare
SOME-THING ELSE... SOME-THING ELSE...
!

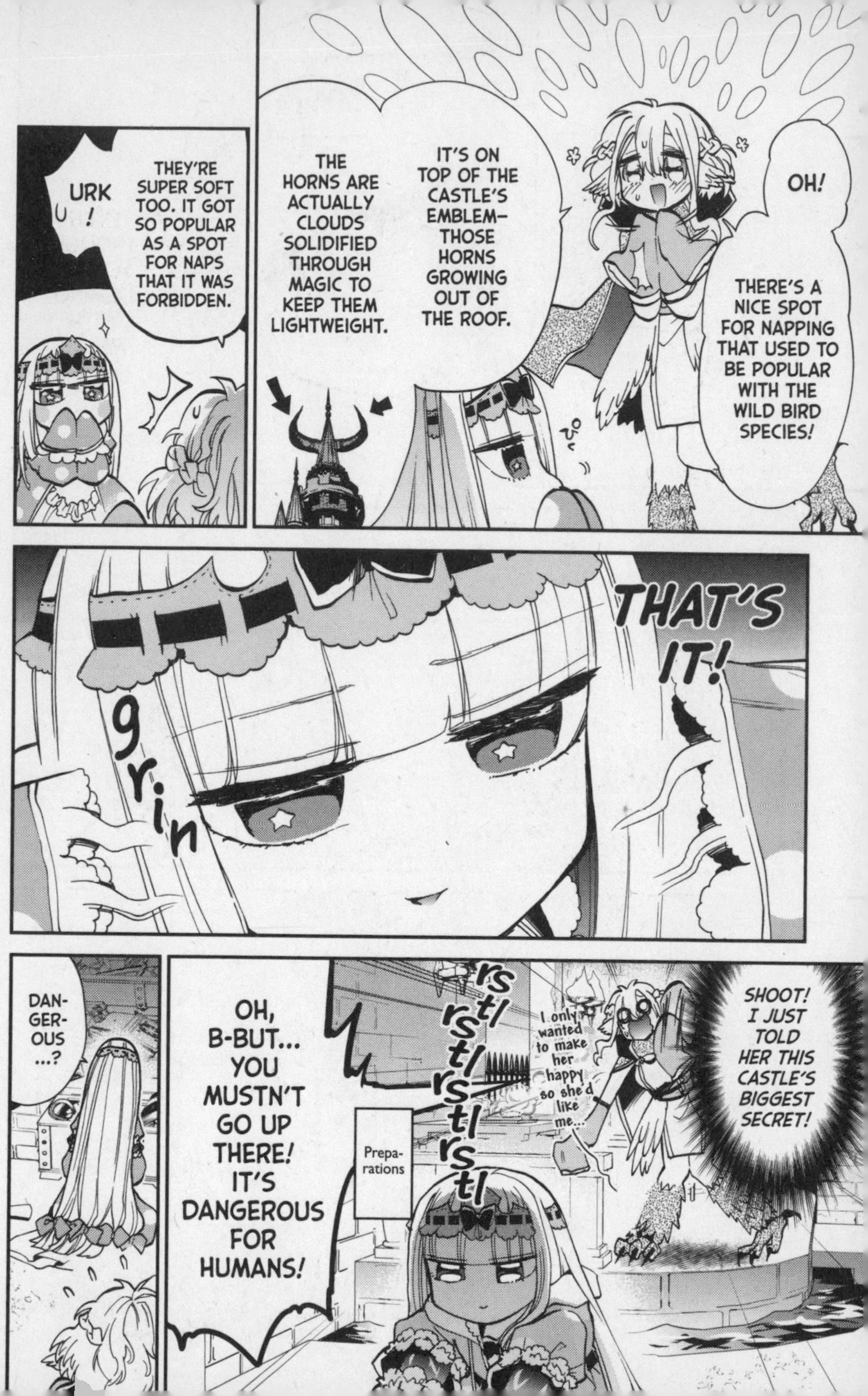
OH!
THERE'S A NICE SPOT FOR NAPPING THAT USED TO BE POPULAR WITH THE WILD BIRD SPECIES!
IT'S ON TOP OF THE CASTLE'S EMBLEM—THOSE HORNS GROWING OUT OF THE ROOF.
THE HORNS ARE ACTUALLY CLOUDS SOLIDIFIED THROUGH MAGIC TO KEEP THEM LIGHTWEIGHT.
THEY'RE SUPER SOFT TOO. IT GOT SO POPULAR AS A SPOT FOR NAPS THAT IT WAS FORBIDDEN.
URK!
THAT'S IT!
grin
SHOOT! I JUST TOLD HER THIS CASTLE'S BIGGEST SECRET!
I only wanted to make her happy so she'd like me...
rstl rstl rstl rstl
OH, B-BUT... YOU MUSTN'T GO UP THERE! IT'S DANGEROUS FOR HUMANS!
Prepa-rations
DAN-GER-OUS...?

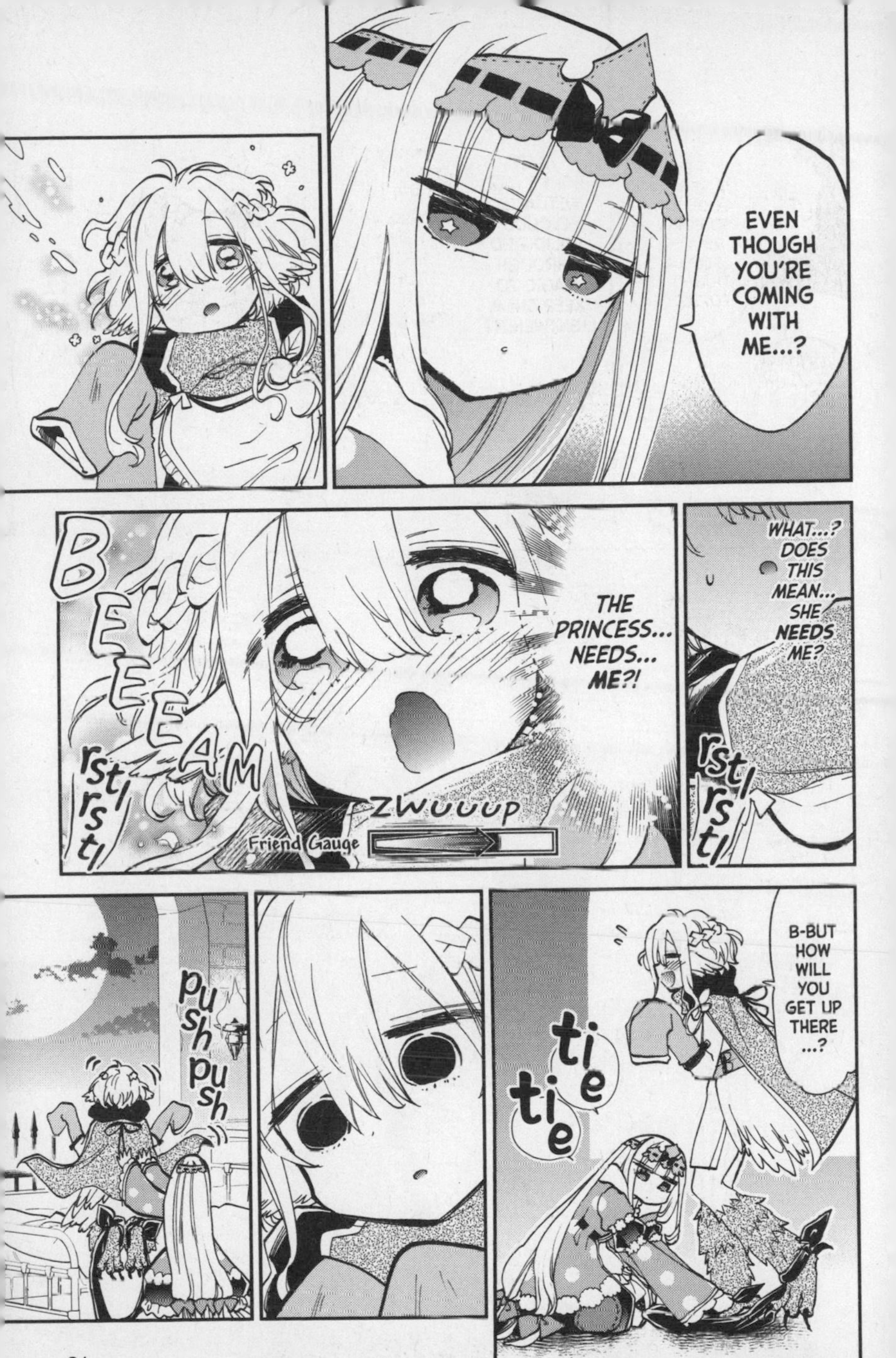
EVEN THOUGH YOU'RE COMING WITH ME...?
WHAT...? DOES THIS MEAN... SHE NEEDS ME?
rstl rstl
THE PRINCESS... NEEDS... ME?!
BEEEEAM
rstl rstl
ZWUUUP
Friend Gauge
B-BUT HOW WILL YOU GET UP THERE ...?
tie tie
push push

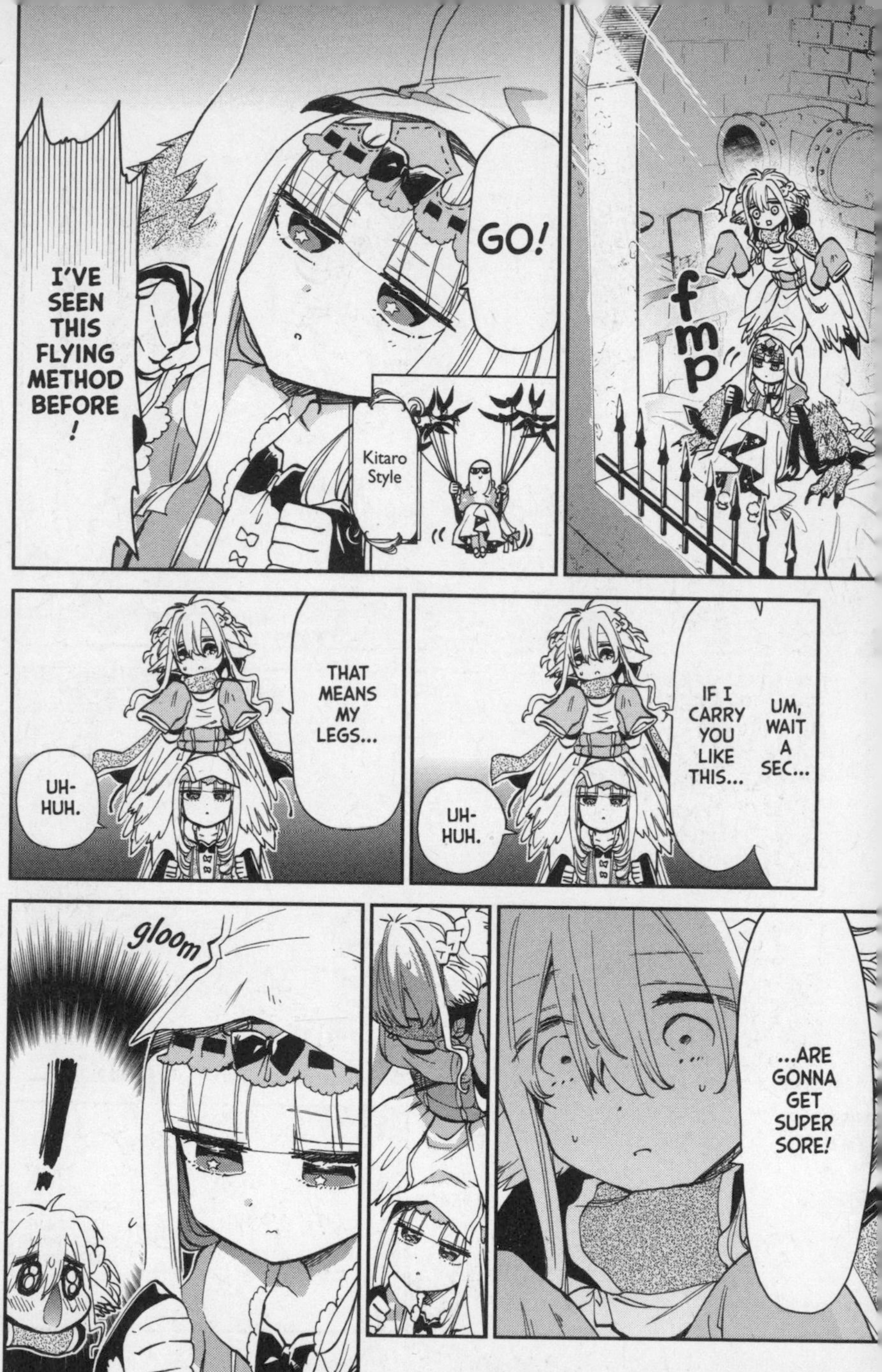
fmp
GO!
Kitaro Style
I'VE SEEN THIS FLYING METHOD BEFORE!
UM, WAIT A SEC...
IF I CARRY YOU LIKE THIS...
UH-HUH.
THAT MEANS MY LEGS...
UH-HUH.
...ARE GONNA GET SUPER SORE!
gloom
!

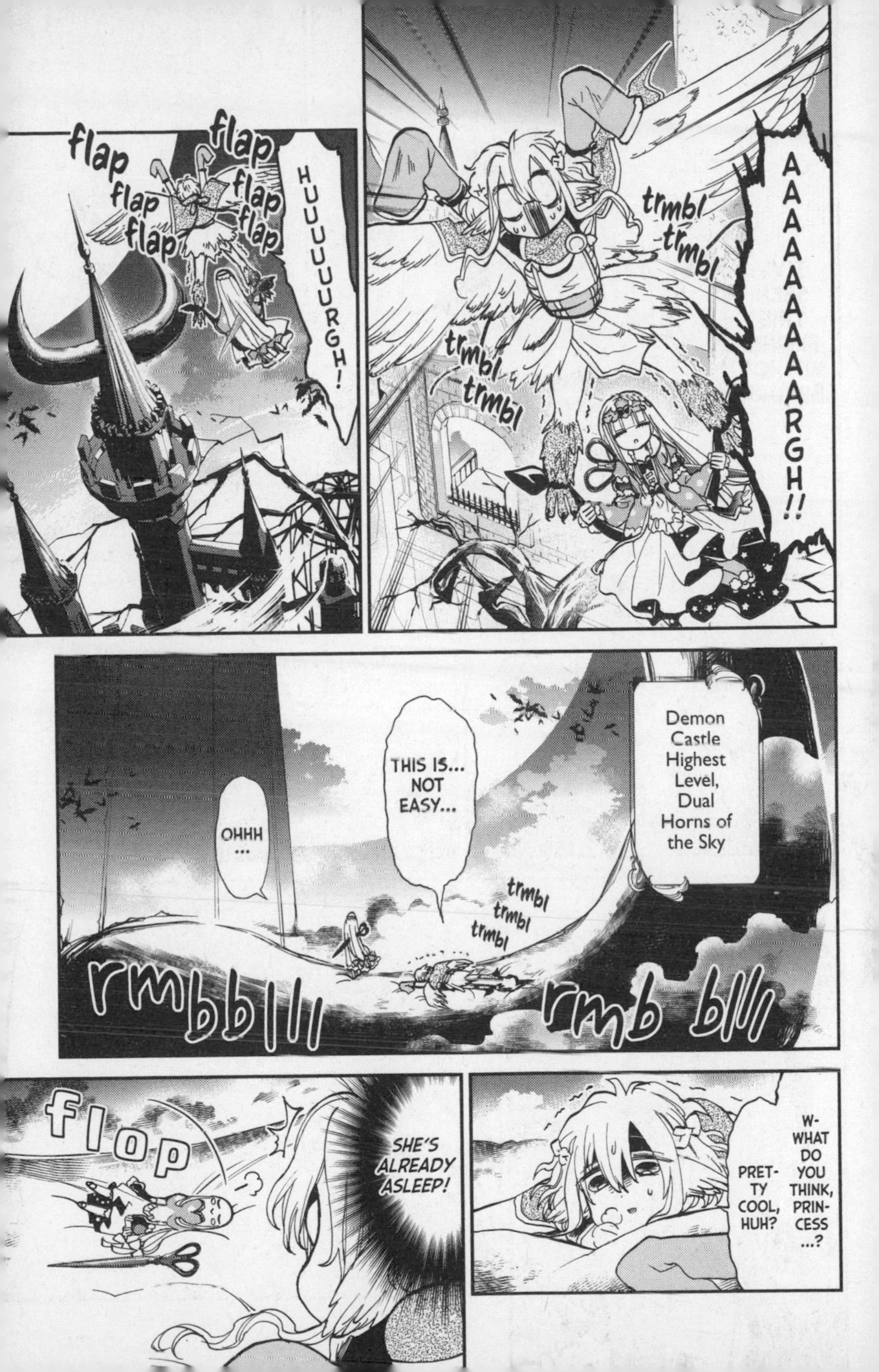
trmbl trmbl
trmbl trmbl
AAAAAAAAAAAARGH!!
flap flap flap flap flap flap
HUUUUUURGH!
Demon Castle Highest Level, Dual Horns of the Sky
trmbl trmbl trmbl
THIS IS... NOT EASY...
OHHH ...
rmbblll
rmb blll
W-WHAT DO YOU THINK, PRINCESS ...?
PRET-TY COOL, HUH?
SHE'S ALREADY ASLEEP!
flop

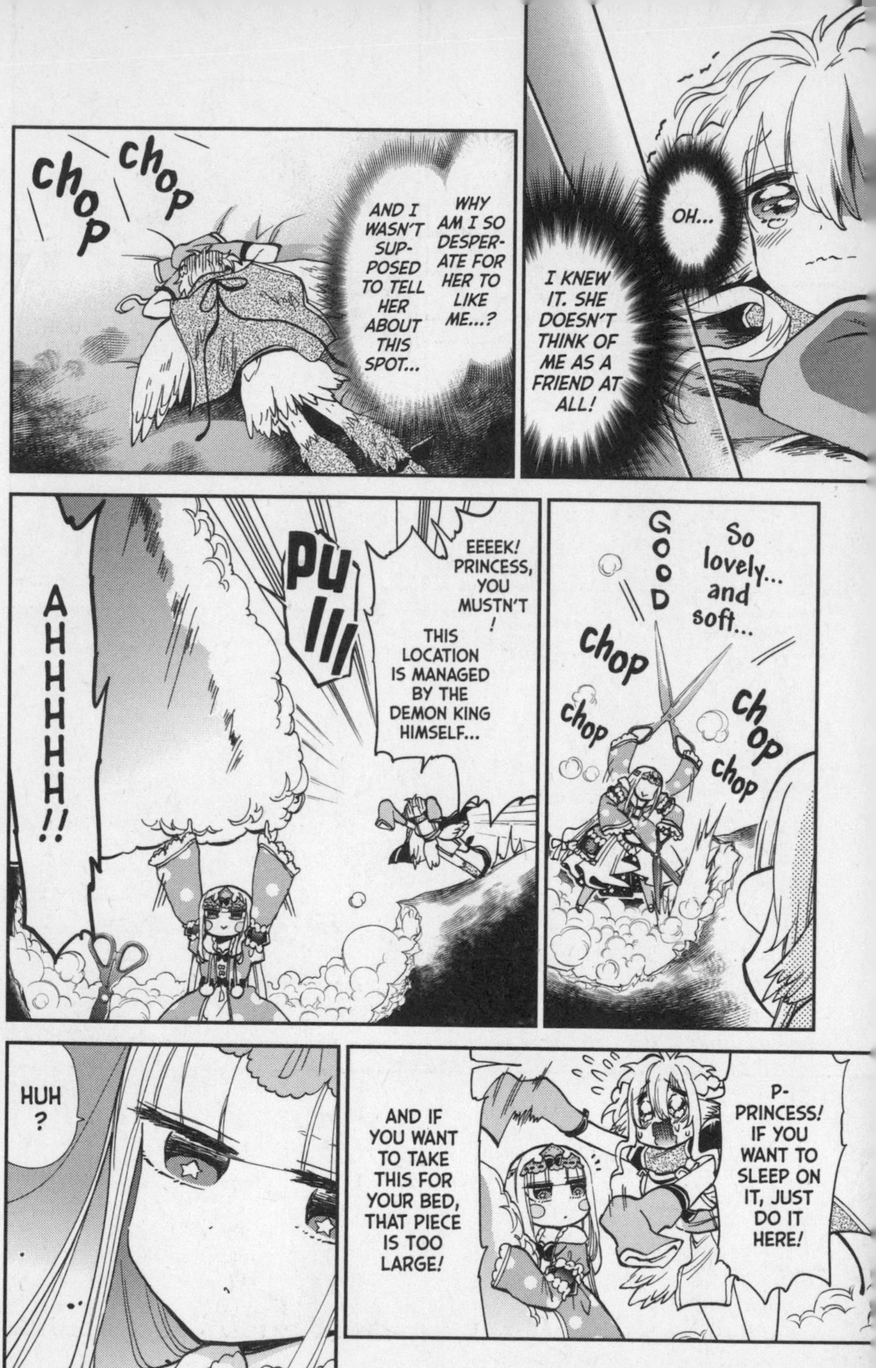
OH...
I KNEW IT. SHE DOESN'T THINK OF ME AS A FRIEND AT ALL!
WHY AM I SO DESPERATE FOR HER TO LIKE ME...?
AND I WASN'T SUPPOSED TO TELL HER ABOUT THIS SPOT...
chop chop chop
So lovely... and soft...
GOOD
chop chop
chop chop
EEEEK! PRINCESS, YOU MUSTN'T!
THIS LOCATION IS MANAGED BY THE DEMON KING HIMSELF...
PULL
AHHHHHH!!
P-PRINCESS! IF YOU WANT TO SLEEP ON IT, JUST DO IT HERE!
AND IF YOU WANT TO TAKE THIS FOR YOUR BED, THAT PIECE IS TOO LARGE!
HUH?

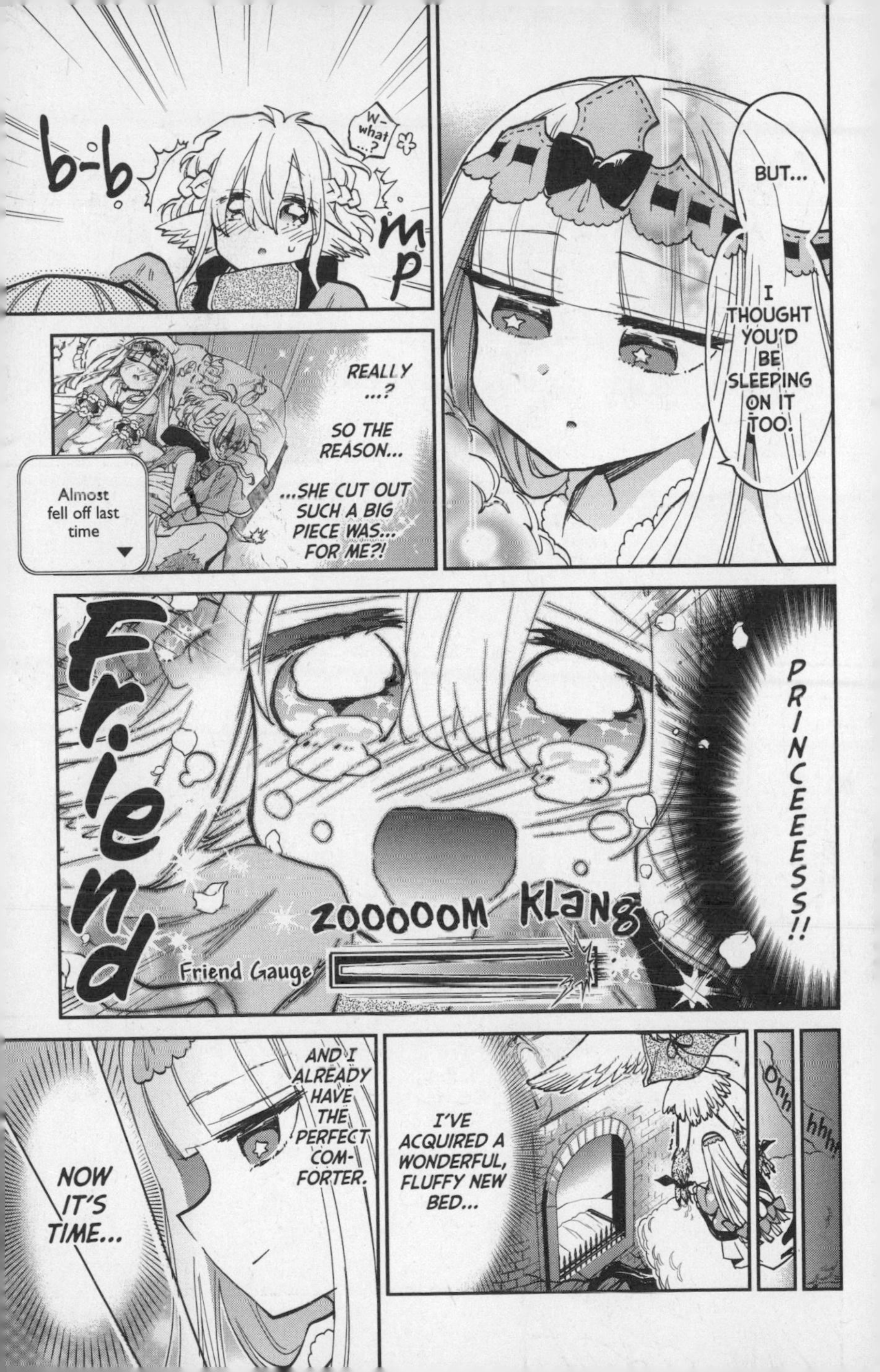
BUT...
I THOUGHT YOU'D BE SLEEPING ON IT TOO.
b-b
W-what ...?
mp
REALLY ...?
SO THE REASON...
...SHE CUT OUT SUCH A BIG PIECE WAS... FOR ME?!
Almost fell off last time
PRINCEEESS!!
Friend
ZOOOOOM
Klang
Friend Gauge
Ohhhhhh!
I'VE ACQUIRED A WONDERFUL, FLUFFY NEW BED...
AND I ALREADY HAVE THE PERFECT COM-FORTER.
NOW IT'S TIME...

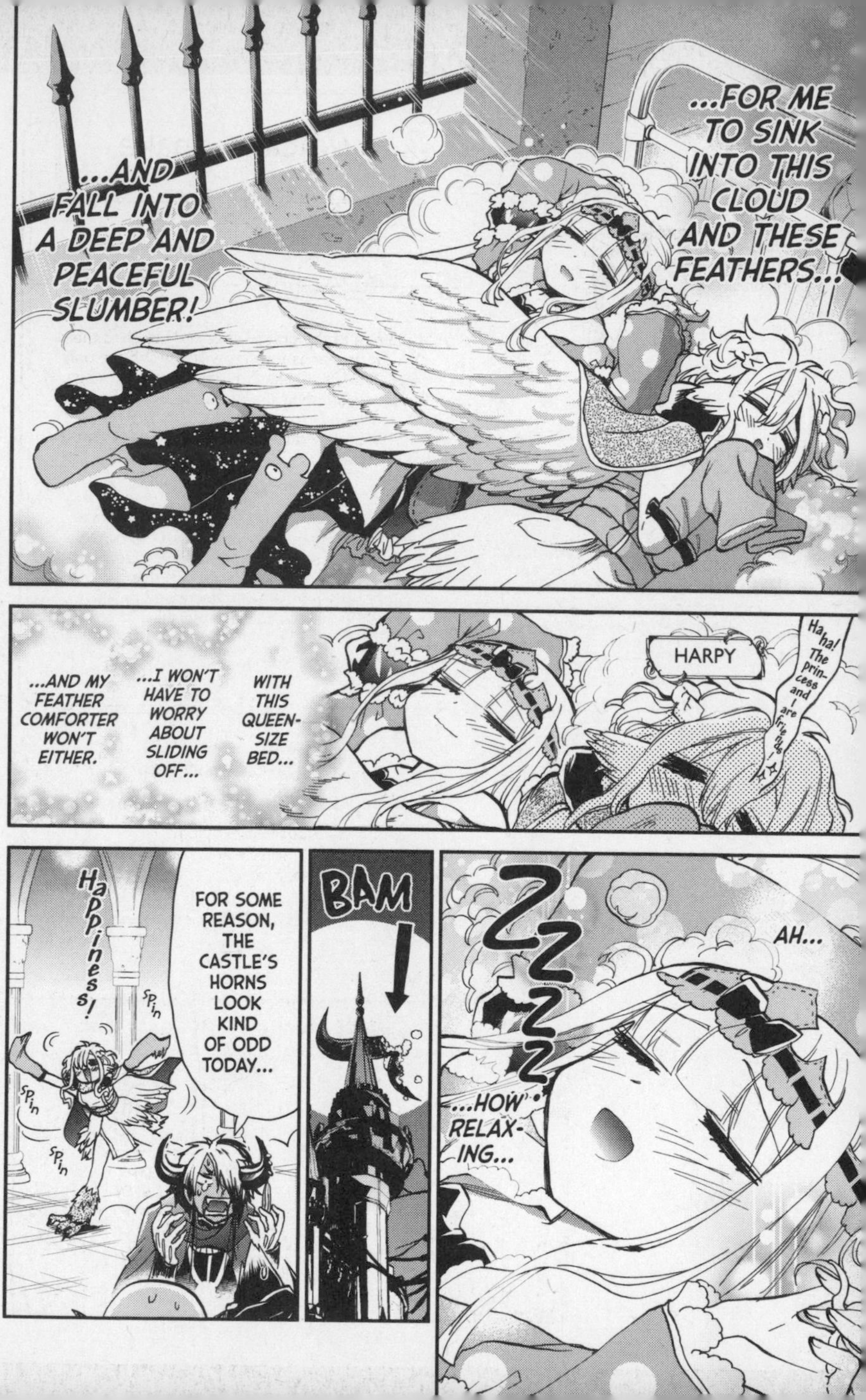
...FOR ME TO SINK INTO THIS CLOUD AND THESE FEATHERS...
...AND FALL INTO A DEEP AND PEACEFUL SLUMBER!
HARPY
Haha! The princess and I are friends!
WITH THIS QUEEN-SIZE BED...
...I WON'T HAVE TO WORRY ABOUT SLIDING OFF...
...AND MY FEATHER COMFORTER WON'T EITHER.
AH...
ZZZ
...HOW RELAXING...
BAM
FOR SOME REASON, THE CASTLE'S HORNS LOOK KIND OF ODD TODAY...
Happiness!
spin
spin
spin

Volcano Snake

Most of his relatives are ordinary dragons.

Speed: ☆☆
Fire Resistance: ☆☆☆☆☆☆☆☆☆☆

A demon of the dragon species. They shed their skin every year as they grow larger and are only called "Volcano Snakes" during their larval stage. The heat from their fire sac is too powerful for their small body to handle before they grow up, so until then they carry a volcano-shaped magical portal on their back for the heat to escape through.

The princess forced this one to shed his skin so she could build her heating device. Unbeknownst to Syalis, fire-resistant skins of this size are extremely hard to come by, so she inadvertently extorted a very useful item from him. The result was that Volcano Snake's body temperature decreased by 180 degrees. But all's well that ends well.

Former problem:
"The hot stones keep disappearing."

Current problem:
"I don't want that girl anywhere near me..."

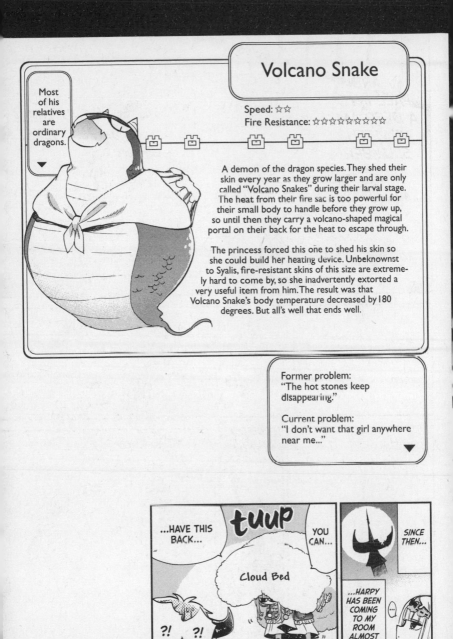

SINCE THEN...
...HARPY HAS BEEN COMING TO MY ROOM ALMOST EVERY DAY.
...
YOU CAN...
tuup
...HAVE THIS BACK...
Cloud Bed
?!
?!

Would you like to change your class?
10 changes remaining

▶Yes

No ▼

Witch

"I can pull anything out of my hat."

▼

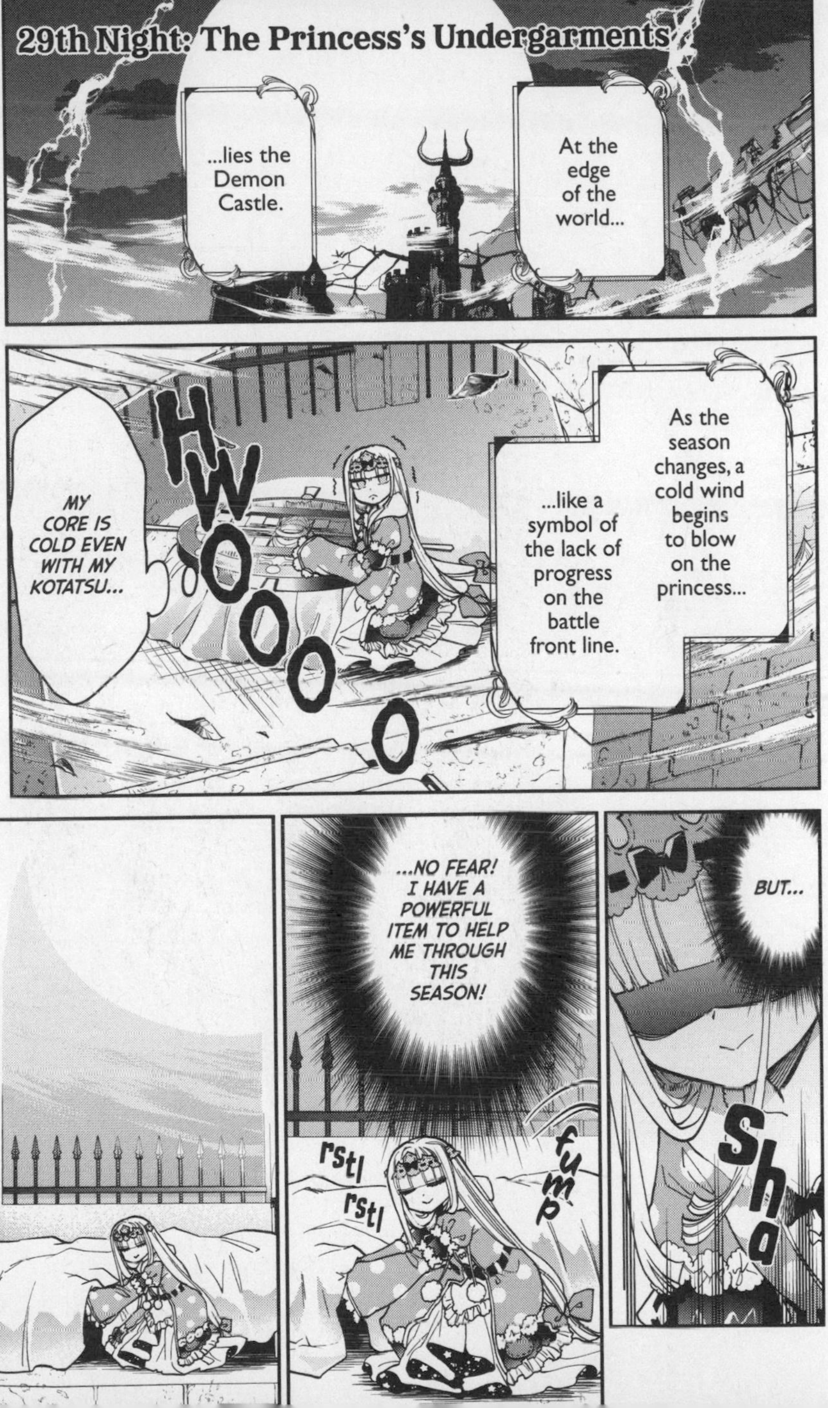
29th Night: The Princess's Undergarments
At the edge of the world...
...lies the Demon Castle.
As the season changes, a cold wind begins to blow on the princess...
...like a symbol of the lack of progress on the battle front line.
HWOOOOO
MY CORE IS COLD EVEN WITH MY KOTATSU...
BUT...
Sha
...NO FEAR! I HAVE A POWERFUL ITEM TO HELP ME THROUGH THIS SEASON!
fump
rstl
rstl

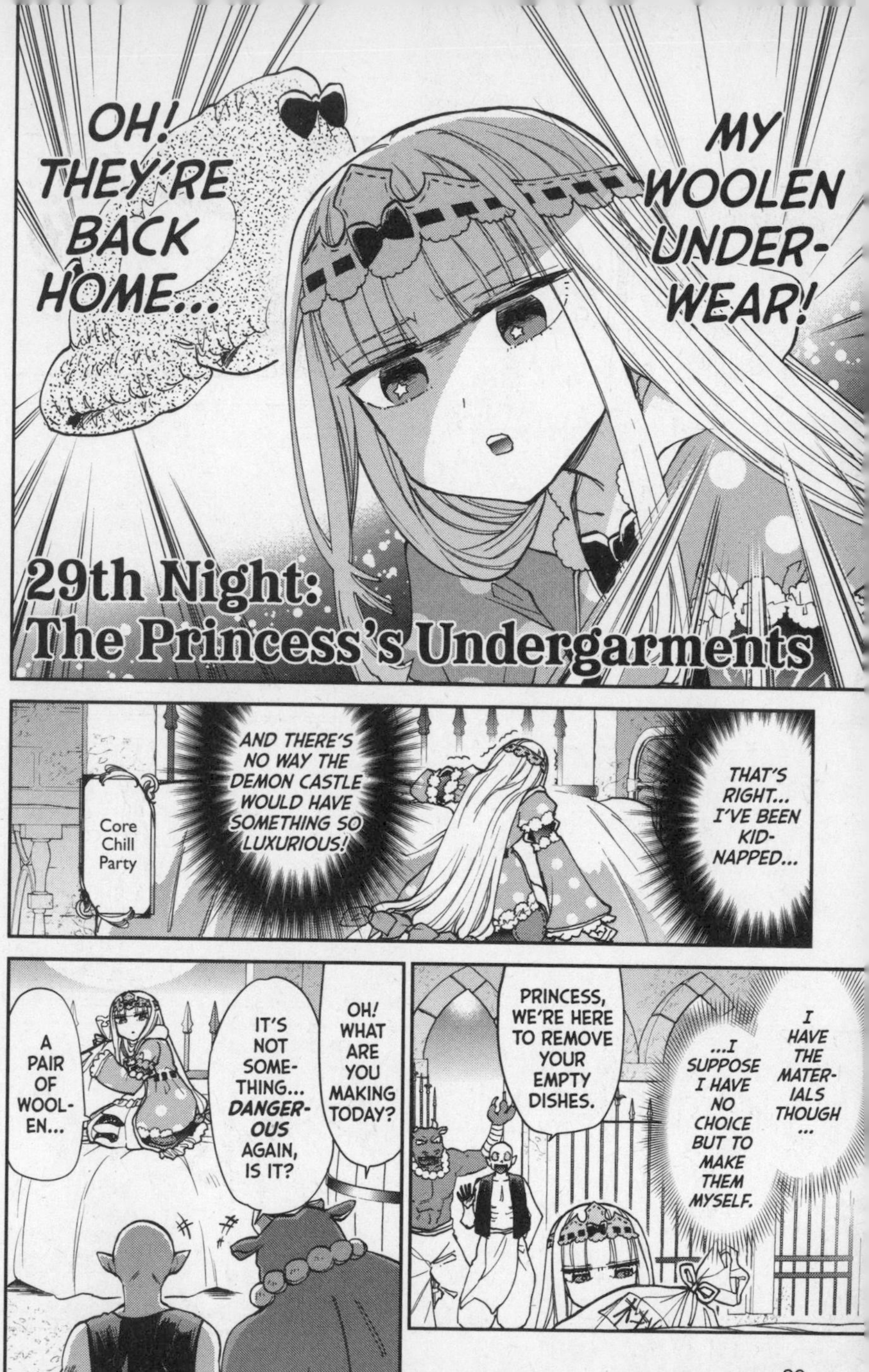
MY WOOLEN UNDER-WEAR!
OH! THEY'RE BACK HOME...
29th Night: The Princess's Undergarments
THAT'S RIGHT... I'VE BEEN KID-NAPPED...
AND THERE'S NO WAY THE DEMON CASTLE WOULD HAVE SOMETHING SO LUXURIOUS!
Core Chill Party
I HAVE THE MATER-IALS THOUGH ...
...I SUPPOSE I HAVE NO CHOICE BUT TO MAKE THEM MYSELF.
PRINCESS, WE'RE HERE TO REMOVE YOUR EMPTY DISHES.
OH! WHAT ARE YOU MAKING TODAY?
IT'S NOT SOME-THING... *DANGER-OUS* AGAIN, IS IT?
A PAIR OF WOOL-EN...

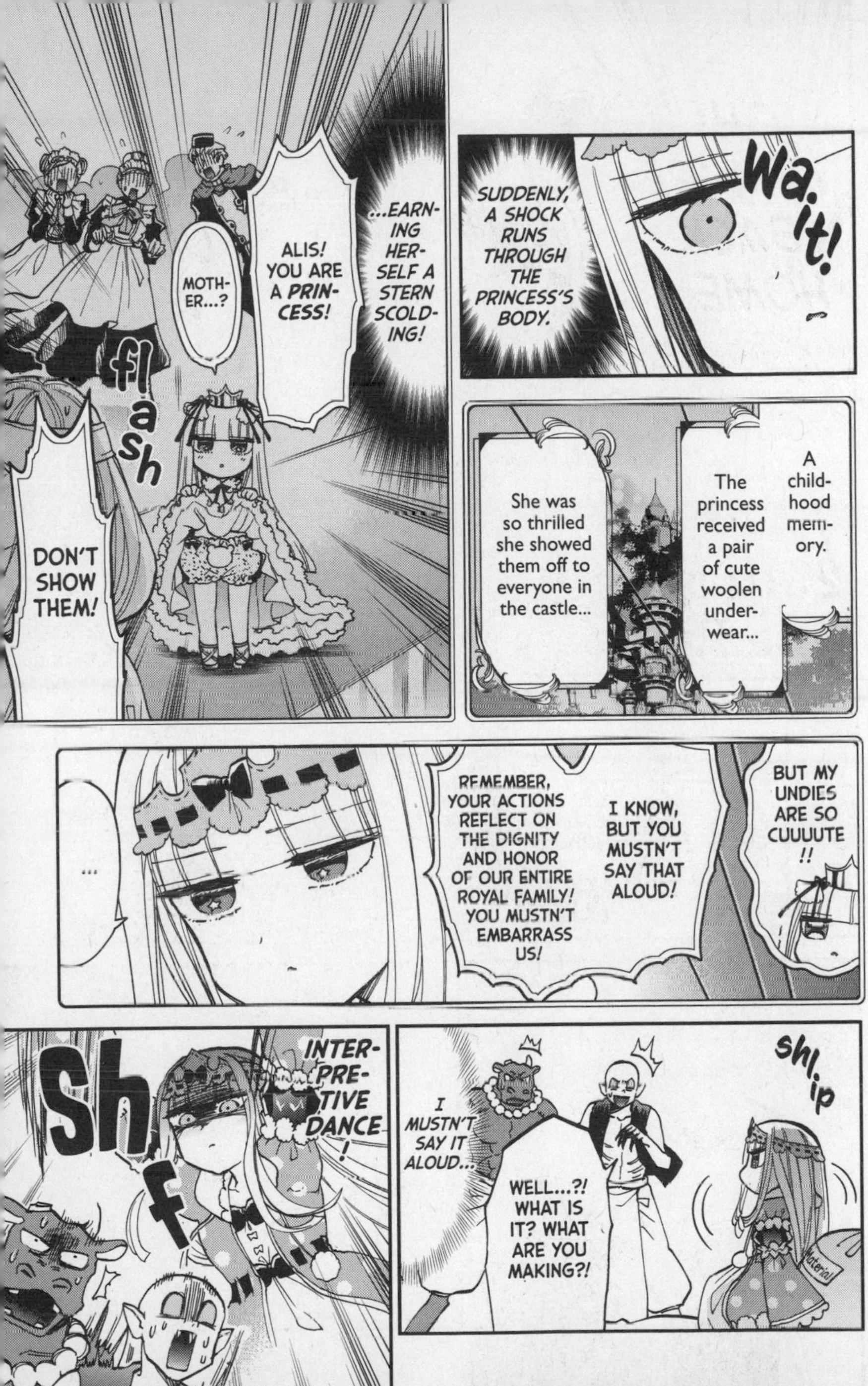
Wait!
SUDDENLY, A SHOCK RUNS THROUGH THE PRINCESS'S BODY.
A childhood memory.
The princess received a pair of cute woolen underwear...
She was so thrilled she showed them off to everyone in the castle...
...EARNING HERSELF A STERN SCOLDING!
ALIS! YOU ARE A PRINCESS!
MOTHER...?
flash
DON'T SHOW THEM!
BUT MY UNDIES ARE SO CUUUUTE !!
I KNOW, BUT YOU MUSTN'T SAY THAT ALOUD!
REMEMBER, YOUR ACTIONS REFLECT ON THE DIGNITY AND HONOR OF OUR ENTIRE ROYAL FAMILY! YOU MUSTN'T EMBARRASS US!
...
shlip
I MUSTN'T SAY IT ALOUD...
WELL...?! WHAT IS IT? WHAT ARE YOU MAKING?!
Material
INTERPRETIVE DANCE!
Shf

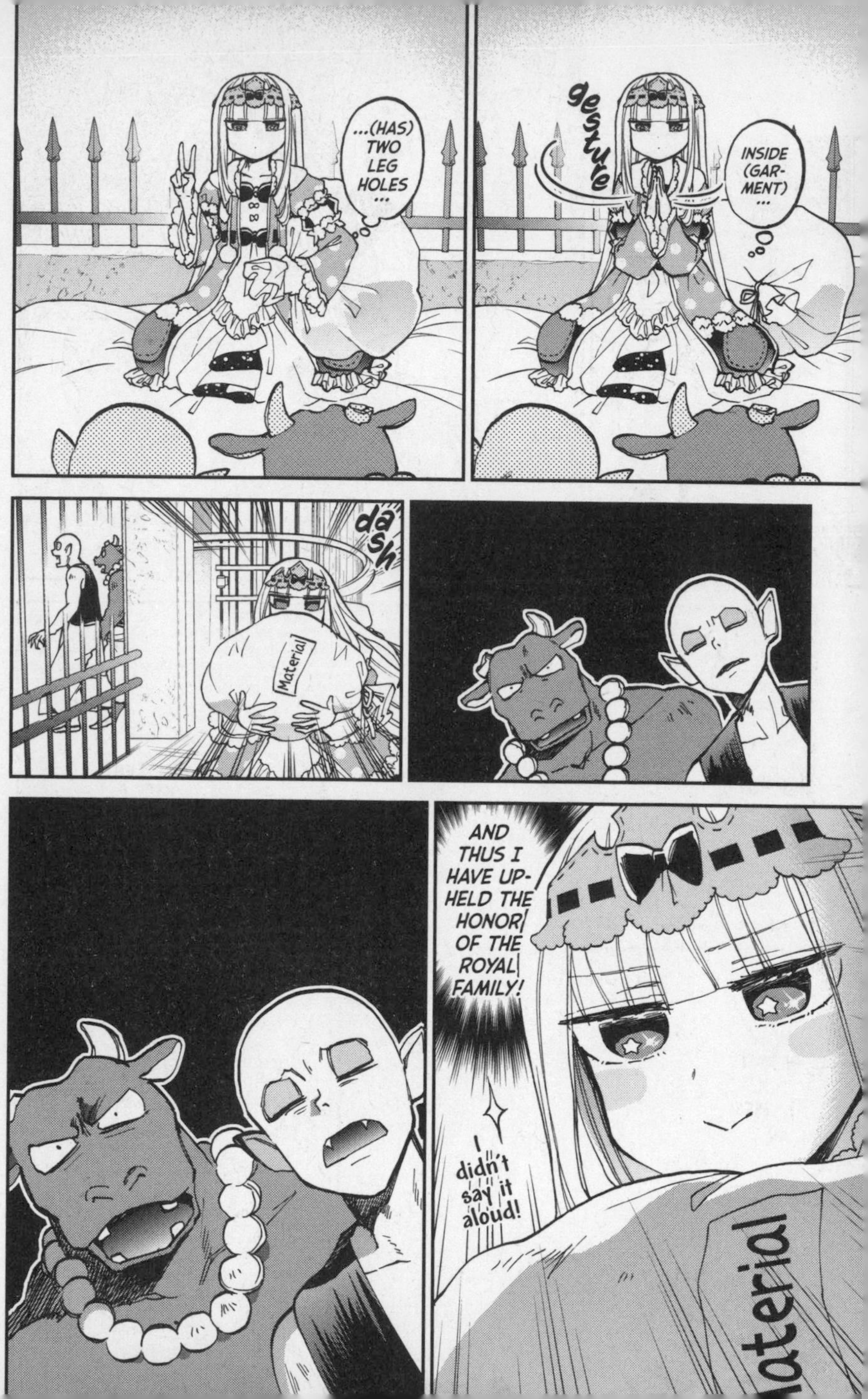
gesture
INSIDE (GARMENT) ...
...(HAS) TWO LEG HOLES ...
dash
Material
AND THUS I HAVE UPHELD THE HONOR OF THE ROYAL FAMILY!
I didn't say it aloud!
Material

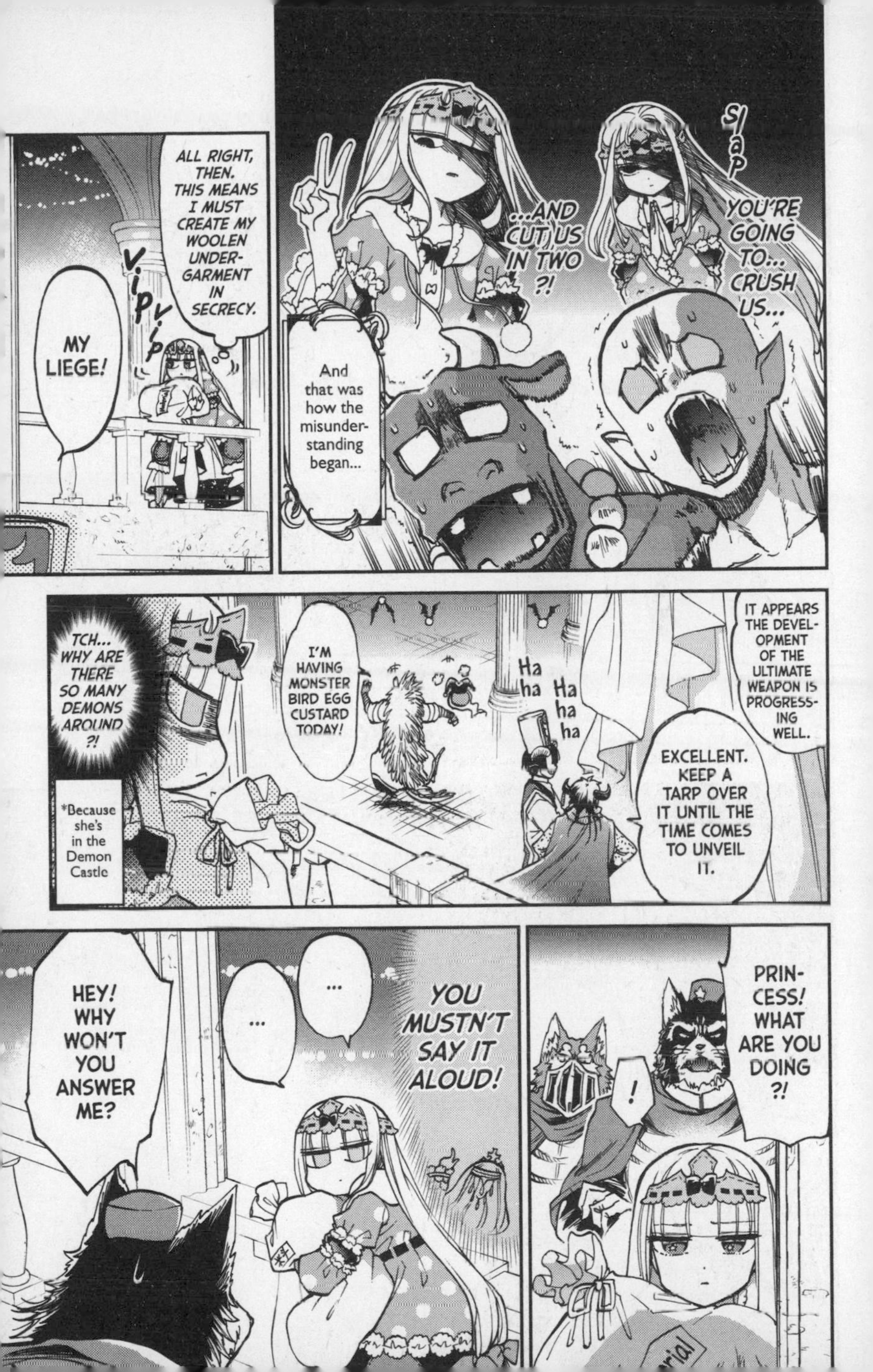
Slap
YOU'RE GOING TO... CRUSH US...
...AND CUT US IN TWO ?!
And that was how the misunderstanding began...
ALL RIGHT, THEN. THIS MEANS I MUST CREATE MY WOOLEN UNDERGARMENT IN SECRECY.
Vip Vip
MY LIEGE!
IT APPEARS THE DEVELOPMENT OF THE ULTIMATE WEAPON IS PROGRESSING WELL.
EXCELLENT. KEEP A TARP OVER IT UNTIL THE TIME COMES TO UNVEIL IT.
Ha ha Ha ha ha
I'M HAVING MONSTER BIRD EGG CUSTARD TODAY!
TCH... WHY ARE THERE SO MANY DEMONS AROUND ?!
*Because she's in the Demon Castle
PRINCESS! WHAT ARE YOU DOING ?!
!
YOU MUSTN'T SAY IT ALOUD!
...
...
HEY! WHY WON'T YOU ANSWER ME?

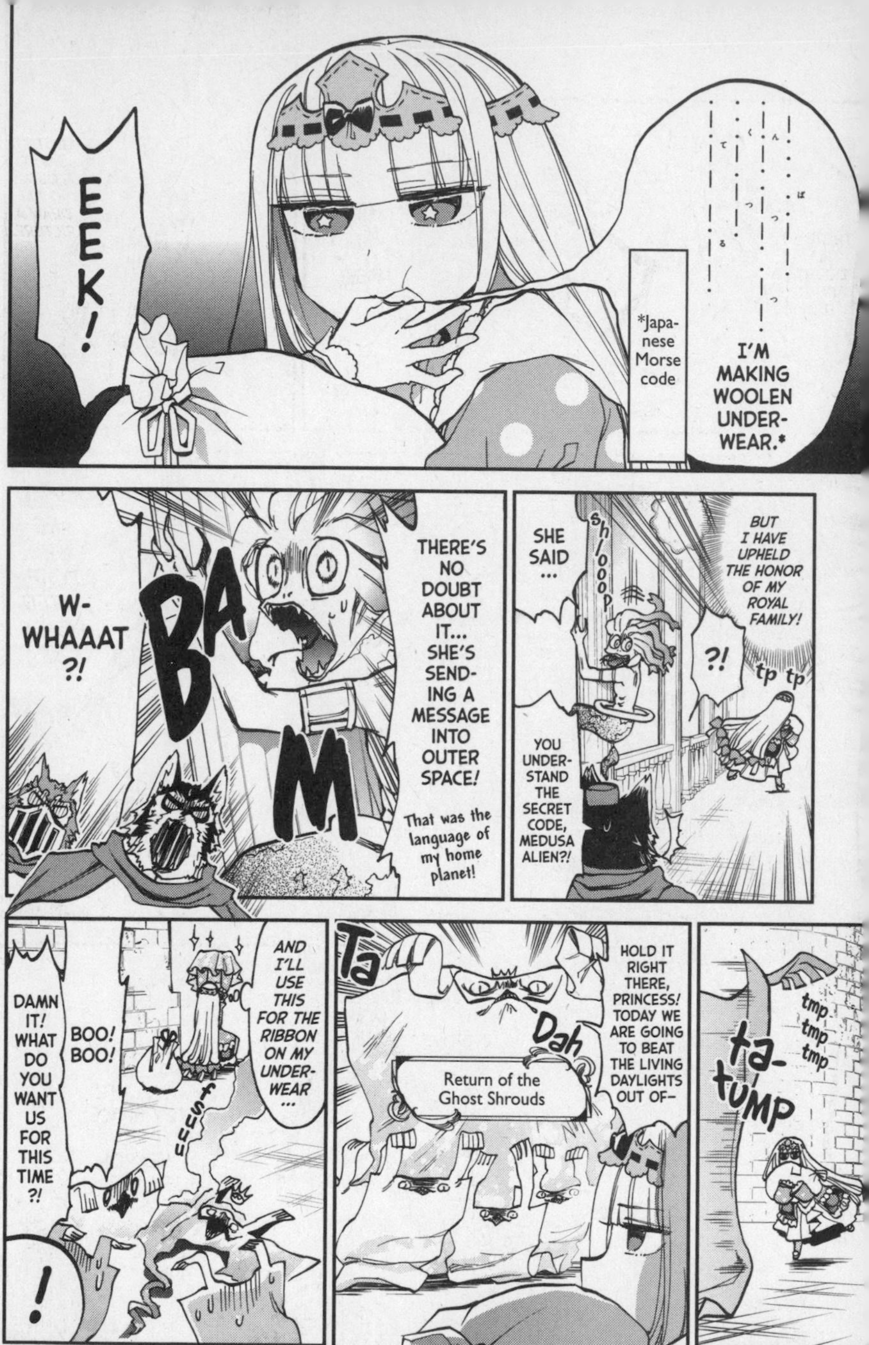
I'M MAKING WOOLEN UNDER-WEAR.*
*Japanese Morse code
EEK!
BUT I HAVE UPHELD THE HONOR OF MY ROYAL FAMILY!
?!
tp tp
SHE SAID ...
sh/ooop
YOU UNDER-STAND THE SECRET CODE, MEDUSA ALIEN?!
THERE'S NO DOUBT ABOUT IT... SHE'S SEND-ING A MESSAGE INTO OUTER SPACE!
That was the language of my home planet!
BAM
W-WHAAAT?!
tmp tmp tmp
ta-tump
HOLD IT RIGHT THERE, PRINCESS! TODAY WE ARE GOING TO BEAT THE LIVING DAYLIGHTS OUT OF–
Ta Dah
Return of the Ghost Shrouds
AND I'LL USE THIS FOR THE RIBBON ON MY UNDER-WEAR ...
fsssss
BOO! BOO!
DAMN IT! WHAT DO YOU WANT US FOR THIS TIME?!
!

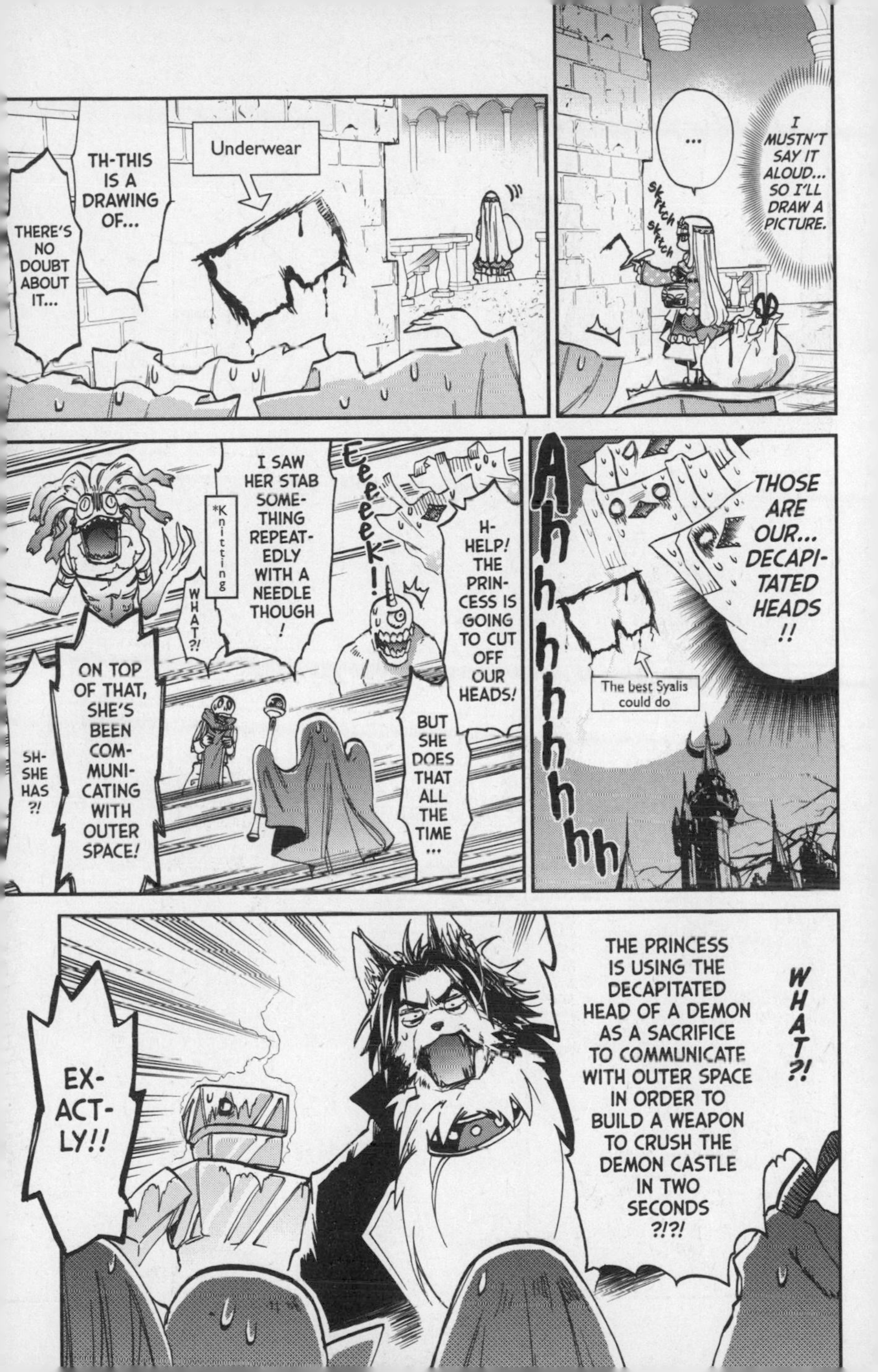
...
I MUSTN'T SAY IT ALOUD... SO I'LL DRAW A PICTURE.
skritch skritch
TH-THIS IS A DRAWING OF...
Underwear
THERE'S NO DOUBT ABOUT IT...
Ahhhhhhhh
THOSE ARE OUR... DECAPITATED HEADS!!
The best Syalis could do
Eeeeek!
H-HELP! THE PRINCESS IS GOING TO CUT OFF OUR HEADS!
BUT SHE DOES THAT ALL THE TIME...
I SAW HER STAB SOMETHING REPEATEDLY WITH A NEEDLE THOUGH!
*Knitting
WHAT?!
ON TOP OF THAT, SHE'S BEEN COMMUNICATING WITH OUTER SPACE!
SH-SHE HAS?!
WHAT?!
THE PRINCESS IS USING THE DECAPITATED HEAD OF A DEMON AS A SACRIFICE TO COMMUNICATE WITH OUTER SPACE IN ORDER TO BUILD A WEAPON TO CRUSH THE DEMON CASTLE IN TWO SECONDS?!?!
EXACTLY!!

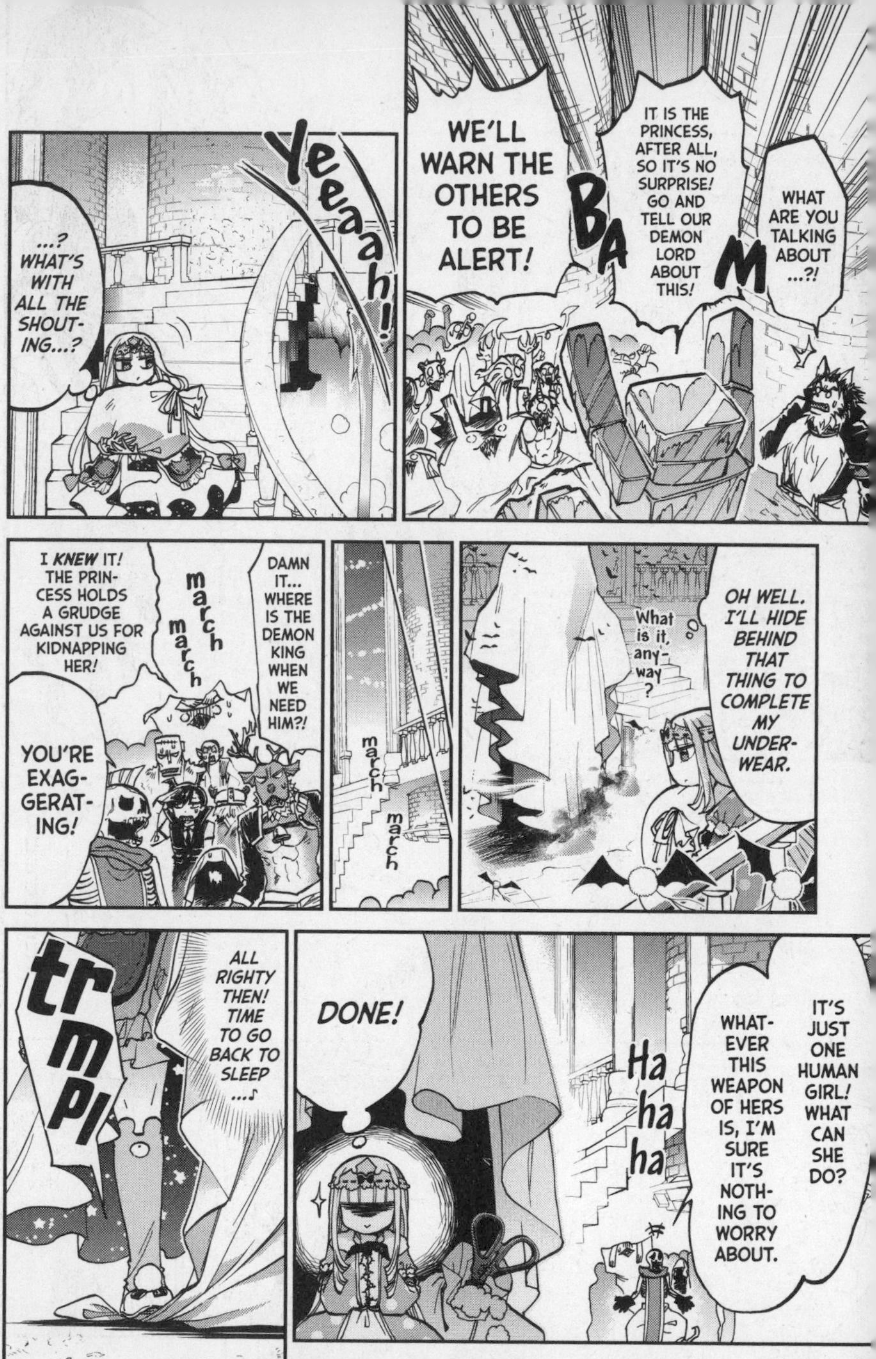
WHAT ARE YOU TALKING ABOUT ...?!
IT IS THE PRINCESS, AFTER ALL, SO IT'S NO SURPRISE! GO AND TELL OUR DEMON LORD ABOUT THIS!
BAM
WE'LL WARN THE OTHERS TO BE ALERT!
Yeeaaah!
...? WHAT'S WITH ALL THE SHOUTING...?
OH WELL. I'LL HIDE BEHIND THAT THING TO COMPLETE MY UNDERWEAR.
What is it, anyway?
march march
DAMN IT... WHERE IS THE DEMON KING WHEN WE NEED HIM?!
I KNEW IT! THE PRINCESS HOLDS A GRUDGE AGAINST US FOR KIDNAPPING HER!
march march march
YOU'RE EXAGGERATING!
IT'S JUST ONE HUMAN GIRL! WHAT CAN SHE DO?
WHATEVER THIS WEAPON OF HERS IS, I'M SURE IT'S NOTHING TO WORRY ABOUT.
Ha ha ha
DONE!
ALL RIGHTY THEN! TIME TO GO BACK TO SLEEP ...♪
trmp!

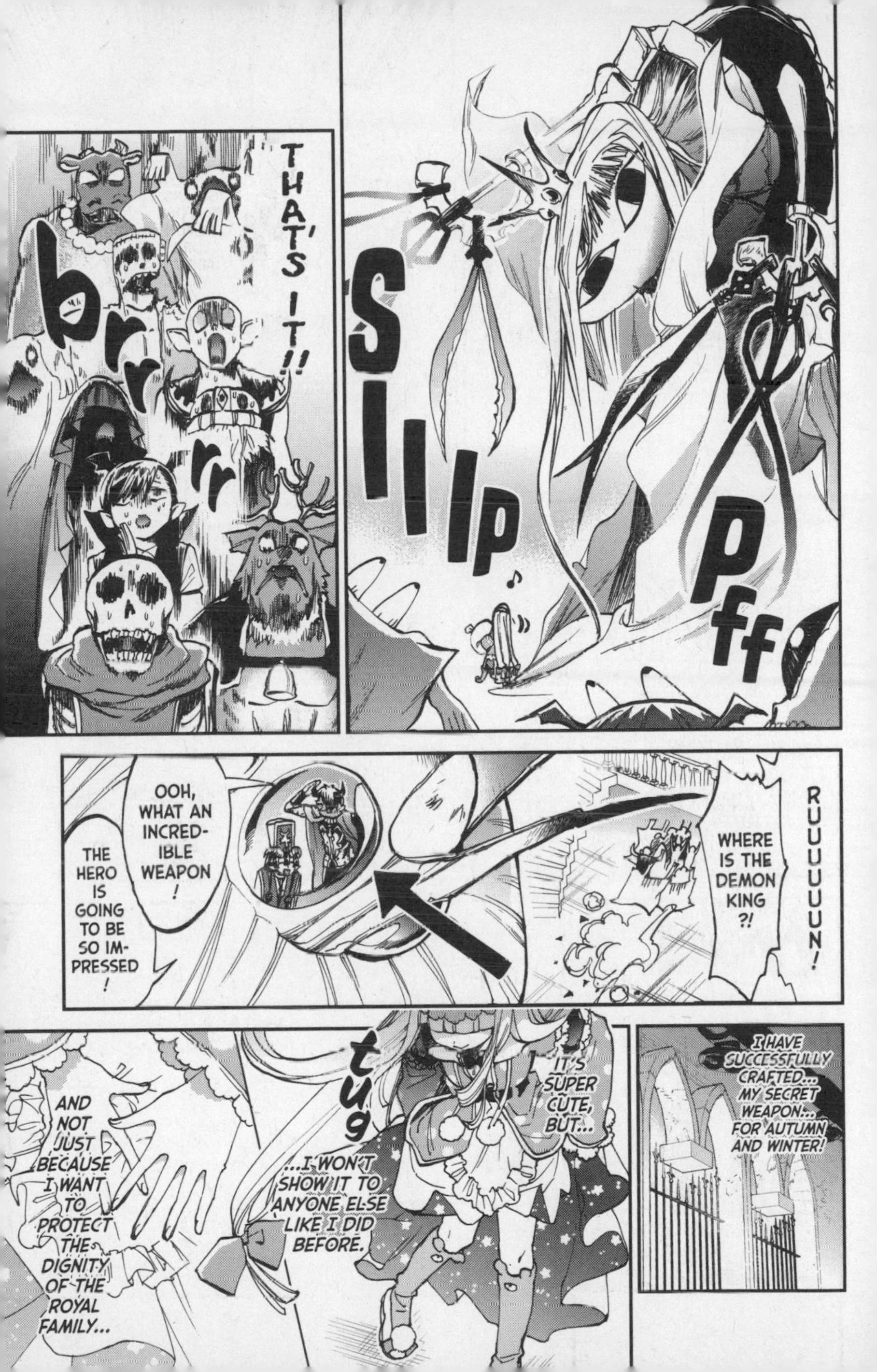
SLIIP
Pff
THAT'S IT!!
brrrr
RUUUUUUN!
WHERE IS THE DEMON KING?!
OOH, WHAT AN INCREDIBLE WEAPON!
THE HERO IS GOING TO BE SO IMPRESSED!
I HAVE SUCCESSFULLY CRAFTED... MY SECRET WEAPON... FOR AUTUMN AND WINTER!
IT'S SUPER CUTE, BUT...
tug
...I WON'T SHOW IT TO ANYONE ELSE LIKE I DID BEFORE.
AND NOT JUST BECAUSE I WANT TO PROTECT THE DIGNITY OF THE ROYAL FAMILY...

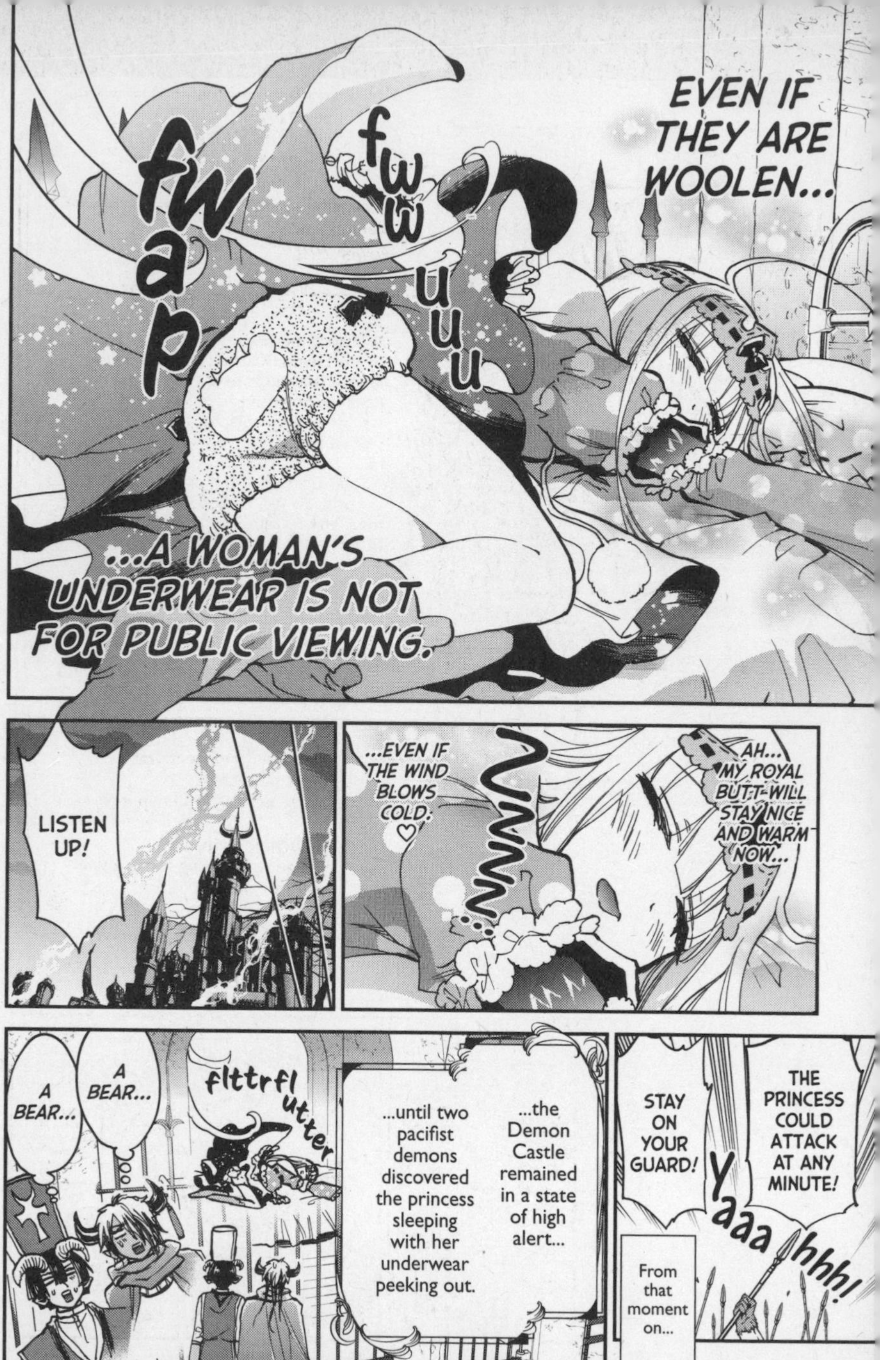
EVEN IF THEY ARE WOOLEN...
fwwuuu
fwap
...A WOMAN'S UNDERWEAR IS NOT FOR PUBLIC VIEWING.
AH... MY ROYAL BUTT WILL STAY NICE AND WARM NOW...
...EVEN IF THE WIND BLOWS COLD. ♡
LISTEN UP!
THE PRINCESS COULD ATTACK AT ANY MINUTE!
STAY ON YOUR GUARD!
Yaaahhh!
From that moment on...
...the Demon Castle remained in a state of high alert...
...until two pacifist demons discovered the princess sleeping with her underwear peeking out.
flttrflutter
A BEAR...
A BEAR...

Evil Scissors Princess

Sleepy Princess: ☆☆☆☆☆☆
Power: ?????

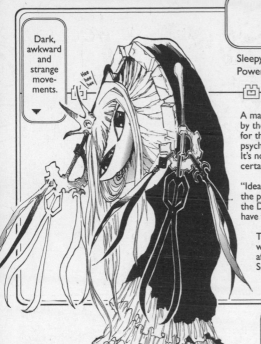

Dark, awkward and strange move-ments.
Hee hee hee

A magical mechanical weapon developed by the Demon Castle's upper echelons for the sole purpose of causing the hero psychological damage.
It's not very durable, but it resembles a certain someone...

"Ideally the hero, Dawner, will mistake it for the princess turned into a cyborg," stated the Demon King. But thus far, only demons have fallen for it.

The Demon King seemed full of glee when he said, "I'm going to send this after the hero when the time comes!" So it's probably undamaged.

Problem before it was completed:
"Where will we keep it?"

Current problem:
"I get the feeling it has a will of its own..."

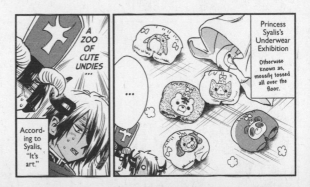

Princess Syalis's Underwear Exhibition
Otherwise known as, messily tossed all over the floor.
...
A ZOO OF CUTE UNDIES...
According to Syalis, "It's art."

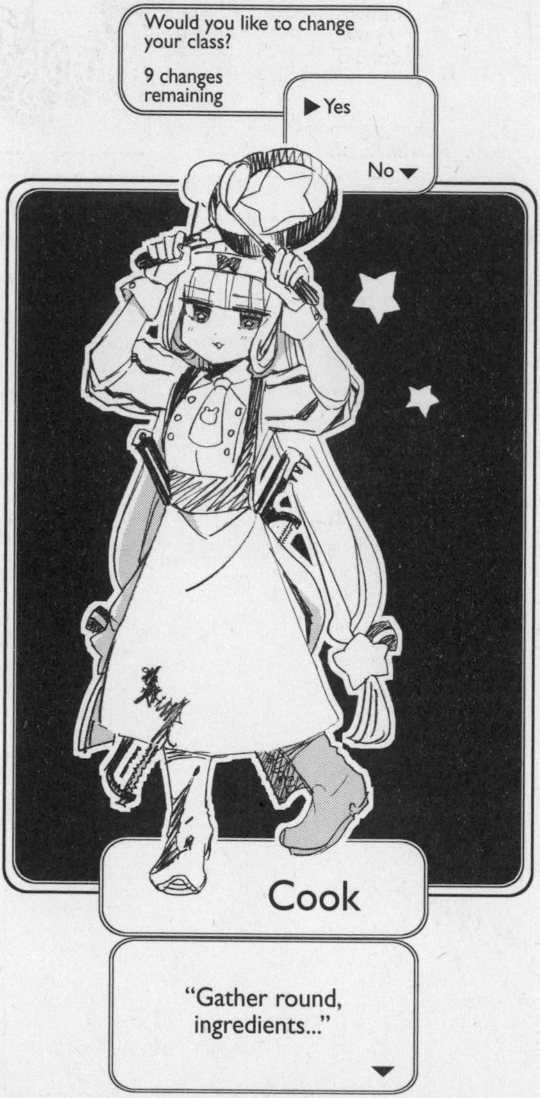
Would you like to change your class?
9 changes remaining
▶Yes
No
Cook
"Gather round, ingredients..."

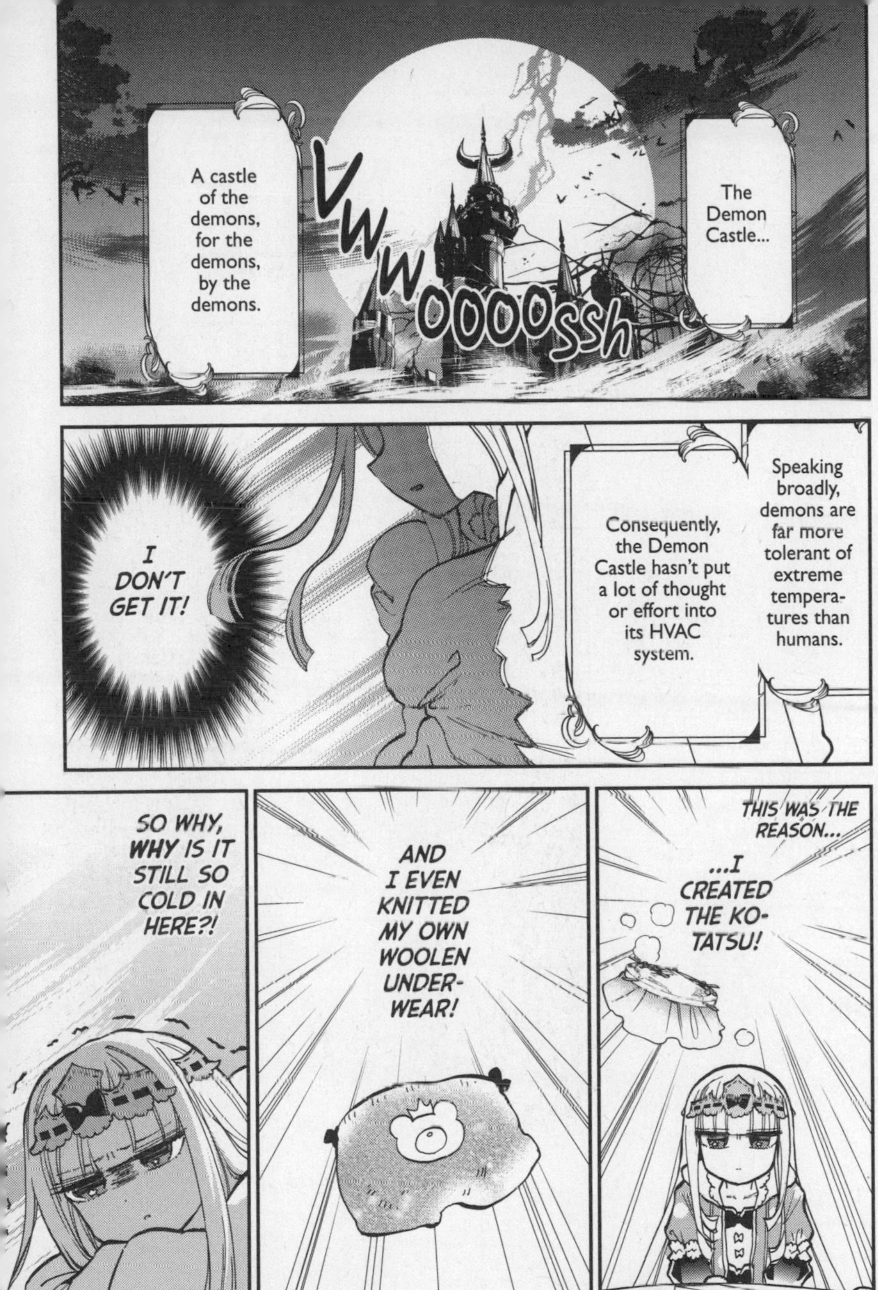
The Demon Castle...
VWWOOOOSSH
A castle of the demons, for the demons, by the demons.
Speaking broadly, demons are far more tolerant of extreme tempera- tures than humans.
Consequently, the Demon Castle hasn't put a lot of thought or effort into its HVAC system.
I DON'T GET IT!
THIS WAS THE REASON...
...I CREATED THE KO- TATSU!
AND I EVEN KNITTED MY OWN WOOLEN UNDER- WEAR!
SO WHY, WHY IS IT STILL SO COLD IN HERE?!

30th Night: Let's Remodel Your Window!

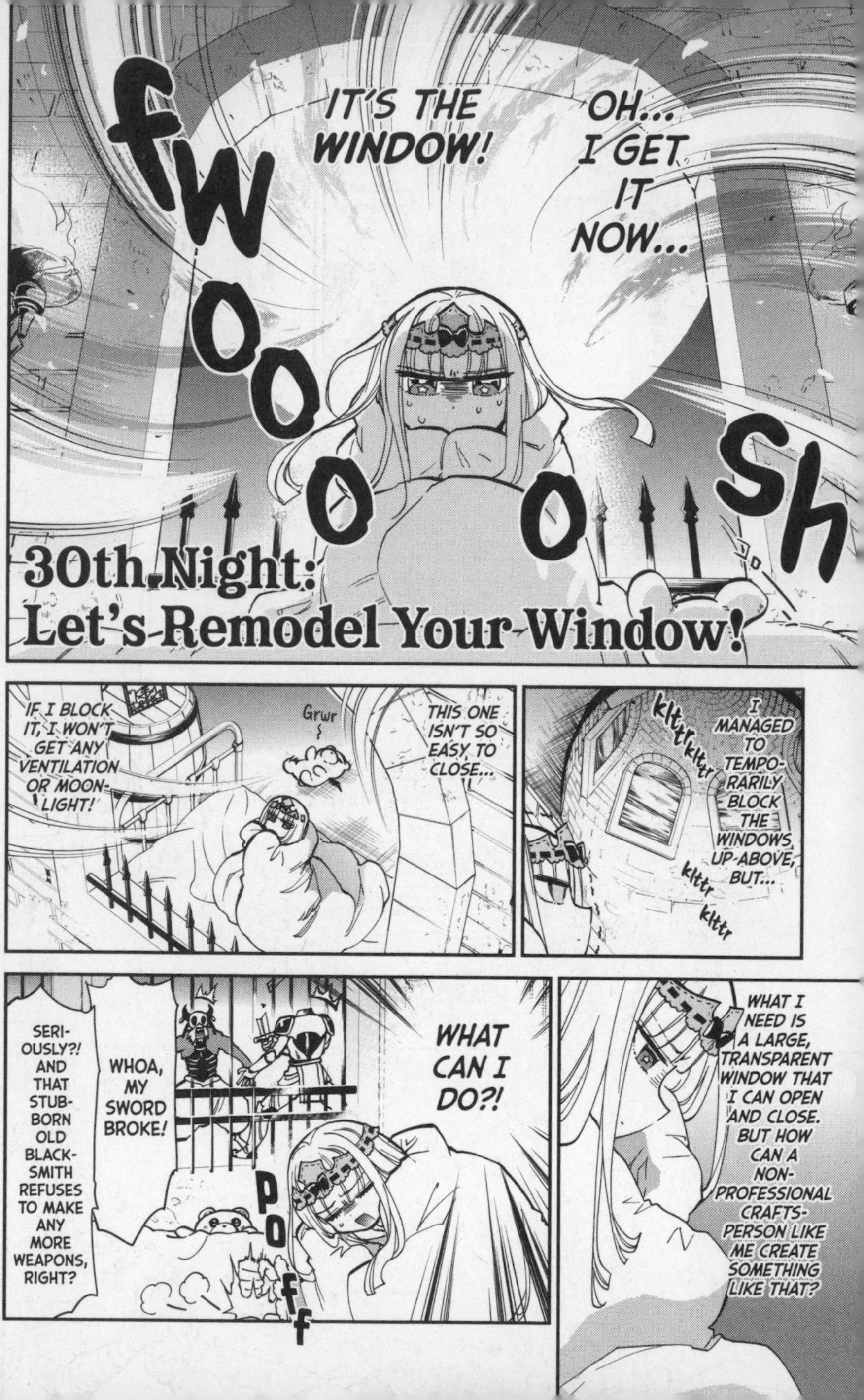
OH... I GET IT NOW...
IT'S THE WINDOW!
fWOOOOSh
30th Night: Let's Remodel Your Window!
kltt rkltt r
I MANAGED TO TEMPORARILY BLOCK THE WINDOWS UP ABOVE, BUT...
klttr klttr
THIS ONE ISN'T SO EASY TO CLOSE...
Grwr
IF I BLOCK IT, I WON'T GET ANY VENTILATION OR MOONLIGHT!
WHAT I NEED IS A LARGE, TRANSPARENT WINDOW THAT I CAN OPEN AND CLOSE. BUT HOW CAN A NON-PROFESSIONAL CRAFTSPERSON LIKE ME CREATE SOMETHING LIKE THAT?
WHAT CAN I DO?!
WHOA, MY SWORD BROKE!
SERIOUSLY?! AND THAT STUBBORN OLD BLACKSMITH REFUSES TO MAKE ANY MORE WEAPONS, RIGHT?
poff

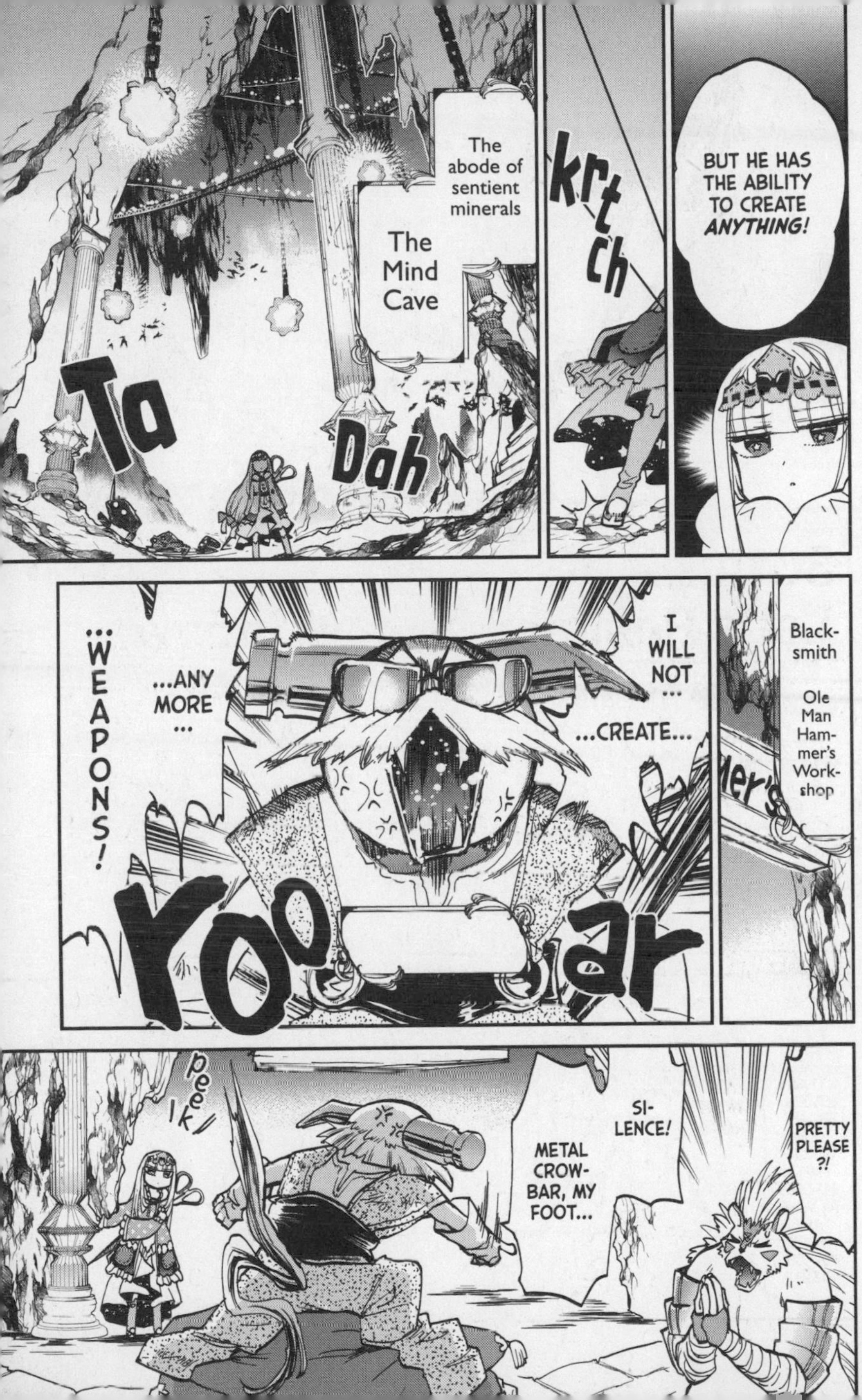
BUT HE HAS THE ABILITY TO CREATE *ANYTHING!*
krtch
The abode of sentient minerals
The Mind Cave
Ta
Dah
Blacksmith
Ole Man Hammer's Workshop
mer's
I WILL NOT ...
...CREATE...
...ANY MORE ...
...WEAPONS!
Roo ar
PRETTY PLEASE ?!
SI-LENCE!
METAL CROW-BAR, MY FOOT...
peeek!

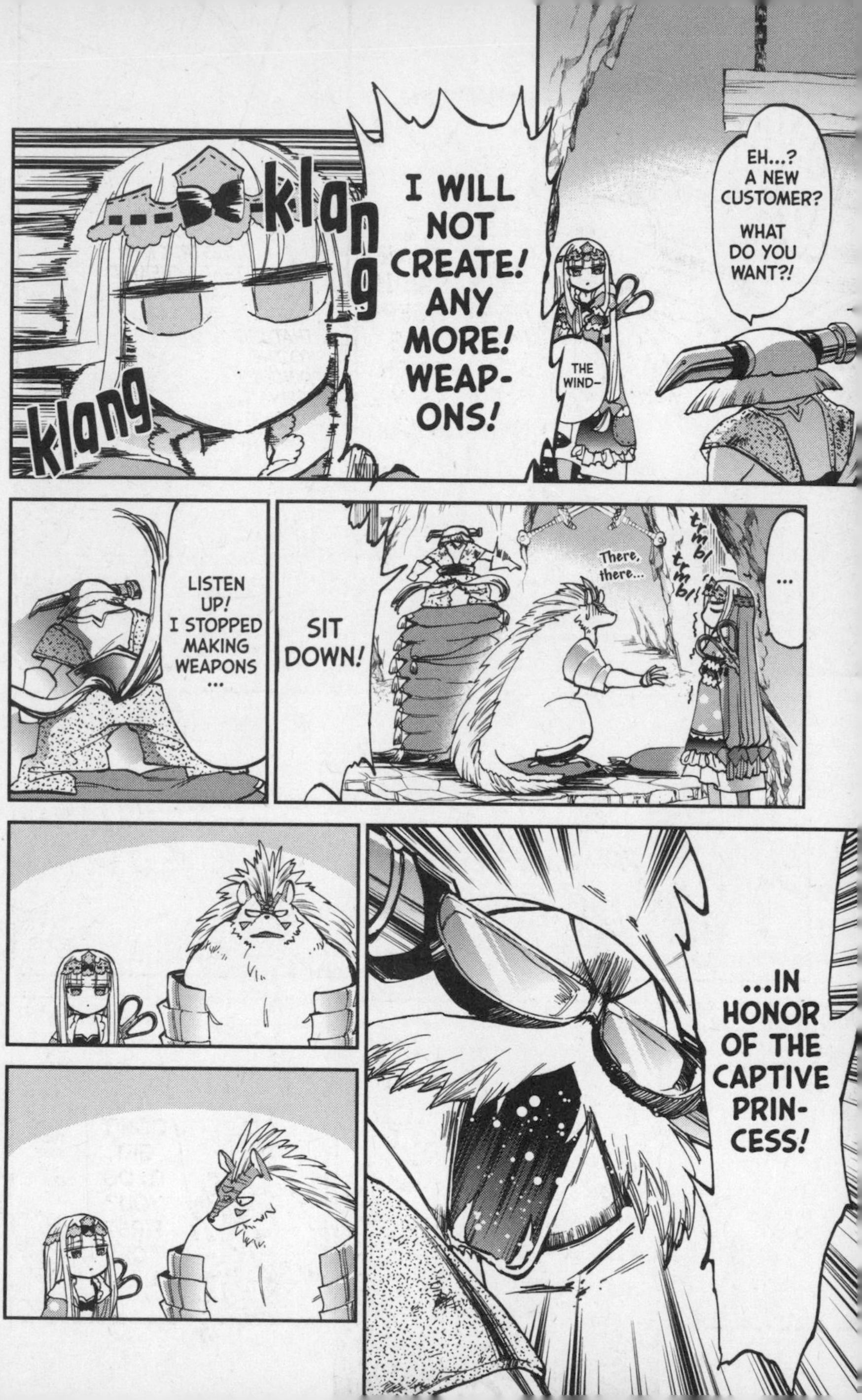
EH...? A NEW CUSTOMER?
WHAT DO YOU WANT?!
THE WIND-
I WILL NOT CREATE! ANY MORE! WEAPONS!
---klang
klang
trmbl trmbl
There, there...
...
SIT DOWN!
LISTEN UP! I STOPPED MAKING WEAPONS ...
...IN HONOR OF THE CAPTIVE PRIN-CESS!

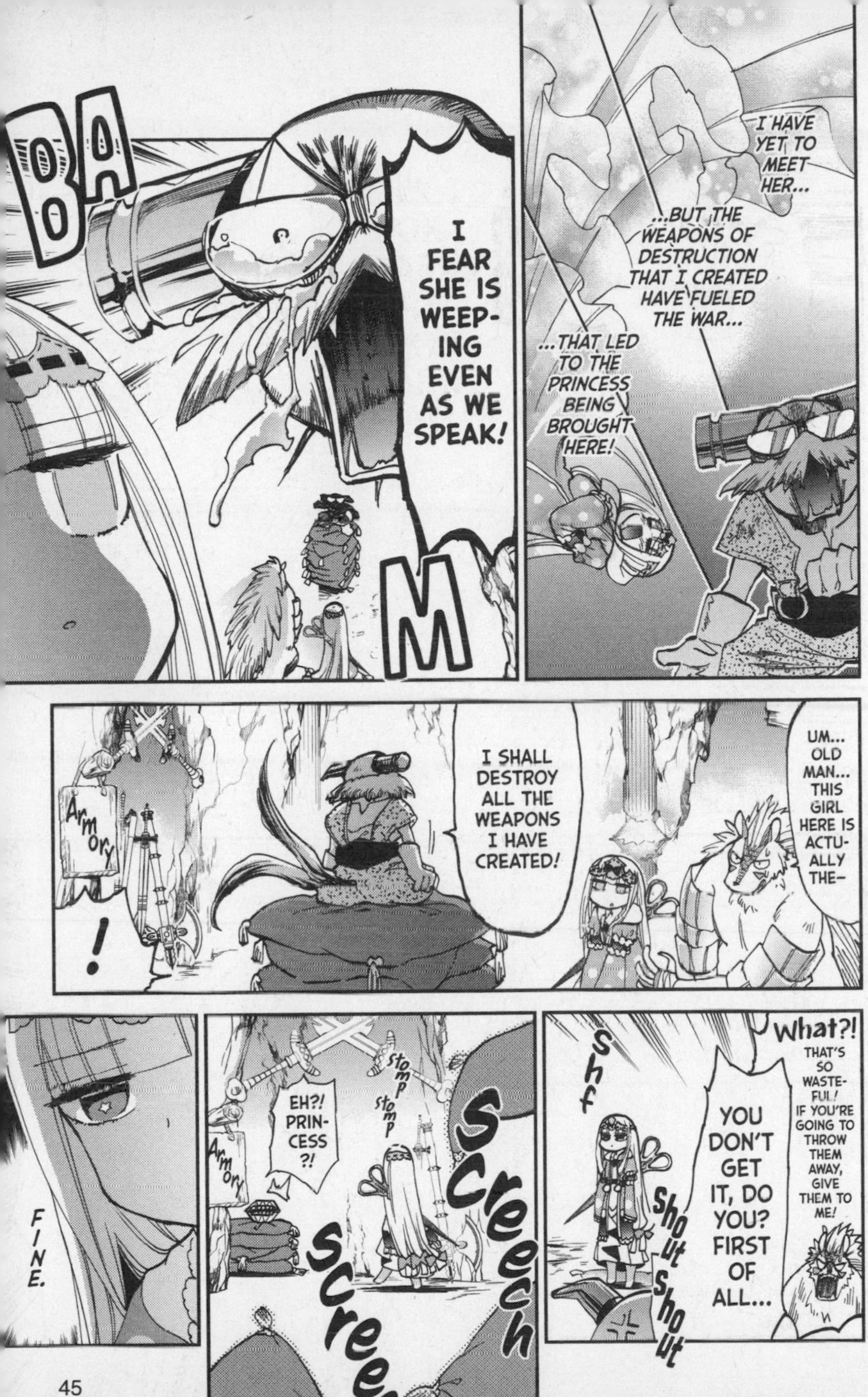
I HAVE YET TO MEET HER...
...BUT THE WEAPONS OF DESTRUCTION THAT I CREATED HAVE FUELED THE WAR...
...THAT LED TO THE PRINCESS BEING BROUGHT HERE!
BAO
I FEAR SHE IS WEEPING EVEN AS WE SPEAK!
M
UM... OLD MAN... THIS GIRL HERE IS ACTUALLY THE–
I SHALL DESTROY ALL THE WEAPONS I HAVE CREATED!
Armory
!
What?!
THAT'S SO WASTEFUL! IF YOU'RE GOING TO THROW THEM AWAY, GIVE THEM TO ME!
Shf
YOU DON'T GET IT, DO YOU? FIRST OF ALL...
Shout shout
stomp stomp
EH?! PRINCESS?!
Screech screech
Armory
FINE.

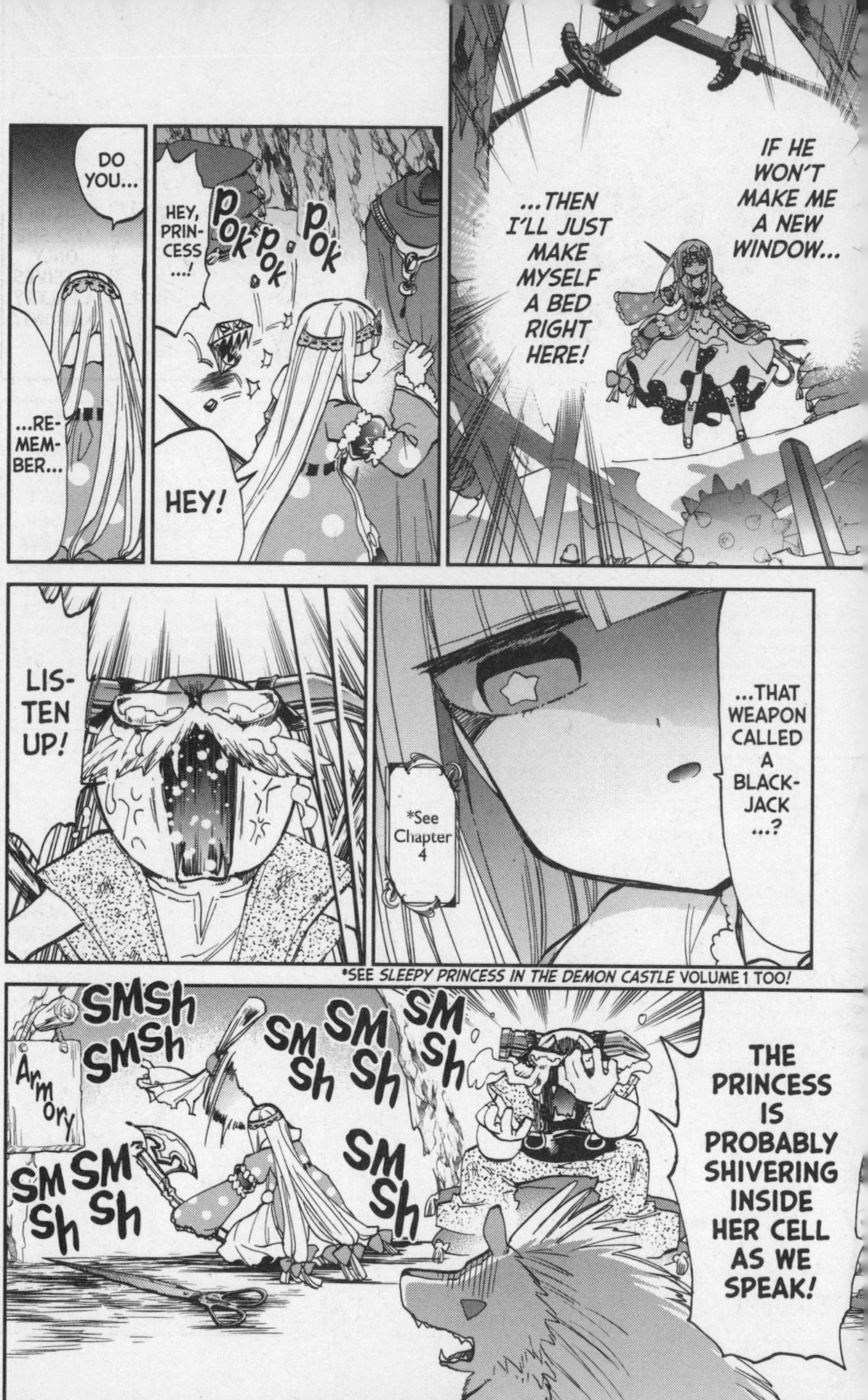
IF HE WON'T MAKE ME A NEW WINDOW...
...THEN I'LL JUST MAKE MYSELF A BED RIGHT HERE!
POK
POK
POK
HEY, PRINCESS...!
HEY!
DO YOU...
...REMEMBER...
...THAT WEAPON CALLED A BLACKJACK...?
*See Chapter 4
LISTEN UP!
THE PRINCESS IS PROBABLY SHIVERING INSIDE HER CELL AS WE SPEAK!
SMSH
SMSH
SMSH
SMSH
SMSH
SMSH
SMSH
Armory

*SEE *SLEEPY PRINCESS IN THE DEMON CASTLE* VOLUME 1 TOO!

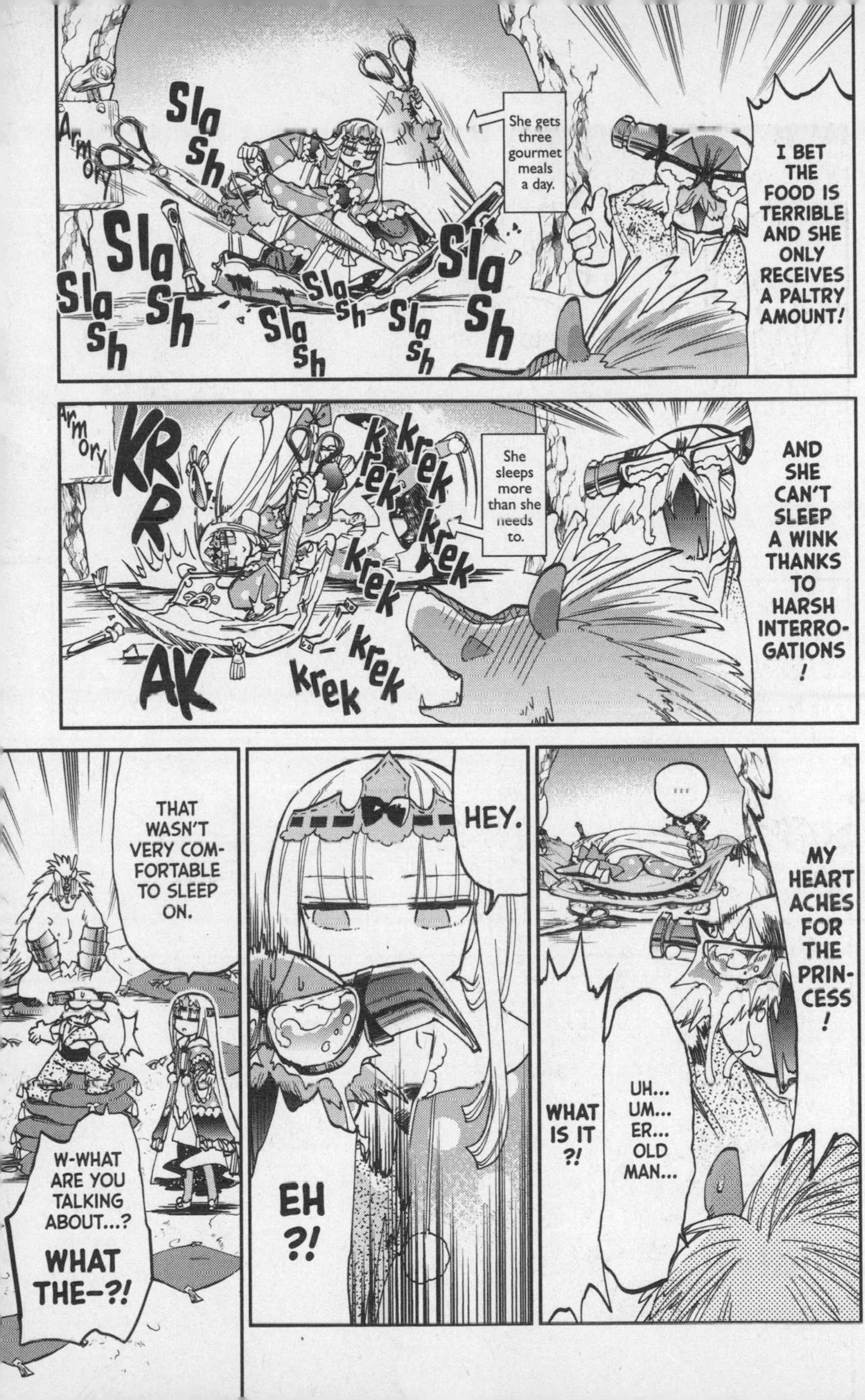
I BET THE FOOD IS TERRIBLE AND SHE ONLY RECEIVES A PALTRY AMOUNT!
She gets three gourmet meals a day.
Slash Slash Slash Slash Slash Slash Slash Slash
Armory
AND SHE CAN'T SLEEP A WINK THANKS TO HARSH INTERROGATIONS!
She sleeps more than she needs to.
krek krek krek krek krek krek krek
KRRAK
Armory
...
MY HEART ACHES FOR THE PRINCESS!
UH... UM... ER... OLD MAN...
WHAT IS IT?!
HEY.
EH?!
THAT WASN'T VERY COMFORTABLE TO SLEEP ON.
W-WHAT ARE YOU TALKING ABOUT...? WHAT THE–?!

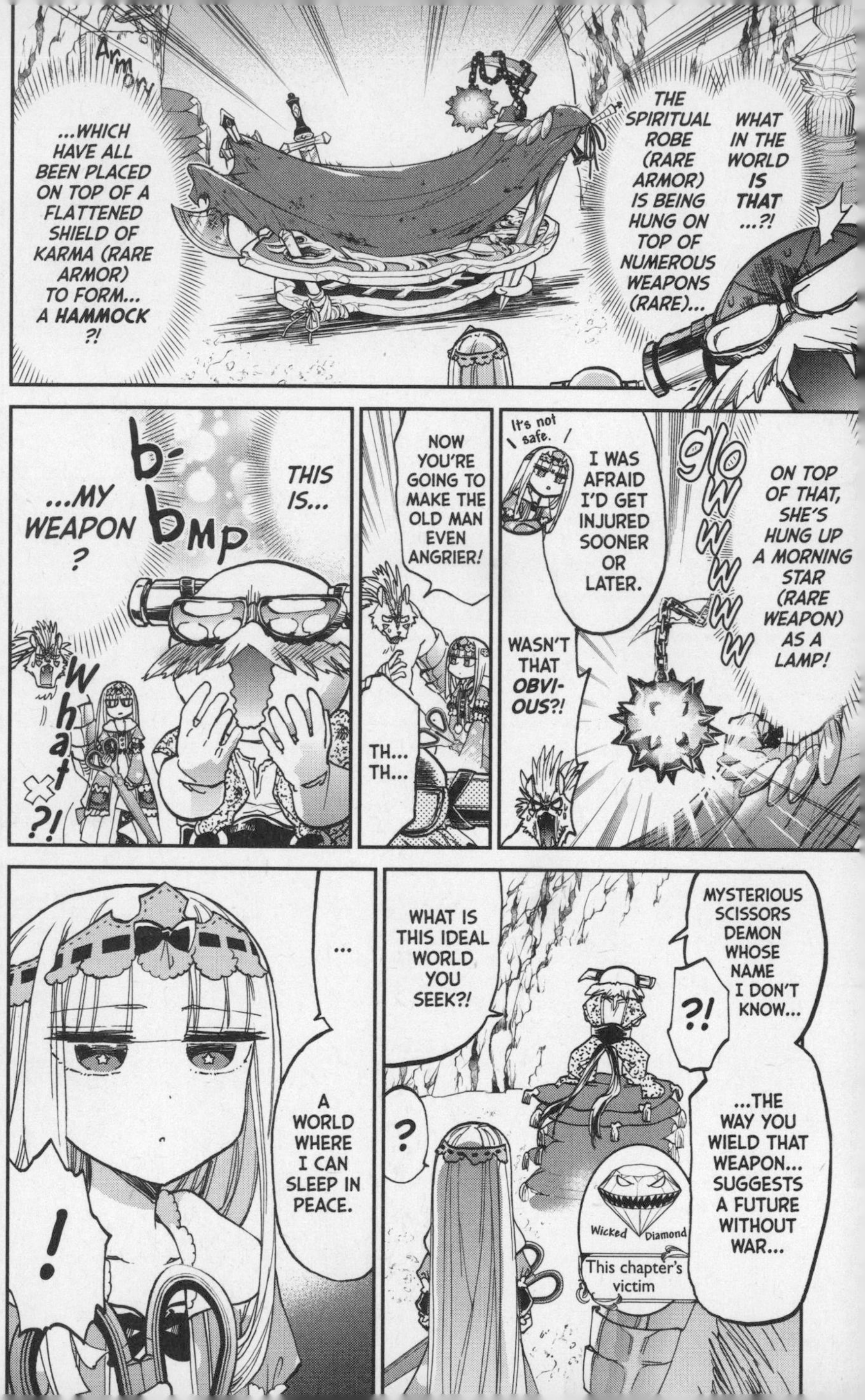
WHAT IN THE WORLD IS THAT ...?!
THE SPIRITUAL ROBE (RARE ARMOR) IS BEING HUNG ON TOP OF NUMEROUS WEAPONS (RARE)...
Armory
...WHICH HAVE ALL BEEN PLACED ON TOP OF A FLATTENED SHIELD OF KARMA (RARE ARMOR) TO FORM... A HAMMOCK ?!
ON TOP OF THAT, SHE'S HUNG UP A MORNING STAR (RARE WEAPON) AS A LAMP!
glowwwwwww
It's not safe.
I WAS AFRAID I'D GET INJURED SOONER OR LATER.
WASN'T THAT OBVIOUS?!
NOW YOU'RE GOING TO MAKE THE OLD MAN EVEN ANGRIER!
TH... TH...
THIS IS...
b-bmp
...MY WEAPON ?
What ×?!
MYSTERIOUS SCISSORS DEMON WHOSE NAME I DON'T KNOW...
?!
WHAT IS THIS IDEAL WORLD YOU SEEK?!
...THE WAY YOU WIELD THAT WEAPON... SUGGESTS A FUTURE WITHOUT WAR...
?
Wicked Diamond
This chapter's victim
...
A WORLD WHERE I CAN SLEEP IN PEACE.
!

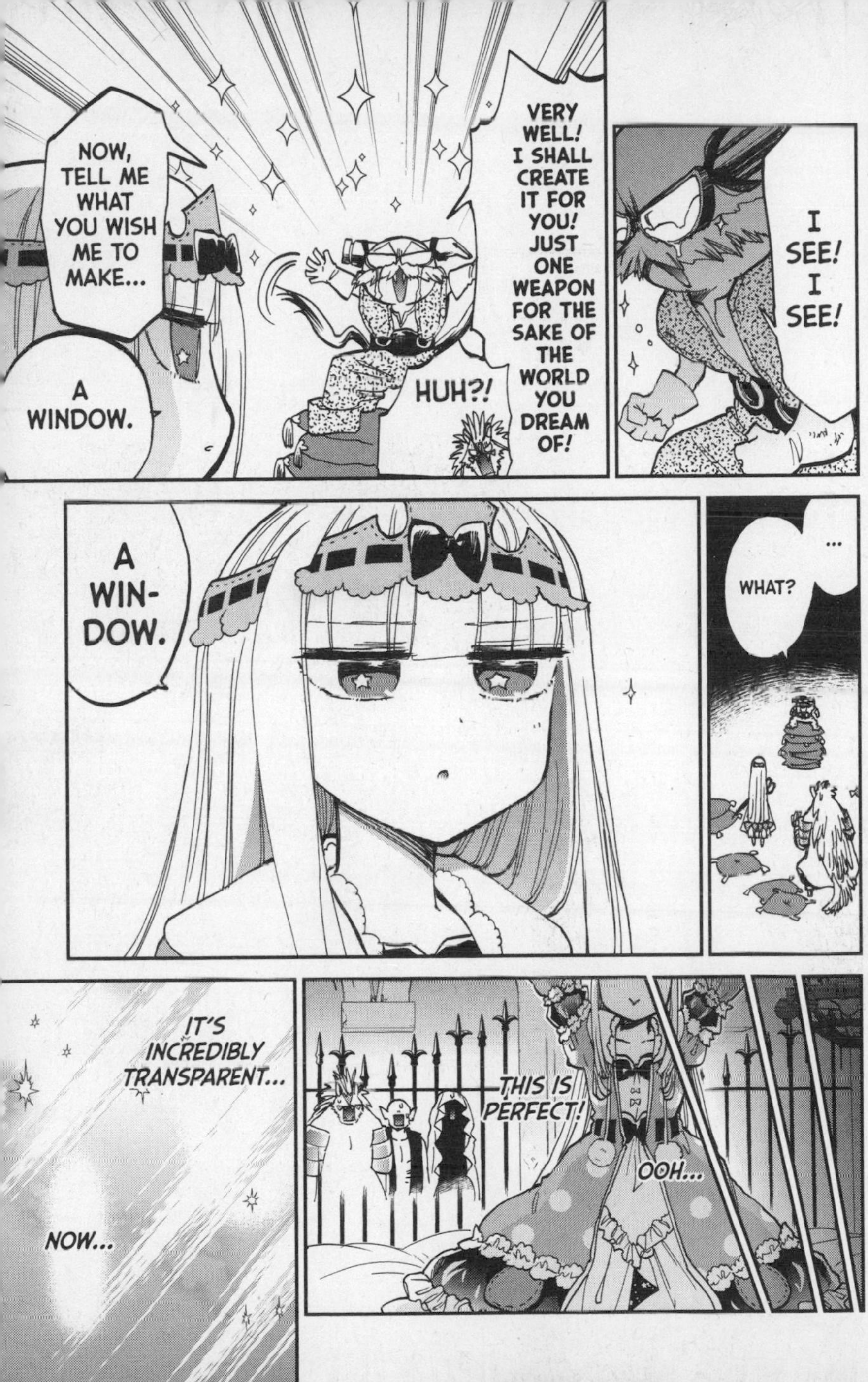
I SEE! I SEE!
VERY WELL! I SHALL CREATE IT FOR YOU! JUST ONE WEAPON FOR THE SAKE OF THE WORLD YOU DREAM OF!
NOW, TELL ME WHAT YOU WISH ME TO MAKE...
A WINDOW.
HUH?!
...
WHAT?
A WIN-DOW.
THIS IS PERFECT!
OOH...
IT'S INCREDIBLY TRANSPARENT...
NOW...

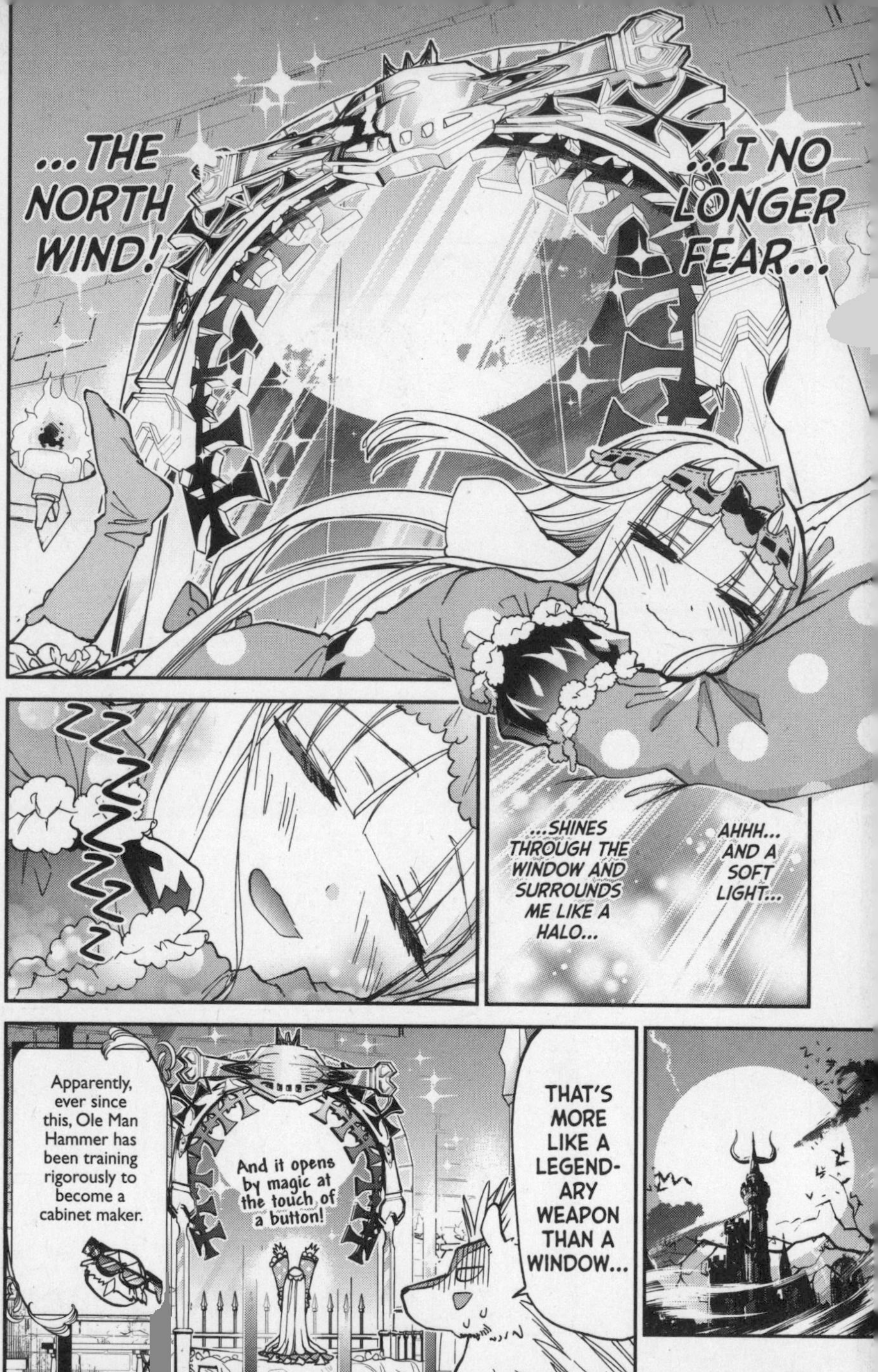
...I NO LONGER FEAR...
...THE NORTH WIND!
AHHH... AND A SOFT LIGHT...
...SHINES THROUGH THE WINDOW AND SURROUNDS ME LIKE A HALO...
THAT'S MORE LIKE A LEGENDARY WEAPON THAN A WINDOW...
And it opens by magic at the touch of a button!
Apparently, ever since this, Ole Man Hammer has been training rigorously to become a cabinet maker.

Ole Man Hammer

A dangerous old man.

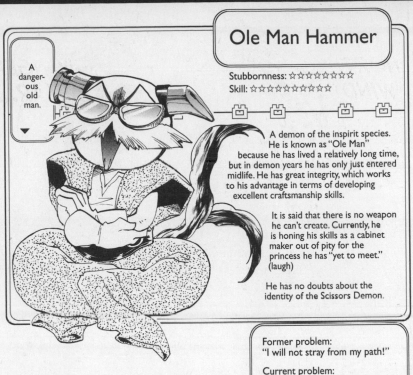

Stubbornness: ☆☆☆☆☆☆☆☆
Skill: ☆☆☆☆☆☆☆☆☆☆

A demon of the inspirit species. He is known as "Ole Man" because he has lived a relatively long time, but in demon years he has only just entered midlife. He has great integrity, which works to his advantage in terms of developing excellent craftsmanship skills.

It is said that there is no weapon he can't create. Currently, he is honing his skills as a cabinet maker out of pity for the princess he has "yet to meet." (laugh)

He has no doubts about the identity of the Scissors Demon.

Former problem:
"I will not stray from my path!"

Current problem:
"The princess might be hungry!"

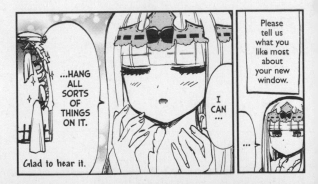

Please tell us what you like most about your new window.
...
I CAN ...
...HANG ALL SORTS OF THINGS ON IT.
Glad to hear it.

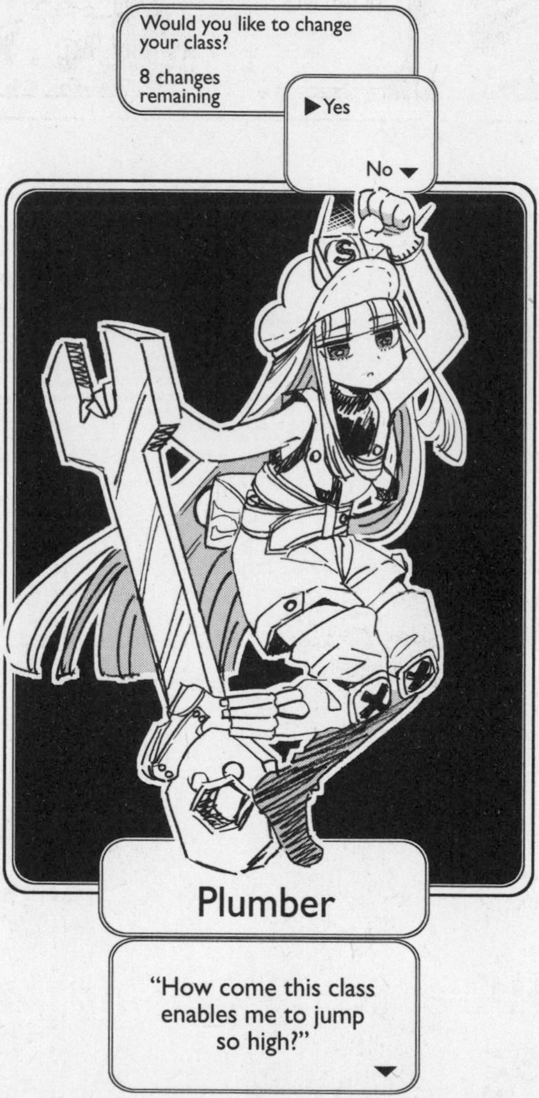
Would you like to change your class?
8 changes remaining
▶Yes
No
Plumber
"How come this class enables me to jump so high?"

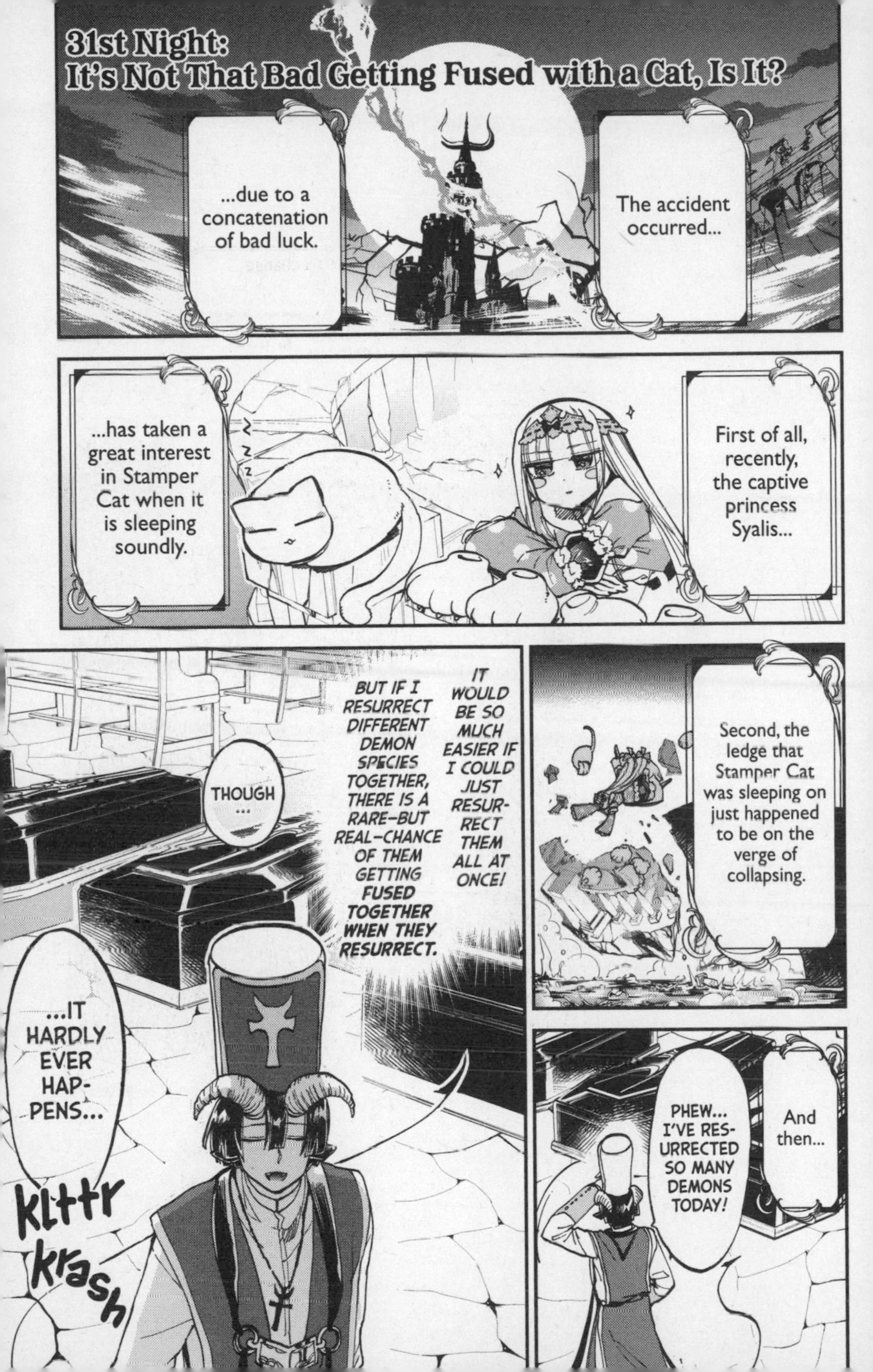
31st Night:
It's Not That Bad Getting Fused with a Cat, Is It?
The accident occurred...
...due to a concatenation of bad luck.
First of all, recently, the captive princess Syalis...
...has taken a great interest in Stamper Cat when it is sleeping soundly.
Second, the ledge that Stamper Cat was sleeping on just happened to be on the verge of collapsing.
And then...
PHEW... I'VE RESURRECTED SO MANY DEMONS TODAY!
IT WOULD BE SO MUCH EASIER IF I COULD JUST RESURRECT THEM ALL AT ONCE!
BUT IF I RESURRECT DIFFERENT DEMON SPECIES TOGETHER, THERE IS A RARE—BUT REAL—CHANCE OF THEM GETTING FUSED TOGETHER WHEN THEY RESURRECT.
THOUGH...
...IT HARDLY EVER HAPPENS...
Klttr
krash

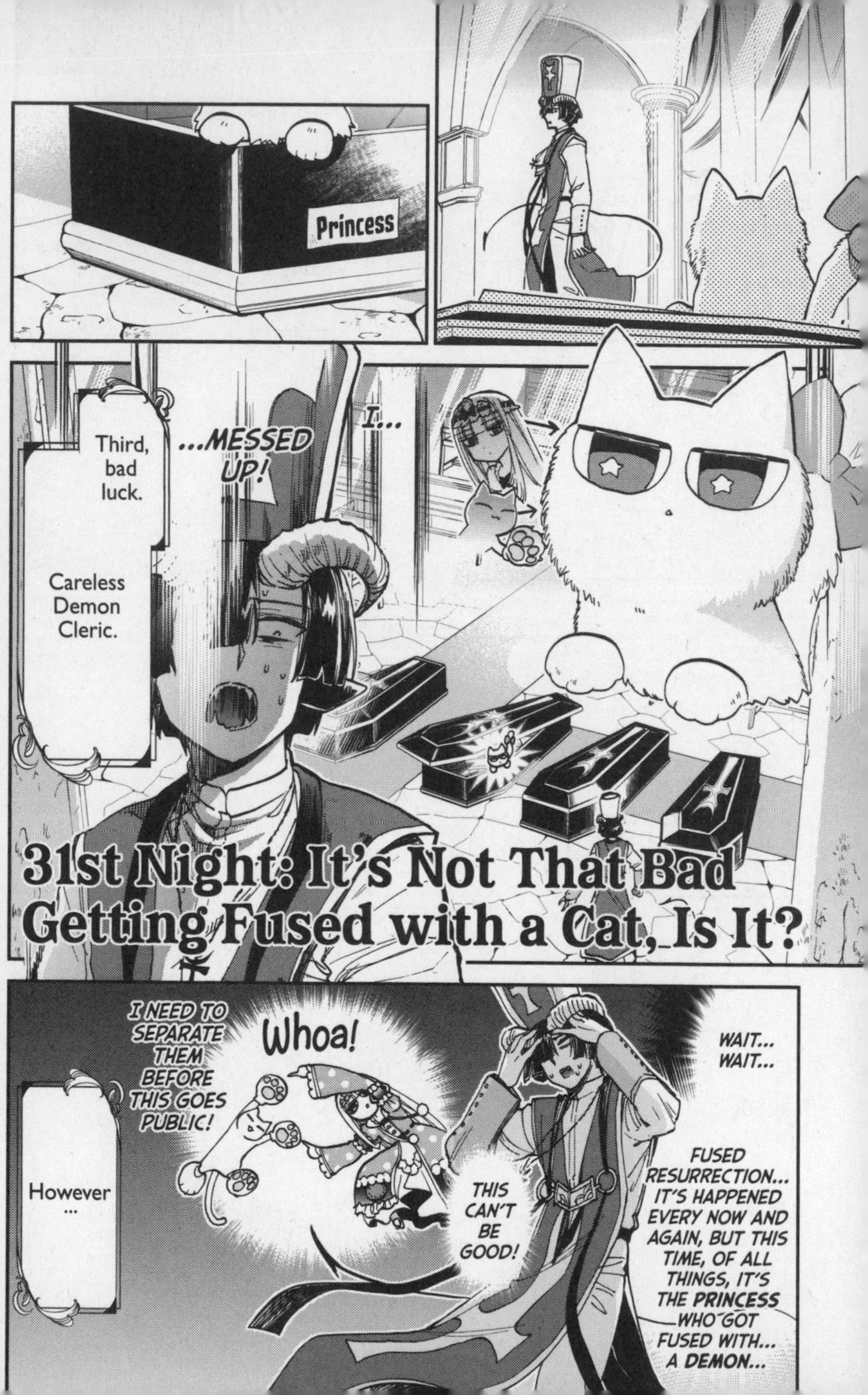
Princess
I...
...MESSED UP!
Third, bad luck.
Careless Demon Cleric.
31st Night: It's Not That Bad Getting Fused with a Cat, Is It?
WAIT... WAIT...
FUSED RESURRECTION... IT'S HAPPENED EVERY NOW AND AGAIN, BUT THIS TIME, OF ALL THINGS, IT'S THE PRINCESS WHO GOT FUSED WITH... A DEMON...
THIS CAN'T BE GOOD!
Whoa!
I NEED TO SEPARATE THEM BEFORE THIS GOES PUBLIC!
However...

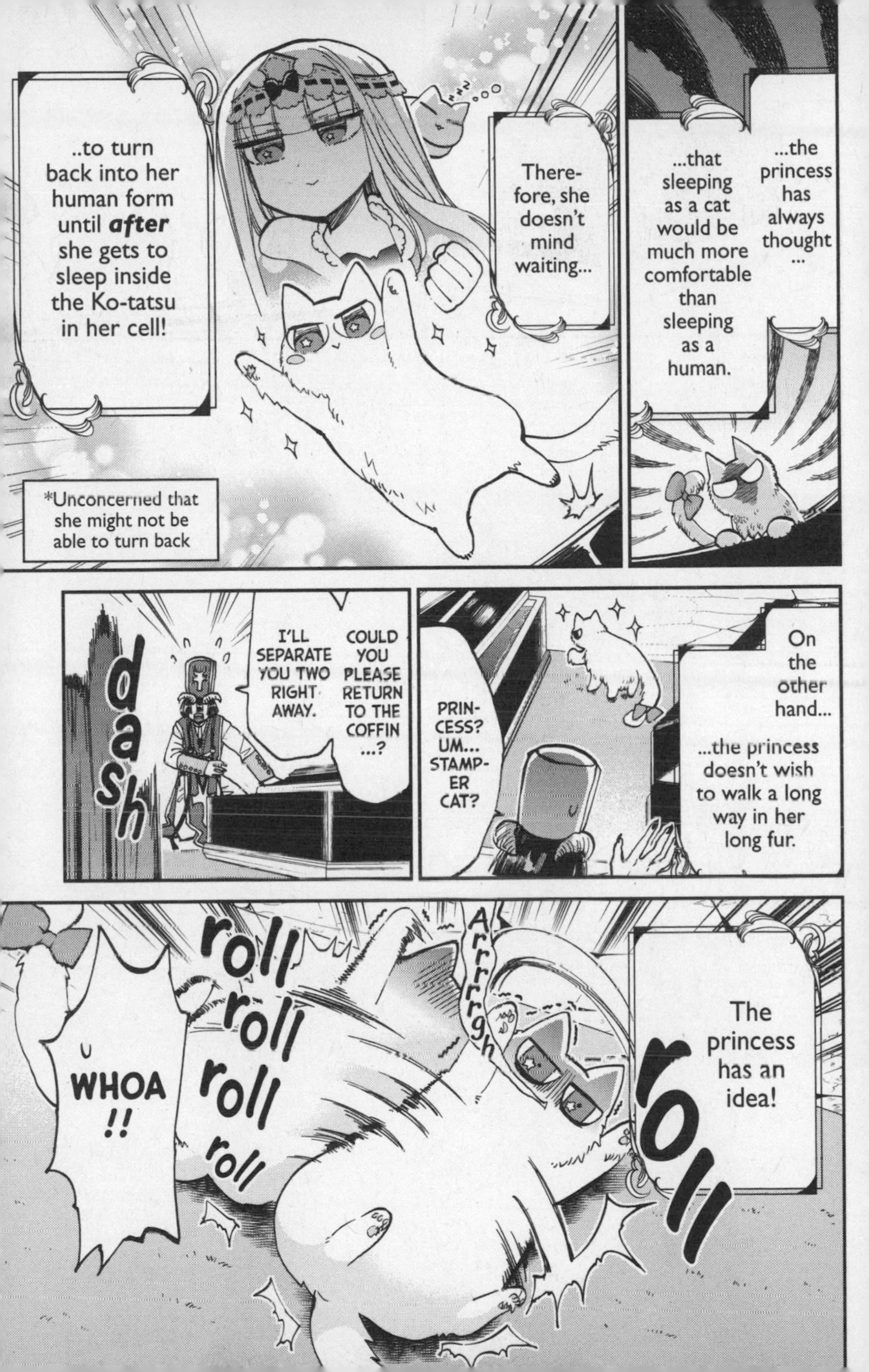
...the princess has always thought...
...that sleeping as a cat would be much more comfortable than sleeping as a human.
Therefore, she doesn't mind waiting...
..to turn back into her human form until ***after*** she gets to sleep inside the Ko-tatsu in her cell!
*Unconcerned that she might not be able to turn back
On the other hand...
...the princess doesn't wish to walk a long way in her long fur.
PRIN-CESS? UM... STAMPER CAT?
COULD YOU PLEASE RETURN TO THE COFFIN ...?
I'LL SEPARATE YOU TWO RIGHT AWAY.
dash
The princess has an idea!
roll
Arrrrgh
roll roll roll roll
WHOA !!

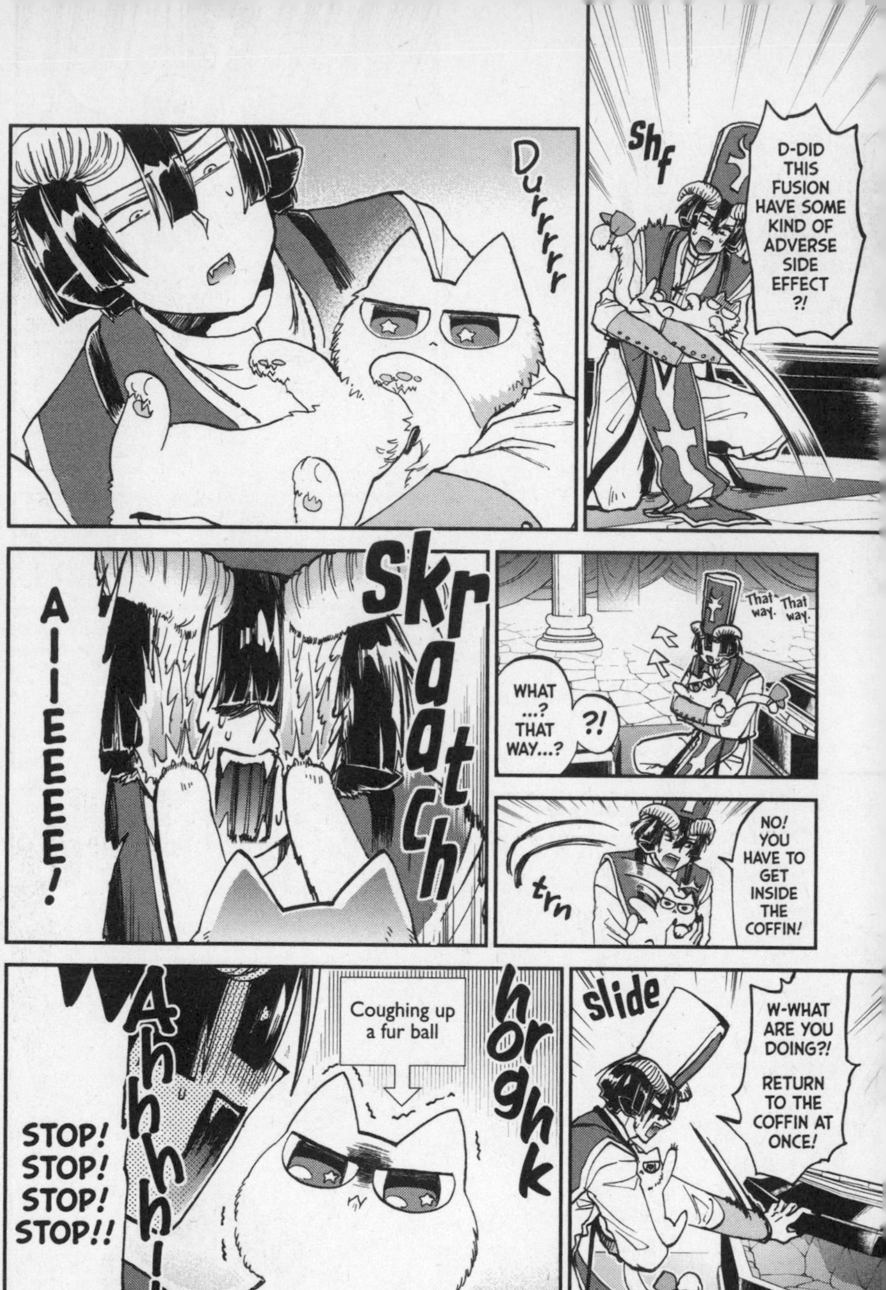
Shf
D-DID THIS FUSION HAVE SOME KIND OF ADVERSE SIDE EFFECT ?!
Durrrrr
That way.
That way.
?!
WHAT ...? THAT WAY...?
trn
NO! YOU HAVE TO GET INSIDE THE COFFIN!
Skrraatch
AIIEEEE!
slide
W-WHAT ARE YOU DOING?!
RETURN TO THE COFFIN AT ONCE!
horgunk
Coughing up a fur ball
Ahhhh!
STOP! STOP! STOP! STOP!!

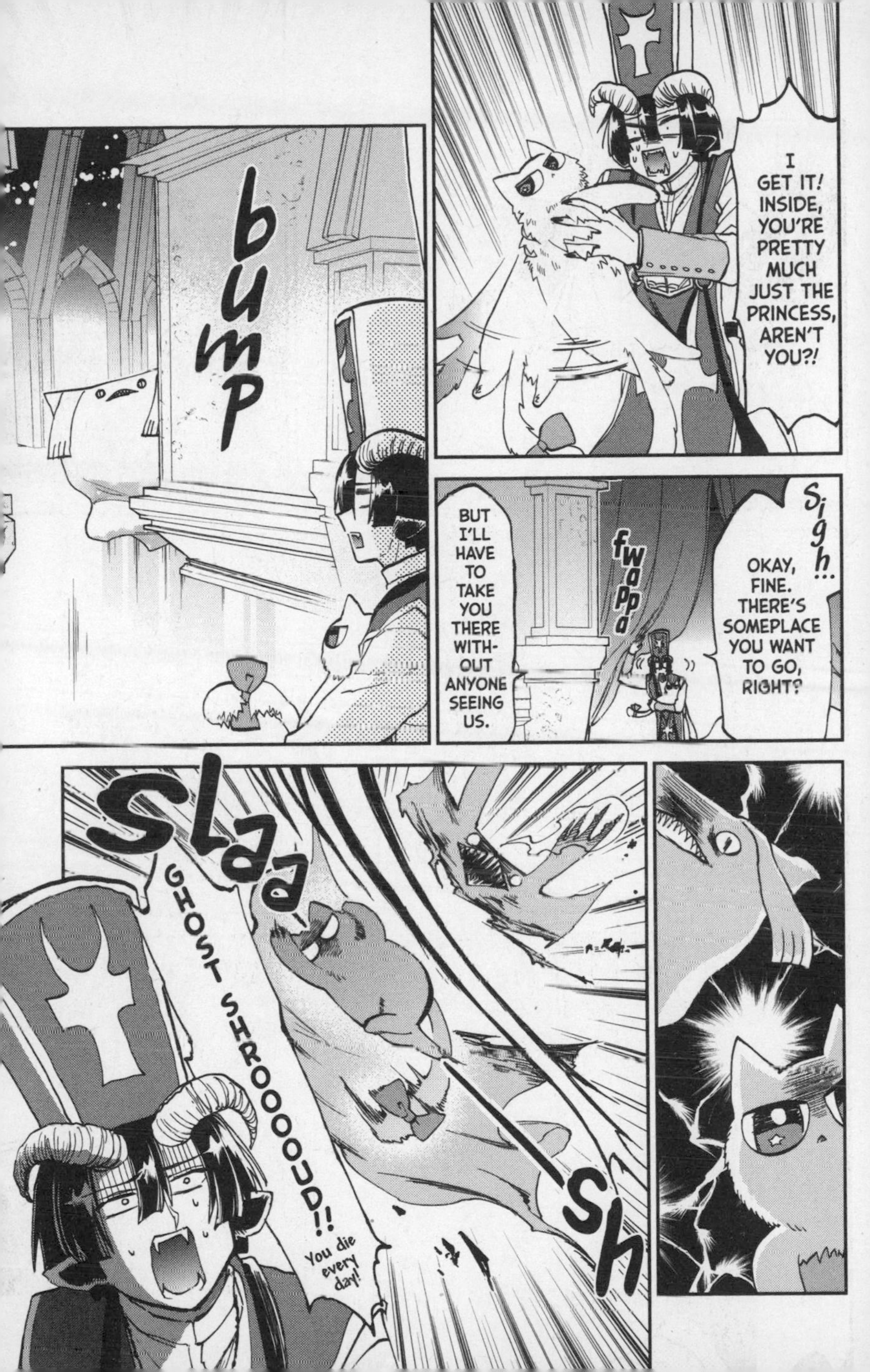
I GET IT! INSIDE, YOU'RE PRETTY MUCH JUST THE PRINCESS, AREN'T YOU?!
Sigh...
OKAY, FINE. THERE'S SOMEPLACE YOU WANT TO GO, RIGHT?
fwappa
BUT I'LL HAVE TO TAKE YOU THERE WITH-OUT ANYONE SEEING US.
bump
Slaa
GHOST SHROOOOUD!!
You die every day!
Sh

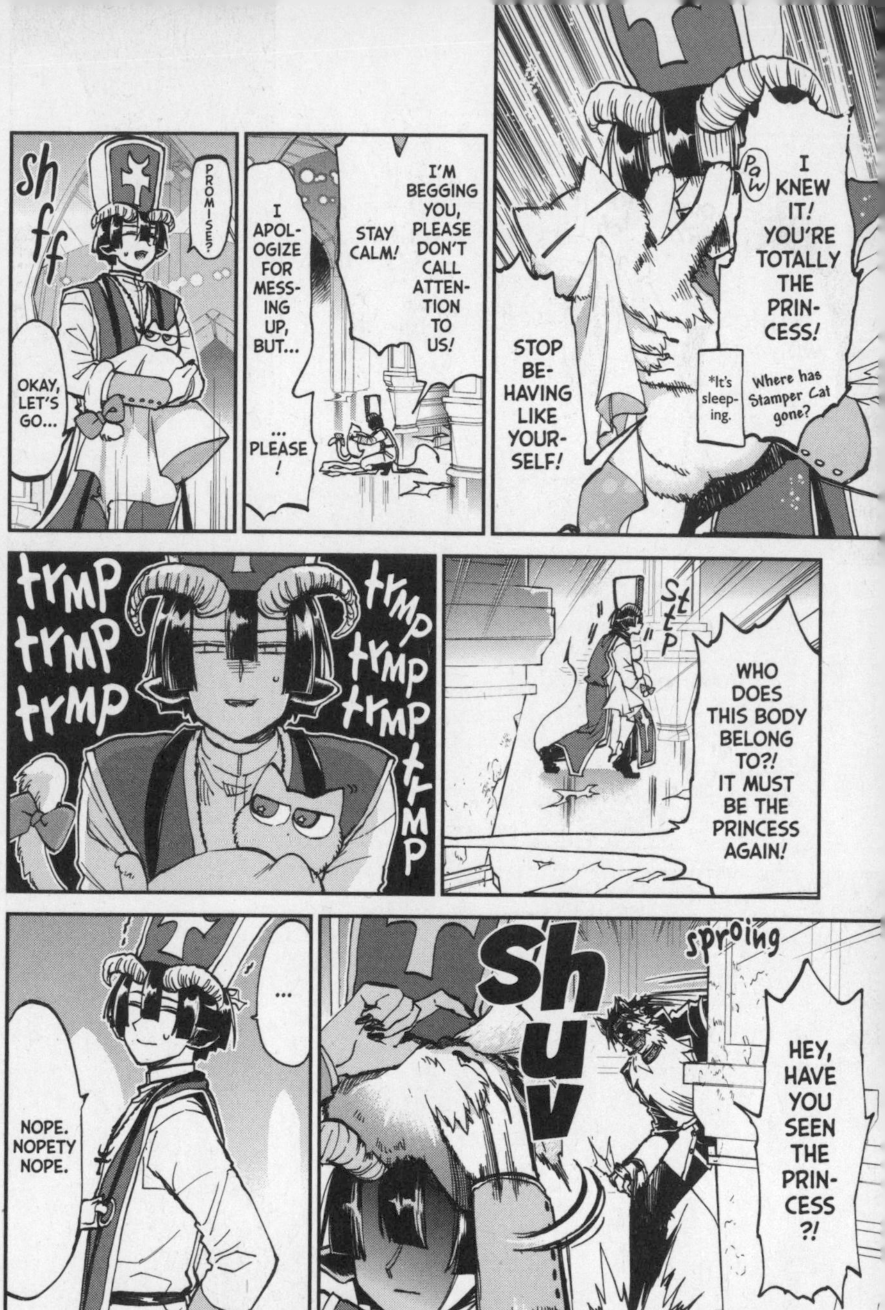
Paw
I KNEW IT! YOU'RE TOTALLY THE PRINCESS!
Where has Stamper Cat gone?
*It's sleeping.
STOP BEHAVING LIKE YOURSELF!
I'M BEGGING YOU, PLEASE DON'T CALL ATTENTION TO US!
STAY CALM!
I APOLOGIZE FOR MESSING UP, BUT...
...PLEASE!
PROMISE?
shff
OKAY, LET'S GO...
stp
WHO DOES THIS BODY BELONG TO?! IT MUST BE THE PRINCESS AGAIN!
trmp trmp trmp trmp
trmp trmp trmp
sproing
HEY, HAVE YOU SEEN THE PRINCESS?!
Shuv
...
NOPE. NOPETY NOPE.

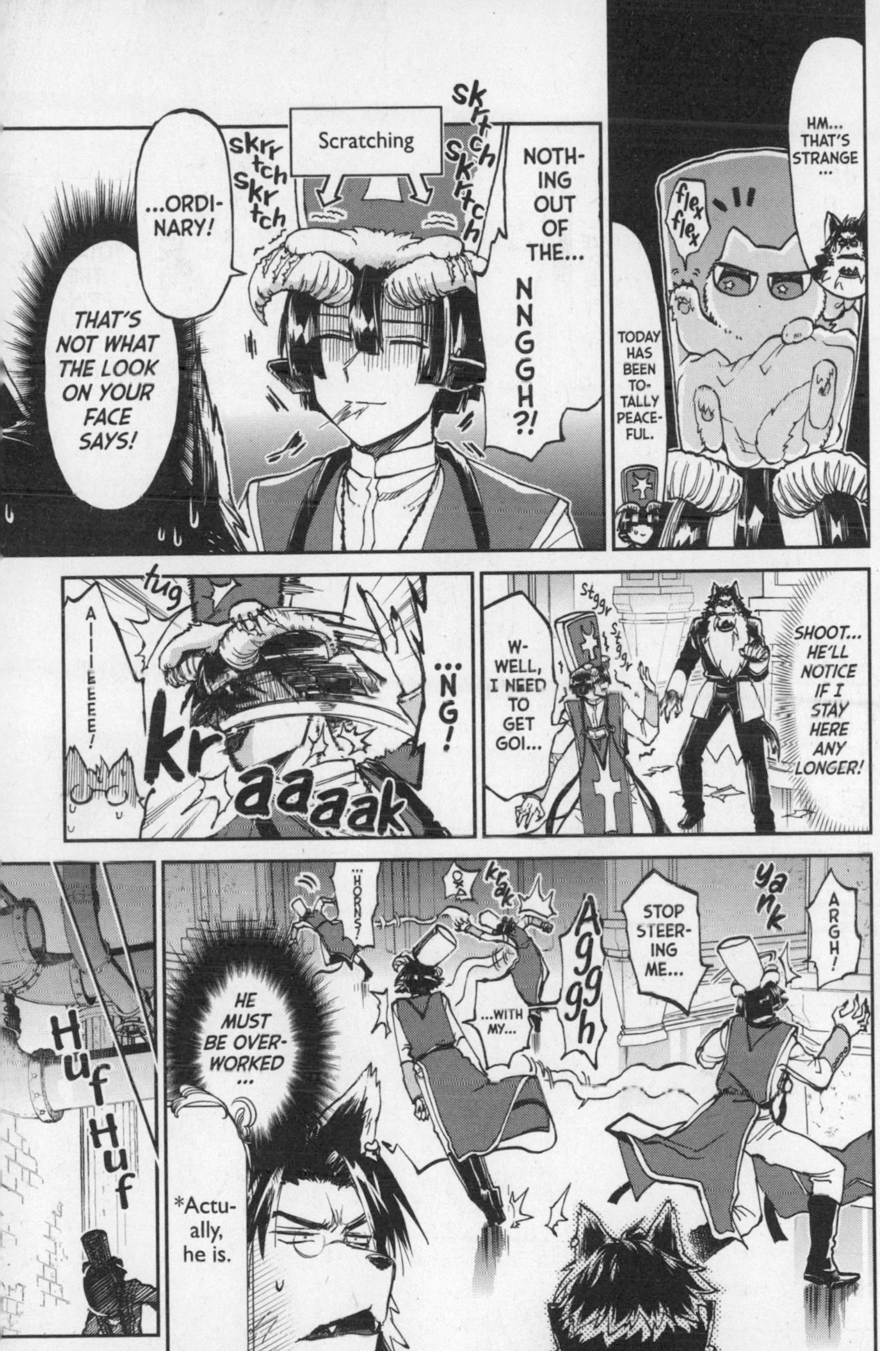
HM... THAT'S STRANGE...
flex flex
TODAY HAS BEEN TOTALLY PEACEFUL.
NOTHING OUT OF THE...
Scratching
skrrtch skrrtch
skrrtch skrrtch
...ORDINARY!
NNGGH?!
THAT'S NOT WHAT THE LOOK ON YOUR FACE SAYS!
SHOOT... HE'LL NOTICE IF I STAY HERE ANY LONGER!
stggr stggr
W-WELL, I NEED TO GET GOI...
tug
...NG!
AIIIEEEEE!
kraaaaak
yank
ARGH!
STOP STEERING ME...
Agggh
krak
...WITH MY...
...HORNS?!
HE MUST BE OVERWORKED...
*Actually, he is.
Huf Huf

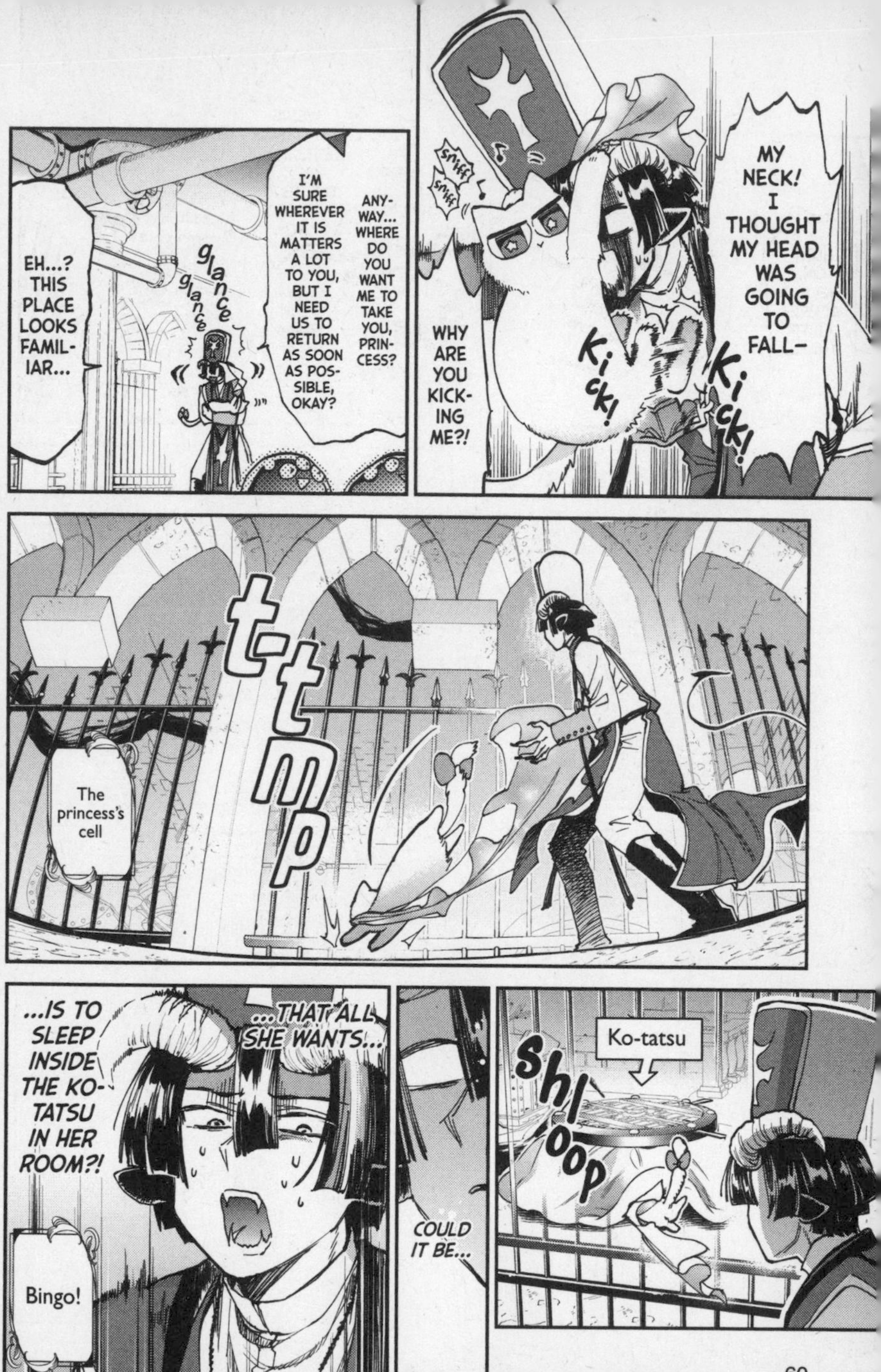
MY NECK! I THOUGHT MY HEAD WAS GOING TO FALL—
sniff
sniff
Kick!
Kick!
WHY ARE YOU KICKING ME?!
ANYWAY... WHERE DO YOU WANT ME TO TAKE YOU, PRINCESS?
I'M SURE WHEREVER IT IS MATTERS A LOT TO YOU, BUT I NEED US TO RETURN AS SOON AS POSSIBLE, OKAY?
glance glance
EH...? THIS PLACE LOOKS FAMILIAR...
t-t-tmp
The princess's cell
Ko-tatsu
shloop
COULD IT BE...
...THAT ALL SHE WANTS...
...IS TO SLEEP INSIDE THE KOTATSU IN HER ROOM?!
Bingo!

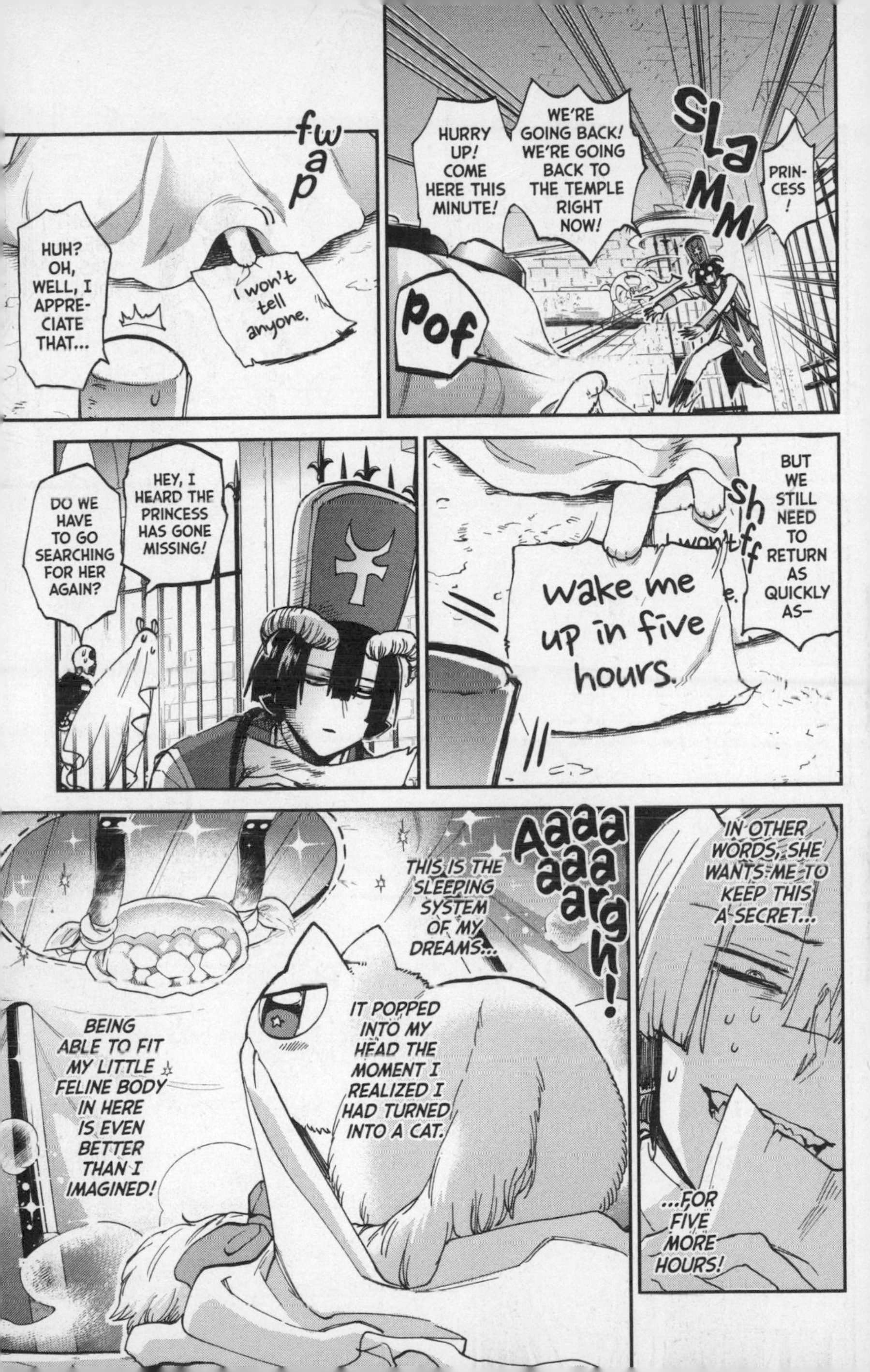
PRIN-CESS!
SLAMM
WE'RE GOING BACK! WE'RE GOING BACK TO THE TEMPLE RIGHT NOW!
HURRY UP! COME HERE THIS MINUTE!
pof
fwap
HUH? OH, WELL, I APPRECIATE THAT...
I won't tell anyone.
BUT WE STILL NEED TO RETURN AS QUICKLY AS—
shiff
wake me up in five hours.
HEY, I HEARD THE PRINCESS HAS GONE MISSING!
DO WE HAVE TO GO SEARCHING FOR HER AGAIN?
IN OTHER WORDS, SHE WANTS ME TO KEEP THIS A SECRET...
...FOR FIVE MORE HOURS!
Aaaaaaaargh!
THIS IS THE SLEEPING SYSTEM OF MY DREAMS...
IT POPPED INTO MY HEAD THE MOMENT I REALIZED I HAD TURNED INTO A CAT.
BEING ABLE TO FIT MY LITTLE FELINE BODY IN HERE IS EVEN BETTER THAN I IMAGINED!

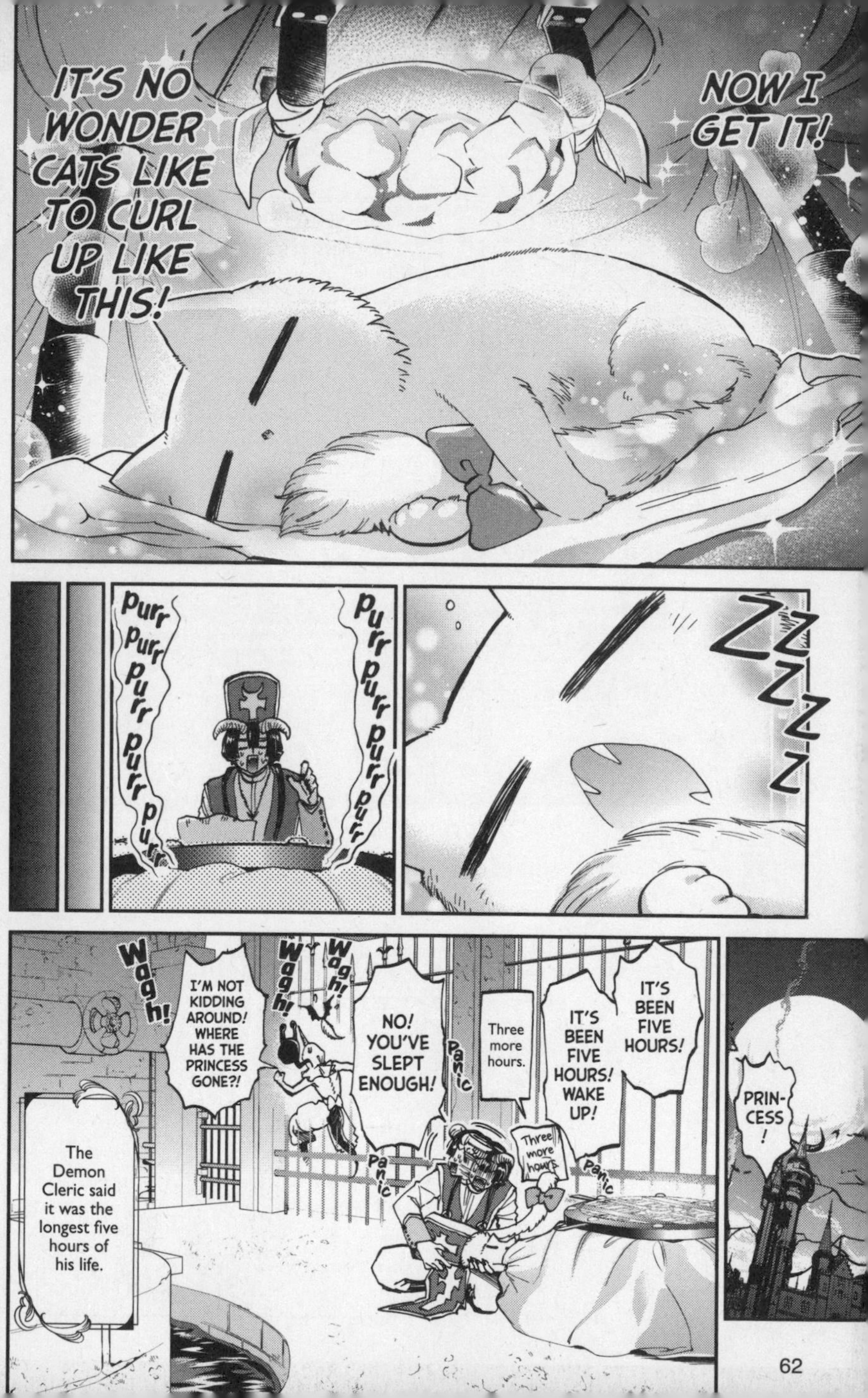
NOW I GET IT!
IT'S NO WONDER CATS LIKE TO CURL UP LIKE THIS!
ZZZZ
purr purr purr purr purr purr purr
purr purr purr purr purr
PRIN-CESS!
IT'S BEEN FIVE HOURS!
IT'S BEEN FIVE HOURS! WAKE UP!
Three more hours.
Three more hours
Panic
Panic
NO! YOU'VE SLEPT ENOUGH!
Panic
Wagh!
Wagh!
I'M NOT KIDDING AROUND! WHERE HAS THE PRINCESS GONE?!
Wagh!
The Demon Cleric said it was the longest five hours of his life.

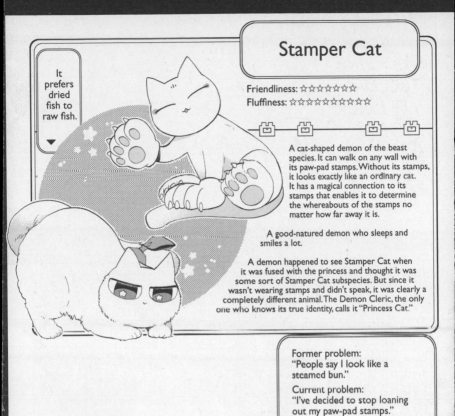

Stamper Cat

Friendliness: ☆☆☆☆☆☆☆
Fluffiness: ☆☆☆☆☆☆☆☆☆☆☆

It prefers dried fish to raw fish.

A cat-shaped demon of the beast species. It can walk on any wall with its paw-pad stamps. Without its stamps, it looks exactly like an ordinary cat. It has a magical connection to its stamps that enables it to determine the whereabouts of the stamps no matter how far away it is.

A good-natured demon who sleeps and smiles a lot.

A demon happened to see Stamper Cat when it was fused with the princess and thought it was some sort of Stamper Cat subspecies. But since it wasn't wearing stamps and didn't speak, it was clearly a completely different animal. The Demon Cleric, the only one who knows its true identity, calls it "Princess Cat."

Former problem:
"People say I look like a steamed bun."

Current problem:
"I've decided to stop loaning out my paw-pad stamps."

PRINCESS, IT'S BEEN FIVE HOURS! COME ON!
fwumf
OOH, SHE'S SO SOFT AND WARM!!
Come on, Prin-cess! Come out!
Ten more hours.
You'll get dehy-drated!
Fluffy...
OH, WHAT THE HECK... I'LL LET HER SLEEP.
SHE'S SO WARM AND FLUFFY I DON'T HAVE THE HEART TO WAKE HER!

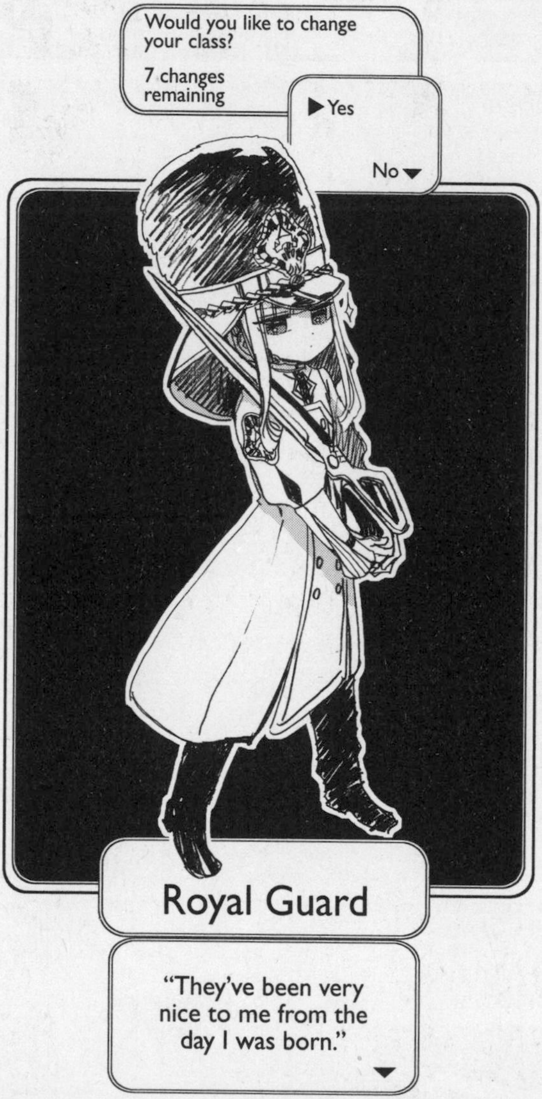
Would you like to change your class?
7 changes remaining
▶Yes
No
Royal Guard
"They've been very nice to me from the day I was born."

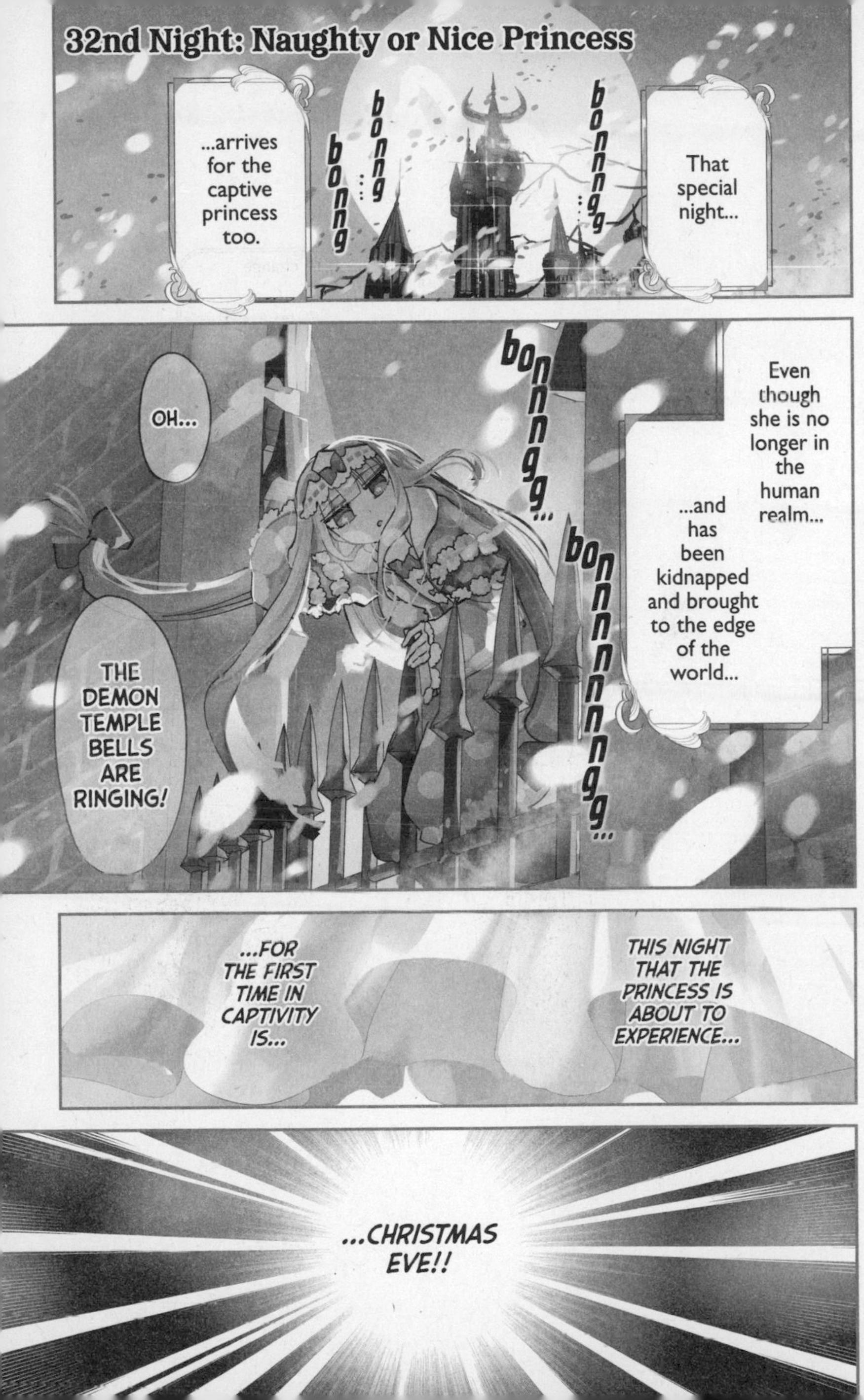
32nd Night: Naughty or Nice Princess
That special night...
bonnngg...
bong...
bong
...arrives for the captive princess too.
Even though she is no longer in the human realm...
...and has been kidnapped and brought to the edge of the world...
bonnnngg...
bonnnnnnnnngg...
OH...
THE DEMON TEMPLE BELLS ARE RINGING!
THIS NIGHT THAT THE PRINCESS IS ABOUT TO EXPERIENCE...
...FOR THE FIRST TIME IN CAPTIVITY IS...
...CHRISTMAS EVE!!

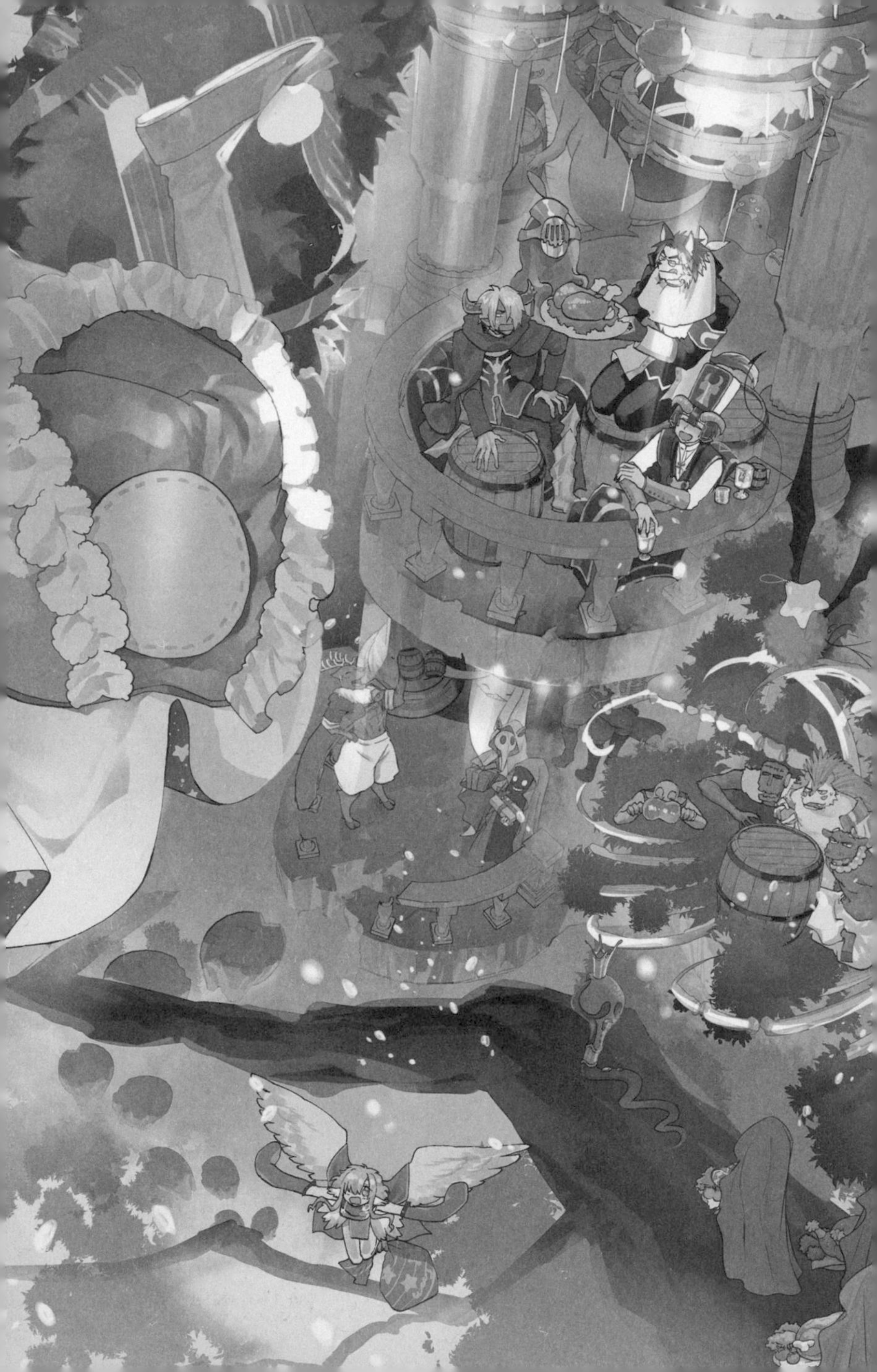

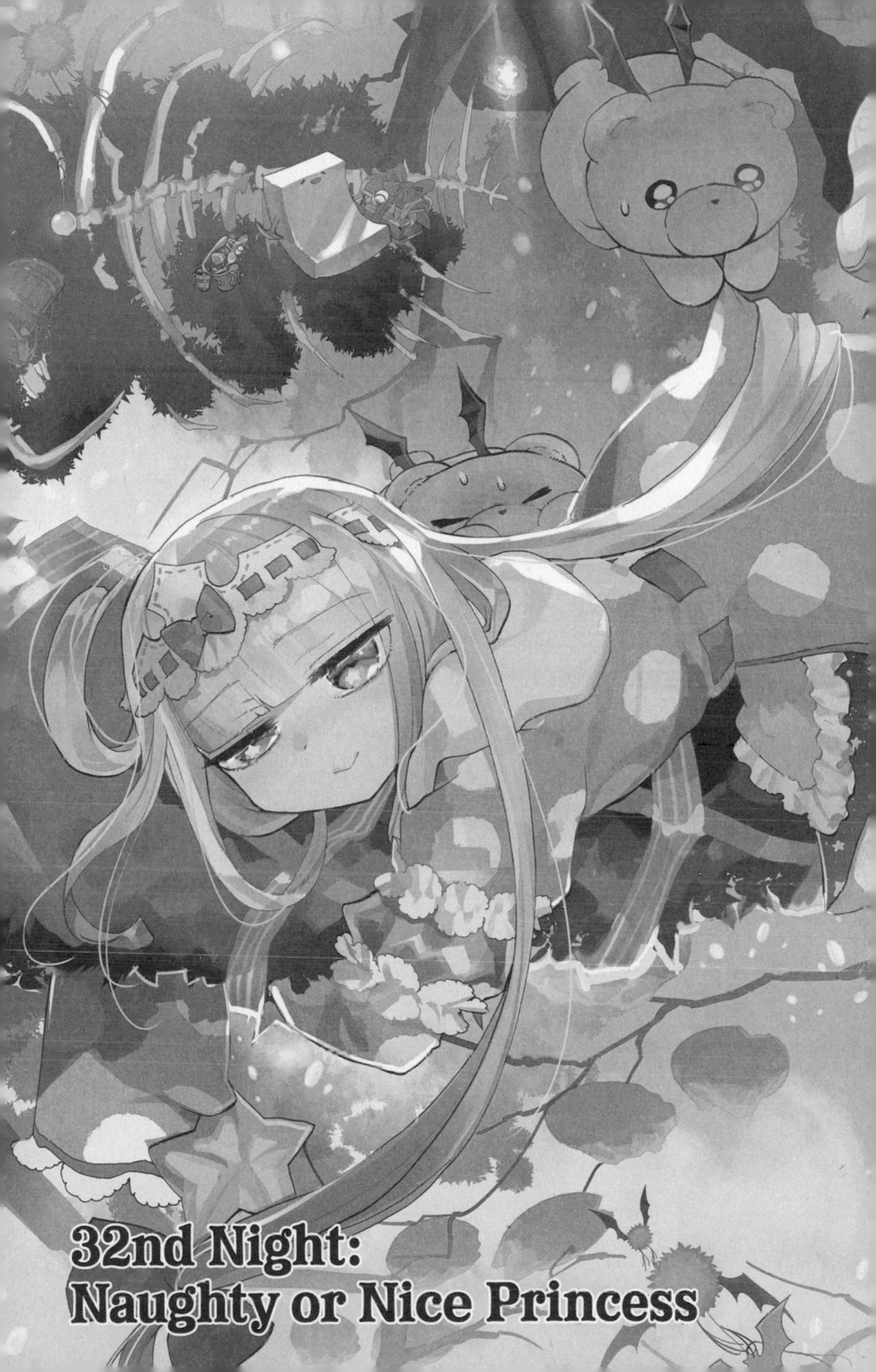

32nd Night: Naughty or Nice Princess

SLEEPY PRINCESS
IN THE DEMON CASTLE

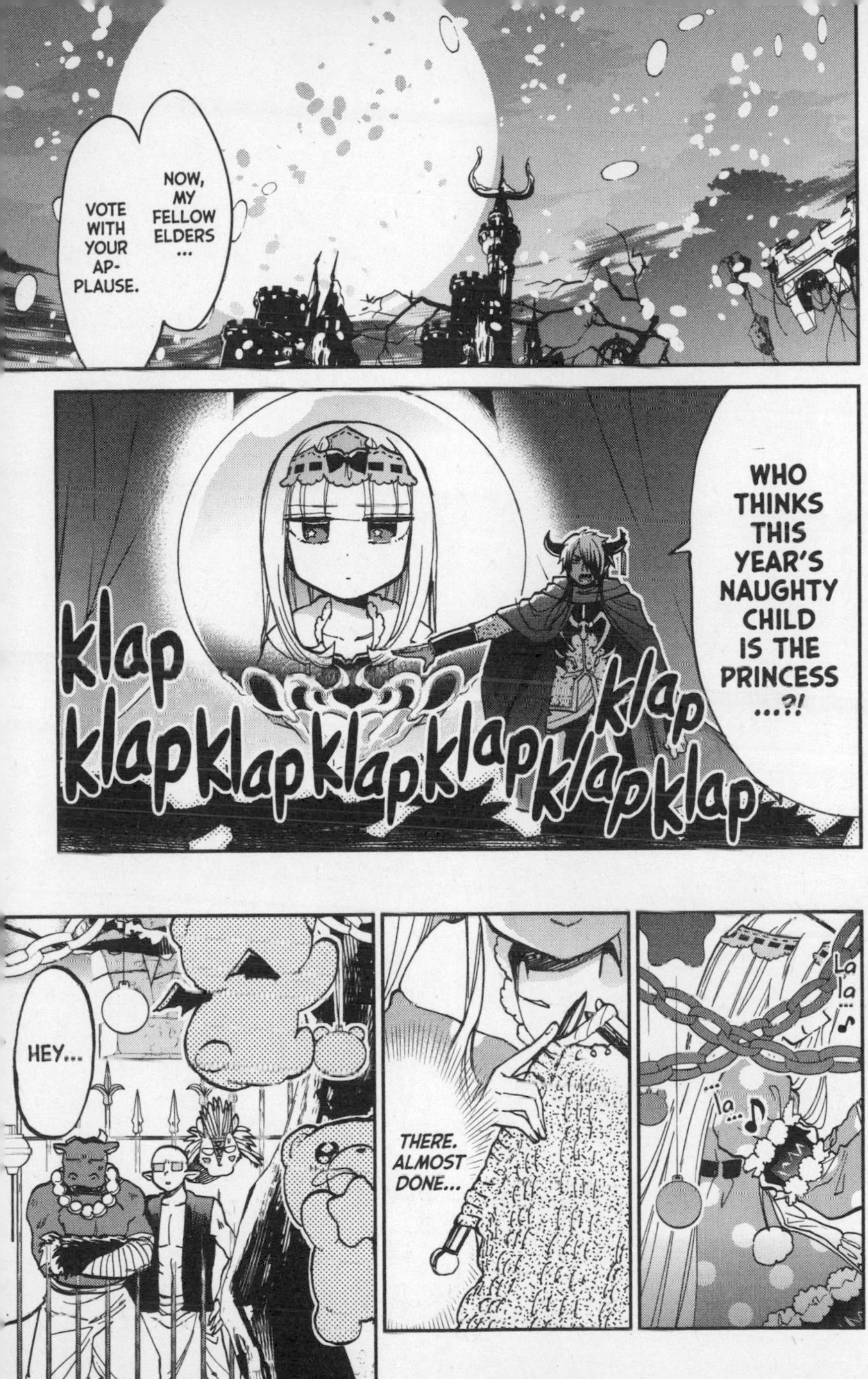
NOW, MY FELLOW ELDERS ...
VOTE WITH YOUR AP-PLAUSE.
WHO THINKS THIS YEAR'S NAUGHTY CHILD IS THE PRINCESS ...?!
klap klap klap klap klap klap klap klap
La la ... ♪
... la ... ♪
THERE. ALMOST DONE...
HEY...

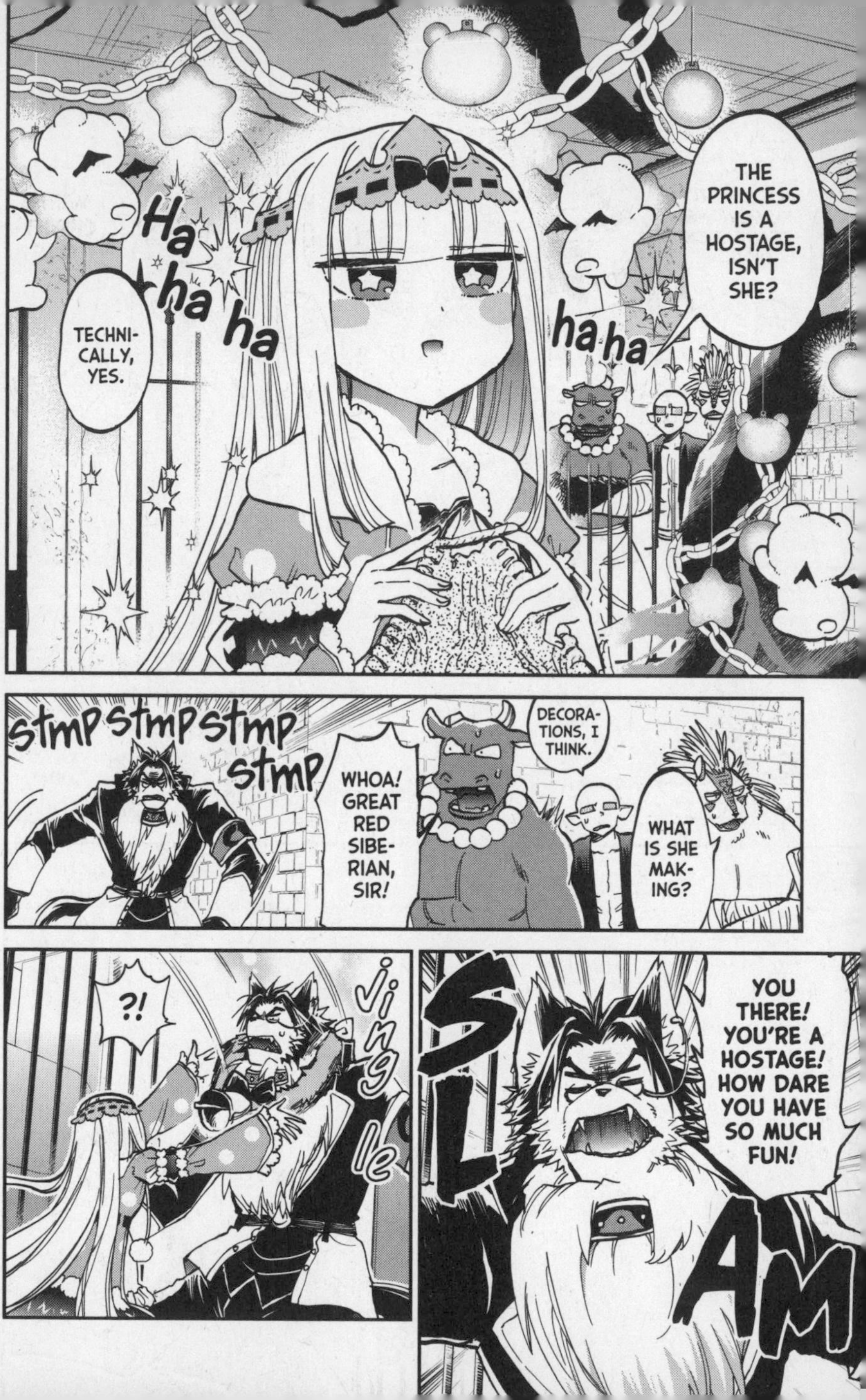
THE PRINCESS IS A HOSTAGE, ISN'T SHE?
ha ha
Ha ha ha ha
TECHNI-CALLY, YES.
WHAT IS SHE MAK-ING?
DECORA-TIONS, I THINK.
WHOA! GREAT RED SIBE-RIAN, SIR!
stmp stmp stmp stmp
YOU THERE! YOU'RE A HOSTAGE! HOW DARE YOU HAVE SO MUCH FUN!
SLAM
jingle
?!

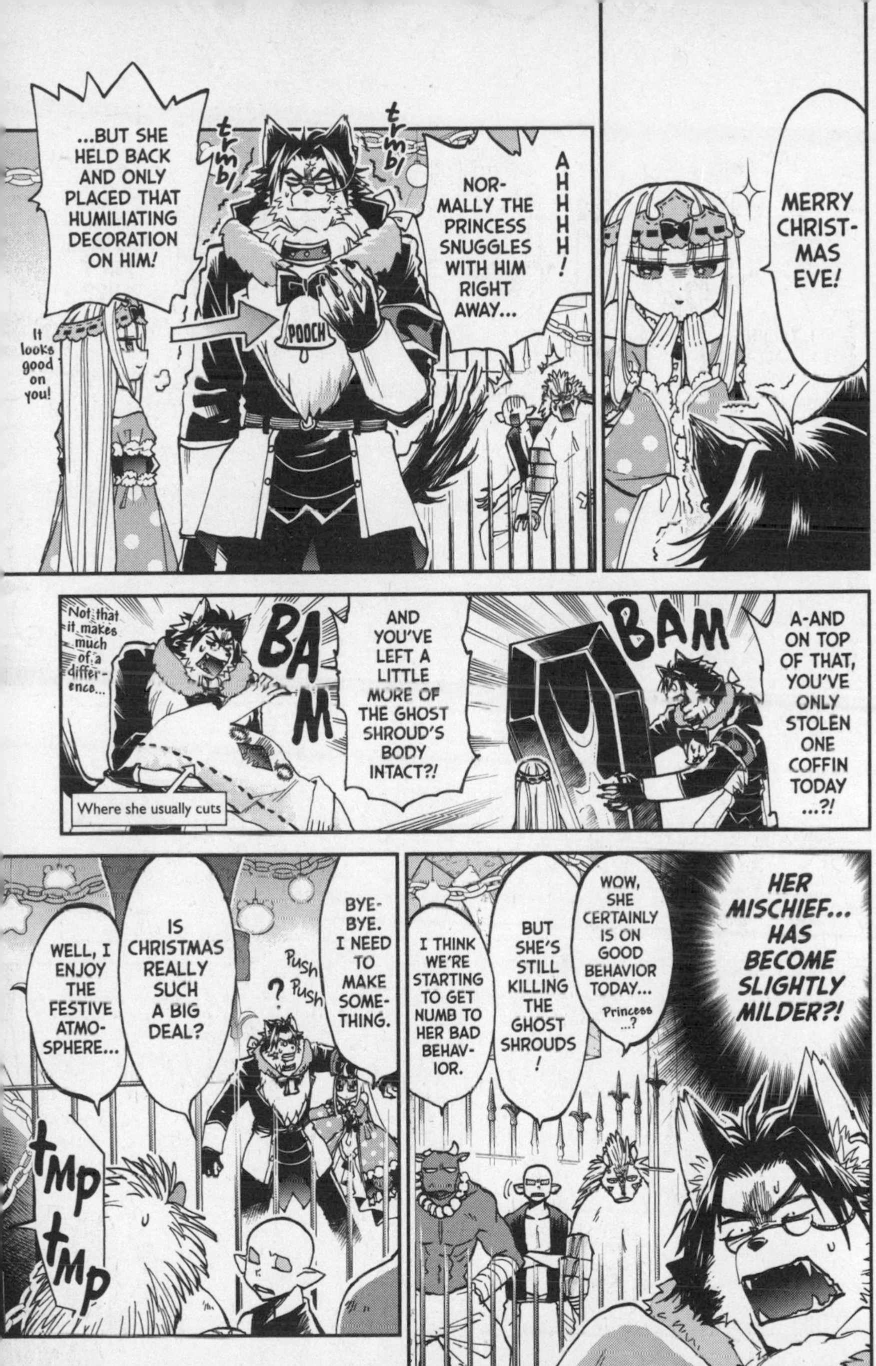
MERRY CHRISTMAS EVE!
AHHHH!
NORMALLY THE PRINCESS SNUGGLES WITH HIM RIGHT AWAY...
trmbl trmbl
...BUT SHE HELD BACK AND ONLY PLACED THAT HUMILIATING DECORATION ON HIM!
POOCH
It looks good on you!
A-AND ON TOP OF THAT, YOU'VE ONLY STOLEN ONE COFFIN TODAY ...?!
BAM
AND YOU'VE LEFT A LITTLE MORE OF THE GHOST SHROUD'S BODY INTACT?!
BAM
Not that it makes much of a difference...
Where she usually cuts
HER MISCHIEF... HAS BECOME SLIGHTLY MILDER?!
WOW, SHE CERTAINLY IS ON GOOD BEHAVIOR TODAY...
Princess ...?
BUT SHE'S STILL KILLING THE GHOST SHROUDS!
I THINK WE'RE STARTING TO GET NUMB TO HER BAD BEHAVIOR.
BYE-BYE. I NEED TO MAKE SOMETHING.
Push Push
?
IS CHRISTMAS REALLY SUCH A BIG DEAL?
WELL, I ENJOY THE FESTIVE ATMOSPHERE...
tmp tmp

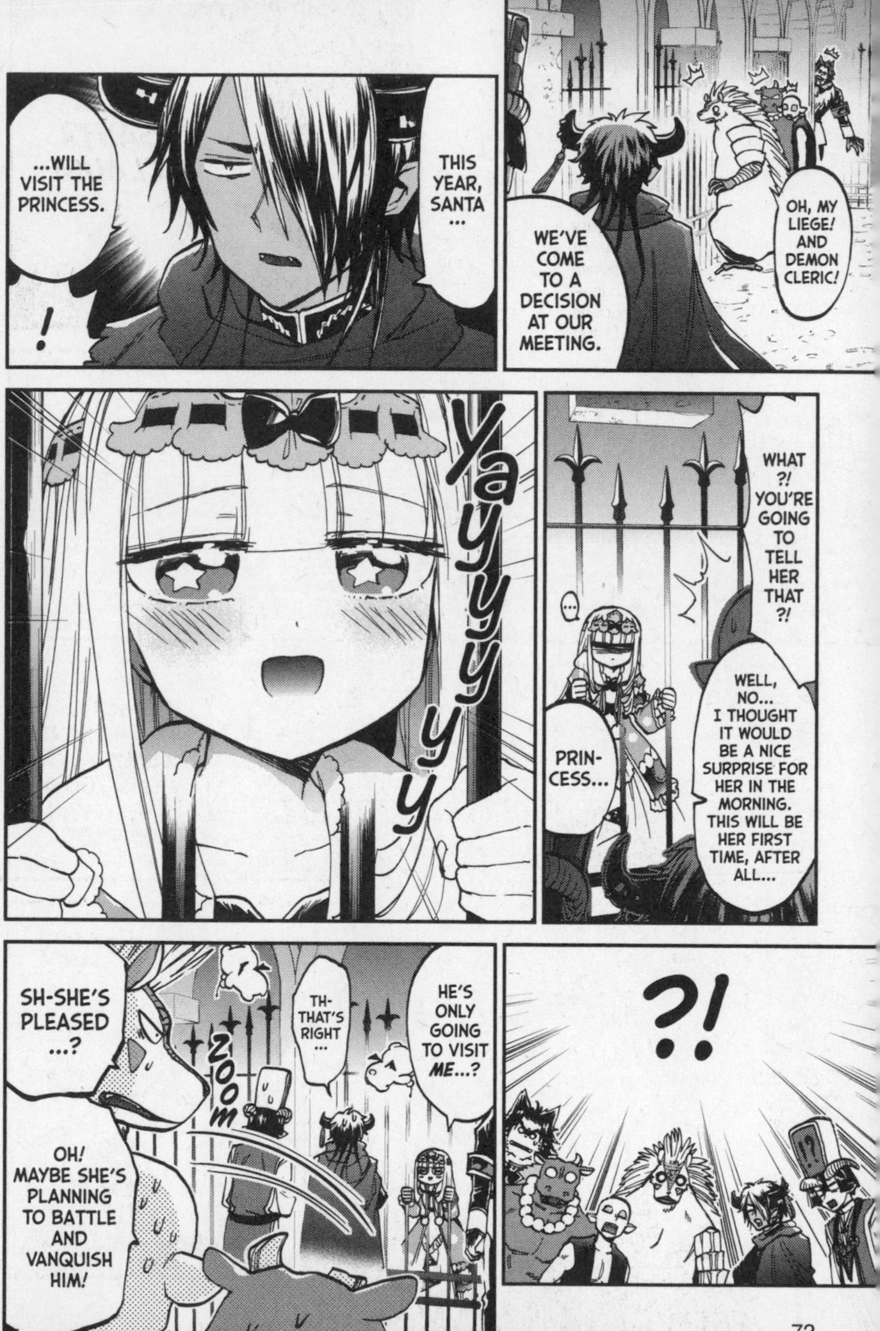
OH, MY LIEGE! AND DEMON CLERIC!
WE'VE COME TO A DECISION AT OUR MEETING.
THIS YEAR, SANTA ...
...WILL VISIT THE PRINCESS.
!
WHAT ?! YOU'RE GOING TO TELL HER THAT ?!
WELL, NO... I THOUGHT IT WOULD BE A NICE SURPRISE FOR HER IN THE MORNING. THIS WILL BE HER FIRST TIME, AFTER ALL...
PRIN-CESS...
...
Yayyyyyy
?!
HE'S ONLY GOING TO VISIT *ME*...?
TH-THAT'S RIGHT ...
ZOOM
SH-SHE'S PLEASED ...?
OH! MAYBE SHE'S PLANNING TO BATTLE AND VANQUISH HIM!

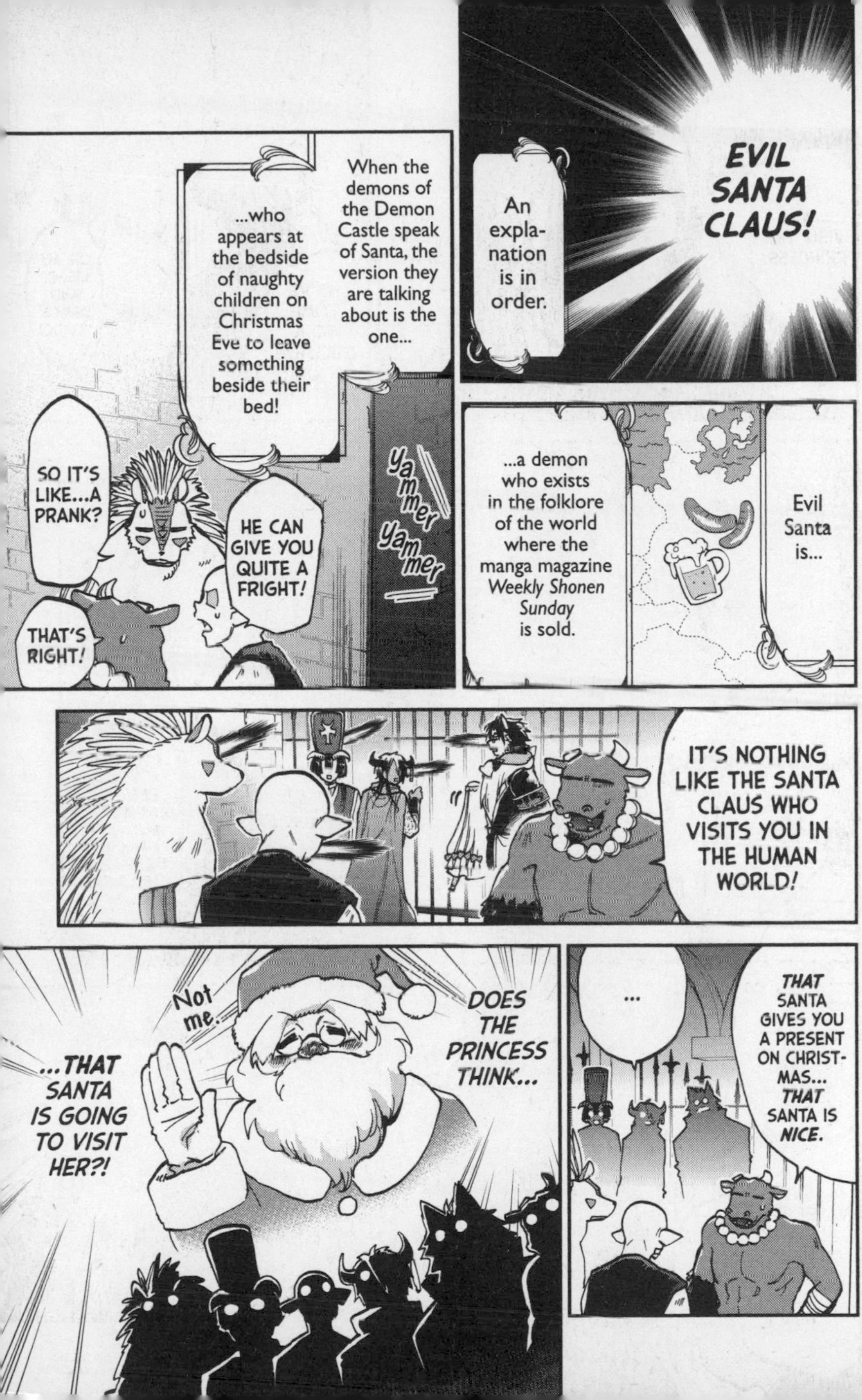
EVIL SANTA CLAUS!
An explanation is in order.
Evil Santa is...
...a demon who exists in the folklore of the world where the manga magazine *Weekly Shonen Sunday* is sold.
When the demons of the Demon Castle speak of Santa, the version they are talking about is the one...
...who appears at the bedside of naughty children on Christmas Eve to leave something beside their bed!
yammer yammer
HE CAN GIVE YOU QUITE A FRIGHT!
SO IT'S LIKE...A PRANK?
THAT'S RIGHT!
IT'S NOTHING LIKE THE SANTA CLAUS WHO VISITS YOU IN THE HUMAN WORLD!
THAT SANTA GIVES YOU A PRESENT ON CHRISTMAS... *THAT* SANTA IS *NICE*.
...
DOES THE PRINCESS THINK...
Not me.
...THAT SANTA IS GOING TO VISIT HER?!

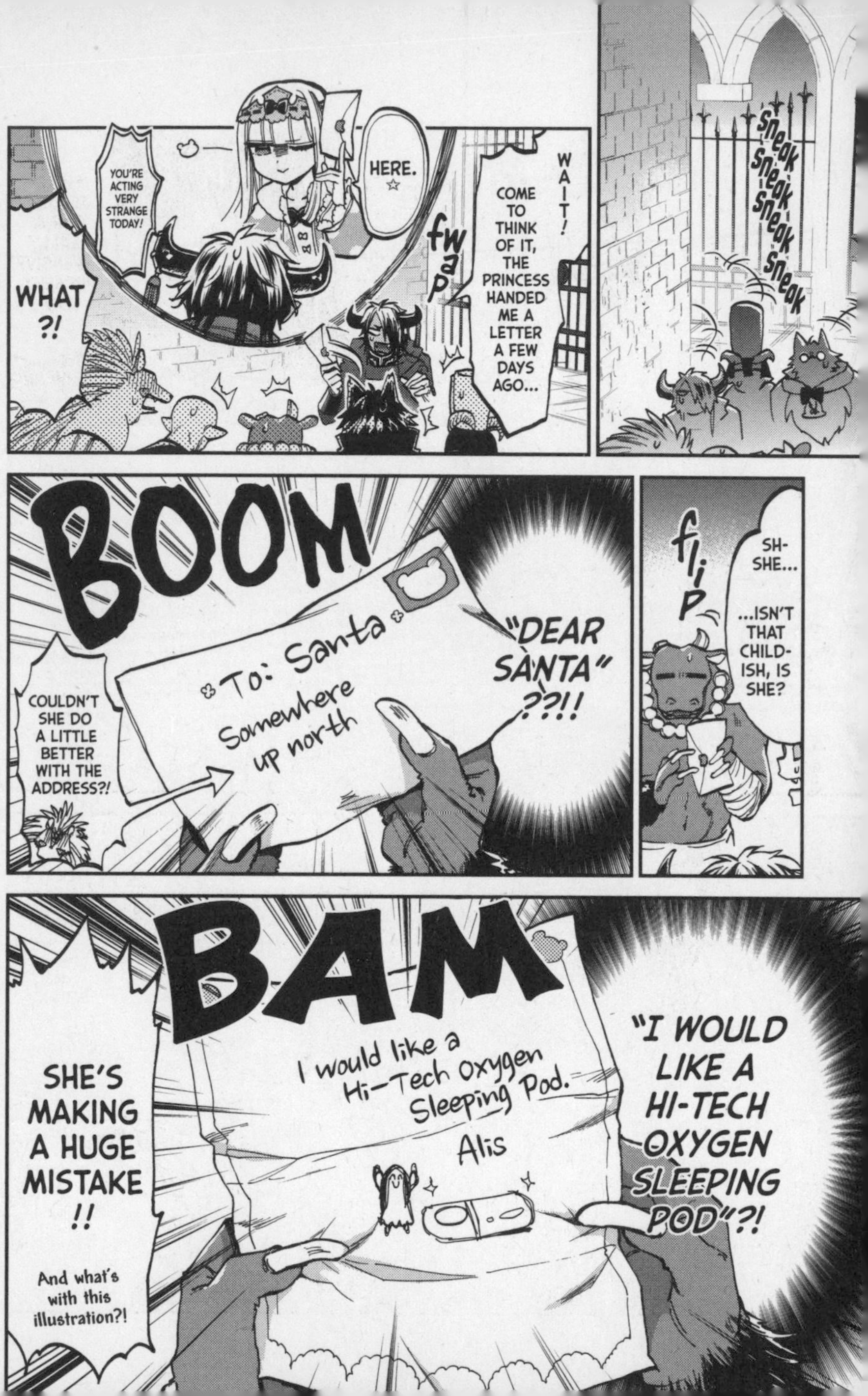
SNEAK SNEAK SNEAK SNEAK SNEAK
WAIT!
COME TO THINK OF IT, THE PRINCESS HANDED ME A LETTER A FEW DAYS AGO...
fwap
HERE. ☆
YOU'RE ACTING VERY STRANGE TODAY!
WHAT?!
flip
SH-SHE...
...ISN'T THAT CHILDISH, IS SHE?
BOOM
"DEAR SANTA"??!!
To: Santa
Somewhere up north
COULDN'T SHE DO A LITTLE BETTER WITH THE ADDRESS?!
BAM
"I WOULD LIKE A HI-TECH OXYGEN SLEEPING POD"?!
I would like a Hi-Tech Oxygen Sleeping Pod.
Alis
SHE'S MAKING A HUGE MISTAKE!!
And what's with this illustration?!

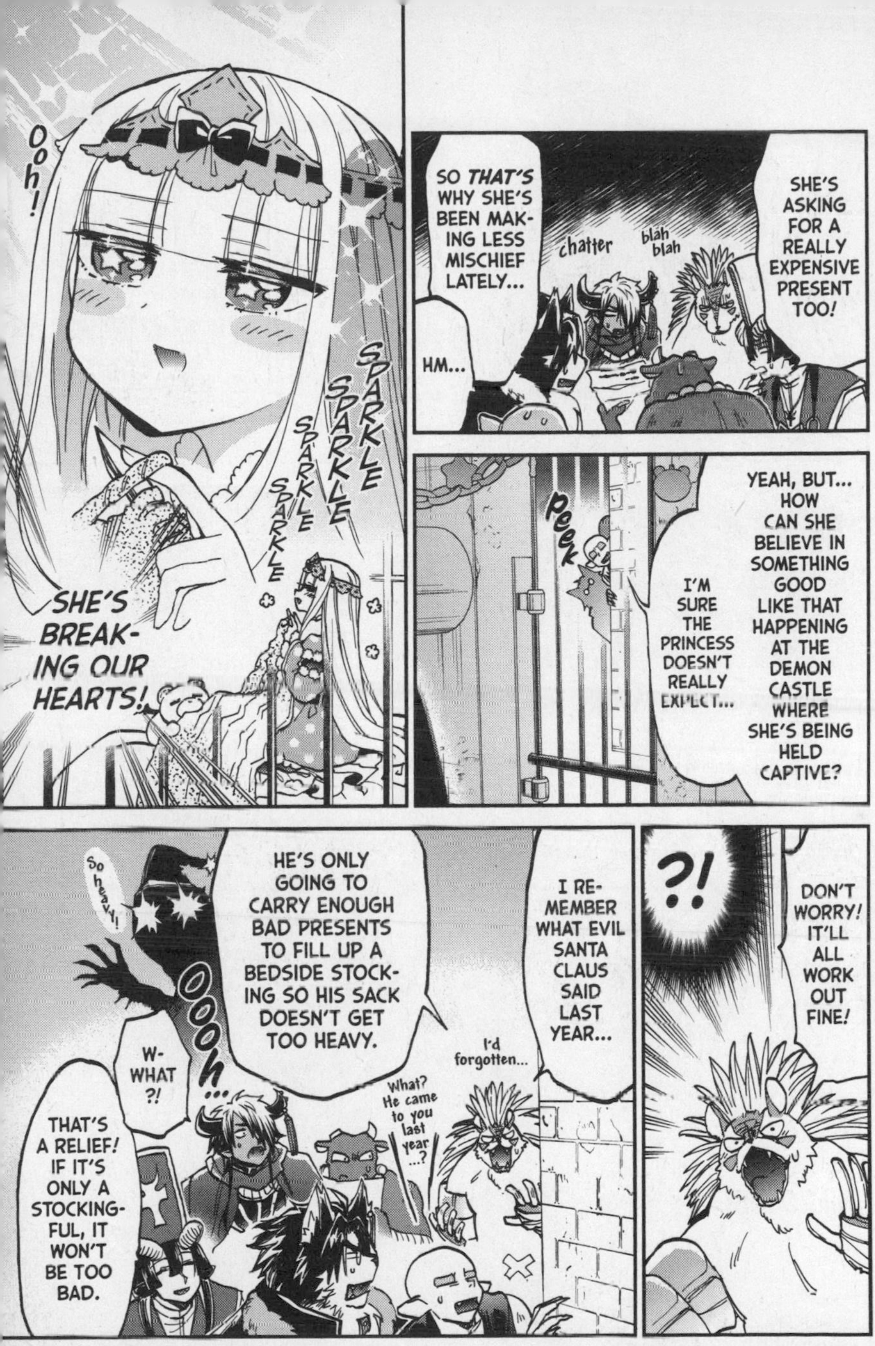
SHE'S ASKING FOR A REALLY EXPENSIVE PRESENT TOO!
blah blah
chatter
SO *THAT'S* WHY SHE'S BEEN MAKING LESS MISCHIEF LATELY...
HM...
YEAH, BUT... HOW CAN SHE BELIEVE IN SOMETHING GOOD LIKE THAT HAPPENING AT THE DEMON CASTLE WHERE SHE'S BEING HELD CAPTIVE?
I'M SURE THE PRINCESS DOESN'T REALLY EXPECT...
peek
Ooh!
SPARKLE SPARKLE SPARKLE SPARKLE
SHE'S BREAKING OUR HEARTS!
DON'T WORRY! IT'LL ALL WORK OUT FINE!
?!
I REMEMBER WHAT EVIL SANTA CLAUS SAID LAST YEAR...
I'd forgotten...
HE'S ONLY GOING TO CARRY ENOUGH BAD PRESENTS TO FILL UP A BEDSIDE STOCKING SO HIS SACK DOESN'T GET TOO HEAVY.
What? He came to you last year...?
So heavy!
Ooooh...
W-WHAT?!
THAT'S A RELIEF! IF IT'S ONLY A STOCKINGFUL, IT WON'T BE TOO BAD.

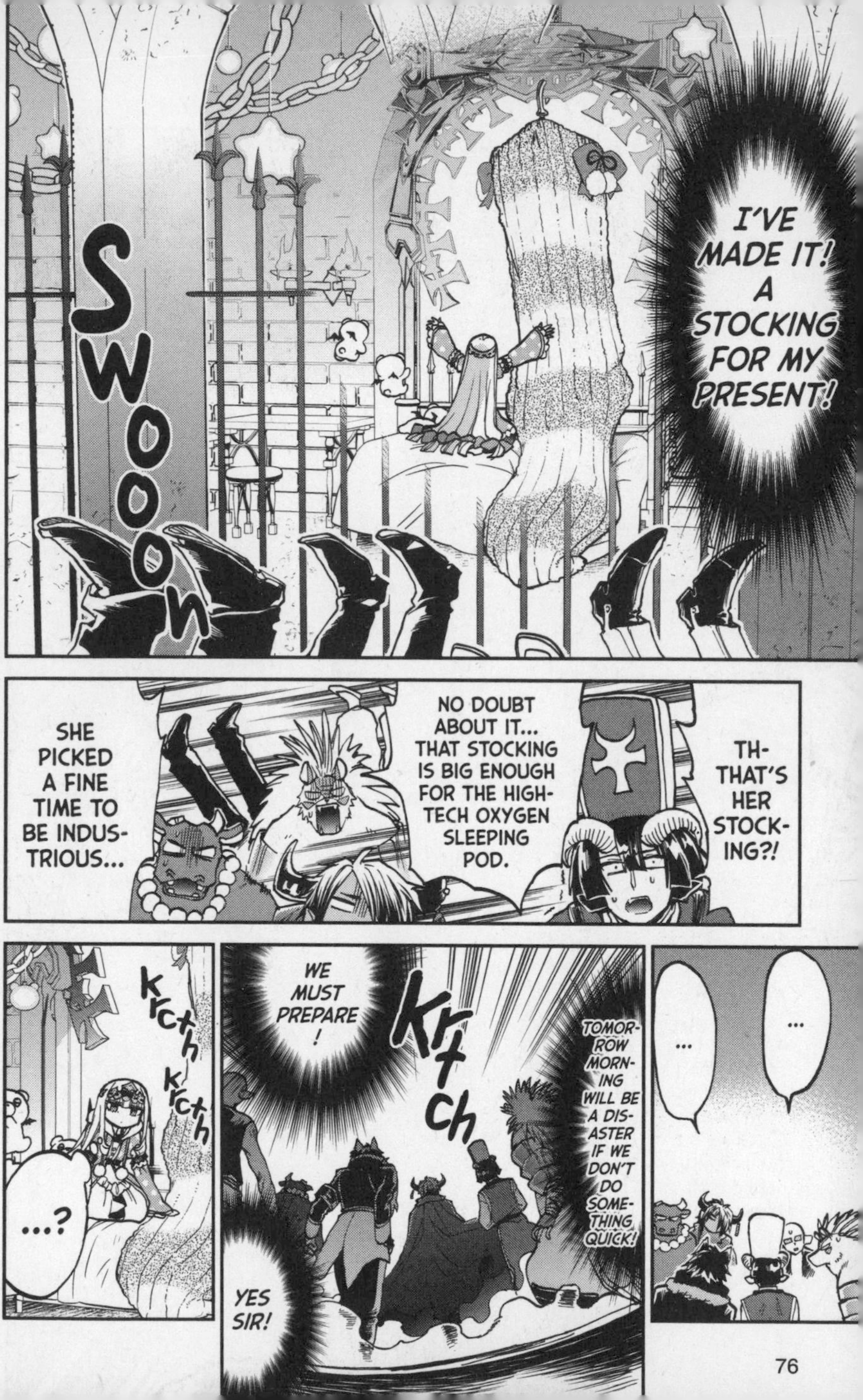
I'VE MADE IT! A STOCKING FOR MY PRESENT!
SWOON
TH-THAT'S HER STOCK-ING?!
NO DOUBT ABOUT IT... THAT STOCKING IS BIG ENOUGH FOR THE HIGH-TECH OXYGEN SLEEPING POD.
SHE PICKED A FINE TIME TO BE INDUS-TRIOUS...
...
...
TOMOR-ROW MORN-ING WILL BE A DIS-ASTER IF WE DON'T DO SOME-THING QUICK!
WE MUST PREPARE!
KRTCH
YES SIR!
KRCTH KRCTH
...?

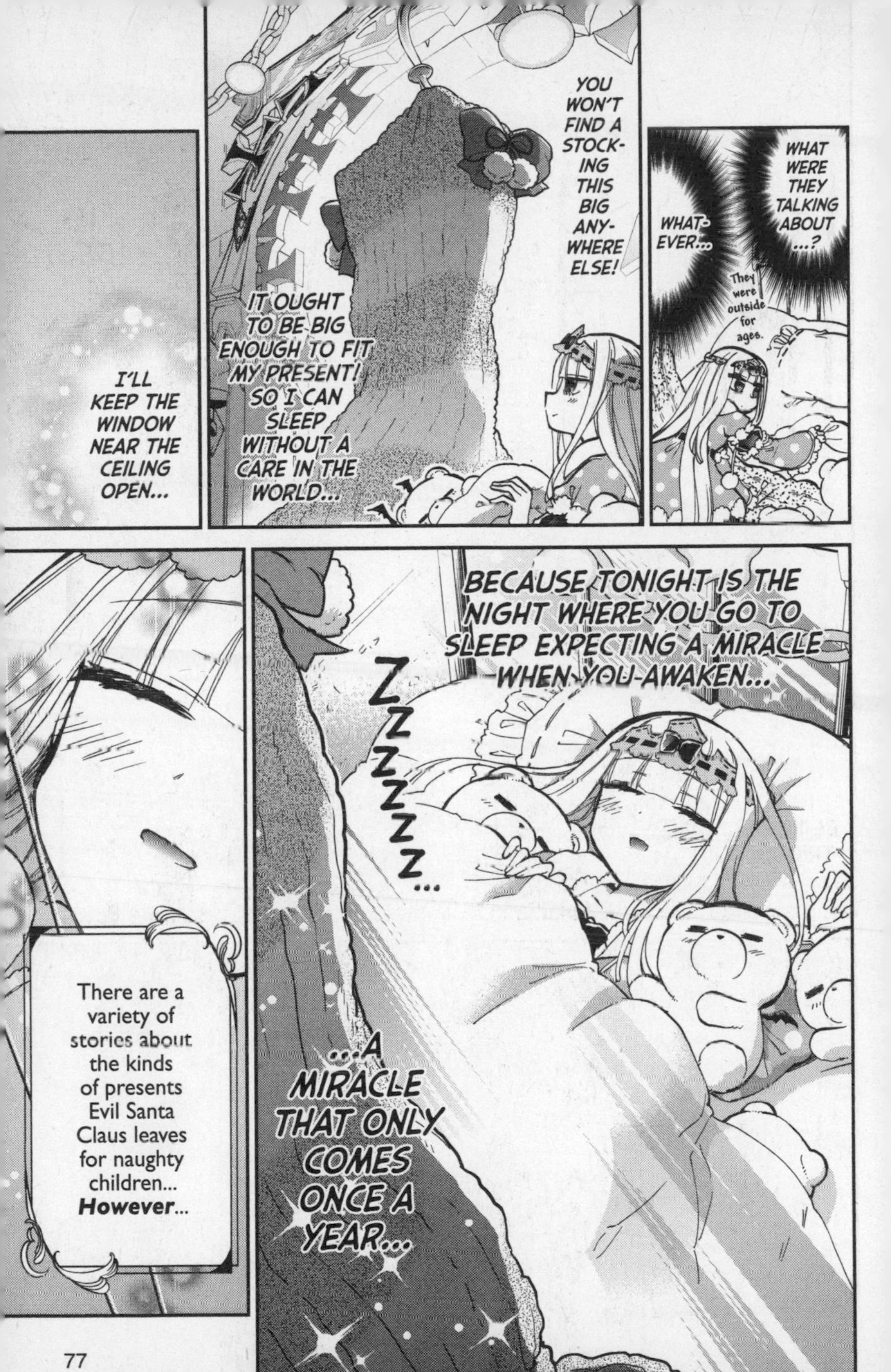
WHAT WERE THEY TALKING ABOUT ...?
WHAT-EVER...
They were outside for ages.
YOU WON'T FIND A STOCK-ING THIS BIG ANY-WHERE ELSE!
IT OUGHT TO BE BIG ENOUGH TO FIT MY PRESENT! SO I CAN SLEEP WITHOUT A CARE IN THE WORLD...
I'LL KEEP THE WINDOW NEAR THE CEILING OPEN...
BECAUSE TONIGHT IS THE NIGHT WHERE YOU GO TO SLEEP EXPECTING A MIRACLE WHEN YOU AWAKEN...
ZZZZZZZ...
...A MIRACLE THAT ONLY COMES ONCE A YEAR...
There are a variety of stories about the kinds of presents Evil Santa Claus leaves for naughty children... **However**...

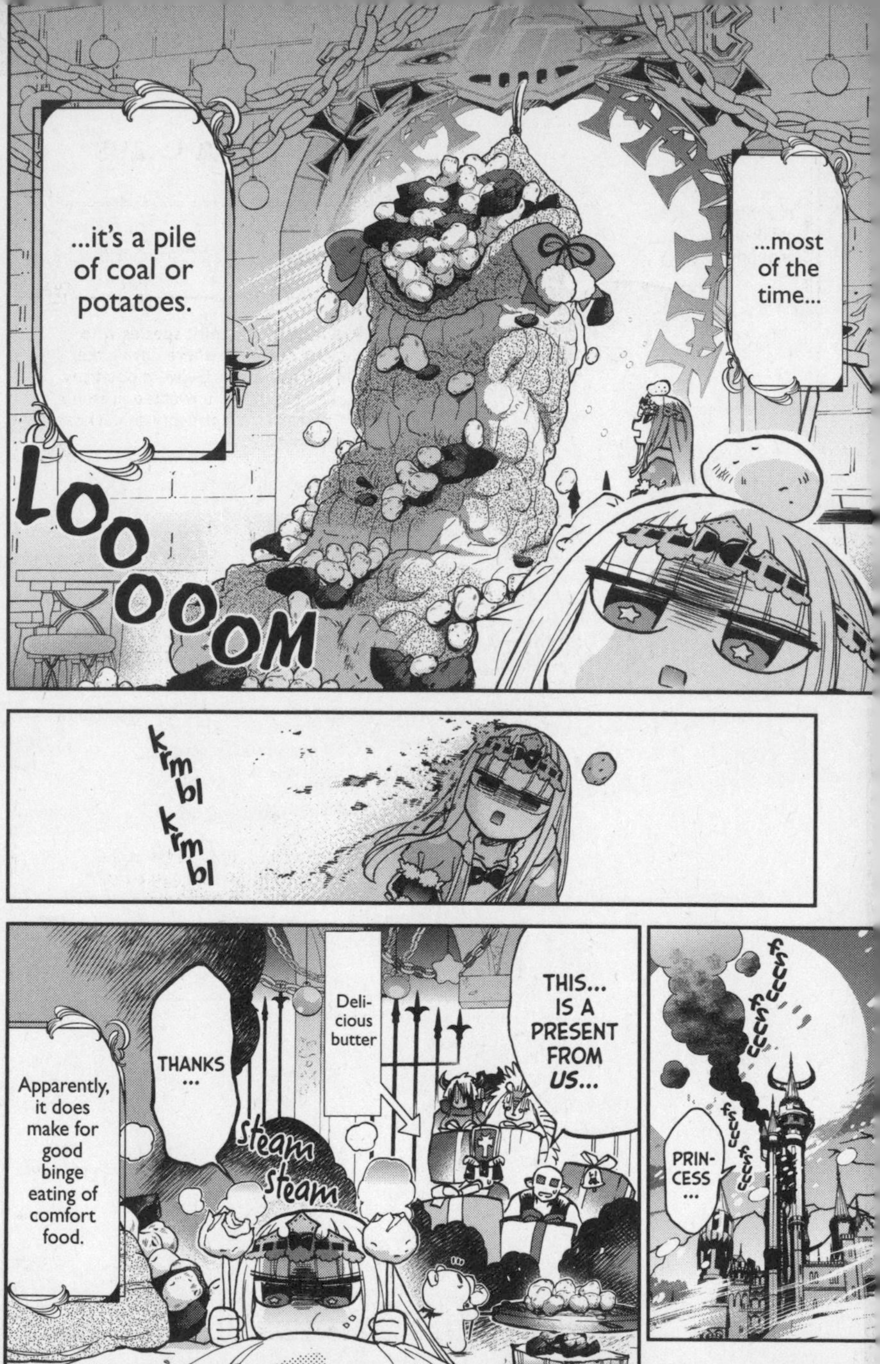
...most of the time...
...it's a pile of coal or potatoes.
LOOOOOOM
krmbl krmbl
fsuuu
PRIN-CESS...
fsuu fsuu
THIS... IS A PRESENT FROM US...
Deli-cious butter
THANKS...
steam steam
Apparently, it does make for good binge eating of comfort food.

Any naughty children around?

Evil Santa Claus

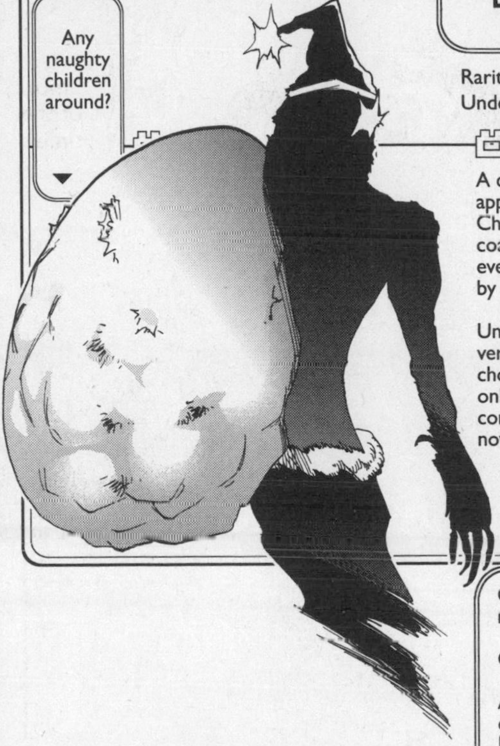

Rarity: ☆☆☆☆☆☆
Undefeatability: ☆☆☆☆☆☆☆☆☆☆

A demon of the spirit species who appears out of nowhere during the Christmas season. Delivers potatoes, coal and assorted unwanted presents every year to the naughty child chosen by committee.

Until last year, the Demon Castle was a very peaceful place, so the demons chosen to be the naughty child were only guilty of trivial mischief. They are confident that they're off the hook now that the princess is here.

Where is he during other seasons? Maybe he's actually living nearby in a different form...

Question to last year's naughty child:

Q: What did you do?

A: I used up all the eggs in the castle to make steamed custard. I lost control. But it was delicious!

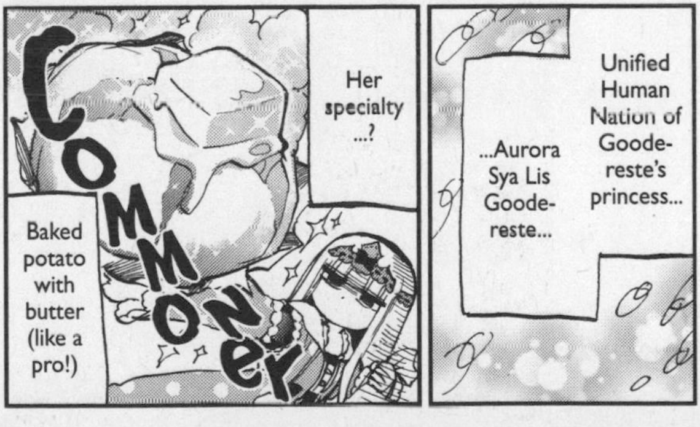
Unified Human Nation of Goodereste's princess...
...Aurora Sya Lis Goodereste...
Her specialty ...?
Baked potato with butter (like a pro!)
COMMONER

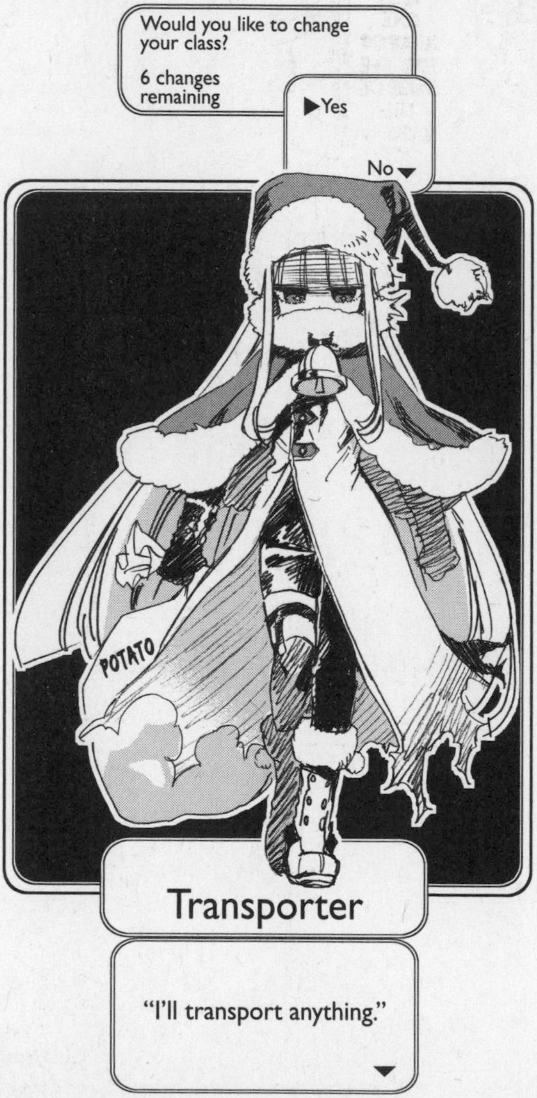
Would you like to change your class?
6 changes remaining
▶Yes
No
POTATO
Transporter
"I'll transport anything."

33rd Night: Don't Take Party Games Too Seriously!

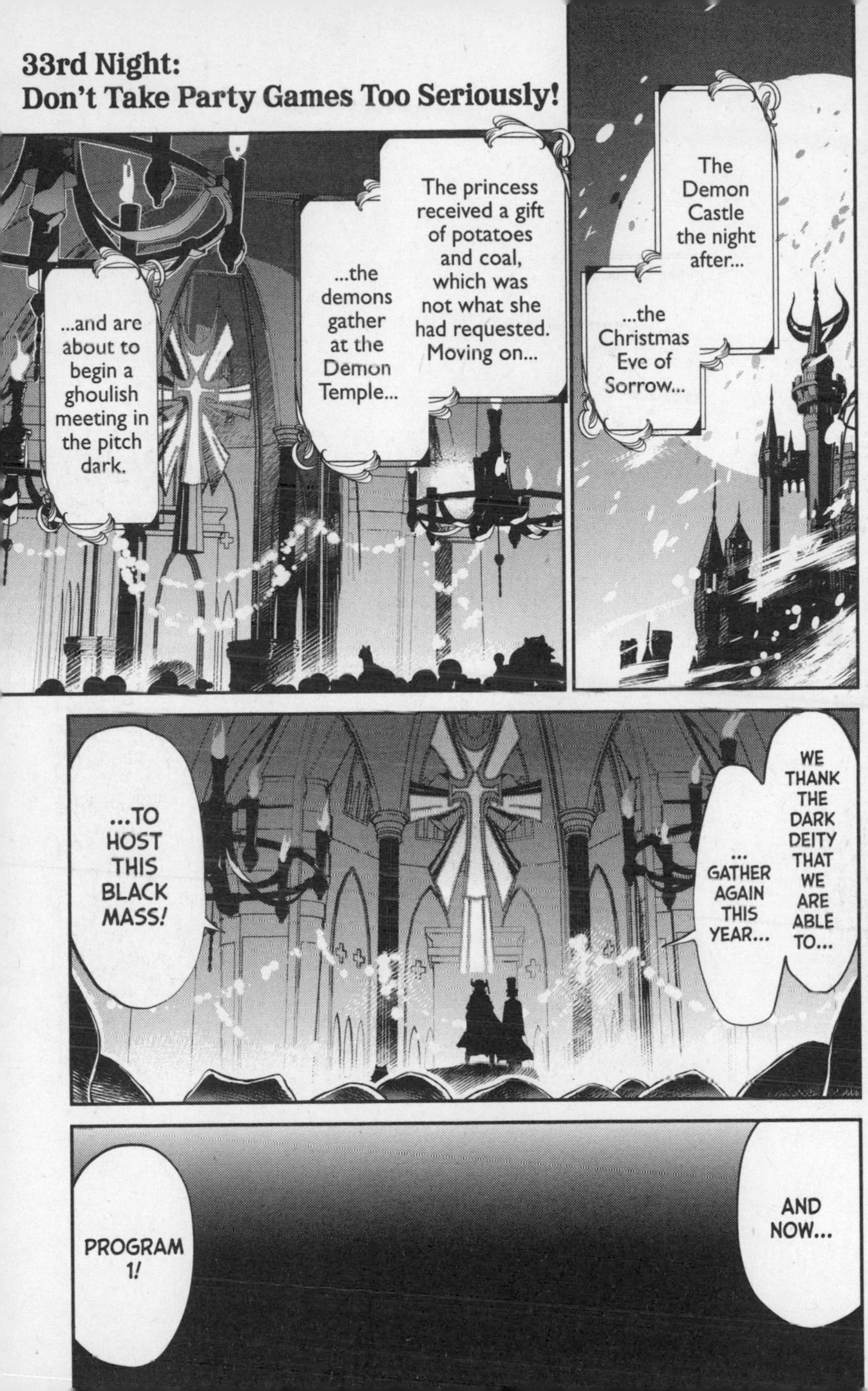
The Demon Castle the night after...
...the Christmas Eve of Sorrow...
The princess received a gift of potatoes and coal, which was not what she had requested. Moving on...
...the demons gather at the Demon Temple...
...and are about to begin a ghoulish meeting in the pitch dark.
WE THANK THE DARK DEITY THAT WE ARE ABLE TO...
...GATHER AGAIN THIS YEAR...
...TO HOST THIS BLACK MASS!
AND NOW...
PROGRAM 1!

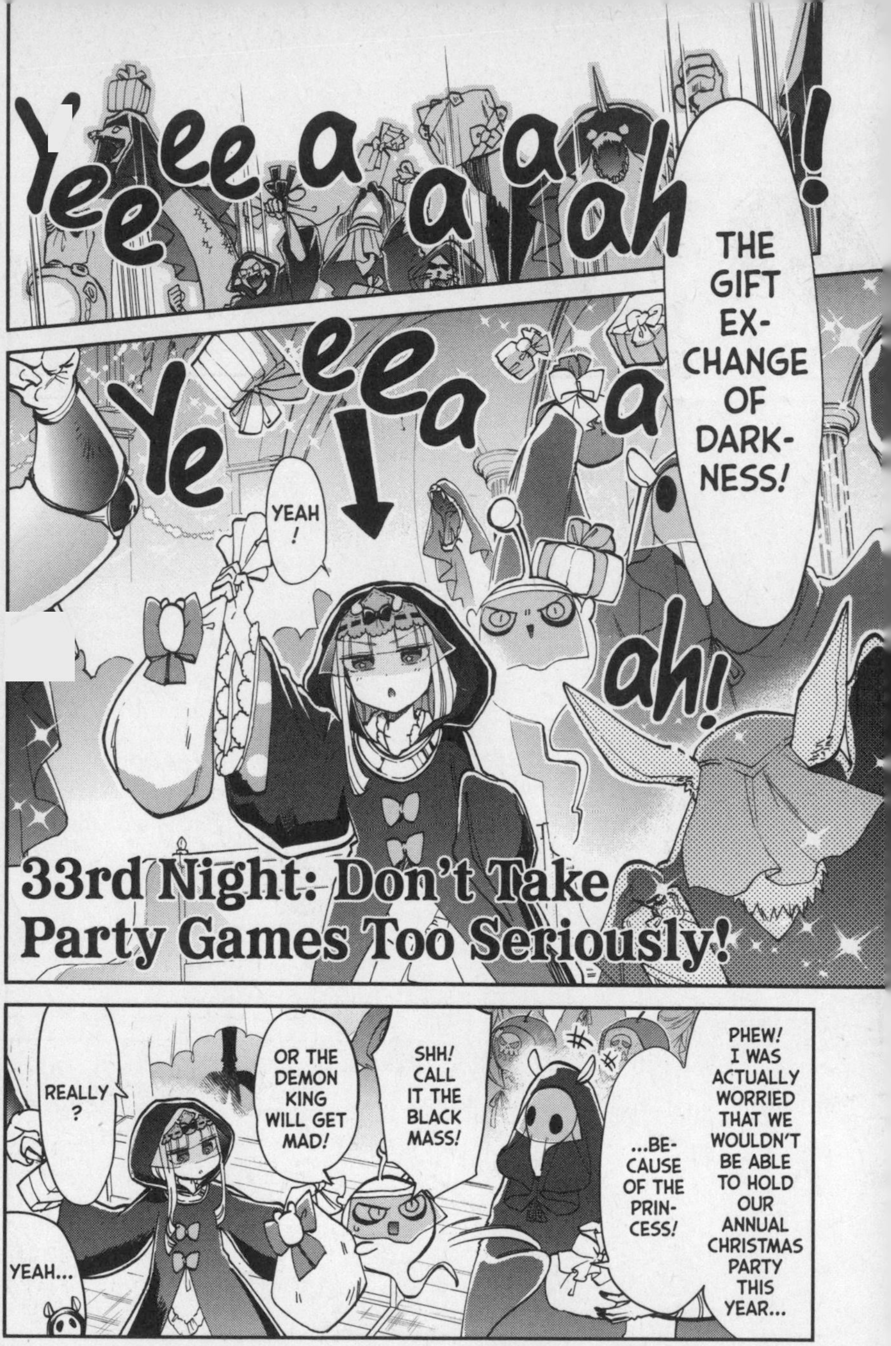
Yeeeeaaaaah!
THE GIFT EX-CHANGE OF DARK-NESS!
Yeeeaaah!
YEAH!
33rd Night: Don't Take Party Games Too Seriously!
PHEW! I WAS ACTUALLY WORRIED THAT WE WOULDN'T BE ABLE TO HOLD OUR ANNUAL CHRISTMAS PARTY THIS YEAR...
...BE-CAUSE OF THE PRIN-CESS!
SHH! CALL IT THE BLACK MASS!
OR THE DEMON KING WILL GET MAD!
REALLY?
YEAH...

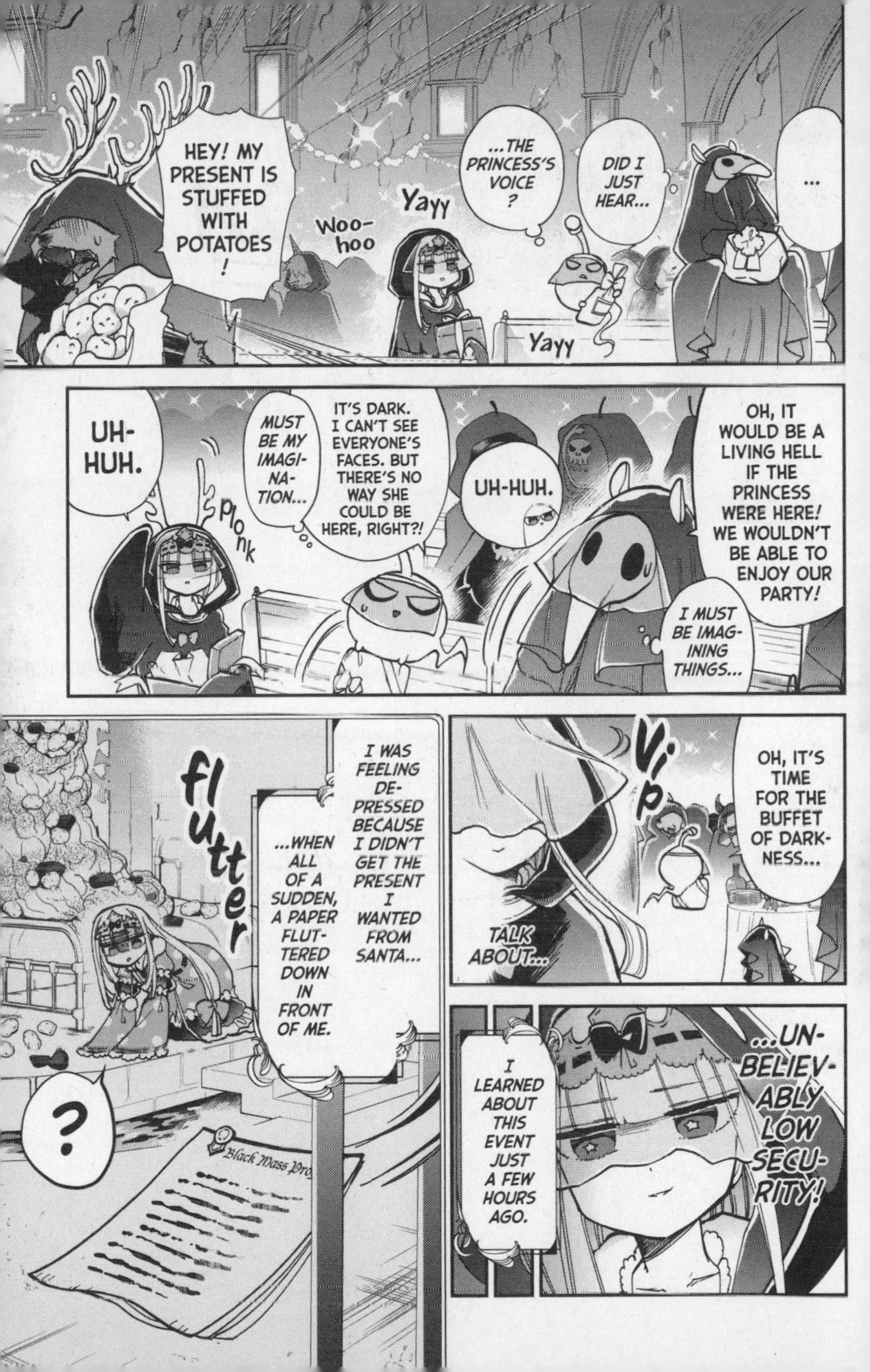
...
DID I JUST HEAR...
...THE PRINCESS'S VOICE?
Yayy
Woo-hoo
HEY! MY PRESENT IS STUFFED WITH POTATOES!
Yayy
OH, IT WOULD BE A LIVING HELL IF THE PRINCESS WERE HERE! WE WOULDN'T BE ABLE TO ENJOY OUR PARTY!
I MUST BE IMAGINING THINGS...
UH-HUH.
IT'S DARK. I CAN'T SEE EVERYONE'S FACES. BUT THERE'S NO WAY SHE COULD BE HERE, RIGHT?!
MUST BE MY IMAGINATION...
Plonk
UH-HUH.
OH, IT'S TIME FOR THE BUFFET OF DARKNESS...
Vip
TALK ABOUT...
...UNBELIEVABLY LOW SECURITY!
I LEARNED ABOUT THIS EVENT JUST A FEW HOURS AGO.
I WAS FEELING DEPRESSED BECAUSE I DIDN'T GET THE PRESENT I WANTED FROM SANTA...
...WHEN ALL OF A SUDDEN, A PAPER FLUTTERED DOWN IN FRONT OF ME.
flutter
?
Black Mass Pro

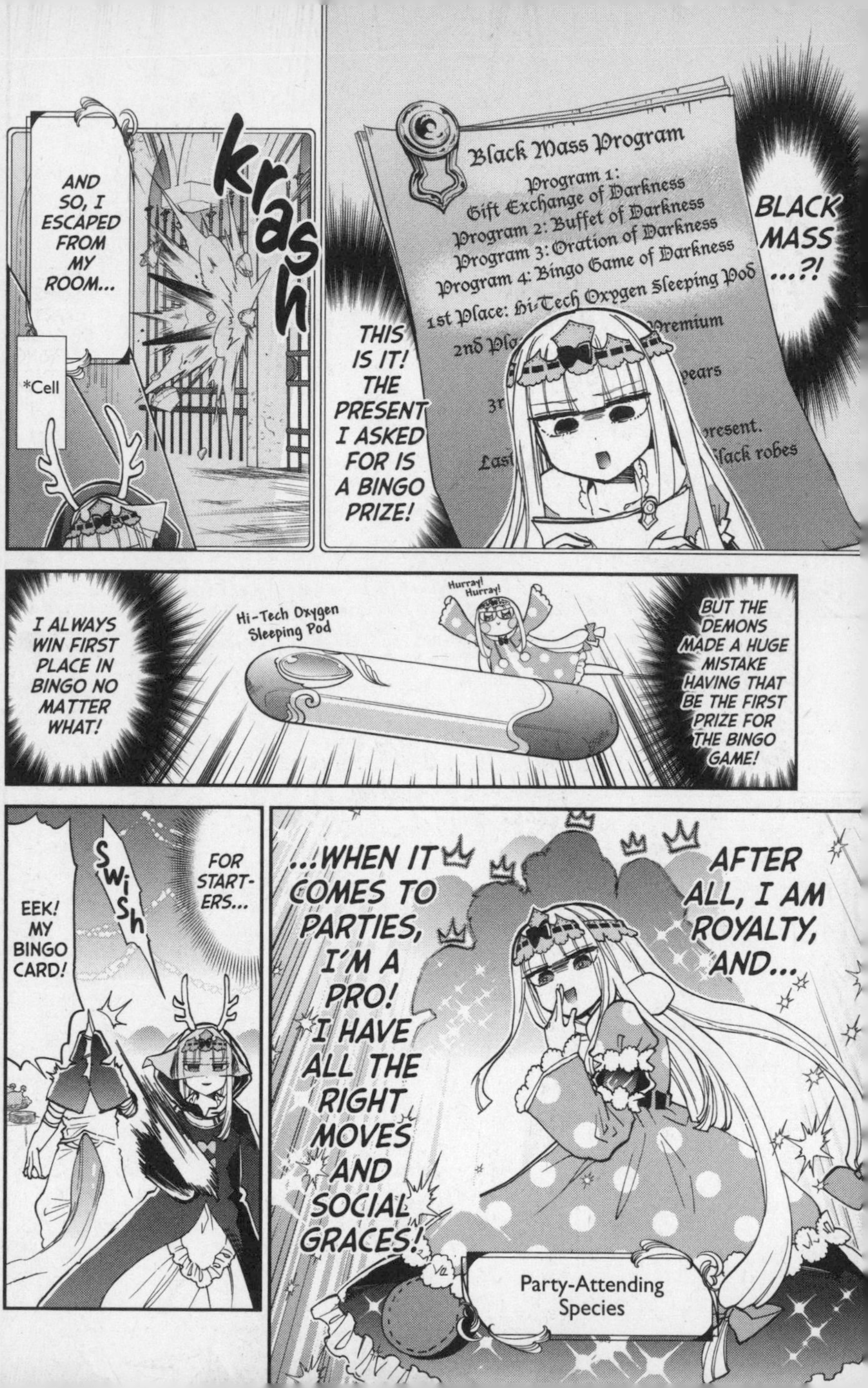
BLACK MASS ...?!
Black Mass Program
Program 1: Gift Exchange of Darkness
Program 2: Buffet of Darkness
Program 3: Oration of Darkness
Program 4: Bingo Game of Darkness
1st Place: Hi-Tech Oxygen Sleeping Pod
Premium
years
present.
black robes
THIS IS IT! THE PRESENT I ASKED FOR IS A BINGO PRIZE!
krash
AND SO, I ESCAPED FROM MY ROOM...
*Cell
BUT THE DEMONS MADE A HUGE MISTAKE HAVING THAT BE THE FIRST PRIZE FOR THE BINGO GAME!
Hurray! Hurray!
Hi-Tech Oxygen Sleeping Pod
I ALWAYS WIN FIRST PLACE IN BINGO NO MATTER WHAT!
AFTER ALL, I AM ROYALTY, AND...
...WHEN IT COMES TO PARTIES, I'M A PRO! I HAVE ALL THE RIGHT MOVES AND SOCIAL GRACES!
Party-Attending Species
FOR STARTERS...
swish
EEK! MY BINGO CARD!

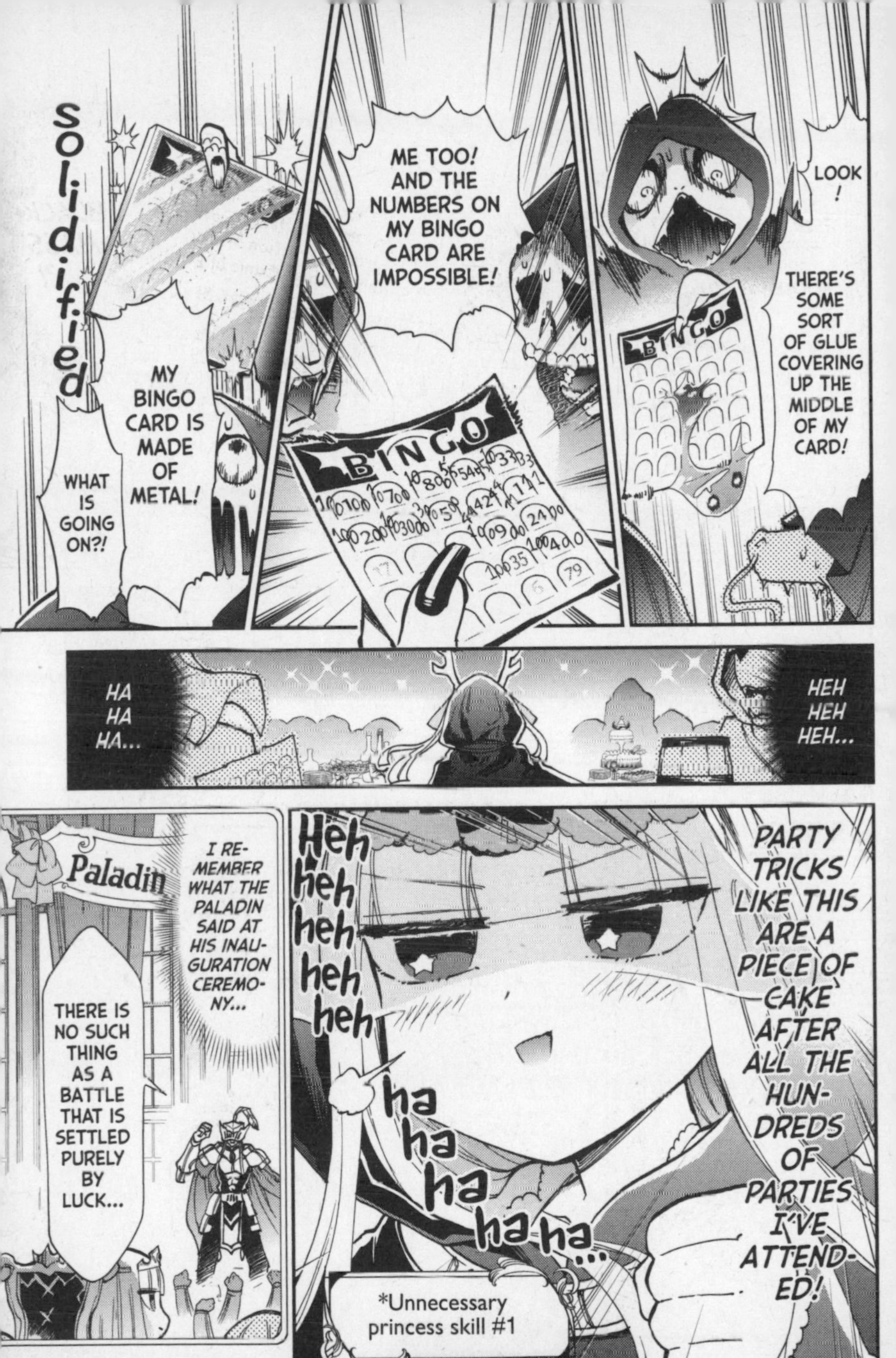
LOOK!
BINGO
THERE'S SOME SORT OF GLUE COVERING UP THE MIDDLE OF MY CARD!
ME TOO! AND THE NUMBERS ON MY BINGO CARD ARE IMPOSSIBLE!
BINGO
solidified
MY BINGO CARD IS MADE OF METAL!
WHAT IS GOING ON?!
HEH HEH HEH...
HA HA HA...
PARTY TRICKS LIKE THIS ARE A PIECE OF CAKE AFTER ALL THE HUNDREDS OF PARTIES I'VE ATTENDED!
Heh heh heh heh heh
ha ha ha ha ha...
*Unnecessary princess skill #1
I REMEMBER WHAT THE PALADIN SAID AT HIS INAUGURATION CEREMONY...
Paladin
THERE IS NO SUCH THING AS A BATTLE THAT IS SETTLED PURELY BY LUCK...

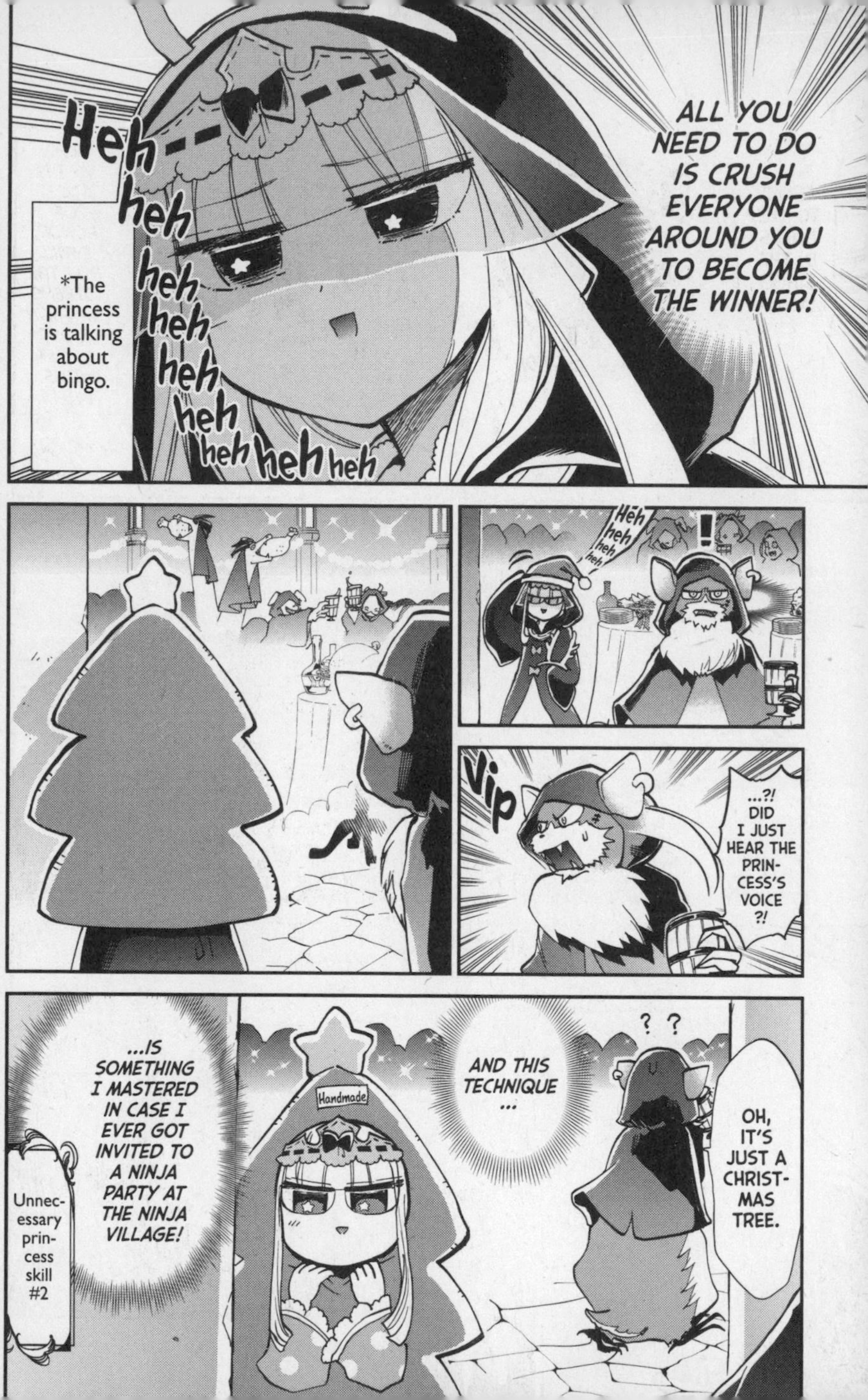
ALL YOU NEED TO DO IS CRUSH EVERYONE AROUND YOU TO BECOME THE WINNER!
Heh heh heh heh heh heh heh heh heh
*The princess is talking about bingo.
Heh heh heh heh
!
Vip
...?! DID I JUST HEAR THE PRIN-CESS'S VOICE ?!
? ?
OH, IT'S JUST A CHRIST-MAS TREE.
AND THIS TECHNIQUE ...
...IS SOMETHING I MASTERED IN CASE I EVER GOT INVITED TO A NINJA PARTY AT THE NINJA VILLAGE!
Handmade
Unnec-essary prin-cess skill #2

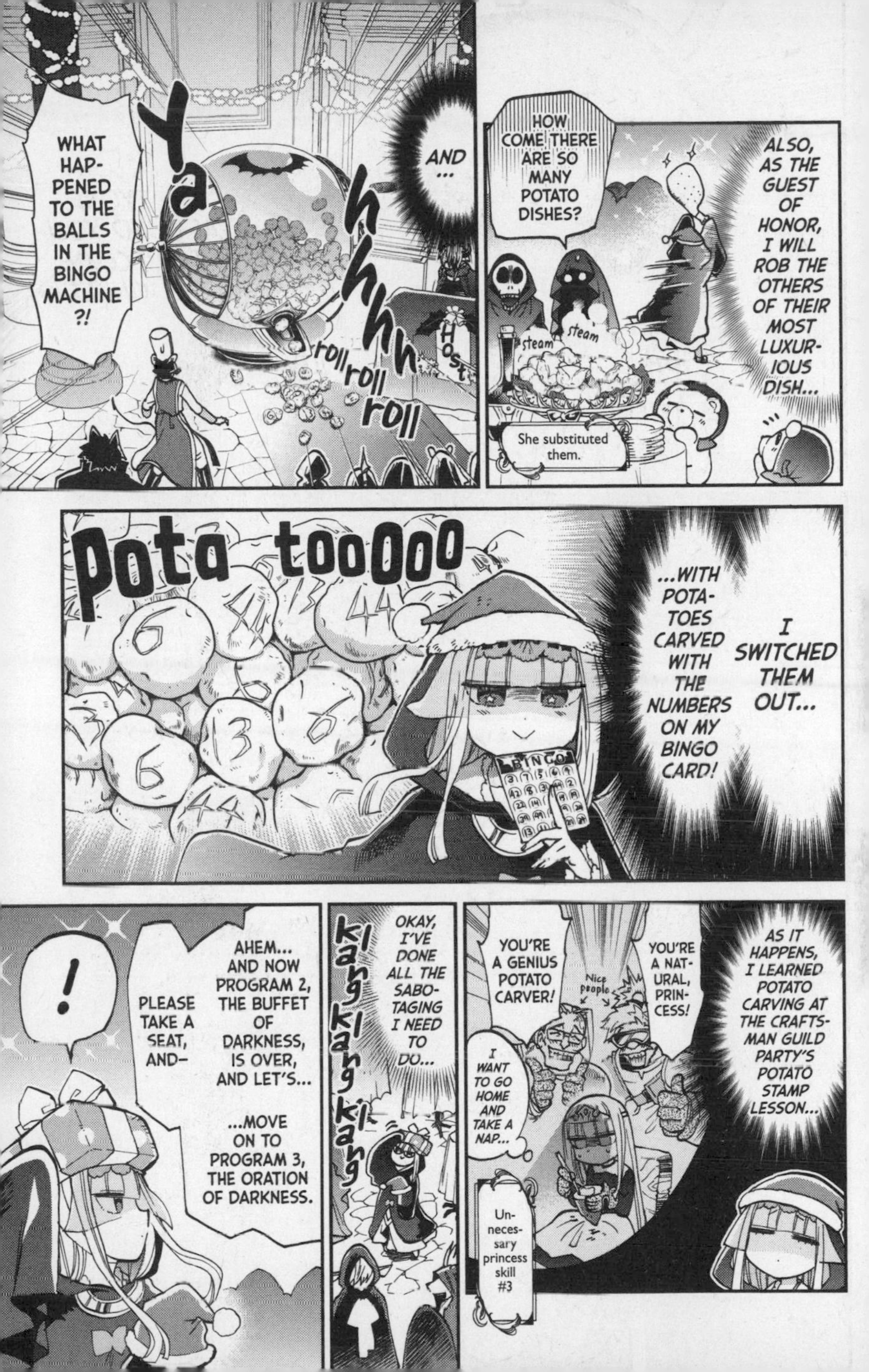
ALSO, AS THE GUEST OF HONOR, I WILL ROB THE OTHERS OF THEIR MOST LUXURIOUS DISH...
HOW COME THERE ARE SO MANY POTATO DISHES?
steam
steam
She substituted them.
AND ...
Yahhhhhn
Host
roll roll roll
WHAT HAPPENED TO THE BALLS IN THE BINGO MACHINE ?!
I SWITCHED THEM OUT...
...WITH POTATOES CARVED WITH THE NUMBERS ON MY BINGO CARD!
pota tooOOO
BINGO
AS IT HAPPENS, I LEARNED POTATO CARVING AT THE CRAFTSMAN GUILD PARTY'S POTATO STAMP LESSON...
YOU'RE A NATURAL, PRINCESS!
Nice people
YOU'RE A GENIUS POTATO CARVER!
I WANT TO GO HOME AND TAKE A NAP...
Unnecessary princess skill #3
OKAY, I'VE DONE ALL THE SABOTAGING I NEED TO DO...
klang klang klang
AHEM... AND NOW PROGRAM 2, THE BUFFET OF DARKNESS, IS OVER, AND LET'S...
PLEASE TAKE A SEAT, AND–
!
...MOVE ON TO PROGRAM 3, THE ORATION OF DARKNESS.

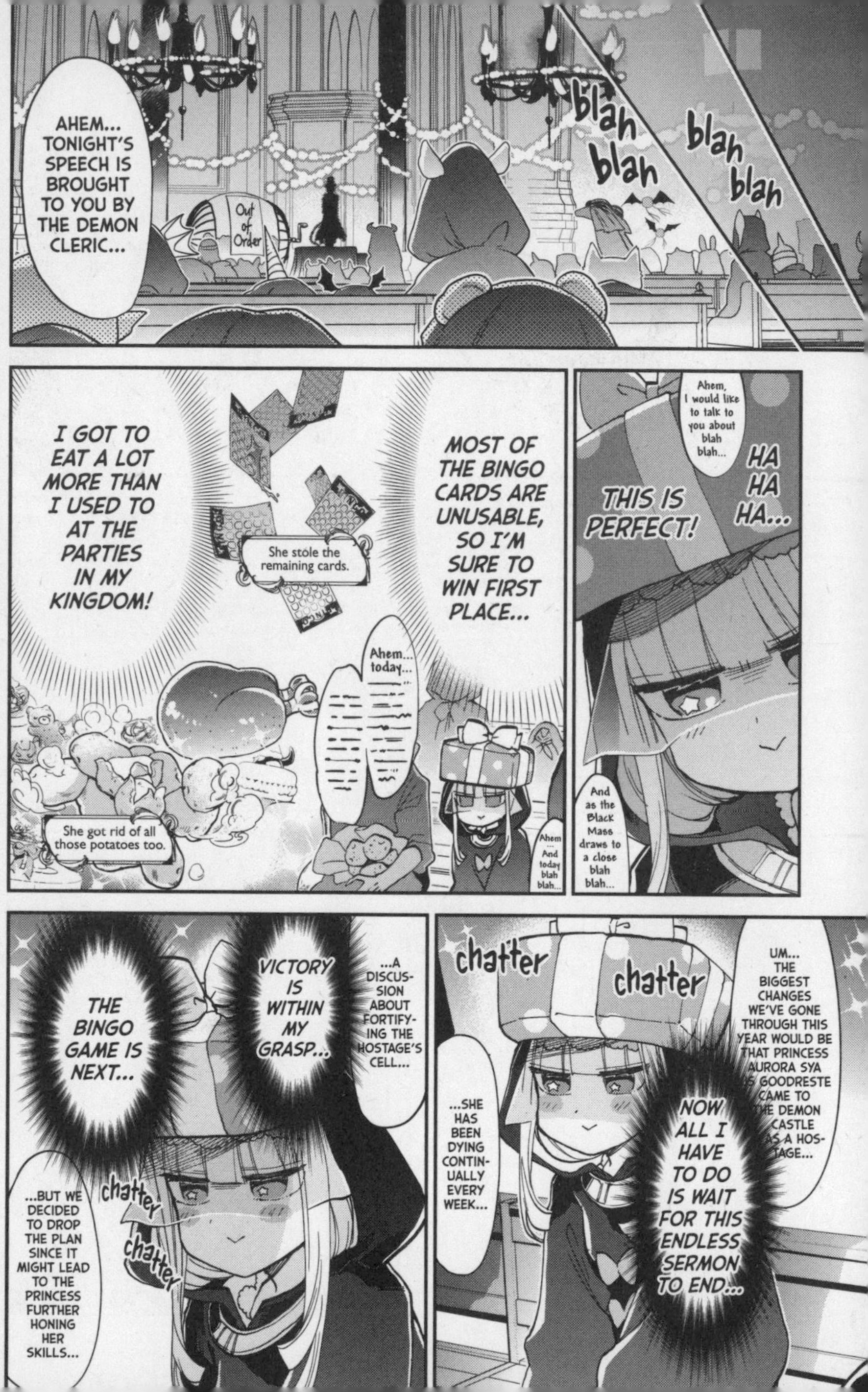
blah blah
blah blah
AHEM... TONIGHT'S SPEECH IS BROUGHT TO YOU BY THE DEMON CLERIC...
Out of Order
Ahem, I would like to talk to you about blah blah...
HA HA HA...
THIS IS PERFECT!
And as the Black Mass draws to a close blah blah...
MOST OF THE BINGO CARDS ARE UNUSABLE, SO I'M SURE TO WIN FIRST PLACE...
I GOT TO EAT A LOT MORE THAN I USED TO AT THE PARTIES IN MY KINGDOM!
She stole the remaining cards.
Ahem... today...
Ahem ... And today blah blah...
She got rid of all those potatoes too.
UM... THE BIGGEST CHANGES WE'VE GONE THROUGH THIS YEAR WOULD BE THAT PRINCESS AURORA SYA S GOODRESTE CAME TO HE DEMON CASTLE AS A HOS-TAGE...
chatter
chatter
NOW ALL I HAVE TO DO IS WAIT FOR THIS ENDLESS SERMON TO END...
...SHE HAS BEEN DYING CONTINUALLY EVERY WEEK...
...A DISCUSSION ABOUT FORTIFYING THE HOSTAGE'S CELL...
VICTORY IS WITHIN MY GRASP...
THE BINGO GAME IS NEXT...
...BUT WE DECIDED TO DROP THE PLAN SINCE IT MIGHT LEAD TO THE PRINCESS FURTHER HONING HER SKILLS...
chatter
chatter

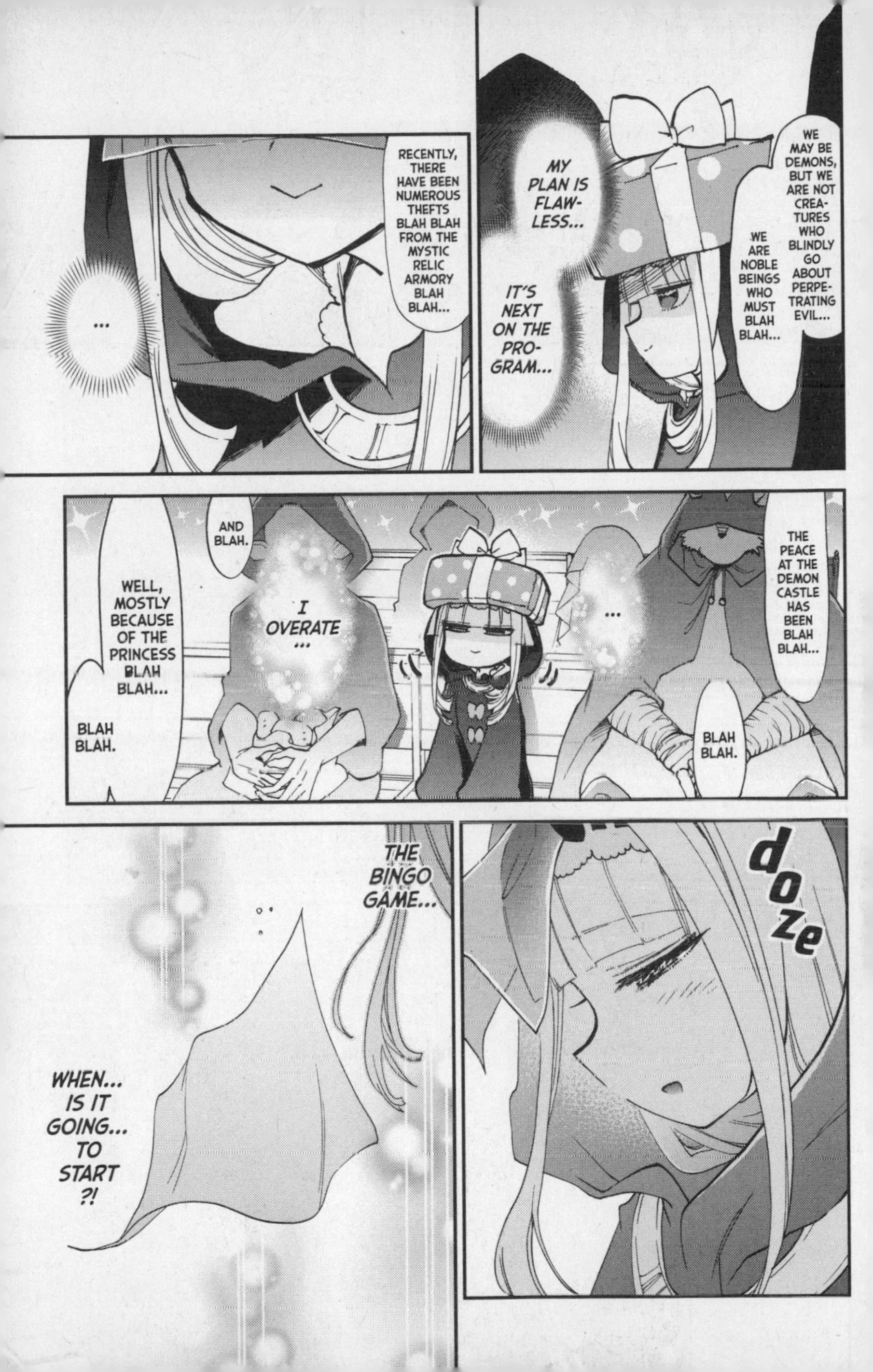
WE MAY BE DEMONS, BUT WE ARE NOT CREATURES WHO BLINDLY GO ABOUT PERPETRATING EVIL...
WE ARE NOBLE BEINGS WHO MUST BLAH BLAH...
MY PLAN IS FLAWLESS...
IT'S NEXT ON THE PROGRAM...
RECENTLY, THERE HAVE BEEN NUMEROUS THEFTS BLAH BLAH FROM THE MYSTIC RELIC ARMORY BLAH BLAH...
...
THE PEACE AT THE DEMON CASTLE HAS BEEN BLAH BLAH...
BLAH BLAH.
...
I OVERATE...
AND BLAH.
WELL, MOSTLY BECAUSE OF THE PRINCESS BLAH BLAH...
BLAH BLAH.
doze
THE BINGO GAME...
WHEN... IS IT GOING... TO START?!

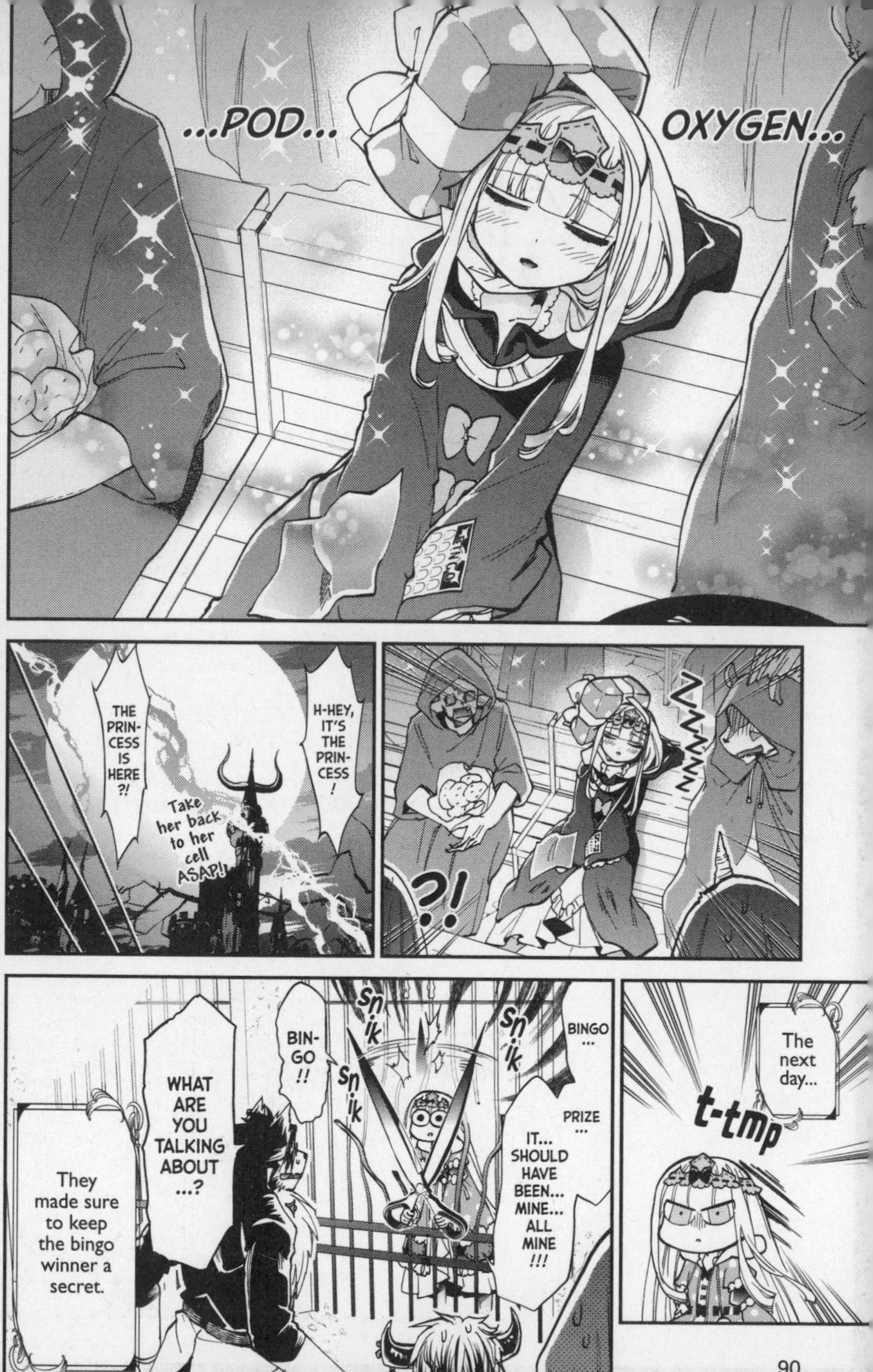

OXYGEN...
...POD...
ZZZZZ
?!
H-HEY, IT'S THE PRIN-CESS!
THE PRIN-CESS IS HERE?!
Take her back to her cell ASAP!
The next day...
t-tmp
BINGO...
snik
PRIZE...
IT... SHOULD HAVE BEEN... MINE... ALL MINE!!!
snik
BIN-GO!!
snik
WHAT ARE YOU TALKING ABOUT...?
They made sure to keep the bingo winner a secret.

Black Mass

Evil: ☆

Participation: ☆☆☆☆☆☆☆☆☆☆

There were potatoes every-where this year.

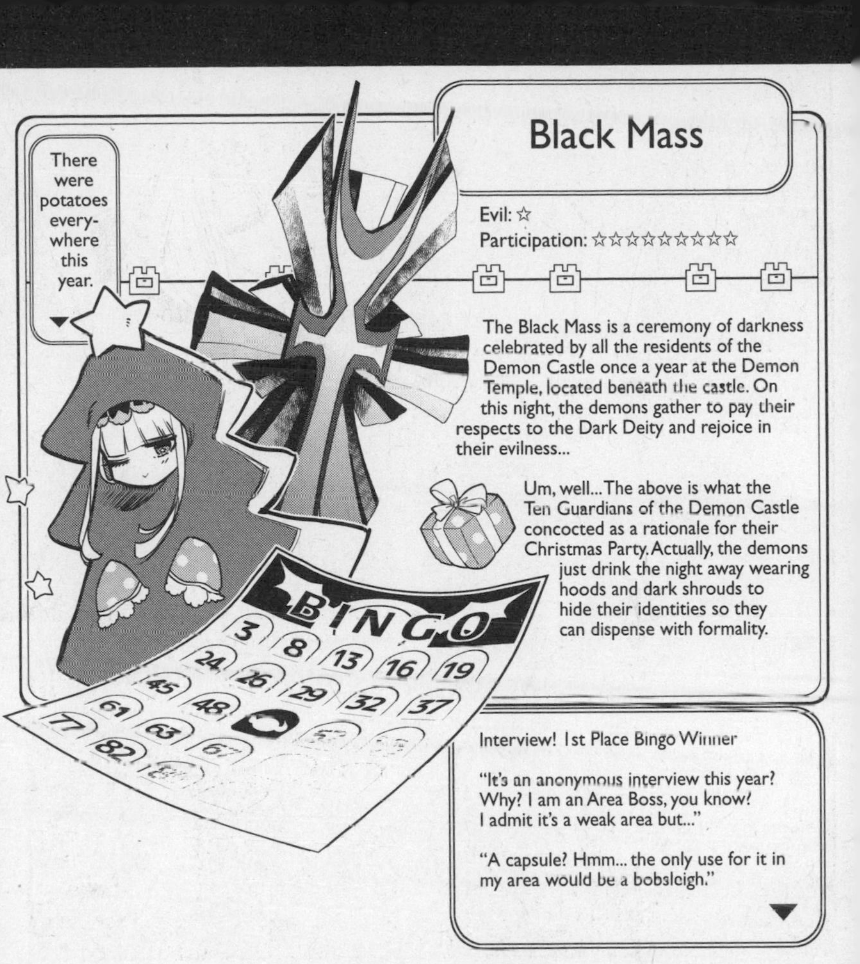
BINGO

The Black Mass is a ceremony of darkness celebrated by all the residents of the Demon Castle once a year at the Demon Temple, located beneath the castle. On this night, the demons gather to pay their respects to the Dark Deity and rejoice in their evilness...

Um, well... The above is what the Ten Guardians of the Demon Castle concocted as a rationale for their Christmas Party. Actually, the demons just drink the night away wearing hoods and dark shrouds to hide their identities so they can dispense with formality.

Interview! 1st Place Bingo Winner

"It's an anonymous interview this year? Why? I am an Area Boss, you know! I admit it's a weak area but..."

"A capsule? Hmm... the only use for it in my area would be a bobsleigh."

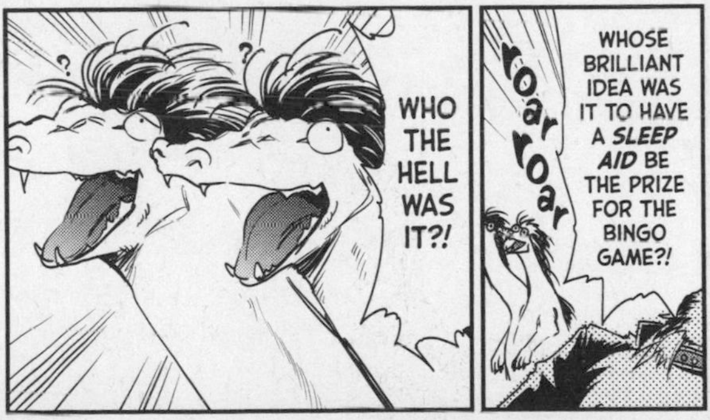
WHOSE BRILLIANT IDEA WAS IT TO HAVE A *SLEEP AID* BE THE PRIZE FOR THE BINGO GAME?!
roar roar roar
WHO THE HELL WAS IT?!

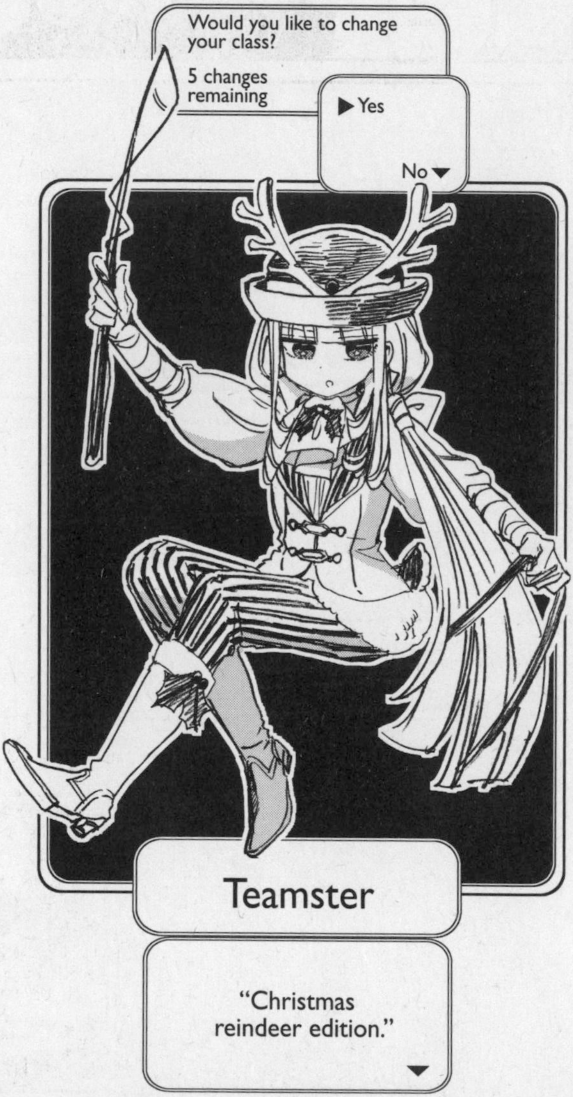
Would you like to change your class?
5 changes remaining
▶Yes
No
Teamster
"Christmas reindeer edition."

34th Night: Puffy ♡ Princess

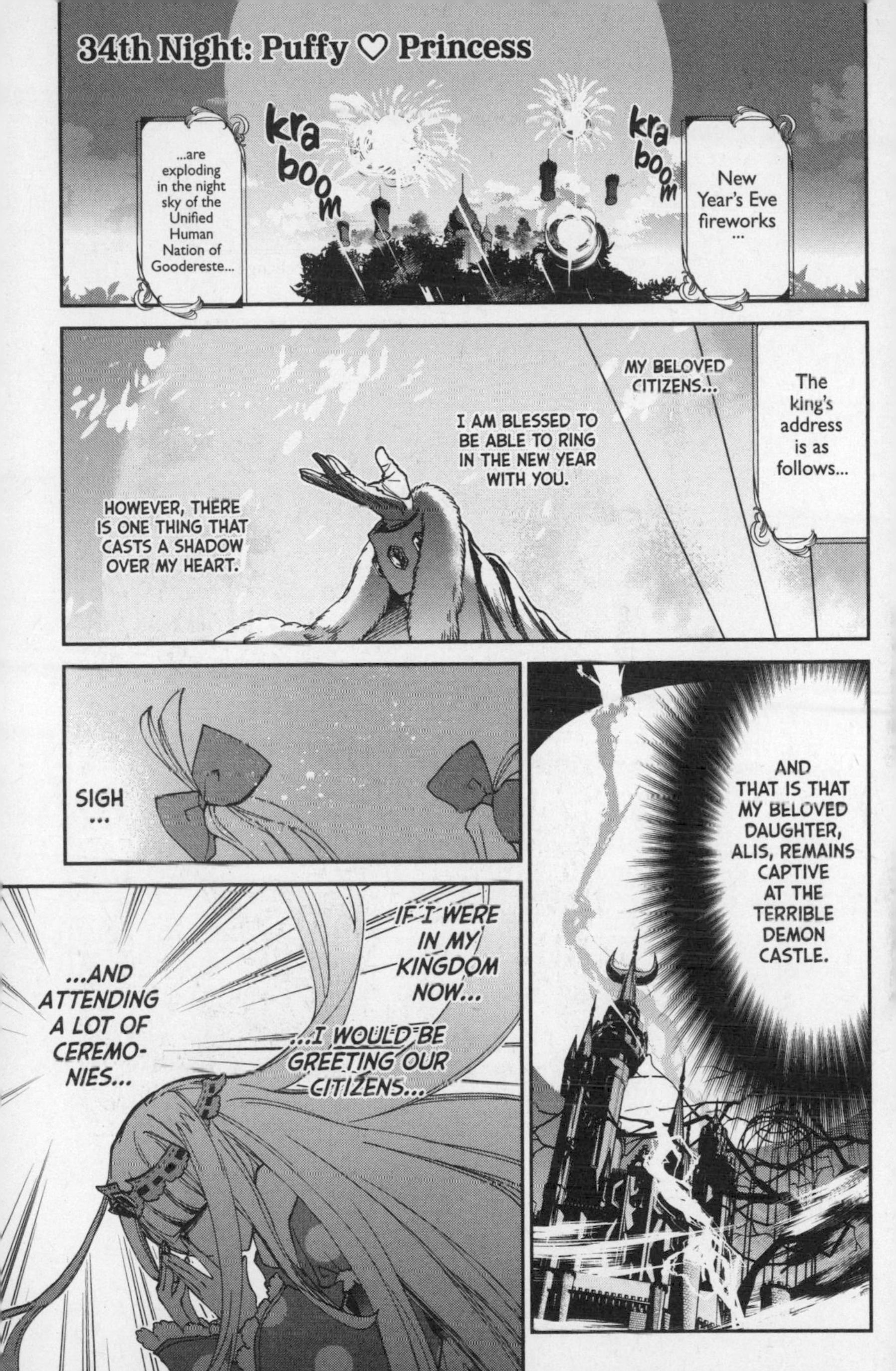

New Year's Eve fireworks ...
kra boom
kra boom
...are exploding in the night sky of the Unified Human Nation of Goodereste...
The king's address is as follows...
MY BELOVED CITIZENS...
I AM BLESSED TO BE ABLE TO RING IN THE NEW YEAR WITH YOU.
HOWEVER, THERE IS ONE THING THAT CASTS A SHADOW OVER MY HEART.
AND THAT IS THAT MY BELOVED DAUGHTER, ALIS, REMAINS CAPTIVE AT THE TERRIBLE DEMON CASTLE.
SIGH ...
IF I WERE IN MY KINGDOM NOW...
...I WOULD BE GREETING OUR CITIZENS...
...AND ATTENDING A LOT OF CEREMONIES...

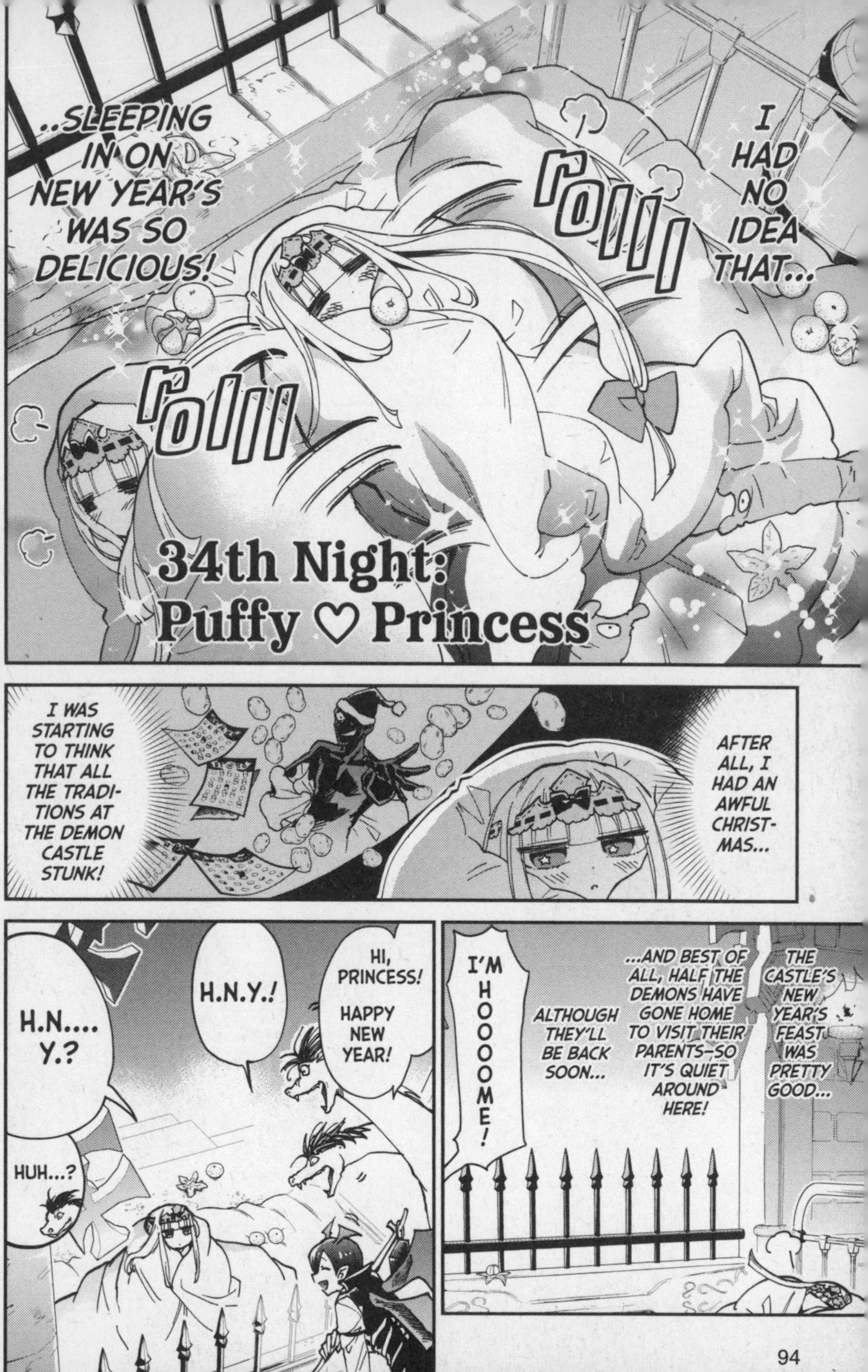
I HAD NO IDEA THAT...
rolll
...SLEEPING IN ON NEW YEAR'S WAS SO DELICIOUS!
rolll
34th Night: Puffy ♡ Princess
AFTER ALL, I HAD AN AWFUL CHRISTMAS...
I WAS STARTING TO THINK THAT ALL THE TRADITIONS AT THE DEMON CASTLE STUNK!
THE CASTLE'S NEW YEAR'S FEAST WAS PRETTY GOOD...
...AND BEST OF ALL, HALF THE DEMONS HAVE GONE HOME TO VISIT THEIR PARENTS—SO IT'S QUIET AROUND HERE!
ALTHOUGH THEY'LL BE BACK SOON...
I'M HOOOOOME!
HI, PRINCESS!
HAPPY NEW YEAR!
H.N.Y.!
H.N.... Y.?
HUH...?

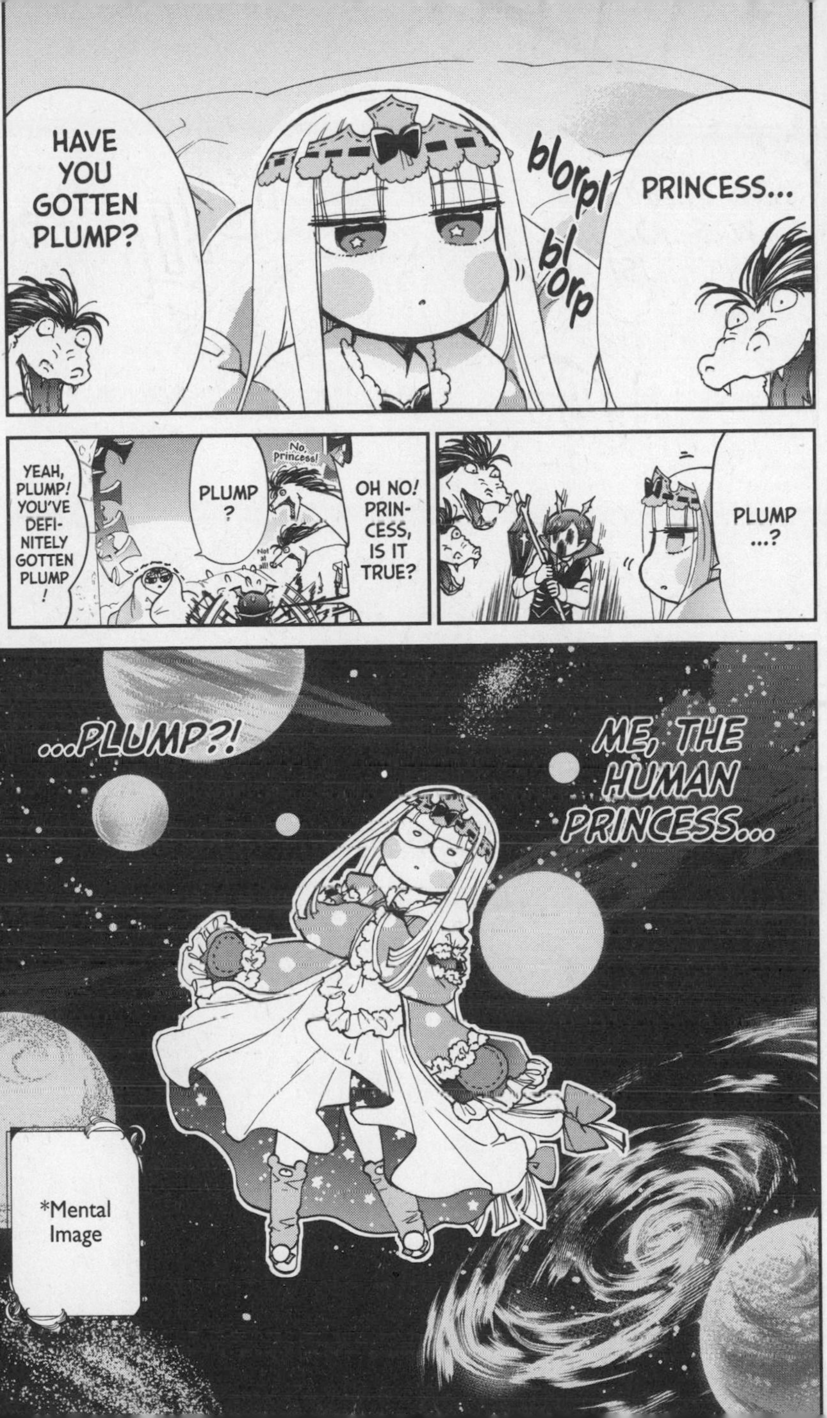
PRINCESS...
blorpl blorp
HAVE YOU GOTTEN PLUMP?
PLUMP ...?
OH NO! PRIN-CESS, IS IT TRUE?
No, princess!
PLUMP ?
Not at all!
YEAH, PLUMP! YOU'VE DEFI-NITELY GOTTEN PLUMP!
ME, THE HUMAN PRINCESS...
...PLUMP?!
*Mental Image

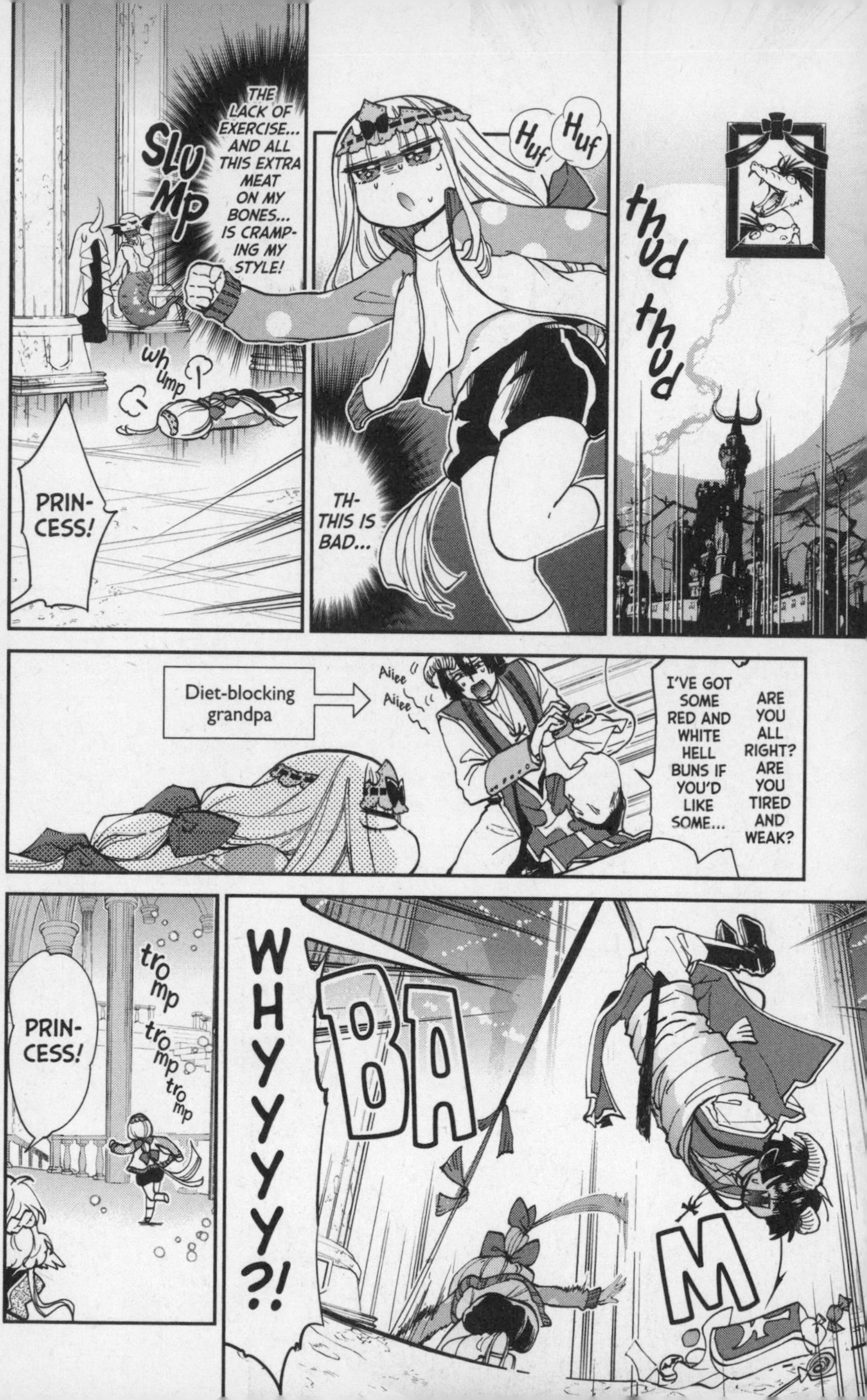
thud thud thud
Huf Huf
TH- THIS IS BAD...
THE LACK OF EXERCISE... AND ALL THIS EXTRA MEAT ON MY BONES... IS CRAMPING MY STYLE!
SLUMP
whump
PRIN- CESS!
ARE YOU ALL RIGHT? ARE YOU TIRED AND WEAK?
I'VE GOT SOME RED AND WHITE HELL BUNS IF YOU'D LIKE SOME...
Aiiee Aiiee
Diet-blocking grandpa
BAM
WHYYYY?!
tromp tromp tromp
PRIN- CESS!

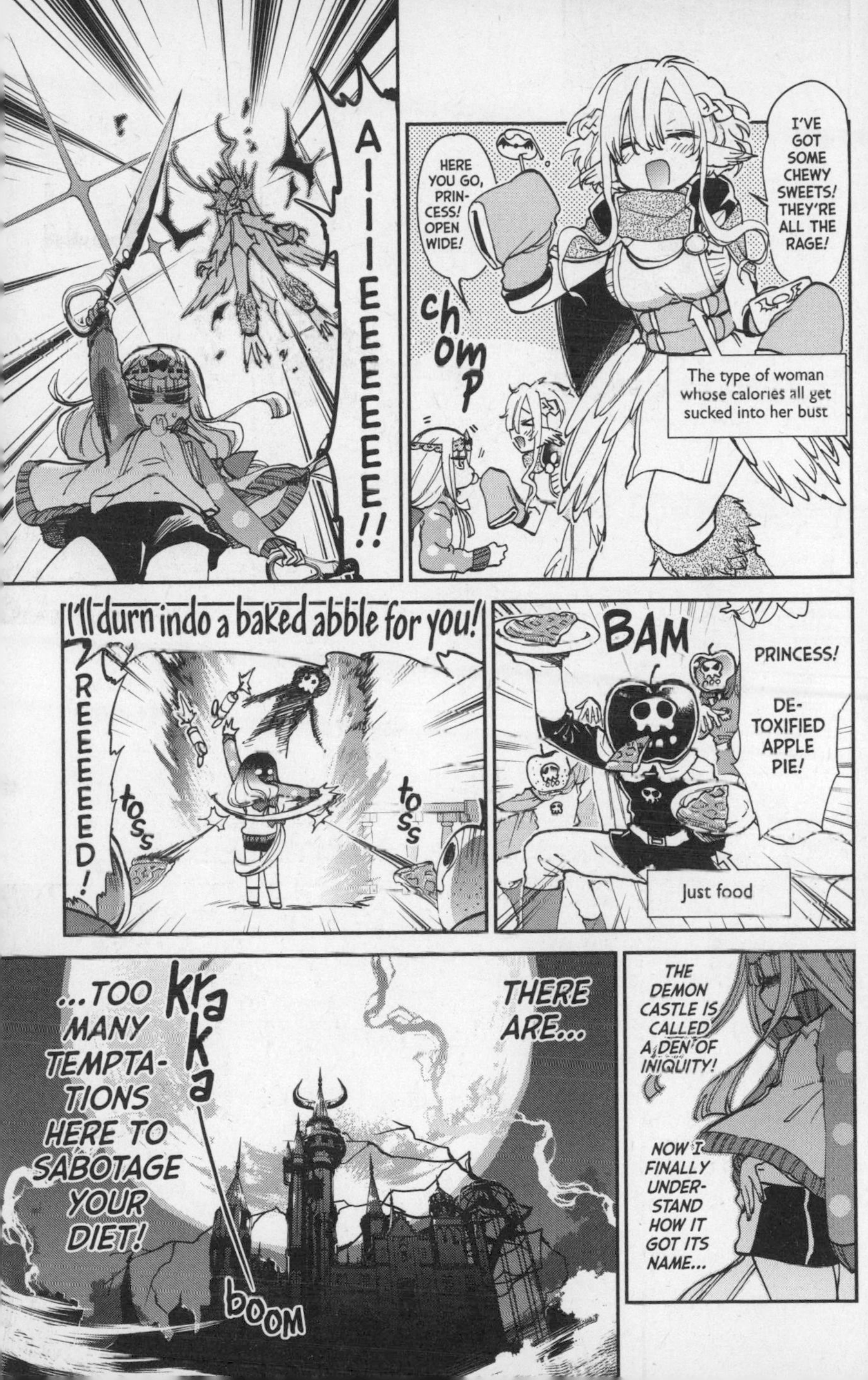
I'VE GOT SOME CHEWY SWEETS! THEY'RE ALL THE RAGE!
HERE YOU GO, PRIN-CESS! OPEN WIDE!
chomp
The type of woman whose calories all get sucked into her bust
AIIIEEEEEEE!!
PRINCESS!
DE-TOXIFIED APPLE PIE!
BAM
Just food
I'll durn indo a baked abble for you!
REEEEEED!
toss
toss
THE DEMON CASTLE IS CALLED A DEN OF INIQUITY!
NOW I FINALLY UNDER-STAND HOW IT GOT ITS NAME...
THERE ARE...
...TOO MANY TEMPTA-TIONS HERE TO SABOTAGE YOUR DIET!
kraka
boom

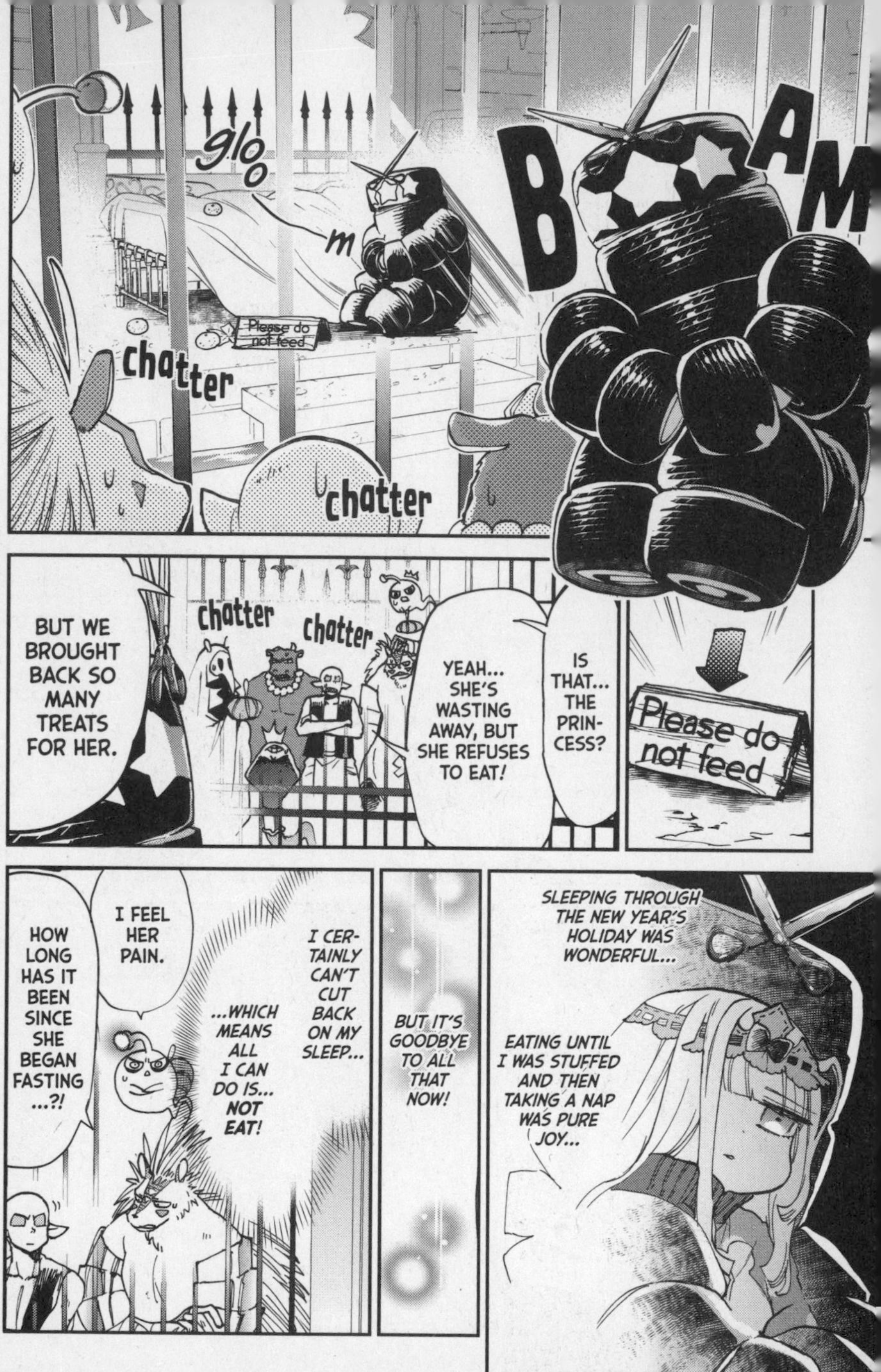
BAM
gloo
m
Please do not feed
chatter
chatter
Please do not feed
IS THAT... THE PRIN-CESS?
YEAH... SHE'S WASTING AWAY, BUT SHE REFUSES TO EAT!
chatter
chatter
BUT WE BROUGHT BACK SO MANY TREATS FOR HER.
SLEEPING THROUGH THE NEW YEAR'S HOLIDAY WAS WONDERFUL...
EATING UNTIL I WAS STUFFED AND THEN TAKING A NAP WAS PURE JOY...
BUT IT'S GOODBYE TO ALL THAT NOW!
I CER-TAINLY CAN'T CUT BACK ON MY SLEEP...
...WHICH MEANS ALL I CAN DO IS... NOT EAT!
I FEEL HER PAIN.
HOW LONG HAS IT BEEN SINCE SHE BEGAN FASTING ...?!

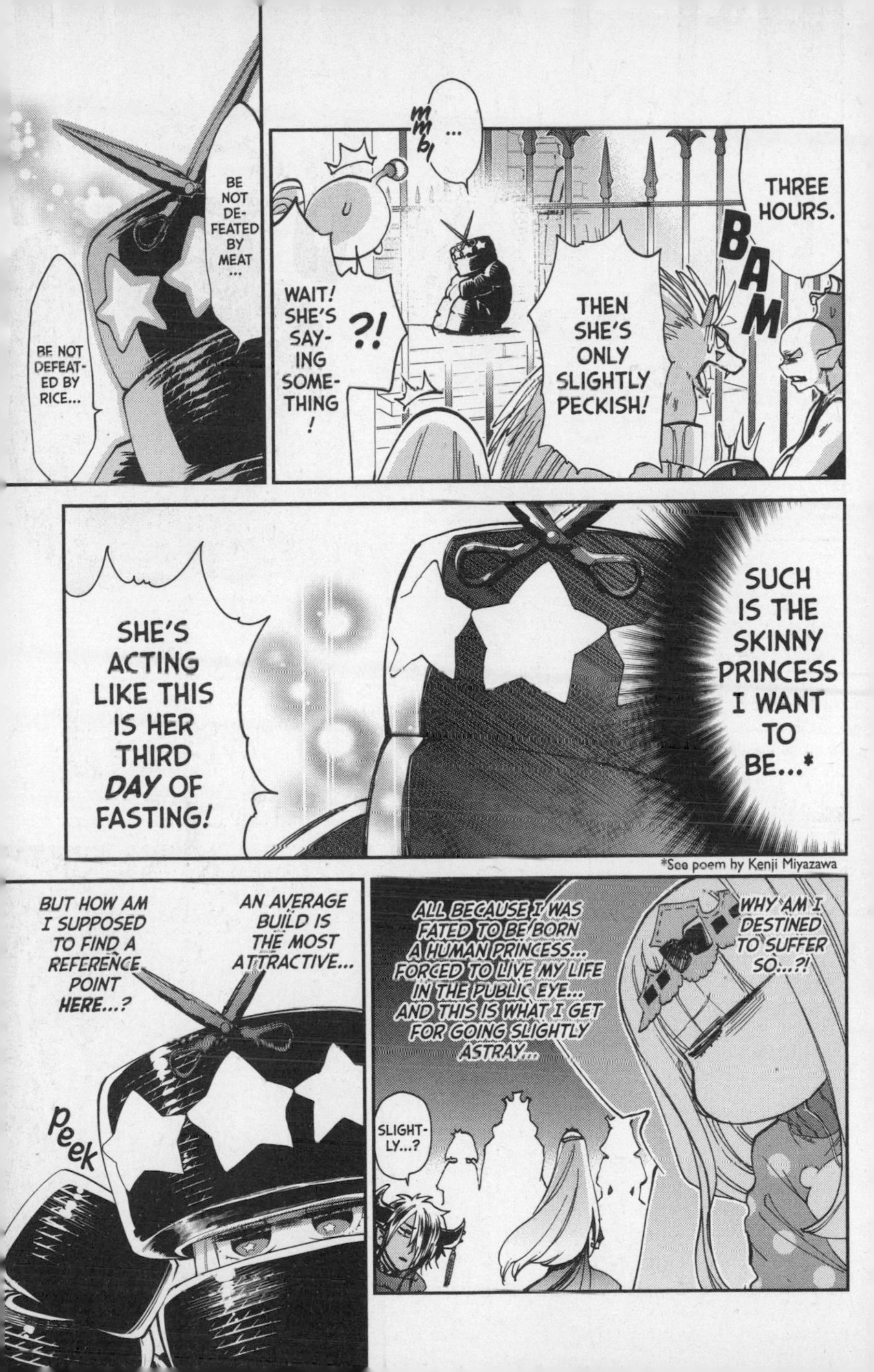
THREE HOURS.
BAM
THEN SHE'S ONLY SLIGHTLY PECKISH!
mmbl
...
WAIT! SHE'S SAYING SOMETHING!
?!
BE NOT DEFEATED BY MEAT...
BE NOT DEFEATED BY RICE...
SUCH IS THE SKINNY PRINCESS I WANT TO BE...*
SHE'S ACTING LIKE THIS IS HER THIRD DAY OF FASTING!
WHY AM I DESTINED TO SUFFER SO...?!
ALL BECAUSE I WAS FATED TO BE BORN A HUMAN PRINCESS... FORCED TO LIVE MY LIFE IN THE PUBLIC EYE... AND THIS IS WHAT I GET FOR GOING SLIGHTLY ASTRAY...
SLIGHTLY...?
AN AVERAGE BUILD IS THE MOST ATTRACTIVE...
BUT HOW AM I SUPPOSED TO FIND A REFERENCE POINT HERE...?
Peek

*See poem by Kenji Miyazawa

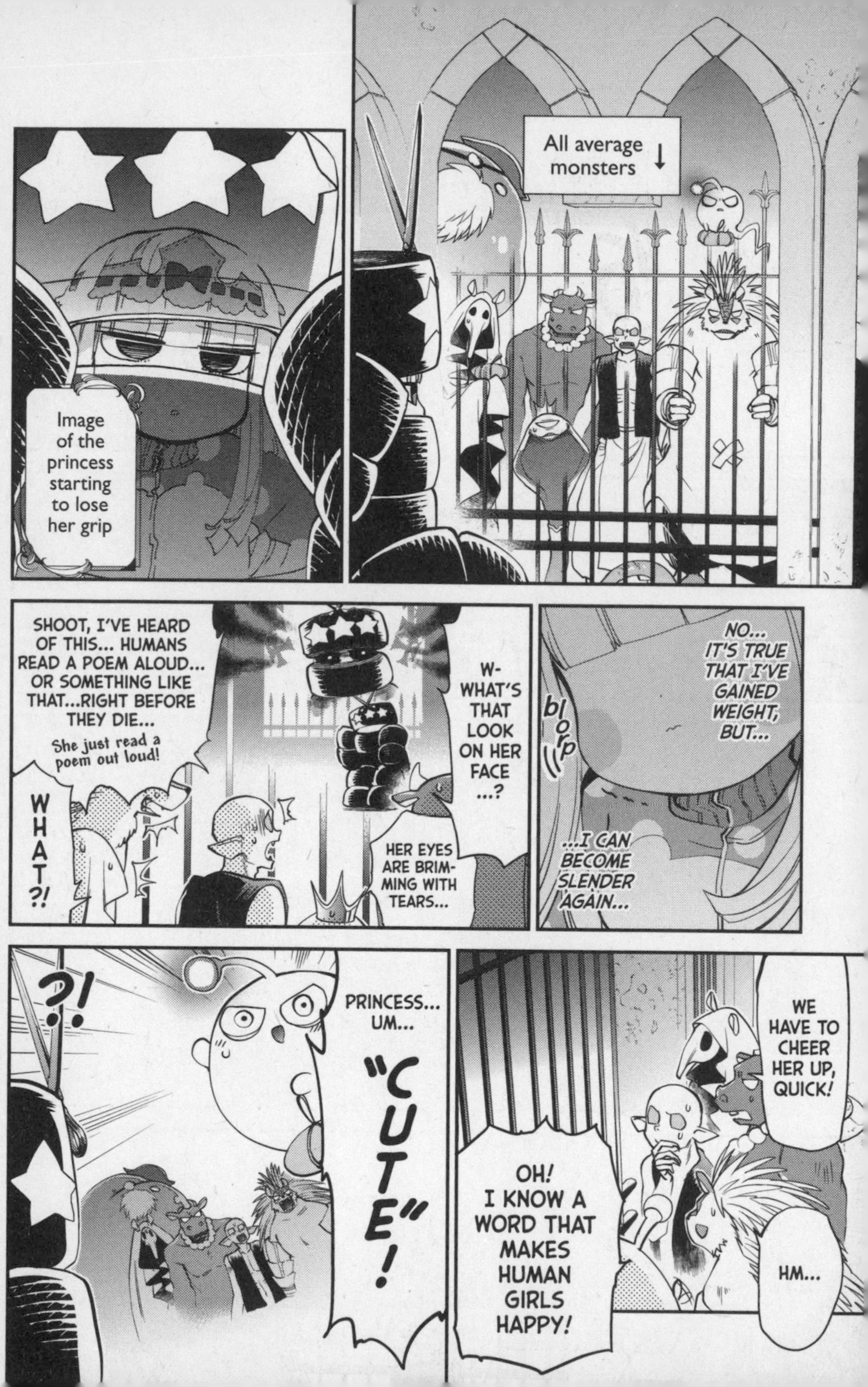
All average monsters ↓
Image of the princess starting to lose her grip
NO... IT'S TRUE THAT I'VE GAINED WEIGHT, BUT...
blorp
...I CAN BECOME SLENDER AGAIN...
W-WHAT'S THAT LOOK ON HER FACE ...?
HER EYES ARE BRIMMING WITH TEARS...
SHOOT, I'VE HEARD OF THIS... HUMANS READ A POEM ALOUD... OR SOMETHING LIKE THAT...RIGHT BEFORE THEY DIE...
She just read a poem out loud!
WHAT?!
WE HAVE TO CHEER HER UP, QUICK!
HM...
OH! I KNOW A WORD THAT MAKES HUMAN GIRLS HAPPY!
PRINCESS... UM...
"CUTE"!
?!

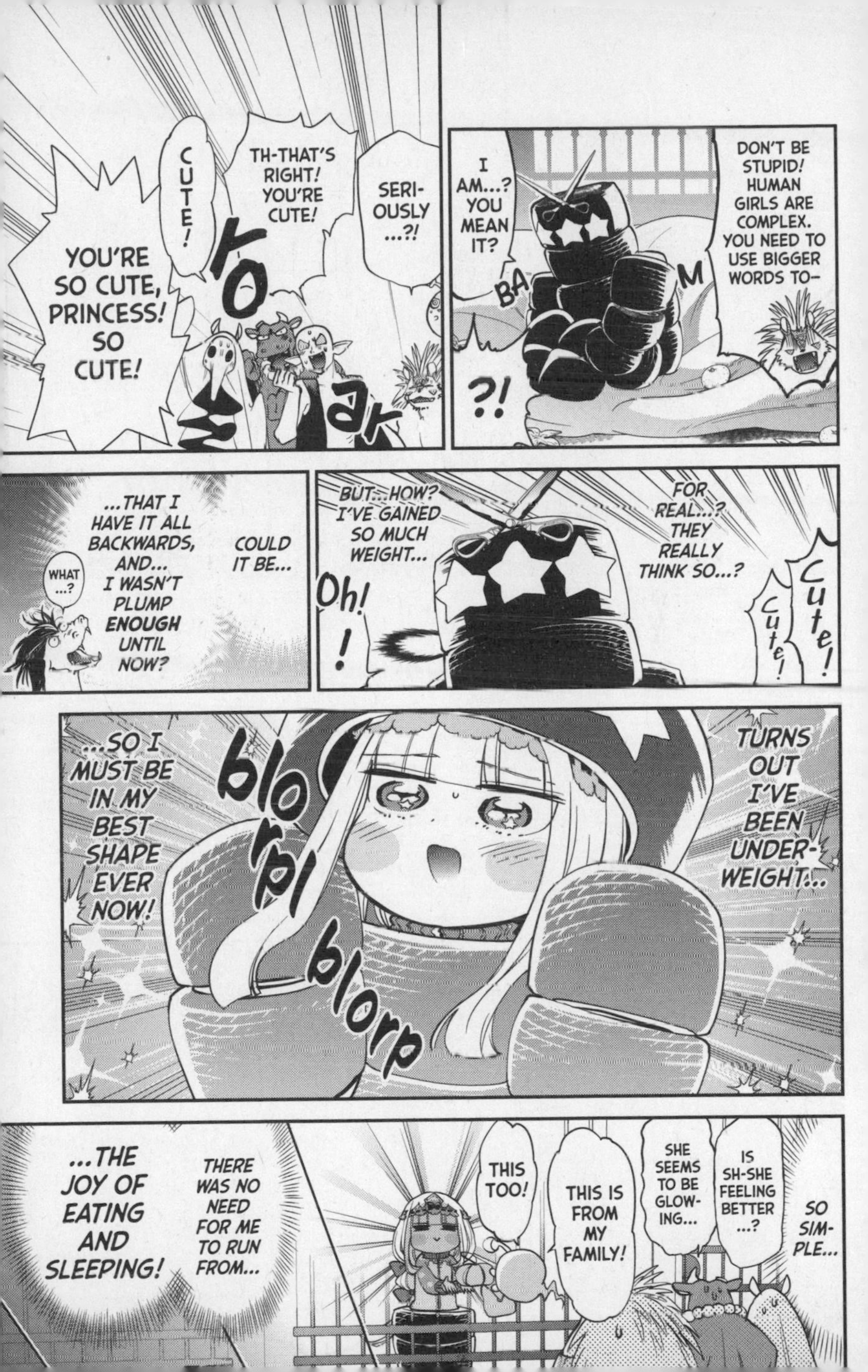
DON'T BE STUPID! HUMAN GIRLS ARE COMPLEX. YOU NEED TO USE BIGGER WORDS TO—
BAM
I AM...? YOU MEAN IT?
?!
SERIOUSLY...?!
TH-THAT'S RIGHT! YOU'RE CUTE!
CUTE!
YOU'RE SO CUTE, PRINCESS! SO CUTE!
YO
Cute!
Cute!
FOR REAL...? THEY REALLY THINK SO...?
BUT... HOW? I'VE GAINED SO MUCH WEIGHT...
Oh!!
COULD IT BE...
...THAT I HAVE IT ALL BACKWARDS, AND... I WASN'T PLUMP ENOUGH UNTIL NOW?
WHAT...?
TURNS OUT I'VE BEEN UNDERWEIGHT...
blorp
blorp
...SO I MUST BE IN MY BEST SHAPE EVER NOW!
SO SIMPLE...
IS SH-SHE FEELING BETTER...?
SHE SEEMS TO BE GLOWING...
THIS IS FROM MY FAMILY!
THIS TOO!
THERE WAS NO NEED FOR ME TO RUN FROM...
...THE JOY OF EATING AND SLEEPING!

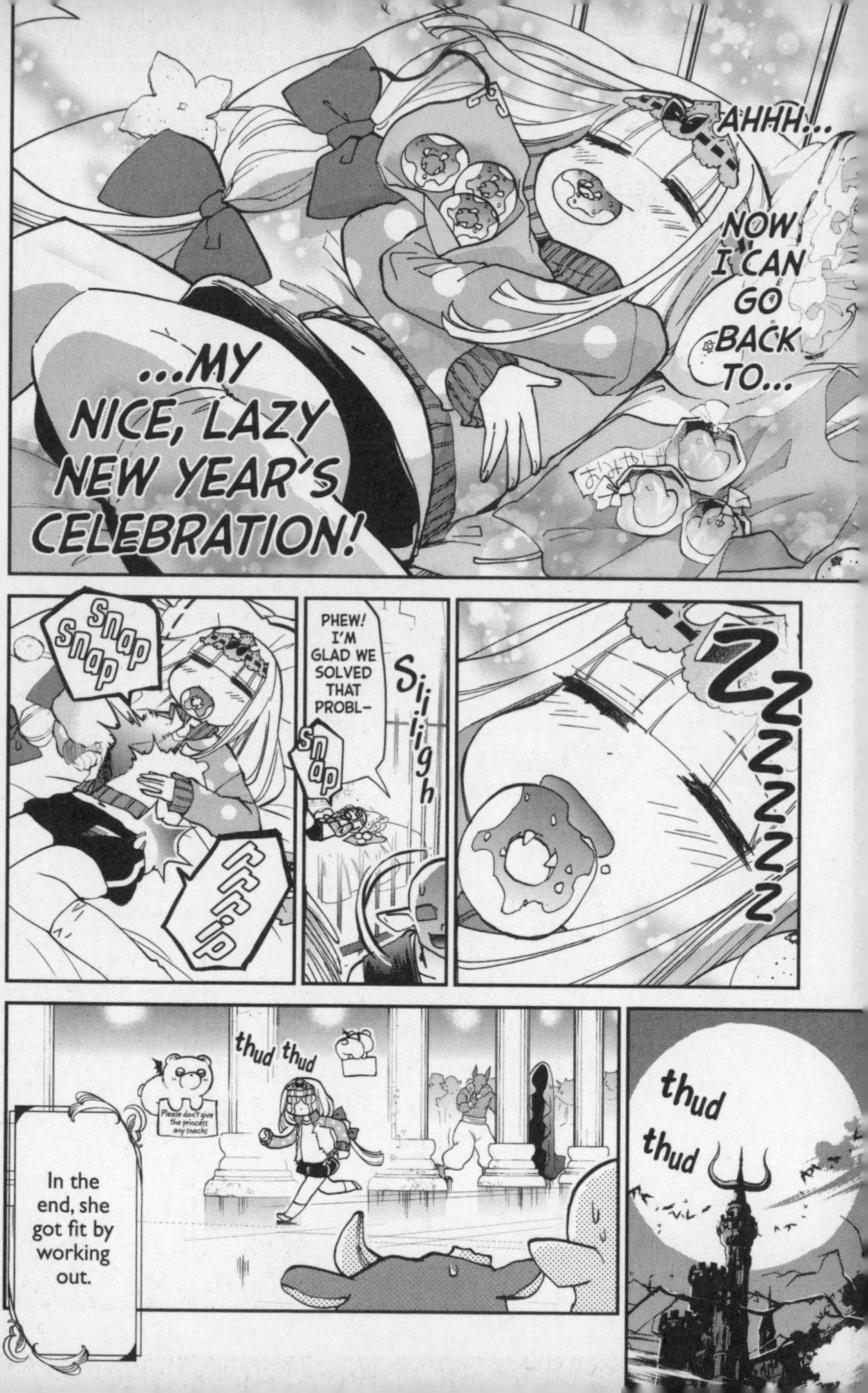
AHHH...
NOW I CAN GO BACK TO...
...MY NICE, LAZY NEW YEAR'S CELEBRATION!
ZZZZZZZ
PHEW! I'M GLAD WE SOLVED THAT PROBL-
Sliiigh
snap
snap snap
rrrrip
thud thud
thud thud
Please don't give the princess any snacks
In the end, she got fit by working out.

I'm not high or any-thing.

Two-Headed Dragon

Stupidity: ☆☆☆☆☆☆☆☆☆

Inappropriate Comments: ☆☆☆☆☆☆☆

A demon of the dragon species. Each of the two heads has a brain, and they can speak to each other. They seem to enjoy conversing, but the people who listen to them get a headache.

Rocket Turtle is his flaky friend. Two-Headed Dragon ends up detonating Rocket Turtle about every other month, but they still have a good relationship because neither of them dwells on the past. That must be nice...

Former problem:
"No one ever asks me about my problems!"

Current problem:
"Problems...? This is the first time anyone has asked me that!"

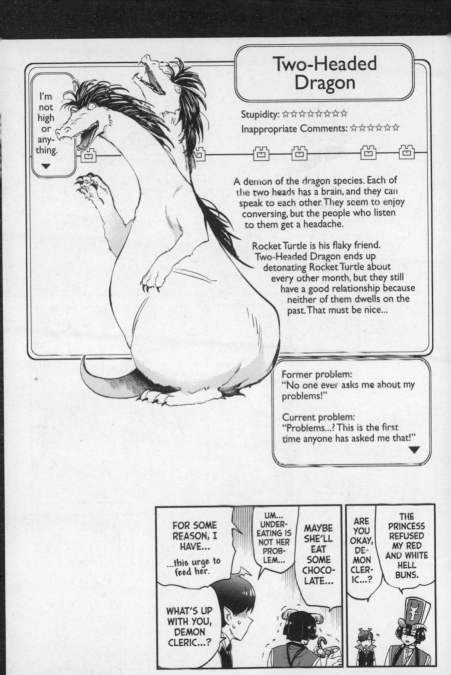

THE PRINCESS REFUSED MY RED AND WHITE HELL BUNS.
ARE YOU OKAY, DE-MON CLER-IC...?
MAYBE SHE'LL EAT SOME CHOCO-LATE...
UM... UNDER-EATING IS NOT HER PROB-LEM...
FOR SOME REASON, I HAVE...
...this urge to feed her.
WHAT'S UP WITH YOU, DEMON CLERIC...?

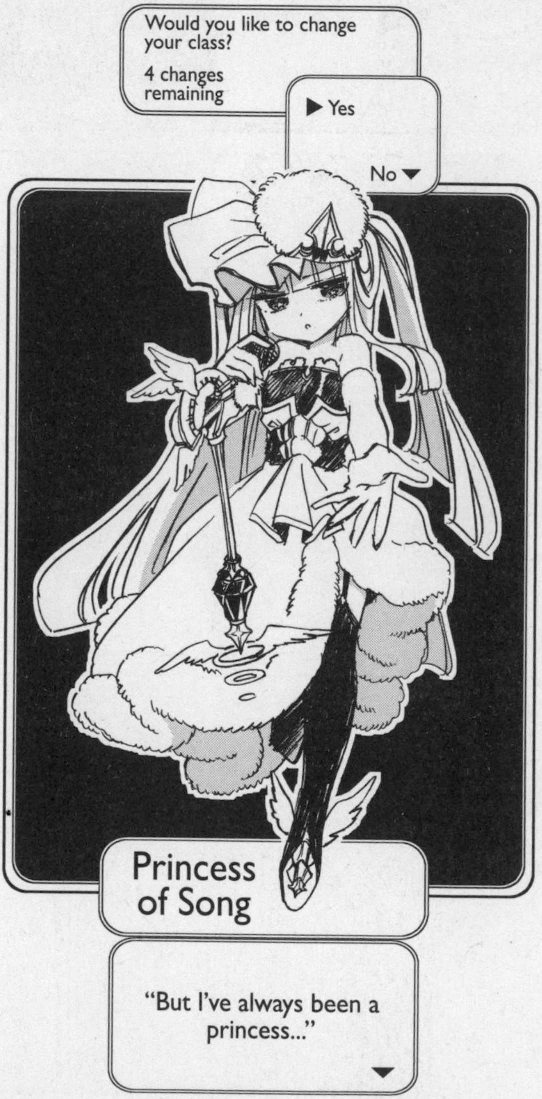
Would you like to change your class?
4 changes remaining
▶ Yes
No ▼
Princess of Song
"But I've always been a princess..."
▼

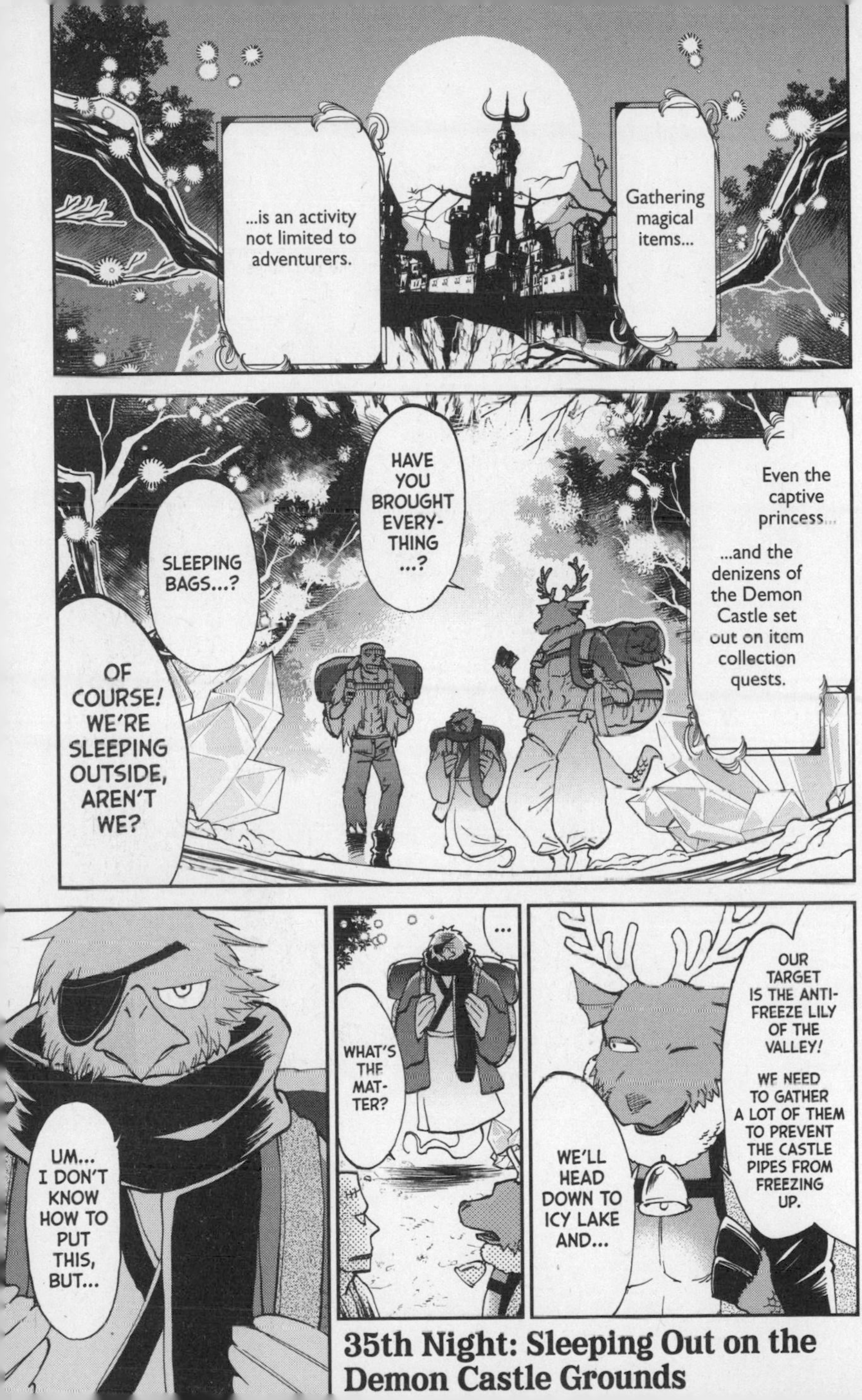
Gathering magical items...
...is an activity not limited to adventurers.
Even the captive princess...
...and the denizens of the Demon Castle set out on item collection quests.
HAVE YOU BROUGHT EVERY-THING...?
SLEEPING BAGS...?
OF COURSE! WE'RE SLEEPING OUTSIDE, AREN'T WE?
OUR TARGET IS THE ANTI-FREEZE LILY OF THE VALLEY!
WE NEED TO GATHER A LOT OF THEM TO PREVENT THE CASTLE PIPES FROM FREEZING UP.
WE'LL HEAD DOWN TO ICY LAKE AND...
...
WHAT'S THE MAT-TER?
UM... I DON'T KNOW HOW TO PUT THIS, BUT...

35th Night: Sleeping Out on the Demon Castle Grounds

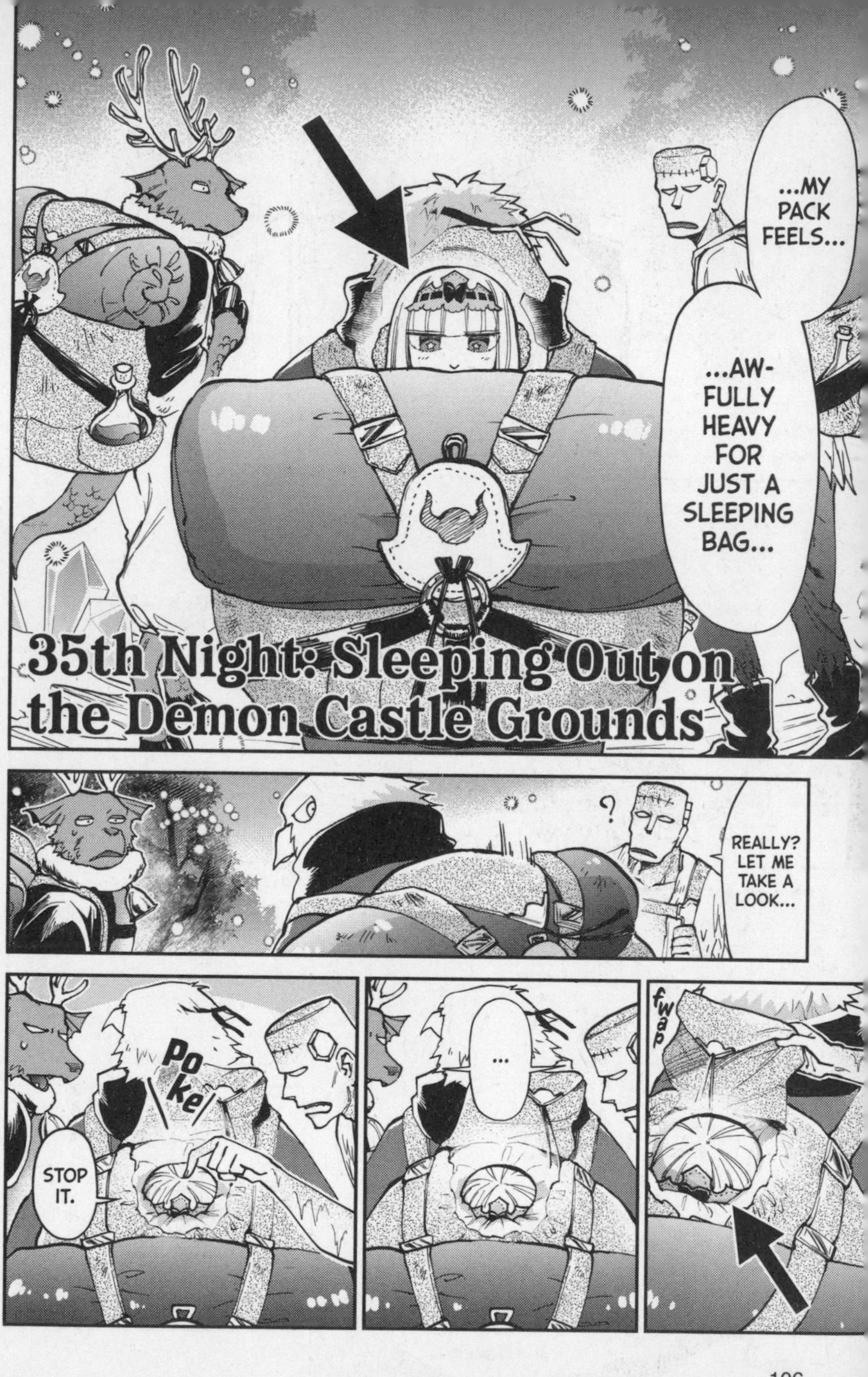
...MY PACK FEELS...
...AW-FULLY HEAVY FOR JUST A SLEEPING BAG...
35th Night: Sleeping Out on the Demon Castle Grounds
REALLY? LET ME TAKE A LOOK...
?
fwap
...
Poke
STOP IT.

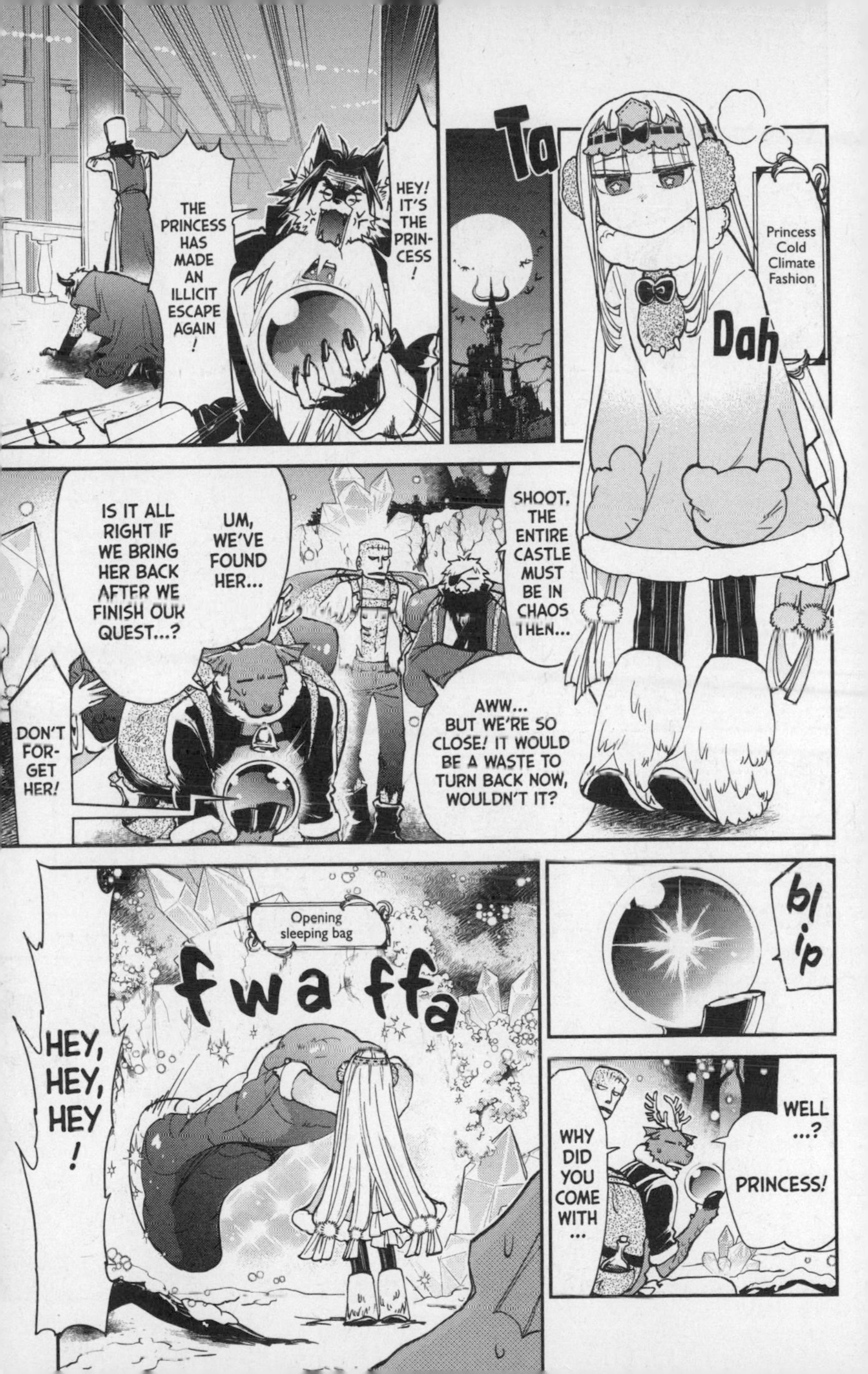
Ta
Dah
Princess Cold Climate Fashion
HEY! IT'S THE PRIN-CESS!
THE PRINCESS HAS MADE AN ILLICIT ESCAPE AGAIN!
SHOOT. THE ENTIRE CASTLE MUST BE IN CHAOS THEN...
UM, WE'VE FOUND HER...
IS IT ALL RIGHT IF WE BRING HER BACK AFTER WE FINISH OUR QUEST...?
AWW... BUT WE'RE SO CLOSE! IT WOULD BE A WASTE TO TURN BACK NOW, WOULDN'T IT?
DON'T FOR-GET HER!
blip
WELL ...? PRINCESS!
WHY DID YOU COME WITH ...
Opening sleeping bag
fwaffa
HEY, HEY, HEY!

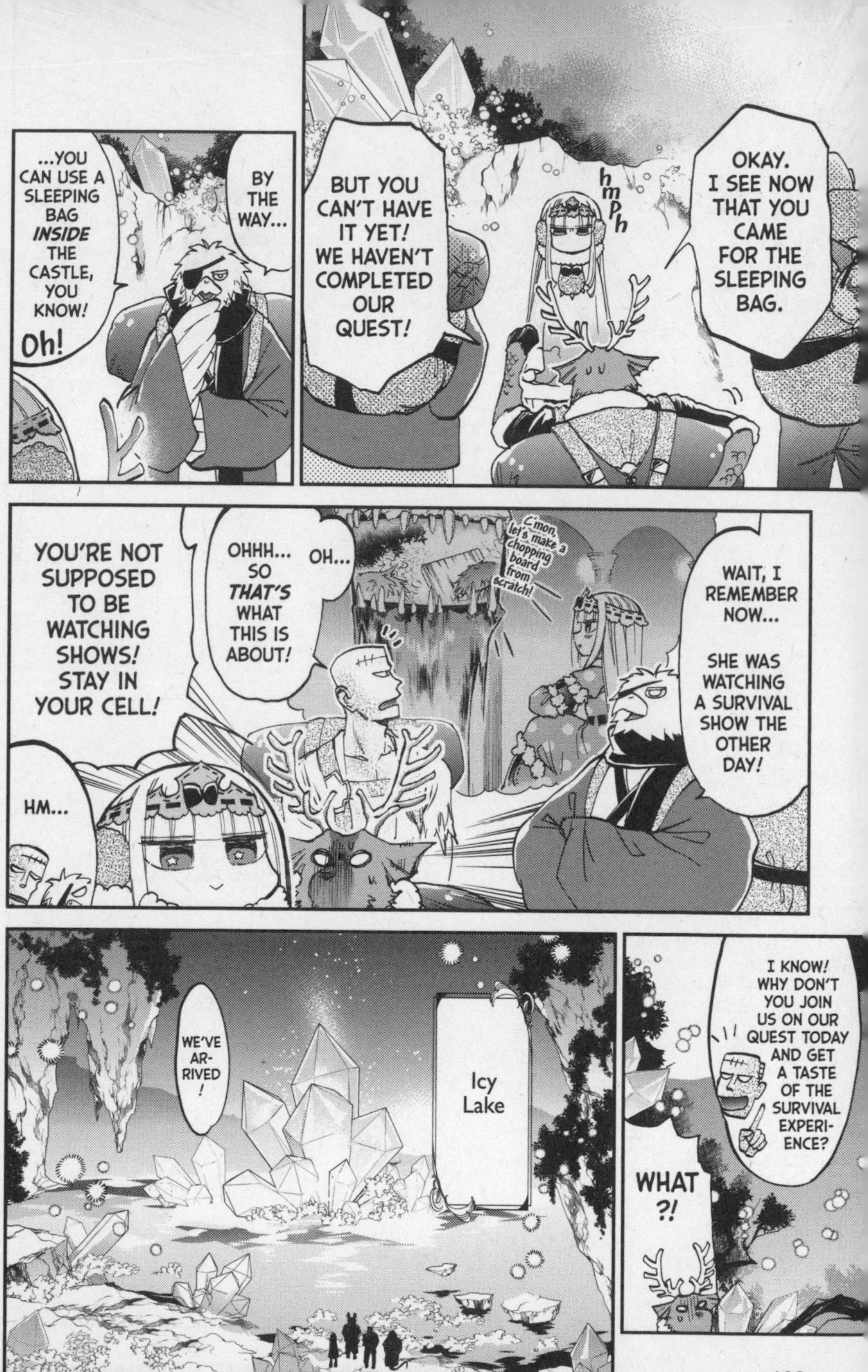
OKAY. I SEE NOW THAT YOU CAME FOR THE SLEEPING BAG.
hmph
BUT YOU CAN'T HAVE IT YET! WE HAVEN'T COMPLETED OUR QUEST!
BY THE WAY...
...YOU CAN USE A SLEEPING BAG *INSIDE* THE CASTLE, YOU KNOW!
Oh!
WAIT, I REMEMBER NOW...
SHE WAS WATCHING A SURVIVAL SHOW THE OTHER DAY!
C'mon, let's make a chopping board from scratch!
OH...
OHHH... SO *THAT'S* WHAT THIS IS ABOUT!
YOU'RE NOT SUPPOSED TO BE WATCHING SHOWS! STAY IN YOUR CELL!
HM...
I KNOW! WHY DON'T YOU JOIN US ON OUR QUEST TODAY AND GET A TASTE OF THE SURVIVAL EXPERIENCE?
WHAT?!
Icy Lake
WE'VE AR-RIVED!

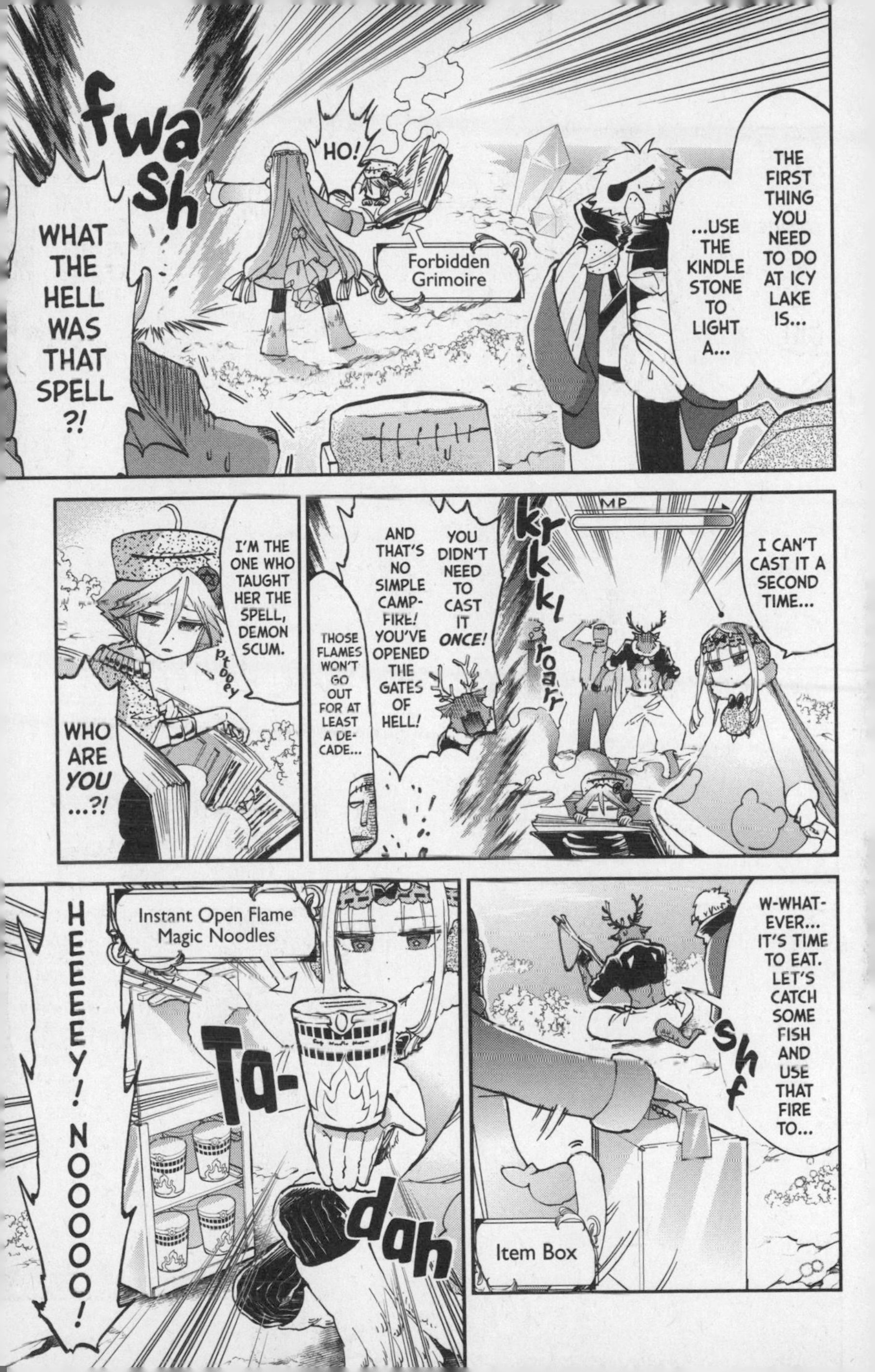
THE FIRST THING YOU NEED TO DO AT ICY LAKE IS...
...USE THE KINDLE STONE TO LIGHT A...
HO!
Forbidden Grimoire
fwash
WHAT THE HELL WAS THAT SPELL?!
MP
I CAN'T CAST IT A SECOND TIME...
krkkkl
roarr
YOU DIDN'T NEED TO CAST IT *ONCE*!
AND THAT'S NO SIMPLE CAMPFIRE! YOU'VE OPENED THE GATES OF HELL!
THOSE FLAMES WON'T GO OUT FOR AT LEAST A DECADE...
I'M THE ONE WHO TAUGHT HER THE SPELL, DEMON SCUM.
ptooey
WHO ARE *YOU*...?!
W-WHATEVER... IT'S TIME TO EAT. LET'S CATCH SOME FISH AND USE THAT FIRE TO...
shf
Item Box
Instant Open Flame Magic Noodles
Ta-dah
HEEEEY! NOOOOO!

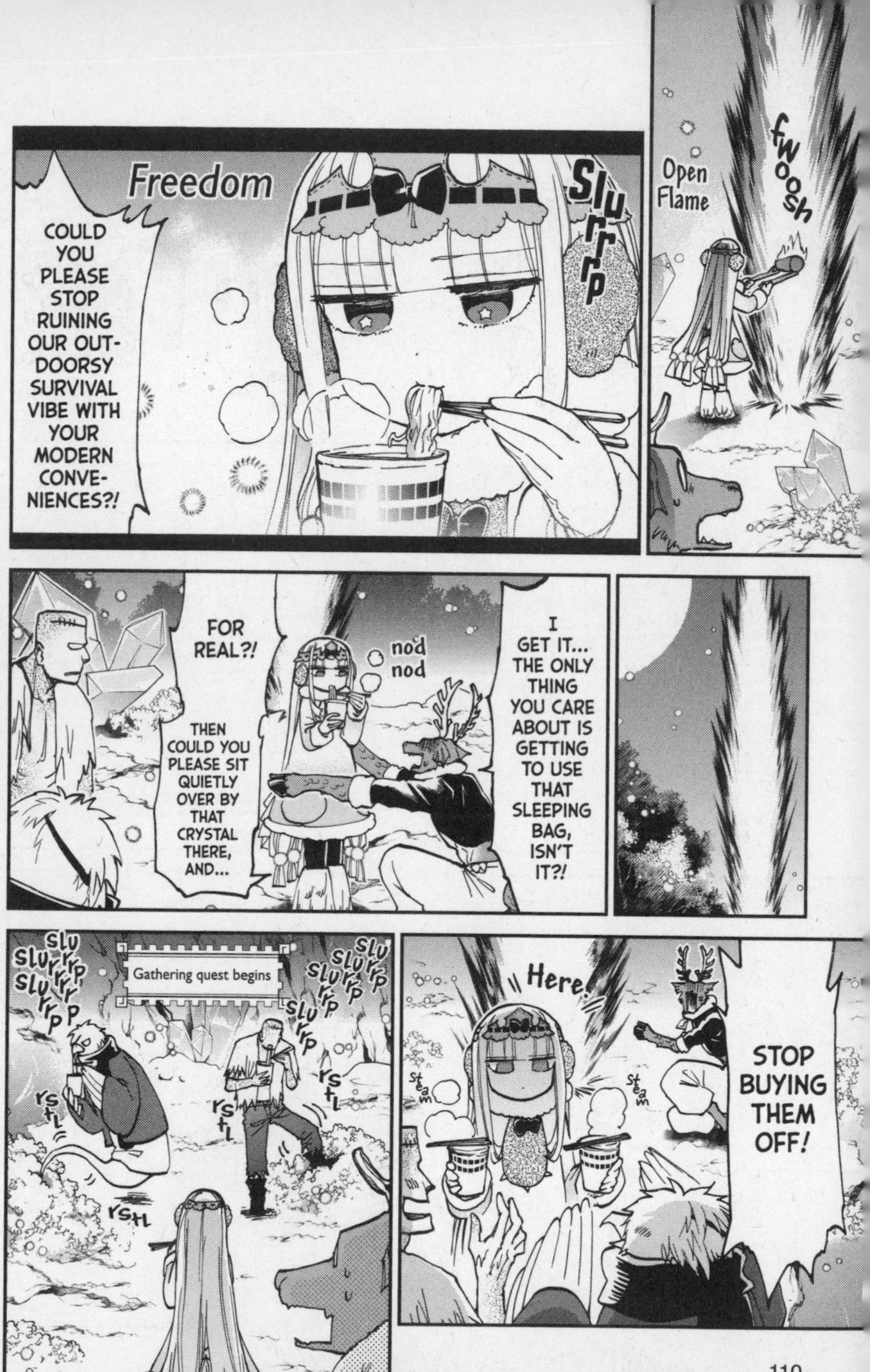

Open Flame
fwoosh
Freedom
Slurrrp
COULD YOU PLEASE STOP RUINING OUR OUT-DOORSY SURVIVAL VIBE WITH YOUR MODERN CONVE-NIENCES?!
I GET IT... THE ONLY THING YOU CARE ABOUT IS GETTING TO USE THAT SLEEPING BAG, ISN'T IT?!
nod nod
FOR REAL?!
THEN COULD YOU PLEASE SIT QUIETLY OVER BY THAT CRYSTAL THERE, AND...
Here
steam
steam
STOP BUYING THEM OFF!
Gathering quest begins
slurrp
slurrrp
slurrrp
slurrrp
slurrrrp
slurrp
rstl
rstl
rstl
rstl

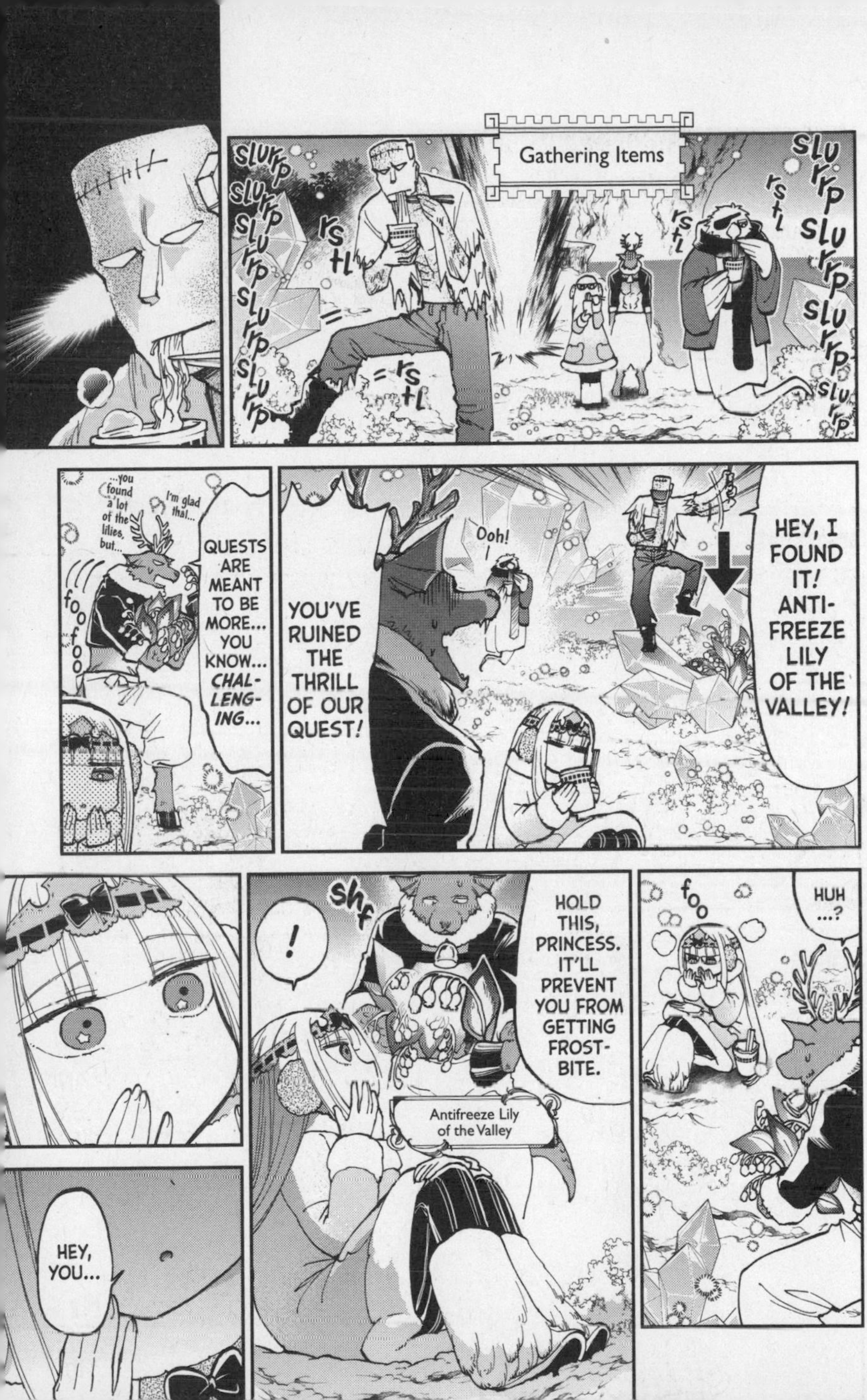
Gathering Items
SLURRP SLURRP SLURRP SLURRP SLURRP
rstl
rstl
SLURRP SLURRP SLURRP SLURRP SLURRP SLURRP
rstl
rstl
HEY, I FOUND IT! ANTI-FREEZE LILY OF THE VALLEY!
Ooh!
YOU'VE RUINED THE THRILL OF OUR QUEST!
QUESTS ARE MEANT TO BE MORE... YOU KNOW... CHAL-LENG-ING...
I'm glad that...
...you found a lot of the lilies, but...
foo foo
HUH ...?
foo
HOLD THIS, PRINCESS. IT'LL PREVENT YOU FROM GETTING FROST-BITE.
shf
!
Antifreeze Lily of the Valley
HEY, YOU...

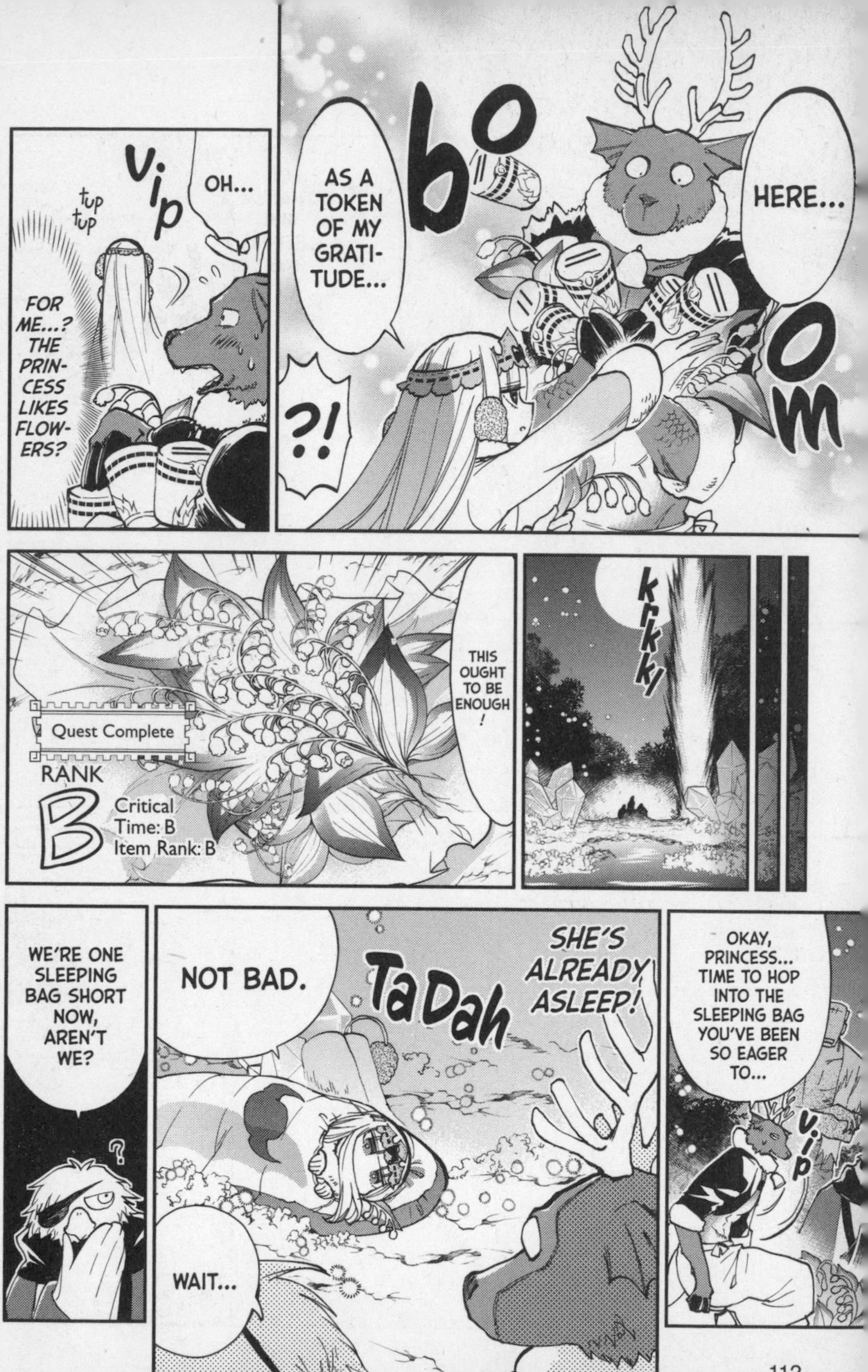
HERE...
boom
AS A TOKEN OF MY GRATITUDE...
?!
vip
OH...
tup tup
FOR ME...? THE PRINCESS LIKES FLOWERS?
krkkk
THIS OUGHT TO BE ENOUGH!
Quest Complete
RANK
B
Critical
Time: B
Item Rank: B
OKAY, PRINCESS... TIME TO HOP INTO THE SLEEPING BAG YOU'VE BEEN SO EAGER TO...
vip
SHE'S ALREADY ASLEEP!
TaDah
NOT BAD.
WAIT...
WE'RE ONE SLEEPING BAG SHORT NOW, AREN'T WE?
?

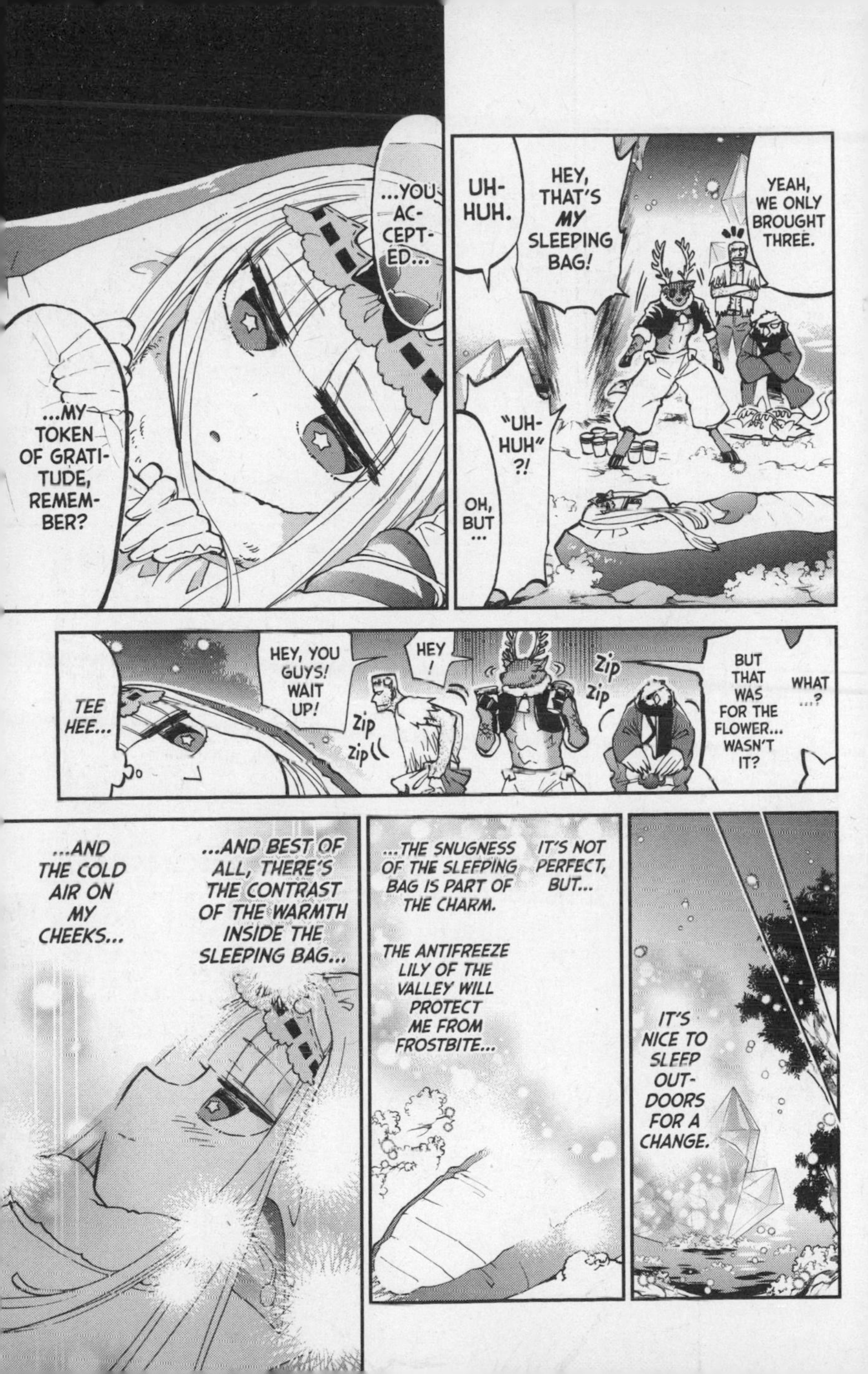

YEAH, WE ONLY BROUGHT THREE.
HEY, THAT'S *MY* SLEEPING BAG!
UH-HUH.
"UH-HUH"?!
OH, BUT...
...YOU ACCEPTED...
...MY TOKEN OF GRATITUDE, REMEMBER?
WHAT...?
BUT THAT WAS FOR THE FLOWER... WASN'T IT?
Zip Zip
HEY!
HEY, YOU GUYS! WAIT UP!
Zip Zip
TEE HEE...
IT'S NICE TO SLEEP OUTDOORS FOR A CHANGE.
IT'S NOT PERFECT, BUT...
...THE SNUGNESS OF THE SLEEPING BAG IS PART OF THE CHARM.
THE ANTIFREEZE LILY OF THE VALLEY WILL PROTECT ME FROM FROSTBITE...
...AND BEST OF ALL, THERE'S THE CONTRAST OF THE WARMTH INSIDE THE SLEEPING BAG...
...AND THE COLD AIR ON MY CHEEKS...

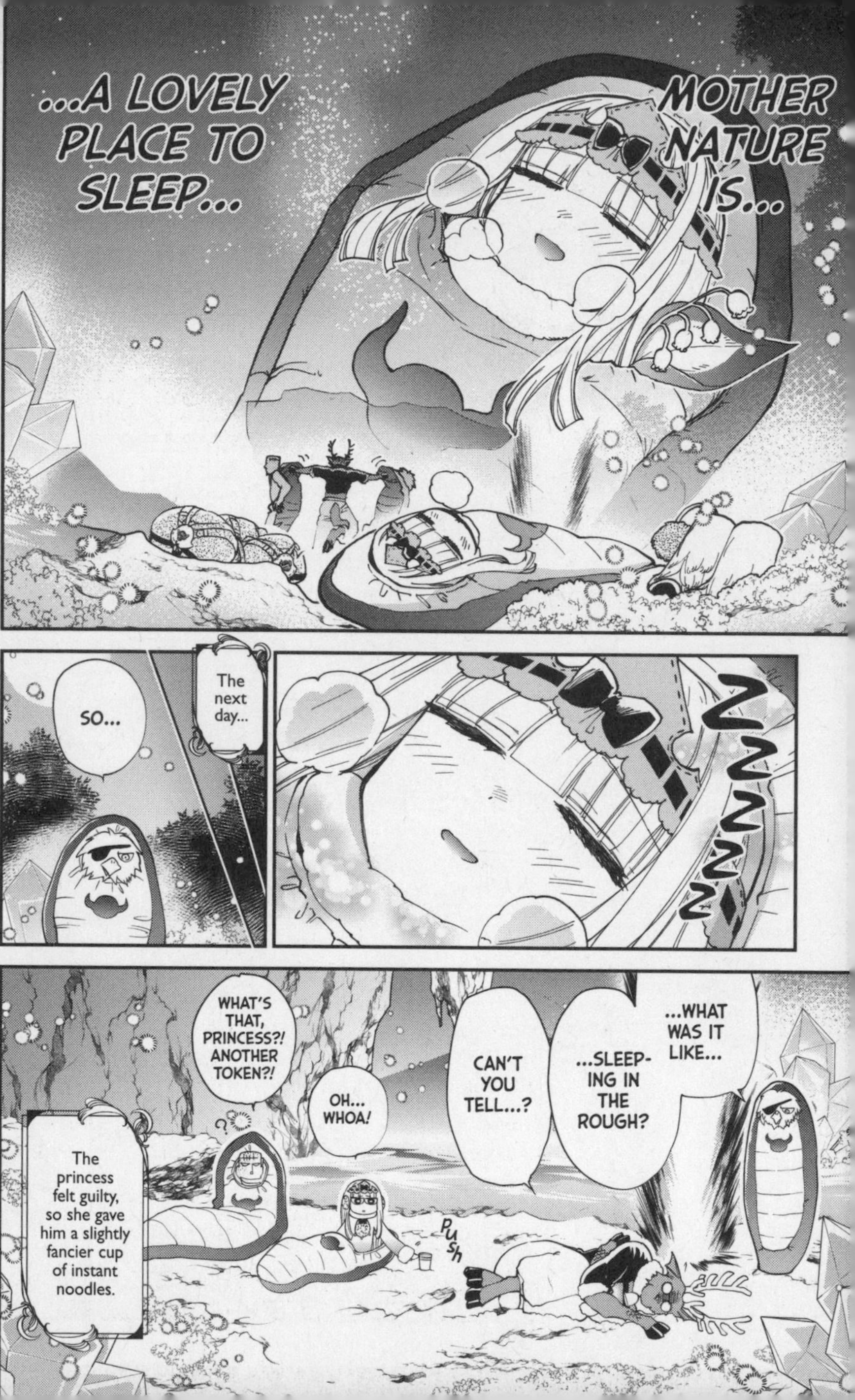
MOTHER NATURE IS...
...A LOVELY PLACE TO SLEEP...
ZZZZZZ
The next day...
SO...
...WHAT WAS IT LIKE...
...SLEEPING IN THE ROUGH?
CAN'T YOU TELL...?
OH... WHOA!
WHAT'S THAT, PRINCESS?! ANOTHER TOKEN?!
?
PUSH
The princess felt guilty, so she gave him a slightly fancier cup of instant noodles.

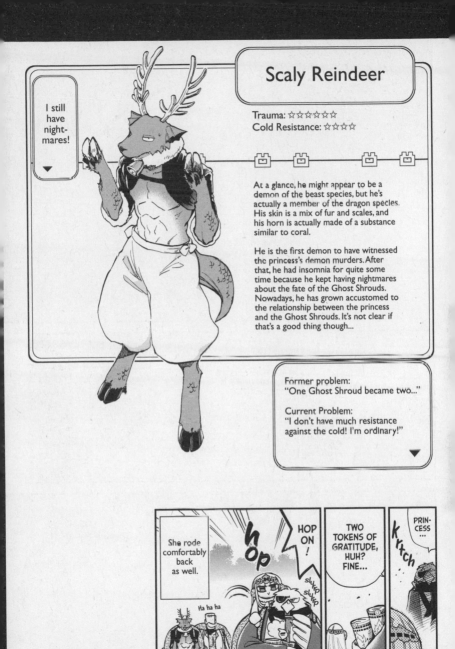

I still have nightmares!

Scaly Reindeer

Trauma: ☆☆☆☆☆☆
Cold Resistance: ☆☆☆☆

At a glance, he might appear to be a demon of the beast species, but he's actually a member of the dragon species. His skin is a mix of fur and scales, and his horn is actually made of a substance similar to coral.

He is the first demon to have witnessed the princess's demon murders. After that, he had insomnia for quite some time because he kept having nightmares about the fate of the Ghost Shrouds. Nowadays, he has grown accustomed to the relationship between the princess and the Ghost Shrouds. It's not clear if that's a good thing though...

Former problem:
"One Ghost Shroud became two..."

Current Problem:
"I don't have much resistance against the cold! I'm ordinary!"

PRIN-CESS ...
krtch
TWO TOKENS OF GRATITUDE, HUH? FINE...
HOP ON!
hop
slurp slurp
She rode comfortably back as well.
Ha ha ha

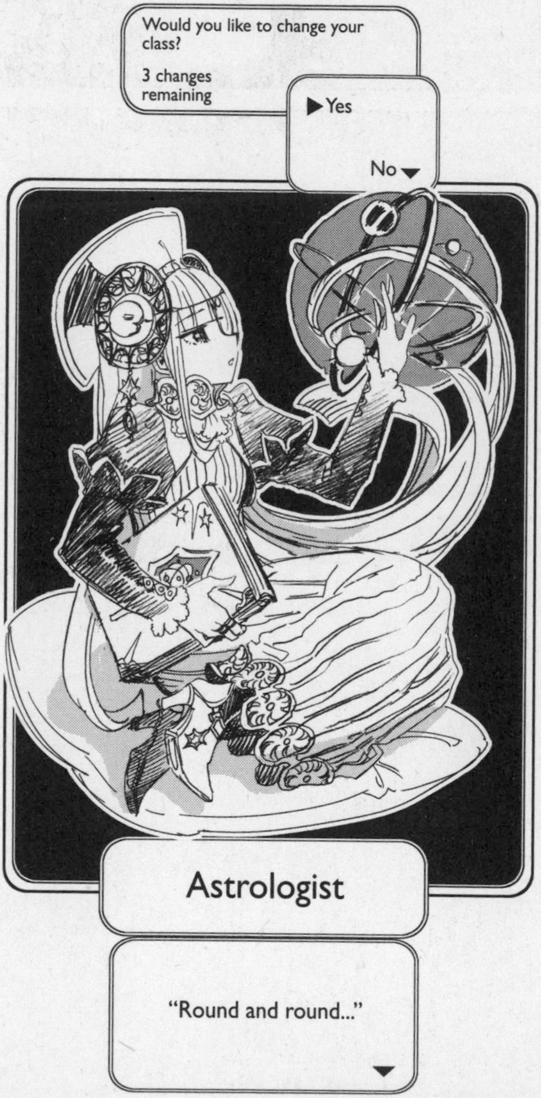
Would you like to change your class?
3 changes remaining
▶Yes
No
Astrologist
"Round and round..."

36th Night: The Divine Move in Her Dreams

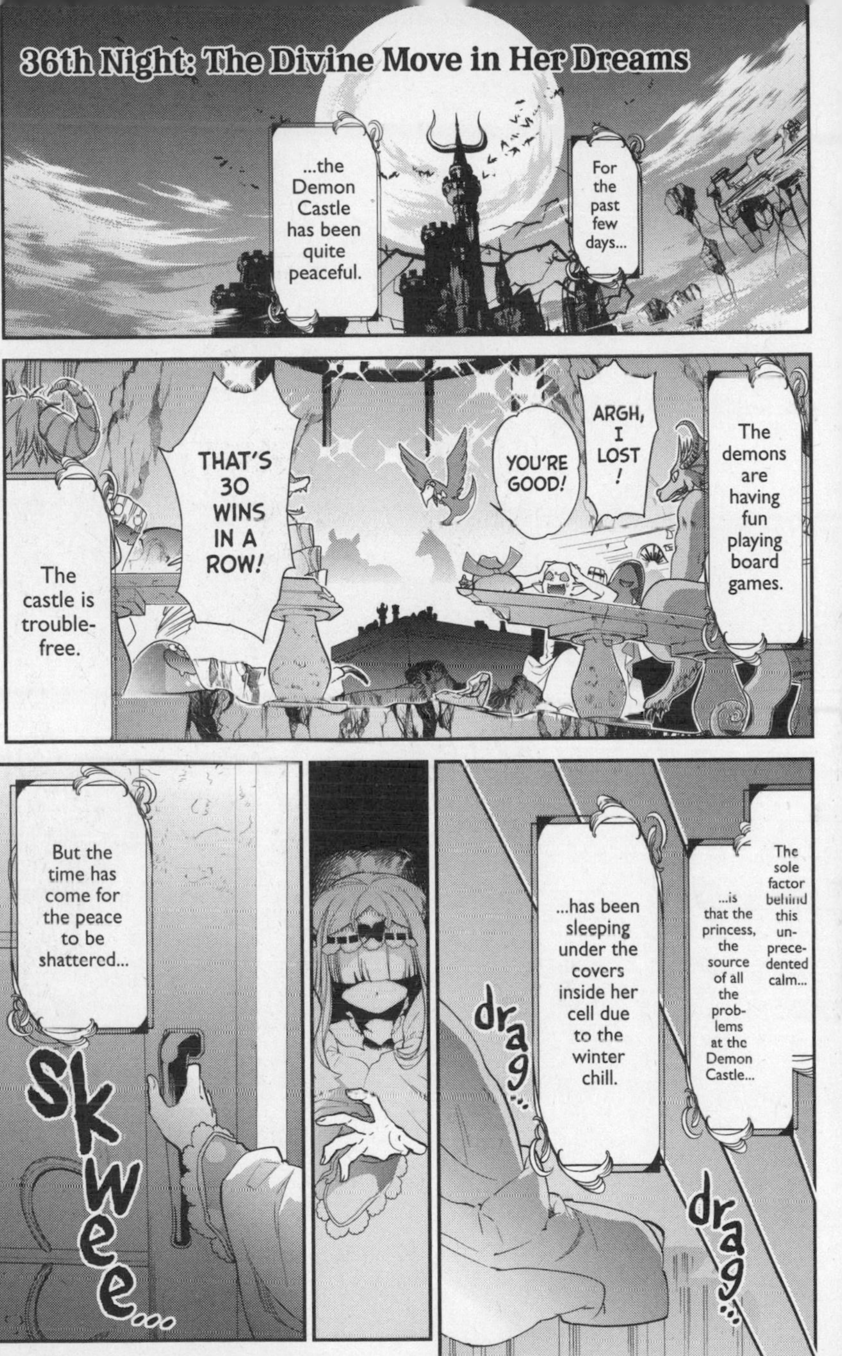
For the past few days...
...the Demon Castle has been quite peaceful.
The demons are having fun playing board games.
ARGH, I LOST!
YOU'RE GOOD!
THAT'S 30 WINS IN A ROW!
The castle is trouble-free.
The sole factor behind this unprecedented calm...
...is that the princess, the source of all the problems at the Demon Castle...
...has been sleeping under the covers inside her cell due to the winter chill.
drag...
drag...
But the time has come for the peace to be shattered...
Skwee...

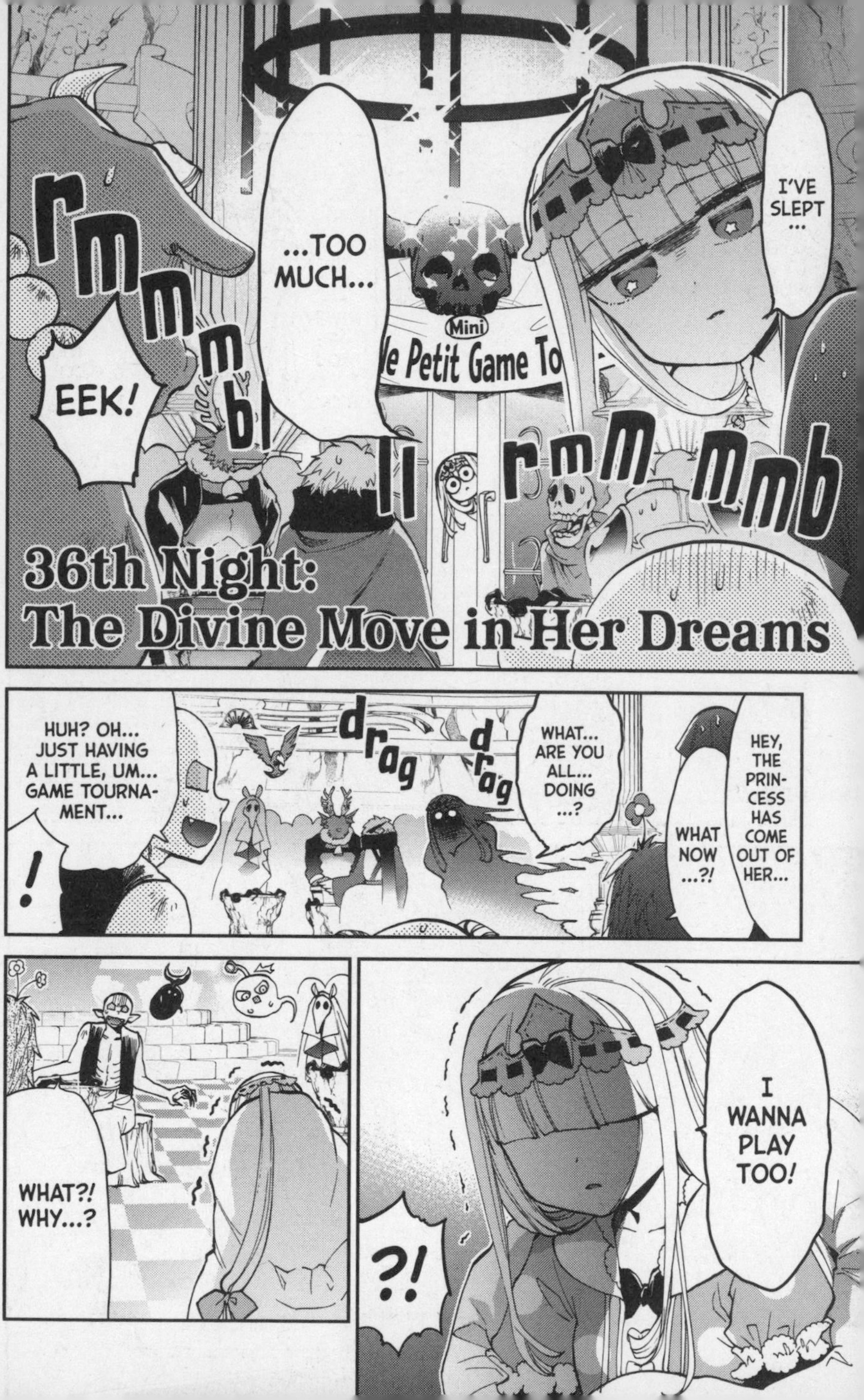
I'VE SLEPT ...
...TOO MUCH...
Mini
Ve Petit Game To
rmmmmbl
rmm mmb
EEK!
36th Night:
The Divine Move in Her Dreams
HEY, THE PRINCESS HAS COME OUT OF HER...
WHAT NOW ...?!
WHAT... ARE YOU ALL... DOING ...?
drag
drag
HUH? OH... JUST HAVING A LITTLE, UM... GAME TOURNAMENT...
!
I WANNA PLAY TOO!
?!
WHAT?! WHY...?

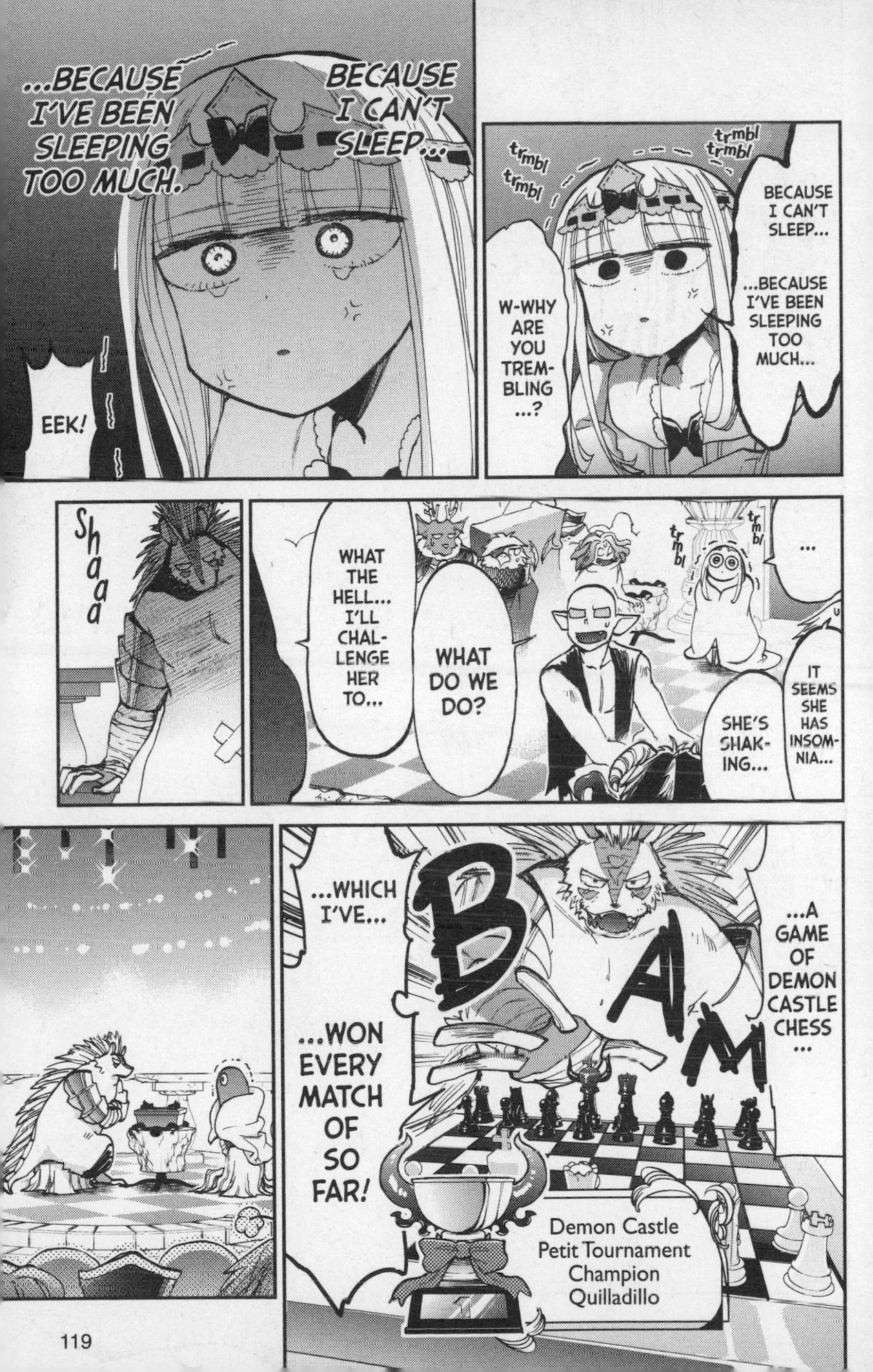
trmbl trmbl
trmbl trmbl
BECAUSE I CAN'T SLEEP...
...BECAUSE I'VE BEEN SLEEPING TOO MUCH...
W-WHY ARE YOU TREM-BLING ...?
BECAUSE I CAN'T SLEEP...
...BECAUSE I'VE BEEN SLEEPING TOO MUCH.
EEK!
trmbl
...
IT SEEMS SHE HAS INSOM-NIA...
SHE'S SHAK-ING...
WHAT DO WE DO?
WHAT THE HELL... I'LL CHAL-LENGE HER TO...
Shaaa
...A GAME OF DEMON CASTLE CHESS ...
BAM
...WHICH I'VE...
...WON EVERY MATCH OF SO FAR!
Demon Castle Petit Tournament Champion Quilladillo

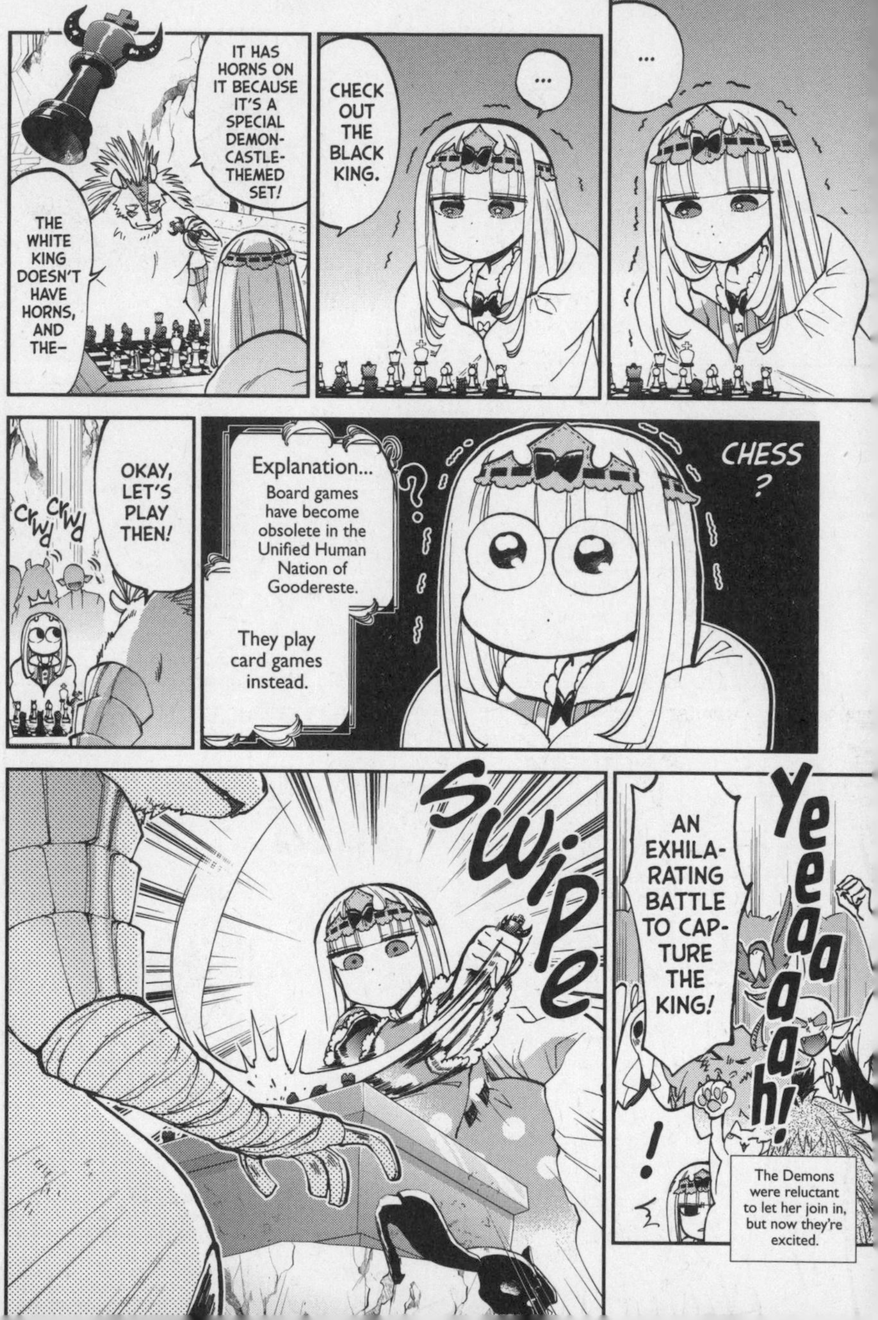
...
...
CHECK OUT THE BLACK KING.
IT HAS HORNS ON IT BECAUSE IT'S A SPECIAL DEMON-CASTLE-THEMED SET!
THE WHITE KING DOESN'T HAVE HORNS, AND THE—
CHESS?
Explanation...
Board games have become obsolete in the Unified Human Nation of Goodereste.
They play card games instead.
OKAY, LET'S PLAY THEN!
CRWD CRWD
Yeeaaaaah!
AN EXHILARATING BATTLE TO CAPTURE THE KING!
!
The Demons were reluctant to let her join in, but now they're excited.
SWIPE

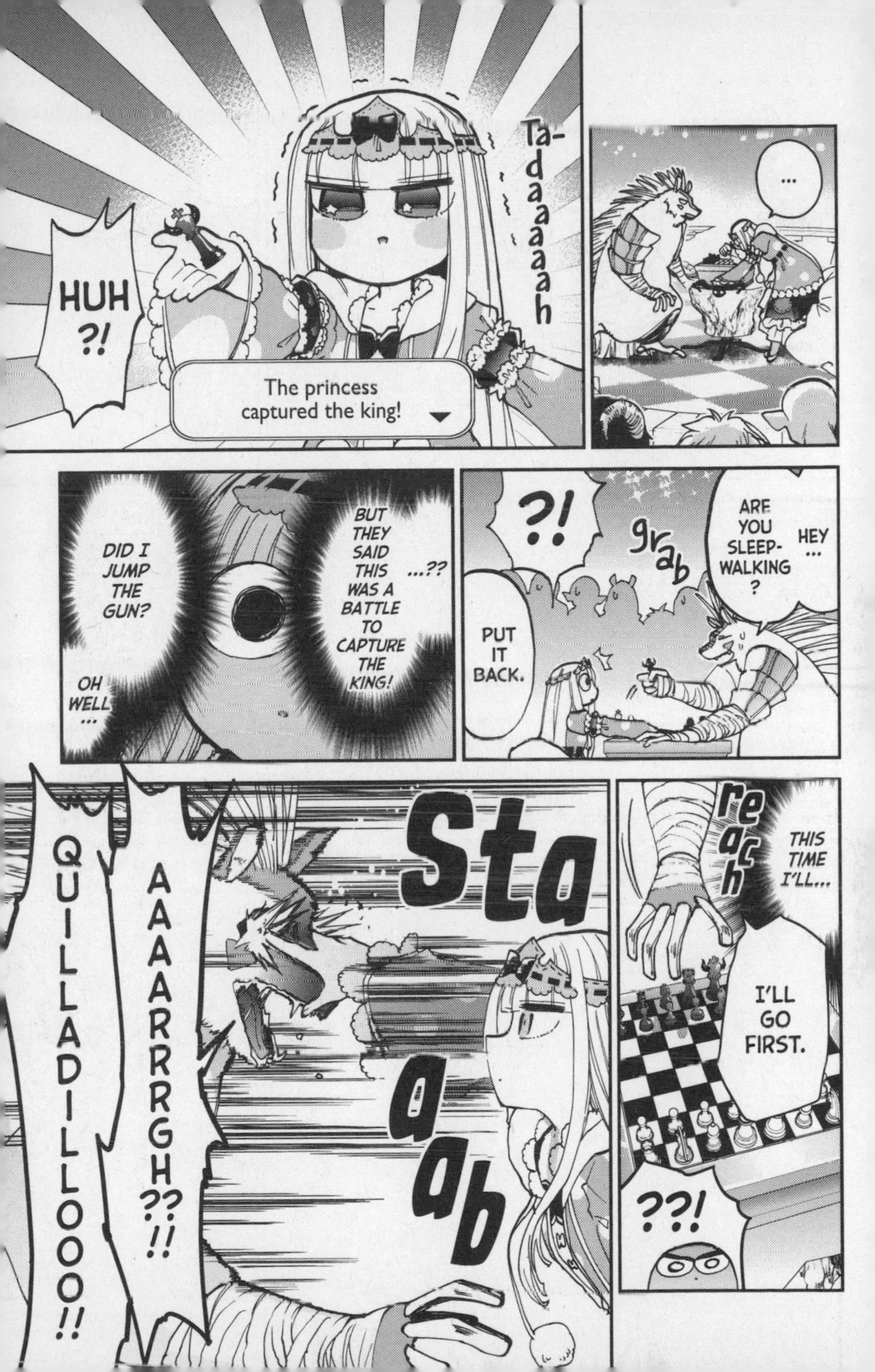
...
Ta-daaaaaah
HUH ?!
The princess captured the king!
HEY ...
ARE YOU SLEEP-WALKING ?
grab
?!
PUT IT BACK.
...??
BUT THEY SAID THIS WAS A BATTLE TO CAPTURE THE KING!
DID I JUMP THE GUN?
OH WELL ...
reach
THIS TIME I'LL...
I'LL GO FIRST.
??!
Staab
AAAARRRGH??!!
QUILLADILLOOO!!

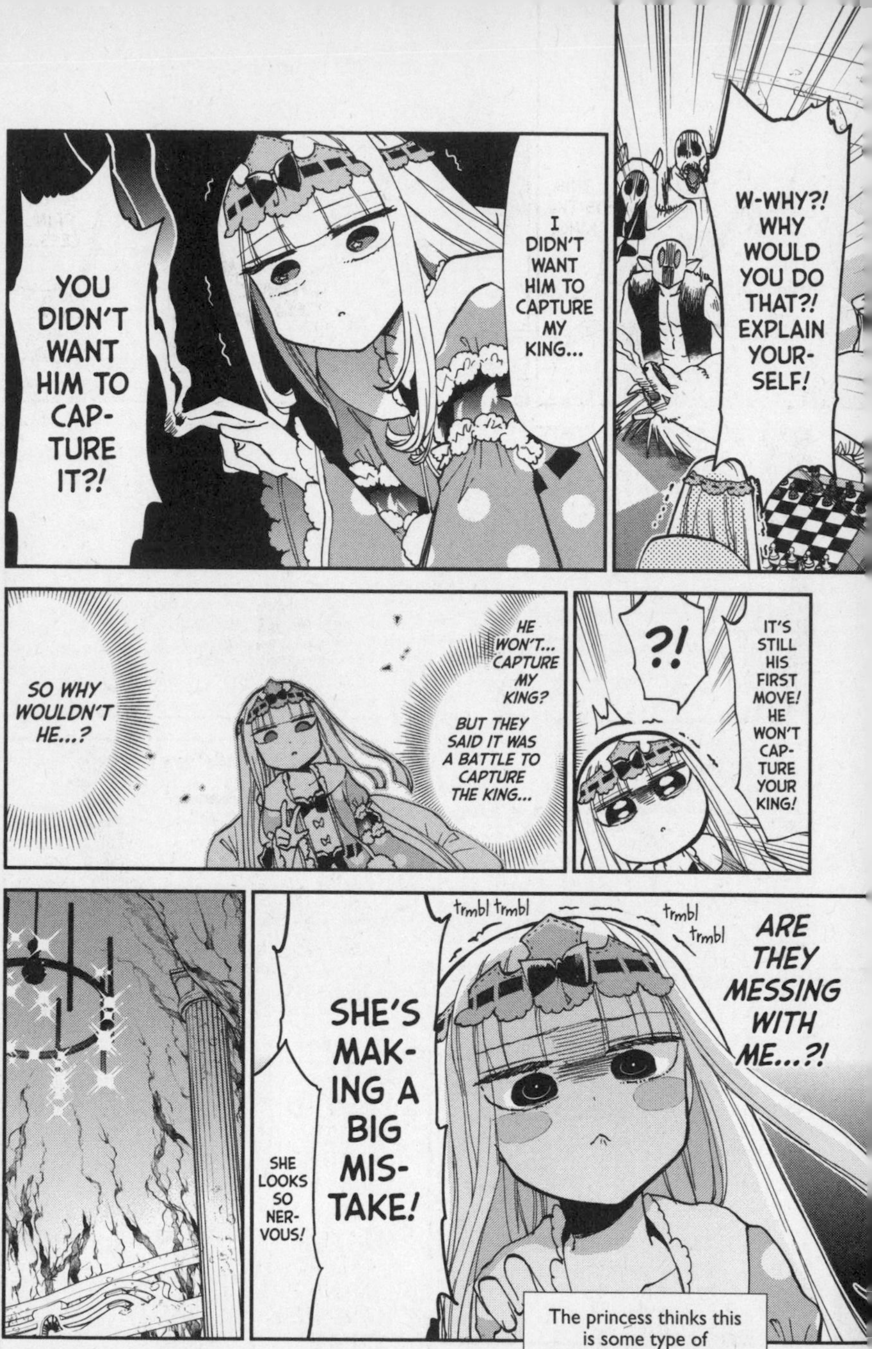
W-WHY?! WHY WOULD YOU DO THAT?! EXPLAIN YOURSELF!
I DIDN'T WANT HIM TO CAPTURE MY KING...
YOU DIDN'T WANT HIM TO CAPTURE IT?!
?!
IT'S STILL HIS FIRST MOVE! HE WON'T CAPTURE YOUR KING!
HE WON'T... CAPTURE MY KING?
BUT THEY SAID IT WAS A BATTLE TO CAPTURE THE KING...
SO WHY WOULDN'T HE...?
ARE THEY MESSING WITH ME...?!
trmbl trmbl
trmbl trmbl
SHE'S MAKING A BIG MISTAKE!
SHE LOOKS SO NERVOUS!

The princess thinks this is some type of slap-and-grab card game.

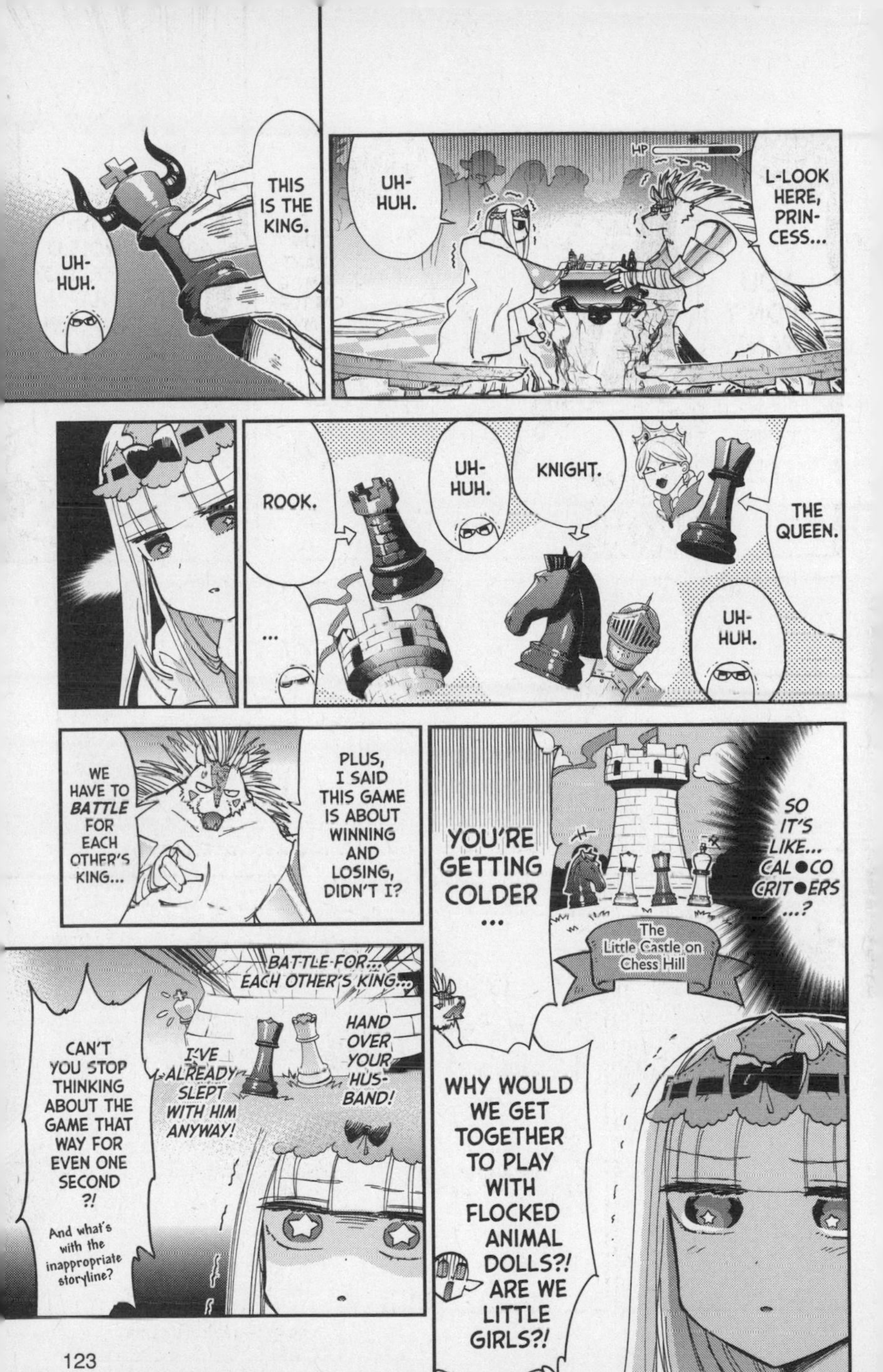
L-LOOK HERE, PRINCESS...
HP
UH-HUH.
THIS IS THE KING.
UH-HUH.
THE QUEEN.
UH-HUH.
KNIGHT.
UH-HUH.
ROOK.
...
SO IT'S LIKE... CAL●CO CRIT●ERS ...?
YOU'RE GETTING COLDER ...
The Little Castle on Chess Hill
PLUS, I SAID THIS GAME IS ABOUT WINNING AND LOSING, DIDN'T I?
WE HAVE TO *BATTLE* FOR EACH OTHER'S KING...
WHY WOULD WE GET TOGETHER TO PLAY WITH FLOCKED ANIMAL DOLLS?! ARE WE LITTLE GIRLS?!
BATTLE FOR... EACH OTHER'S KING...
HAND OVER YOUR HUSBAND!
I'VE ALREADY SLEPT WITH HIM ANYWAY!
CAN'T YOU STOP THINKING ABOUT THE GAME THAT WAY FOR EVEN ONE SECOND?!
And what's with the inappropriate storyline?

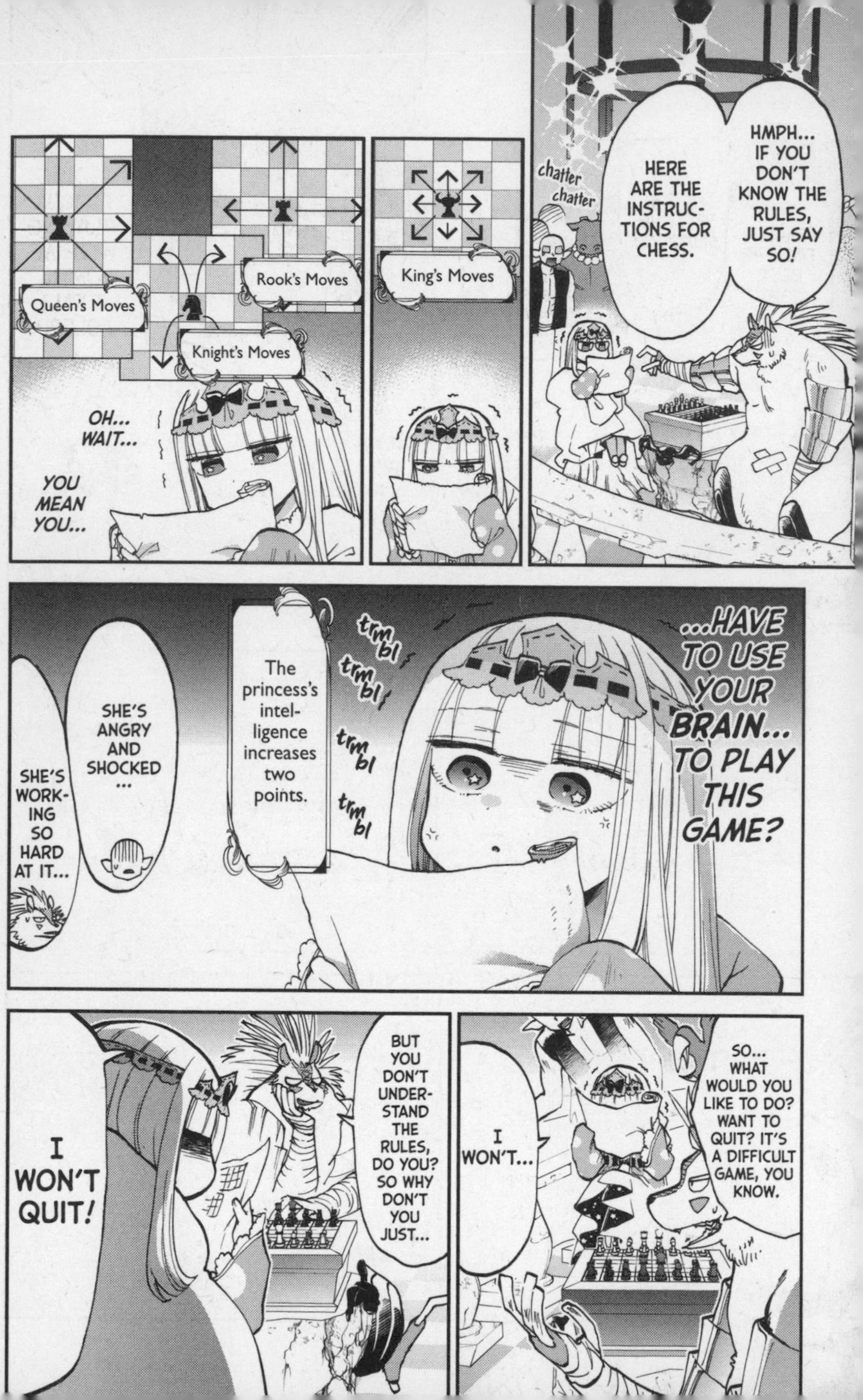
HMPH... IF YOU DON'T KNOW THE RULES, JUST SAY SO!
HERE ARE THE INSTRUCTIONS FOR CHESS.
chatter chatter
King's Moves
Rook's Moves
Queen's Moves
Knight's Moves
OH... WAIT...
YOU MEAN YOU...
...HAVE TO USE YOUR BRAIN... TO PLAY THIS GAME?
trmbl trmbl trmbl trmbl
The princess's intelligence increases two points.
SHE'S ANGRY AND SHOCKED...
SHE'S WORKING SO HARD AT IT...
SO... WHAT WOULD YOU LIKE TO DO? WANT TO QUIT? IT'S A DIFFICULT GAME, YOU KNOW.
I WON'T...
BUT YOU DON'T UNDERSTAND THE RULES, DO YOU? SO WHY DON'T YOU JUST...
I WON'T QUIT!

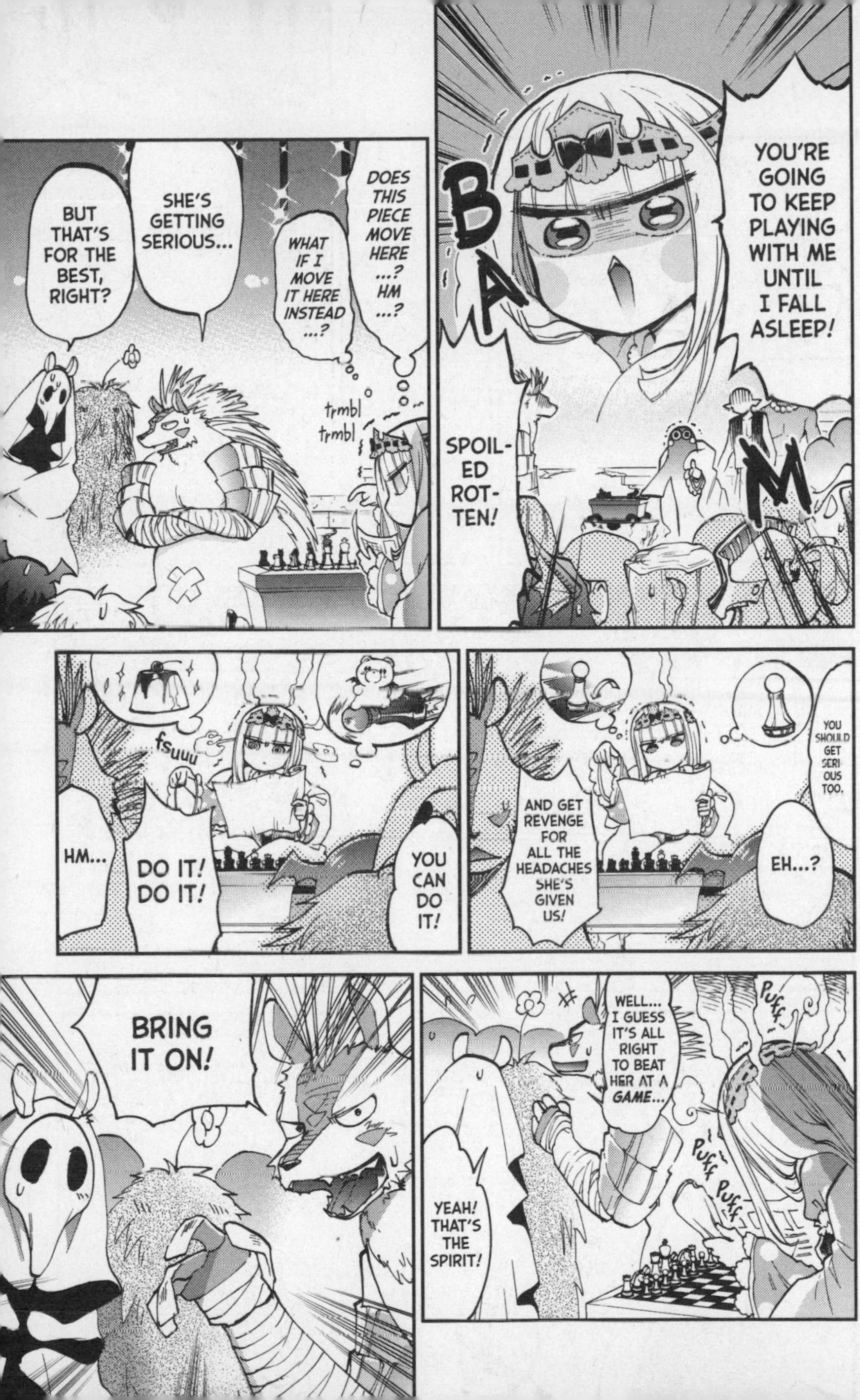
BAM
YOU'RE GOING TO KEEP PLAYING WITH ME UNTIL I FALL ASLEEP!
SPOIL-ED ROT-TEN!
DOES THIS PIECE MOVE HERE ...? HM ...?
WHAT IF I MOVE IT HERE INSTEAD ...?
trmbl trmbl
SHE'S GETTING SERIOUS...
BUT THAT'S FOR THE BEST, RIGHT?
YOU SHOULD GET SERI OUS TOO.
EH...?
AND GET REVENGE FOR ALL THE HEADACHES SHE'S GIVEN US!
fsuuu
YOU CAN DO IT!
DO IT! DO IT!
HM...
Puff
WELL... I GUESS IT'S ALL RIGHT TO BEAT HER AT A GAME...
Puff Puff
YEAH! THAT'S THE SPIRIT!
BRING IT ON!

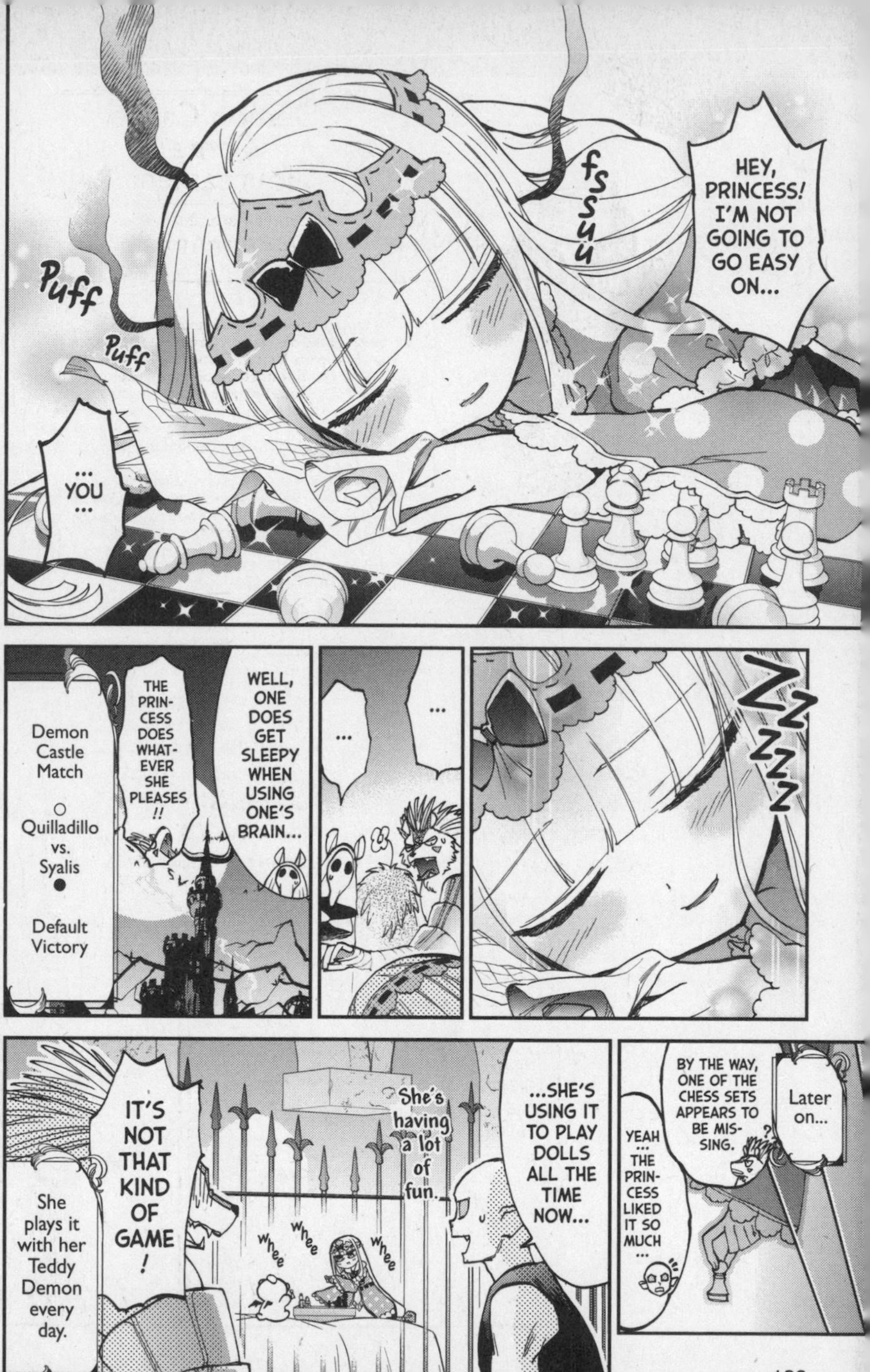
HEY, PRINCESS! I'M NOT GOING TO GO EASY ON...
fssuu
Puff
Puff
... YOU ...
ZZZZZ
...
...
WELL, ONE DOES GET SLEEPY WHEN USING ONE'S BRAIN...
THE PRINCESS DOES WHATEVER SHE PLEASES!!
Demon Castle Match
○ Quilladillo vs. Syalis ●
Default Victory
Later on...
BY THE WAY, ONE OF THE CHESS SETS APPEARS TO BE MISSING.
?
YEAH... THE PRINCESS LIKED IT SO MUCH...
...SHE'S USING IT TO PLAY DOLLS ALL THE TIME NOW...
She's having a lot of fun.
whee
whee
whee
IT'S NOT THAT KIND OF GAME!
She plays it with her Teddy Demon every day.

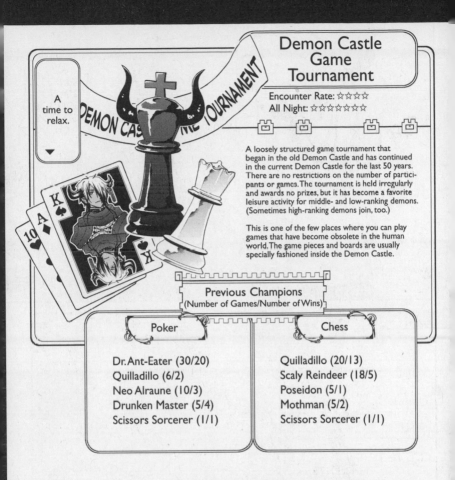

Demon Castle Game Tournament

A time to relax.

▼

DEMON CAS
ME TOURNAMENT

Encounter Rate: ☆☆☆☆
All Night: ☆☆☆☆☆☆☆☆

A loosely structured game tournament that began in the old Demon Castle and has continued in the current Demon Castle for the last 50 years. There are no restrictions on the number of participants or games. The tournament is held irregularly and awards no prizes, but it has become a favorite leisure activity for middle- and low-ranking demons. (Sometimes high-ranking demons join, too.)

This is one of the few places where you can play games that have become obsolete in the human world. The game pieces and boards are usually specially fashioned inside the Demon Castle.

Previous Champions
(Number of Games/Number of Wins)

Poker

Dr. Ant-Eater (30/20)
Quilladillo (6/2)
Neo Alraune (10/3)
Drunken Master (5/4)
Scissors Sorcerer (1/1)

Chess

Quilladillo (20/13)
Scaly Reindeer (18/5)
Poseidon (5/1)
Mothman (5/2)
Scissors Sorcerer (1/1)

HONEY... I'M SORRY...
Queen
Queen
THE HATRED BE- TWEEN US...
...HAS TURNED TO LOVE!
THIS IS REALLY GETTING OUT OF HAND!
Whaaat ?!

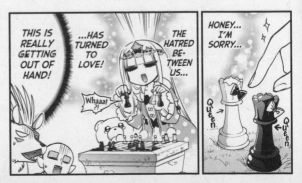

Would you like to change your class?

2 changes remaining

▶Yes

No ▼

Merchant

"This demon is not for sale."

▼

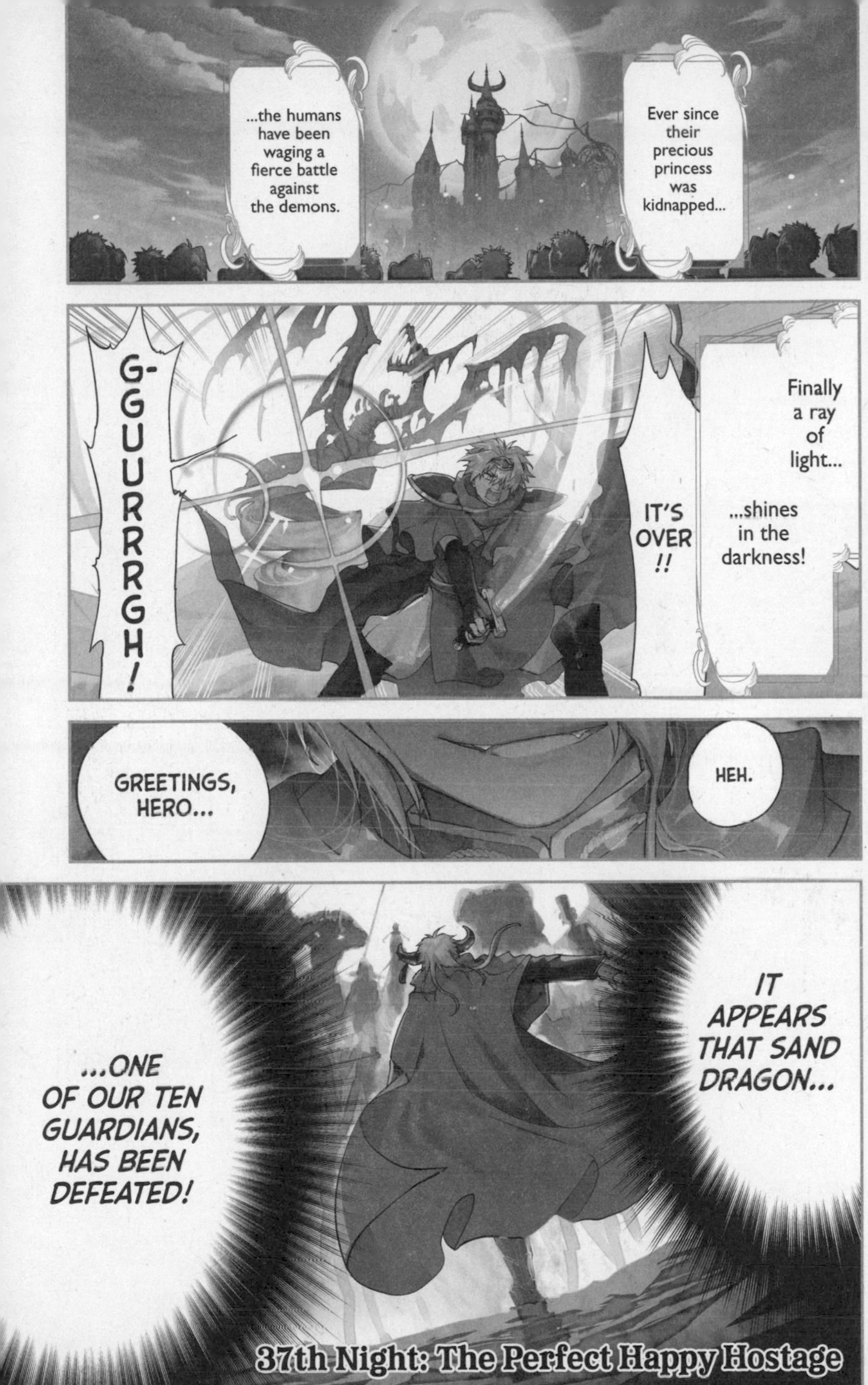
Ever since their precious princess was kidnapped...
...the humans have been waging a fierce battle against the demons.
Finally a ray of light...
...shines in the darkness!
IT'S OVER!!
G-GGUURRRRGH!
HEH.
GREETINGS, HERO...
IT APPEARS THAT SAND DRAGON...
...ONE OF OUR TEN GUARDIANS, HAS BEEN DEFEATED!
37th Night: The Perfect Happy Hostage

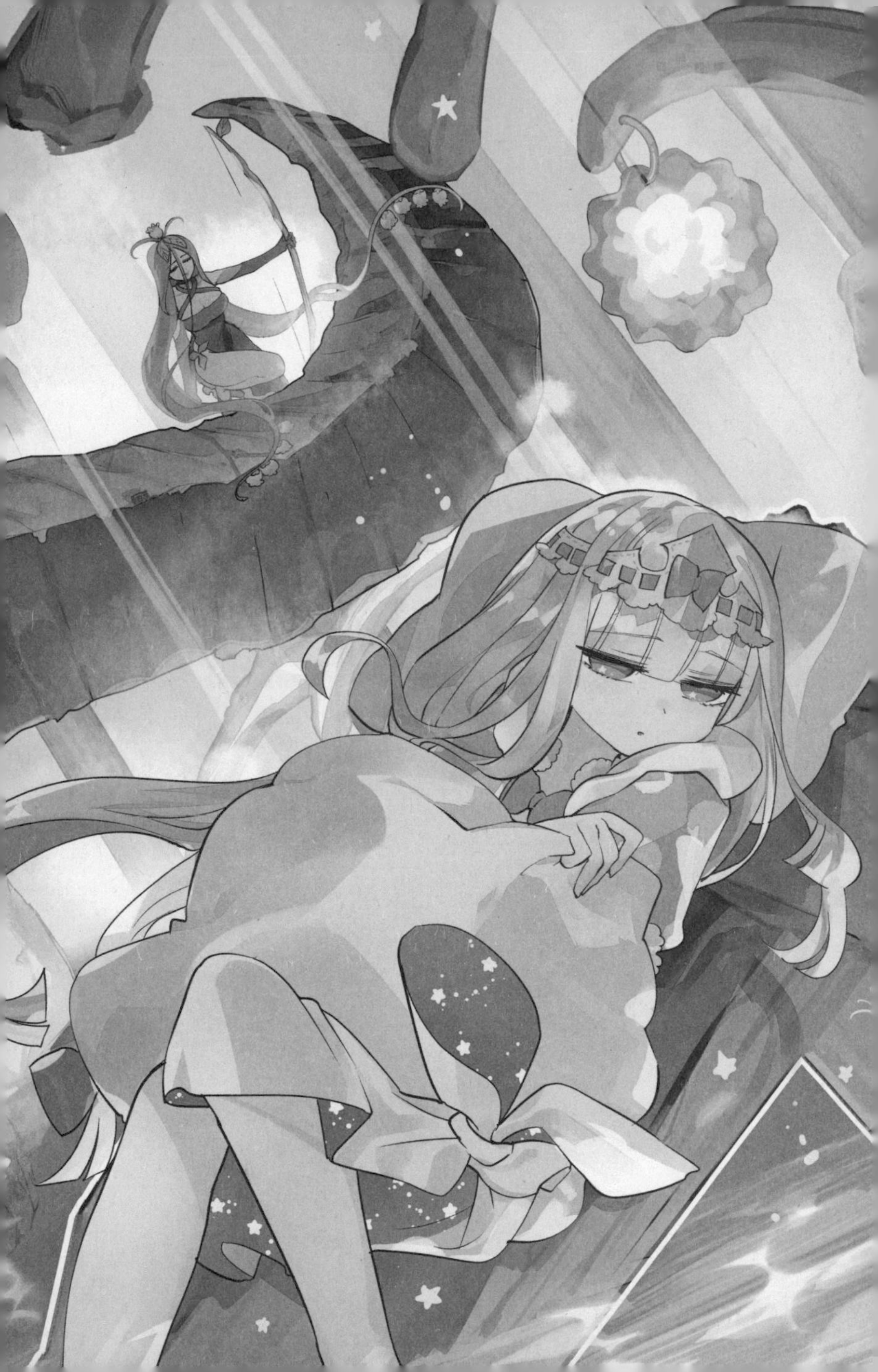

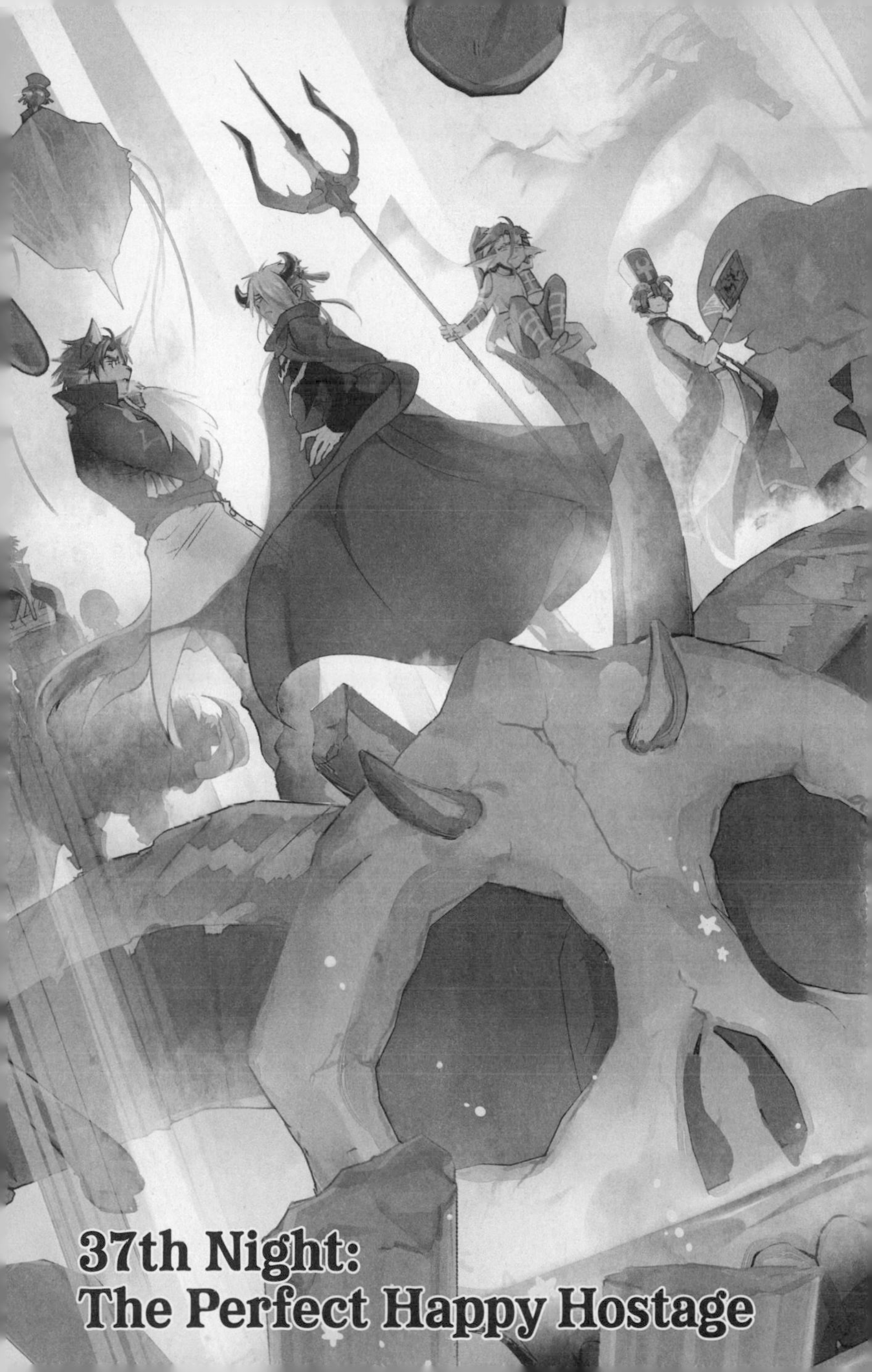

37th Night: The Perfect Happy Hostage

SLEEPY PRINCESS
IN THE DEMON CASTLE

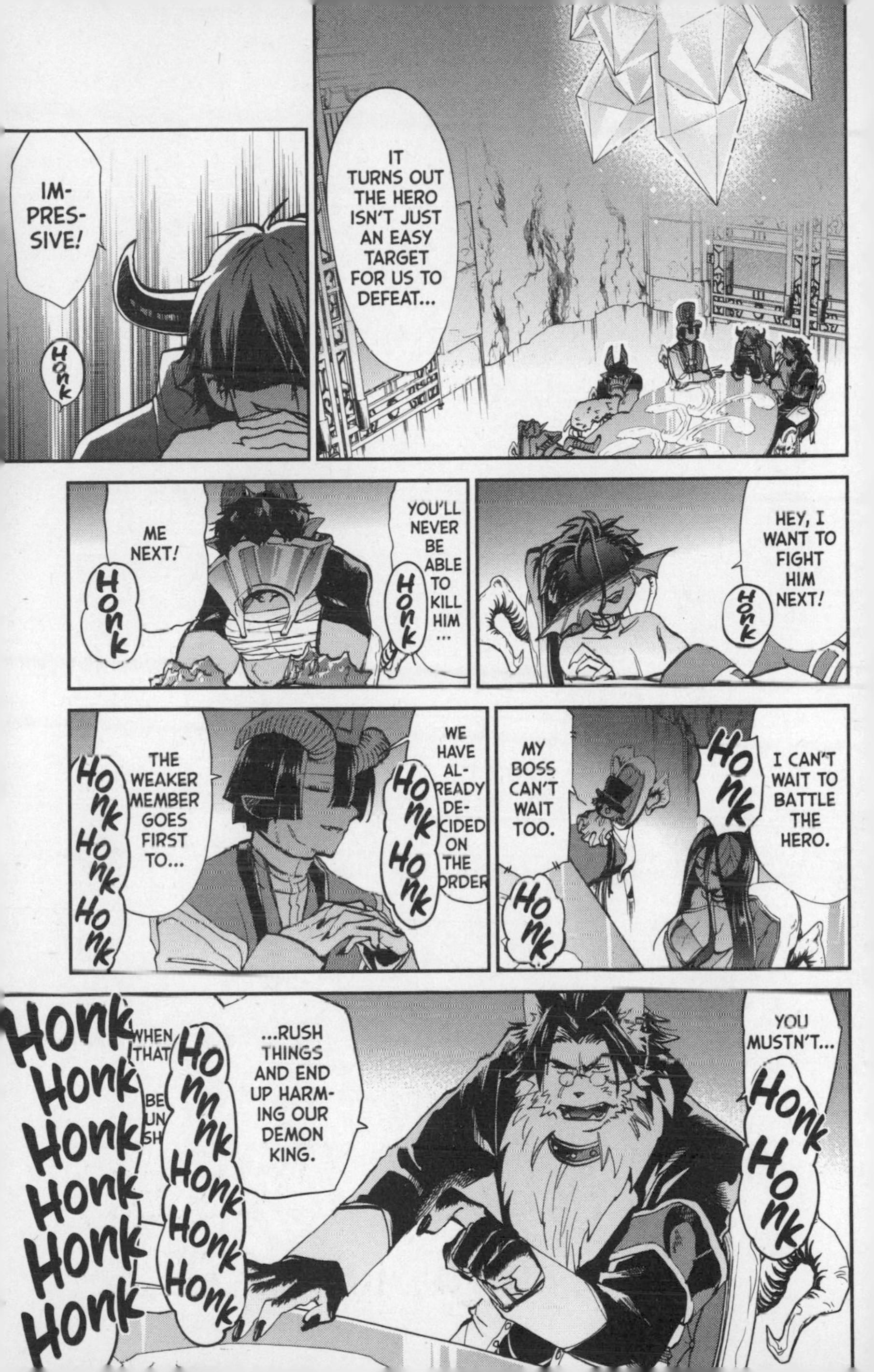
IT TURNS OUT THE HERO ISN'T JUST AN EASY TARGET FOR US TO DEFEAT...
IM-PRES-SIVE!
Honk
HEY, I WANT TO FIGHT HIM NEXT!
Honk
YOU'LL NEVER BE ABLE TO KILL HIM...
Honk
ME NEXT!
Honk
I CAN'T WAIT TO BATTLE THE HERO.
HONK
MY BOSS CAN'T WAIT TOO.
HONK
WE HAVE AL-READY DE-CIDED ON THE ORDER
Honk Honk
THE WEAKER MEMBER GOES FIRST TO...
Honk Honk Honk Honk
YOU MUSTN'T...
Honk Honk Honk
...RUSH THINGS AND END UP HARM-ING OUR DEMON KING.
Honnnk Honk Honk Honk
WHEN THAT
Honk Honk Honk Honk Honk Honk Honk

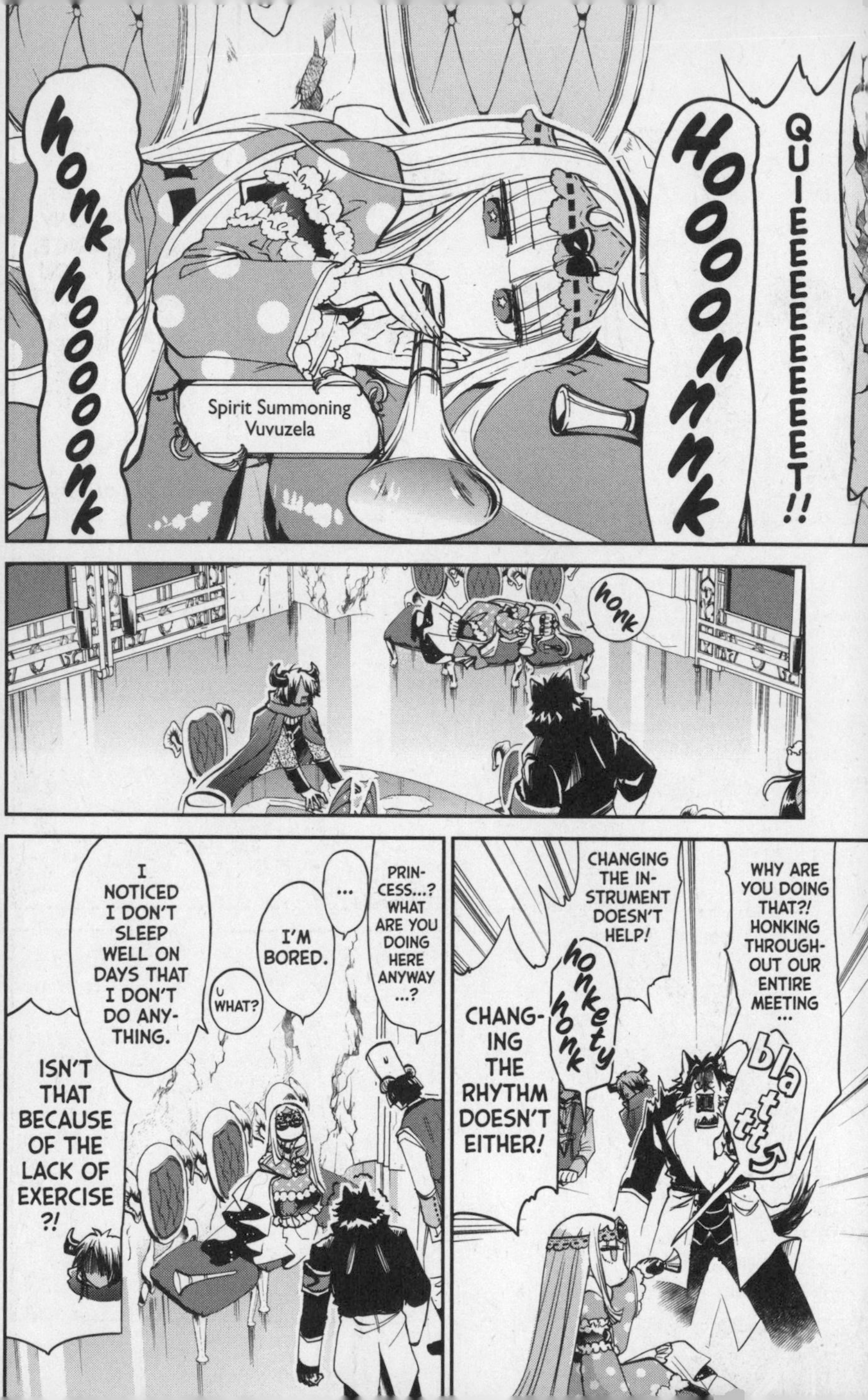
QUIEEEEEEEEET!!
HOOOOnnnk
Spirit Summoning Vuvuzela
honk hooooonk
honk
WHY ARE YOU DOING THAT?! HONKING THROUGHOUT OUR ENTIRE MEETING...
blattt
CHANGING THE INSTRUMENT DOESN'T HELP!
honkety honk
CHANGING THE RHYTHM DOESN'T EITHER!
PRINCESS...? WHAT ARE YOU DOING HERE ANYWAY...?
...
I'M BORED.
WHAT?
I NOTICED I DON'T SLEEP WELL ON DAYS THAT I DON'T DO ANYTHING.
ISN'T THAT BECAUSE OF THE LACK OF EXERCISE?!

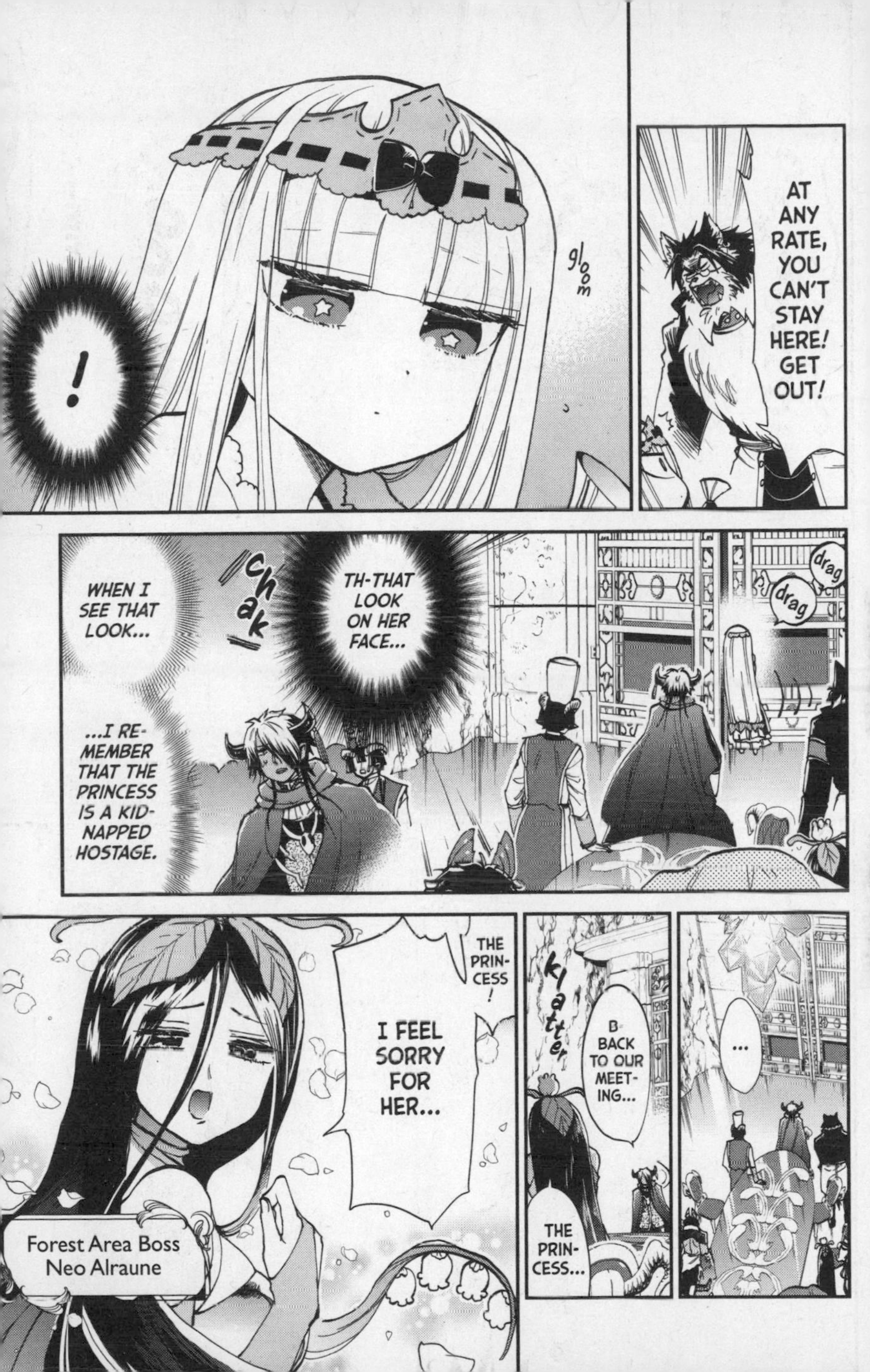
AT ANY RATE, YOU CAN'T STAY HERE! GET OUT!
gloom
!
drag
drag
TH-THAT LOOK ON HER FACE...
chak
WHEN I SEE THAT LOOK...
...I RE-MEMBER THAT THE PRINCESS IS A KID-NAPPED HOSTAGE.
...
B-BACK TO OUR MEET-ING...
klatter
THE PRIN-CESS...
THE PRIN-CESS!
I FEEL SORRY FOR HER...
Forest Area Boss
Neo Alraune

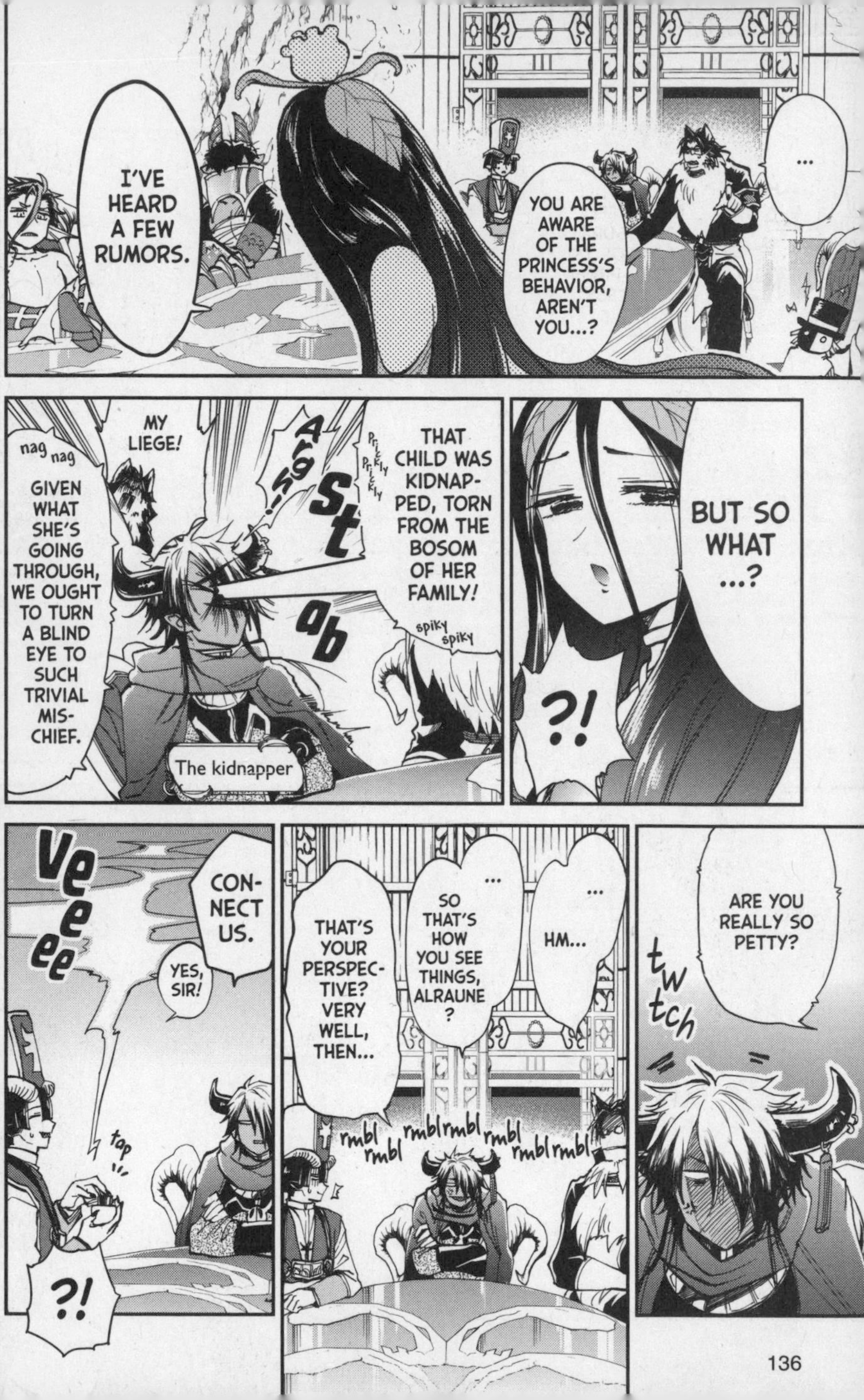
...
YOU ARE AWARE OF THE PRINCESS'S BEHAVIOR, AREN'T YOU...?
I'VE HEARD A FEW RUMORS.
BUT SO WHAT ...?
?!
THAT CHILD WAS KIDNAP-PED, TORN FROM THE BOSOM OF HER FAMILY!
Prickly prickly
spiky spiky
Argh!
Stab
MY LIEGE!
nag nag
GIVEN WHAT SHE'S GOING THROUGH, WE OUGHT TO TURN A BLIND EYE TO SUCH TRIVIAL MIS-CHIEF.
The kidnapper
ARE YOU REALLY SO PETTY?
twitch
... HM...
... SO THAT'S HOW YOU SEE THINGS, ALRAUNE?
THAT'S YOUR PERSPEC-TIVE? VERY WELL, THEN...
rmbl rmbl rmblrmbl rmbl rmblrmbl
CON-NECT US.
YES, SIR!
Veeeee
tap
?!

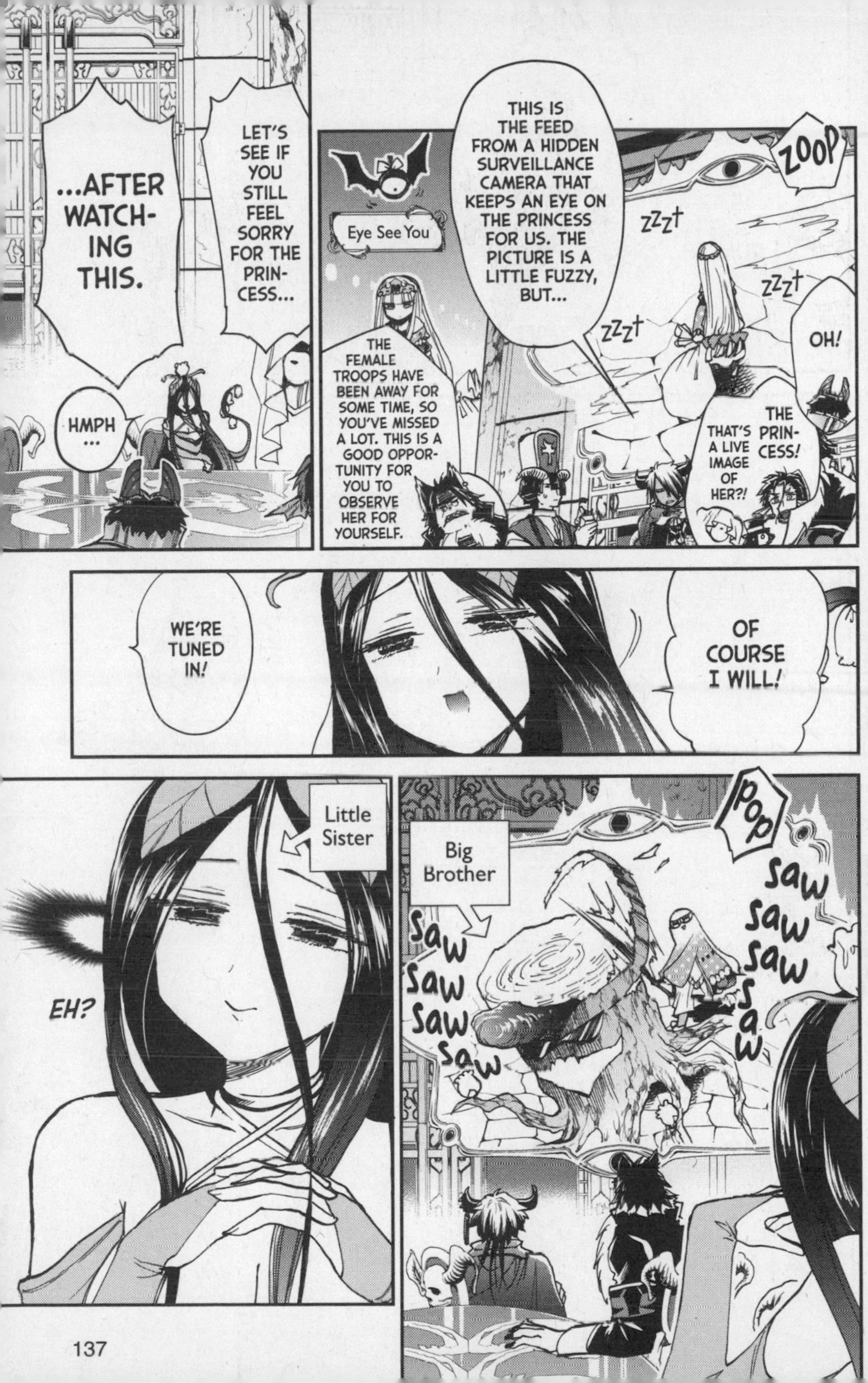
ZOOP
THIS IS THE FEED FROM A HIDDEN SURVEILLANCE CAMERA THAT KEEPS AN EYE ON THE PRINCESS FOR US. THE PICTURE IS A LITTLE FUZZY, BUT...
ZZZ
ZZZ
ZZZ
OH!
THE PRINCESS!
THAT'S A LIVE IMAGE OF HER?!
Eye See You
THE FEMALE TROOPS HAVE BEEN AWAY FOR SOME TIME, SO YOU'VE MISSED A LOT. THIS IS A GOOD OPPORTUNITY FOR YOU TO OBSERVE HER FOR YOURSELF.
LET'S SEE IF YOU STILL FEEL SORRY FOR THE PRINCESS...
...AFTER WATCHING THIS.
HMPH...
OF COURSE I WILL!
WE'RE TUNED IN!
POP
SAW SAW SAW SAW SAW
Big Brother
SAW SAW SAW SAW
Little Sister
EH?

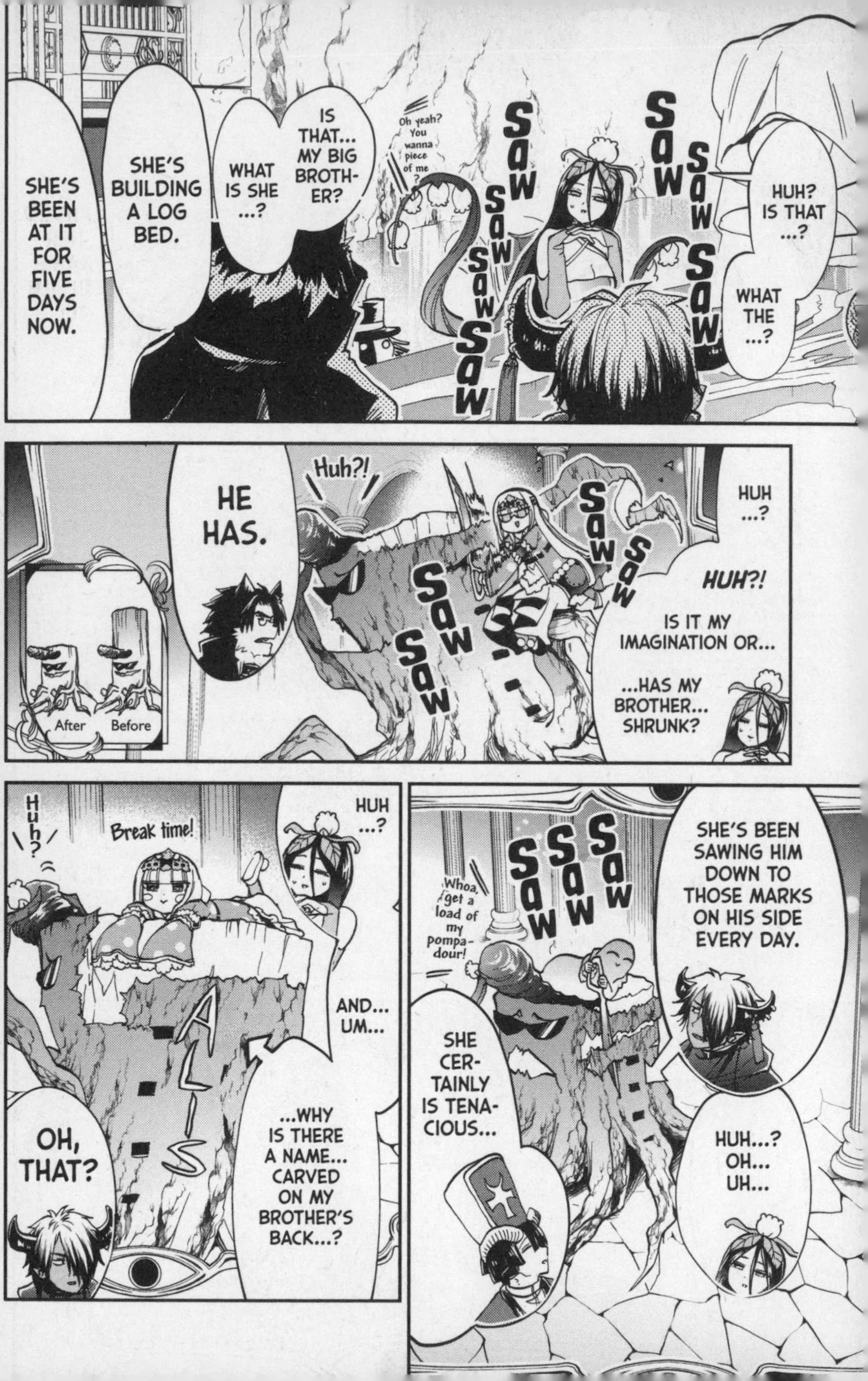
HUH? IS THAT ...?
WHAT THE ...?
Saw Saw Saw Saw
Saw Saw Saw Saw
Oh yeah? You wanna piece of me?
IS THAT... MY BIG BROTHER?
WHAT IS SHE ...?
SHE'S BUILDING A LOG BED.
SHE'S BEEN AT IT FOR FIVE DAYS NOW.
HUH ...?
HUH?!
IS IT MY IMAGINATION OR...
...HAS MY BROTHER... SHRUNK?
Saw Saw Saw Saw
Huh?!
HE HAS.
Before
After
SHE'S BEEN SAWING HIM DOWN TO THOSE MARKS ON HIS SIDE EVERY DAY.
Saw Saw Saw
Saw Saw Saw
Whoa, get a load of my pompadour!
HUH...? OH... UH...
SHE CERTAINLY IS TENACIOUS...
HUH ...?
AND... UM...
Break time!
Huh?
...WHY IS THERE A NAME... CARVED ON MY BROTHER'S BACK...?
OH, THAT?

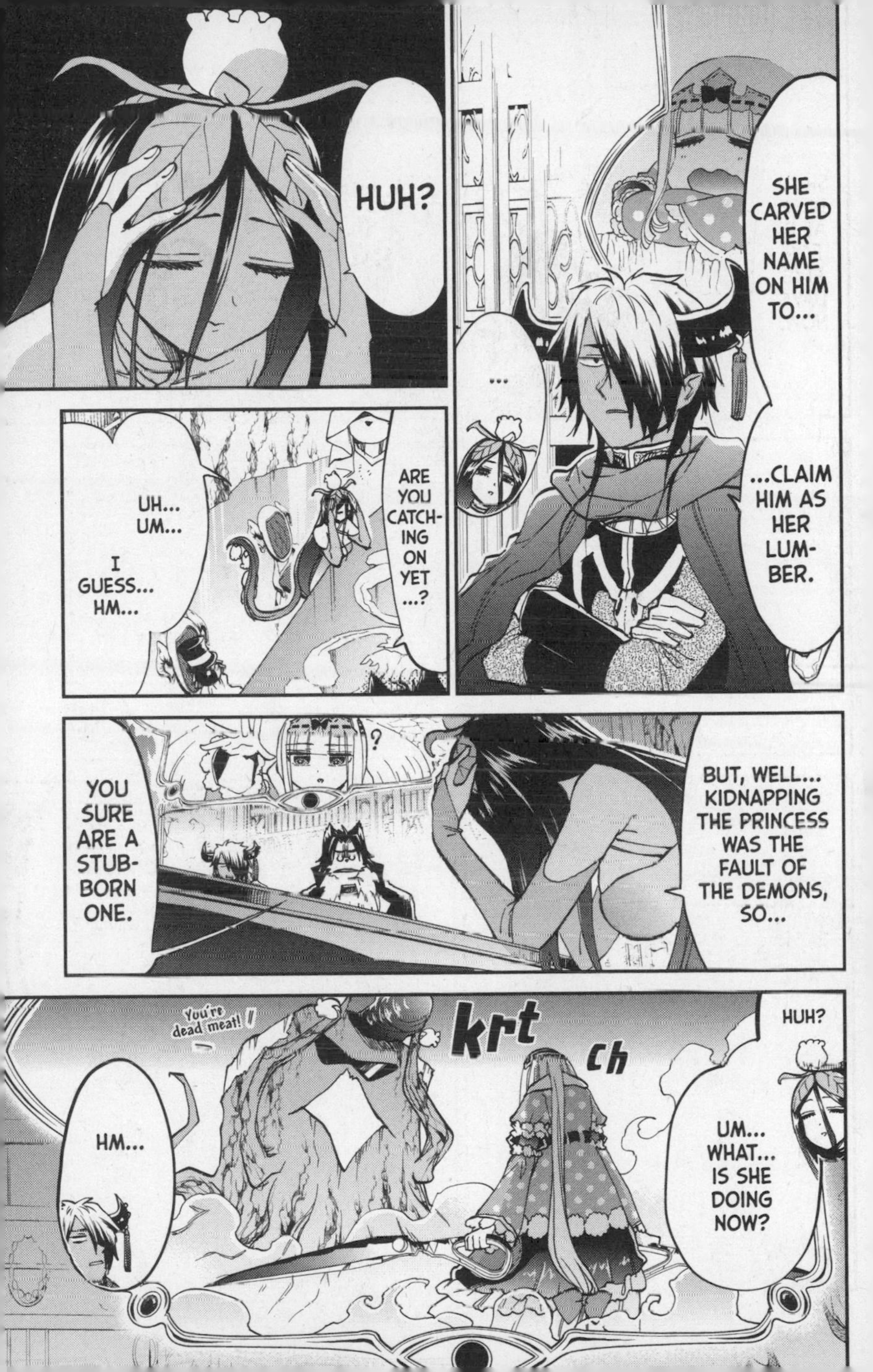

SHE CARVED HER NAME ON HIM TO...
...CLAIM HIM AS HER LUMBER.
...
HUH?
ARE YOU CATCHING ON YET ...?
UH... UM...
I GUESS... HM...
BUT, WELL... KIDNAPPING THE PRINCESS WAS THE FAULT OF THE DEMONS, SO...
?
YOU SURE ARE A STUBBORN ONE.
HUH?
UM... WHAT... IS SHE DOING NOW?
krt
ch
You're dead meat!!
HM...

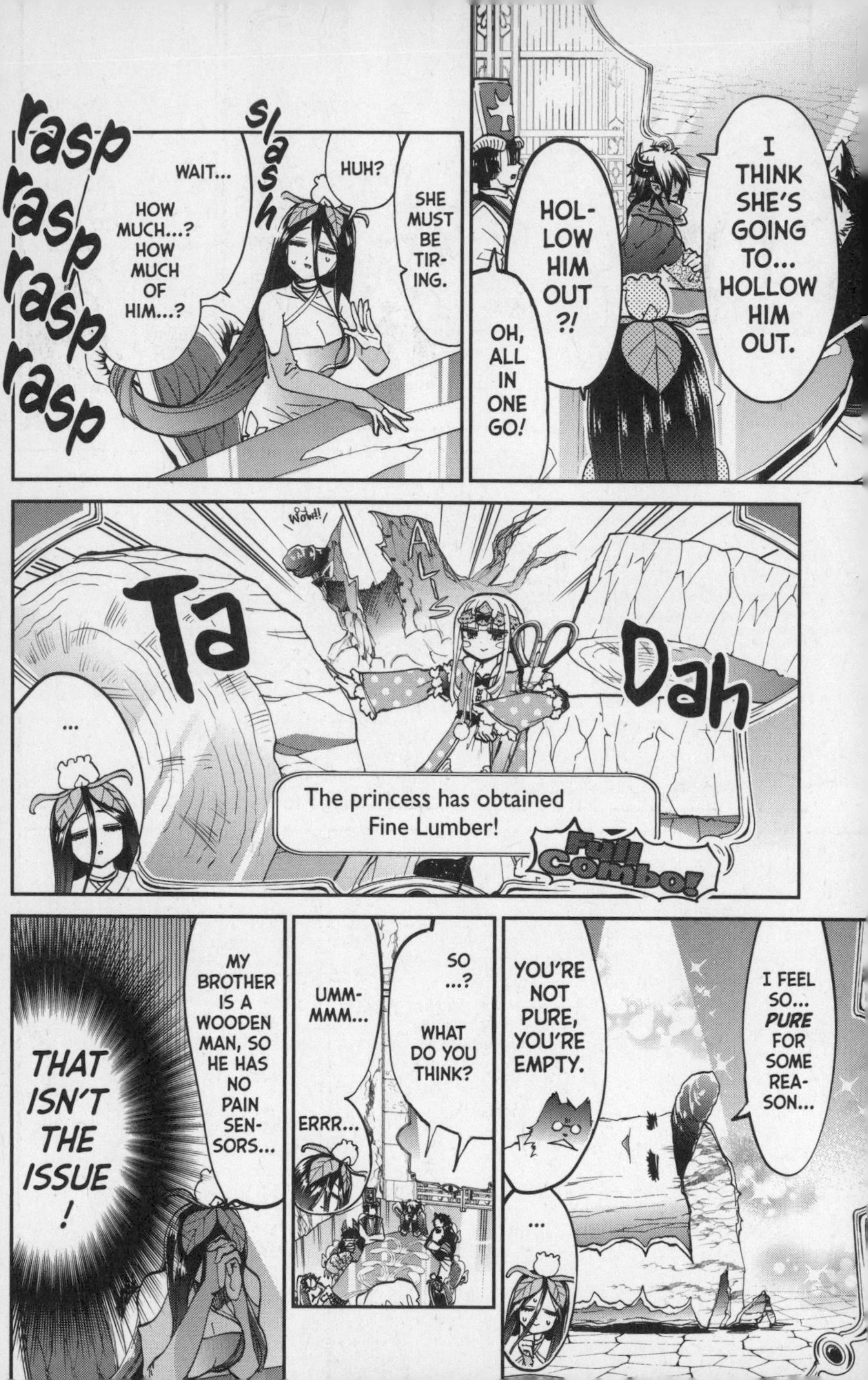
I THINK SHE'S GOING TO... HOLLOW HIM OUT.
HOL-LOW HIM OUT?!
OH, ALL IN ONE GO!
slash
HUH?
SHE MUST BE TIR-ING.
WAIT... HOW MUCH...? HOW MUCH OF HIM...?
rasp rasp rasp rasp rasp
Wow!!
Ta Dah
...
The princess has obtained Fine Lumber!
Full Combo!
I FEEL SO... *PURE* FOR SOME REA-SON...
YOU'RE NOT PURE, YOU'RE EMPTY.
...
SO ...?
WHAT DO YOU THINK?
UMM-MMM...
ERRR...
MY BROTHER IS A WOODEN MAN, SO HE HAS NO PAIN SEN-SORS...
THAT ISN'T THE ISSUE!

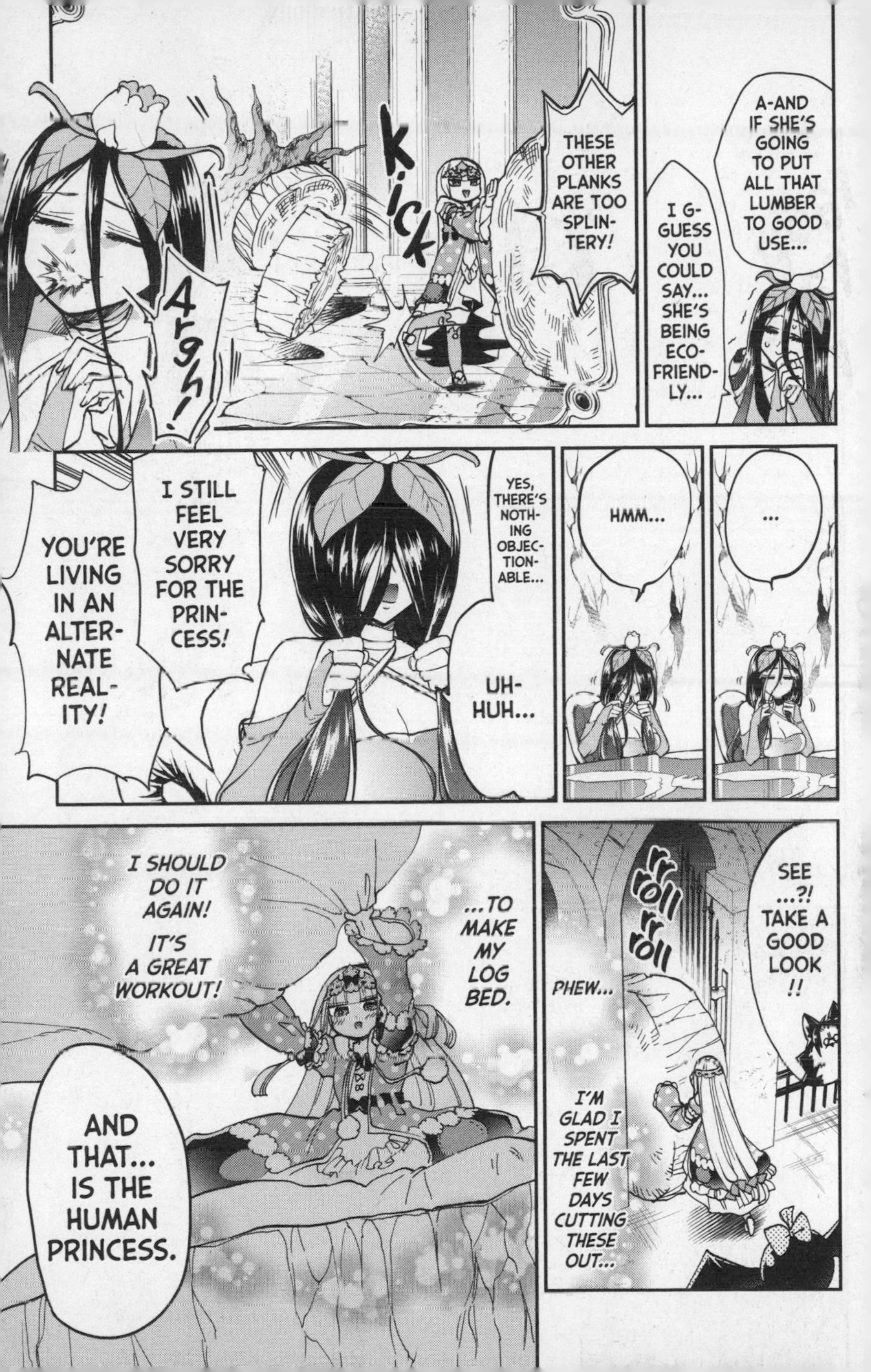
A-AND IF SHE'S GOING TO PUT ALL THAT LUMBER TO GOOD USE...
I G-GUESS YOU COULD SAY... SHE'S BEING ECO-FRIENDLY...
THESE OTHER PLANKS ARE TOO SPLINTERY!
KICK
ARGH!
...
HMM...
YES, THERE'S NOTHING OBJECTIONABLE...
UH-HUH...
I STILL FEEL VERY SORRY FOR THE PRINCESS!
YOU'RE LIVING IN AN ALTERNATE REALITY!
SEE ...?! TAKE A GOOD LOOK!!
ROLL ROLL
PHEW...
I'M GLAD I SPENT THE LAST FEW DAYS CUTTING THESE OUT...
...TO MAKE MY LOG BED.
I SHOULD DO IT AGAIN!
IT'S A GREAT WORKOUT!
AND THAT... IS THE HUMAN PRINCESS.

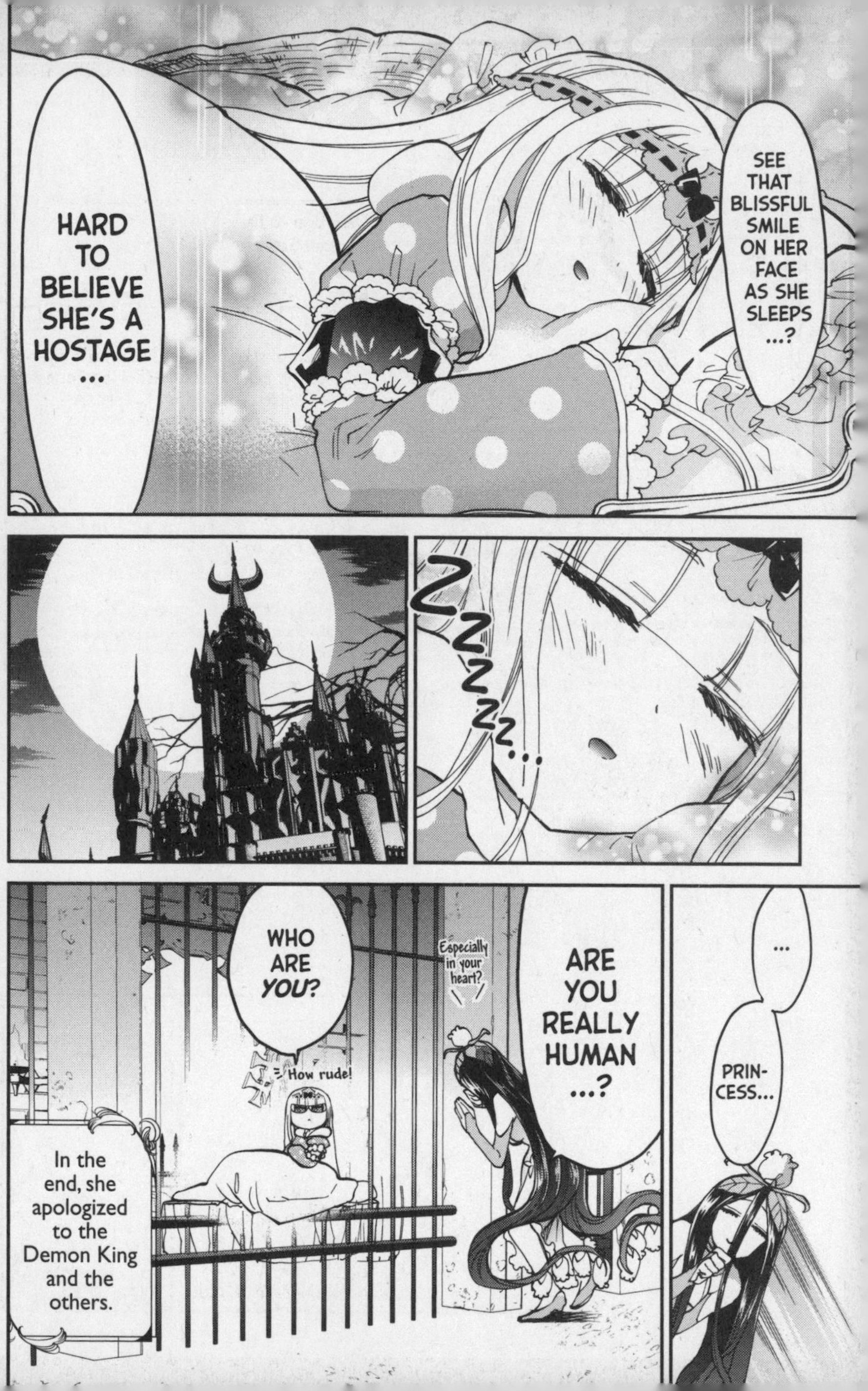
SEE THAT BLISSFUL SMILE ON HER FACE AS SHE SLEEPS ...?
HARD TO BELIEVE SHE'S A HOSTAGE ...
ZZZZZ...
...
PRIN- CESS...
ARE YOU REALLY HUMAN ...?
Especially in your heart?
WHO ARE *YOU*?
How rude!
In the end, she apologized to the Demon King and the others.

Neo Alraune

Devotion to Family: ☆☆☆☆☆☆
Pleasant Scent: ☆☆☆☆☆☆☆☆

In Floriography, she stands for "the return of happiness."

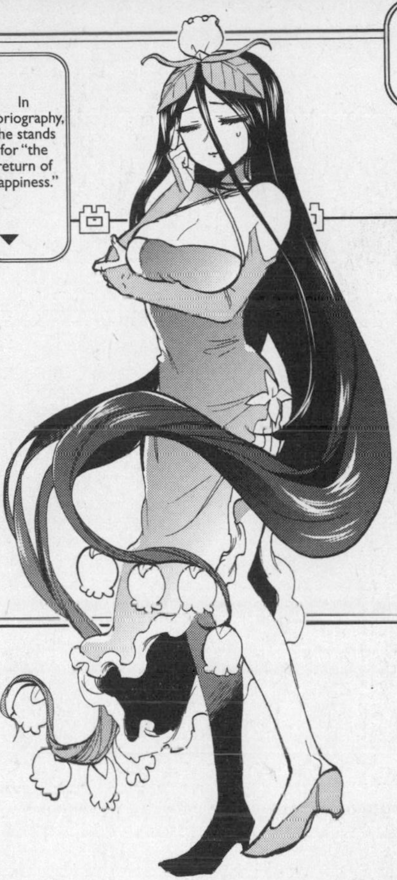

A demon of the plant species who is the boss of the Evil Flower Garden and one of the Demon Castle's Ten Guardians. Her status ailment and charm attacks are brutal.

She is a firm believer in people's intrinsic goodness. Great Red Siberian defends the laws of his master, the Demon King, but she lives by her own laws based on her own sense of right and wrong.

Her older brother is a useless tree trunk, so she uses her position to protect him inside her forest territory.

Former problem:
"I'm worried about my brother."

Current problem:
"I didn't secretly wish for the princess to kill my brother. Really, I didn't."

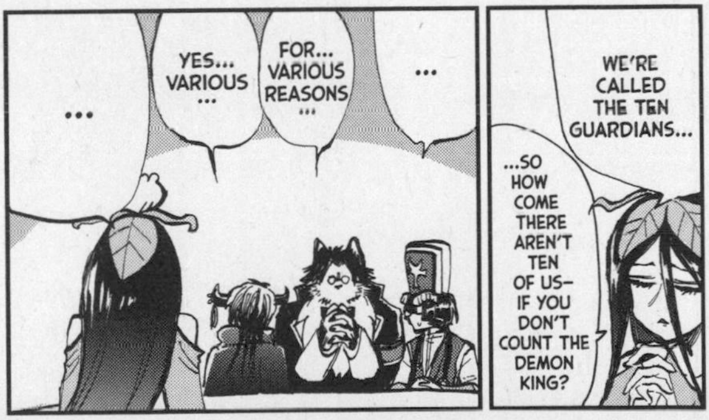
WE'RE CALLED THE TEN GUARDIANS...
...SO HOW COME THERE AREN'T TEN OF US– IF YOU DON'T COUNT THE DEMON KING?
...
FOR... VARIOUS REASONS...
YES... VARIOUS...
...

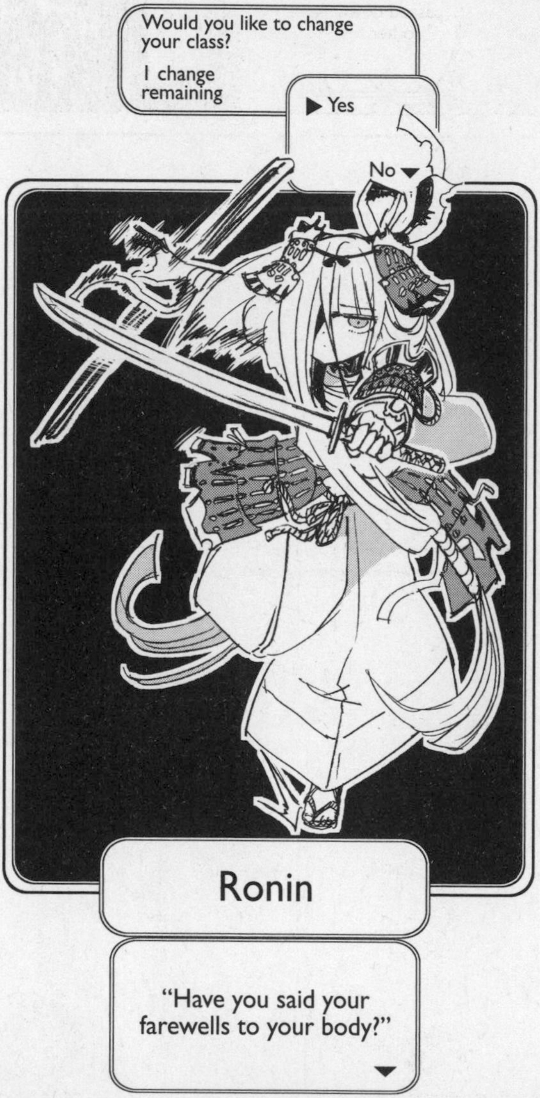
Would you like to change your class?
1 change remaining
▶ Yes
No
Ronin
"Have you said your farewells to your body?"

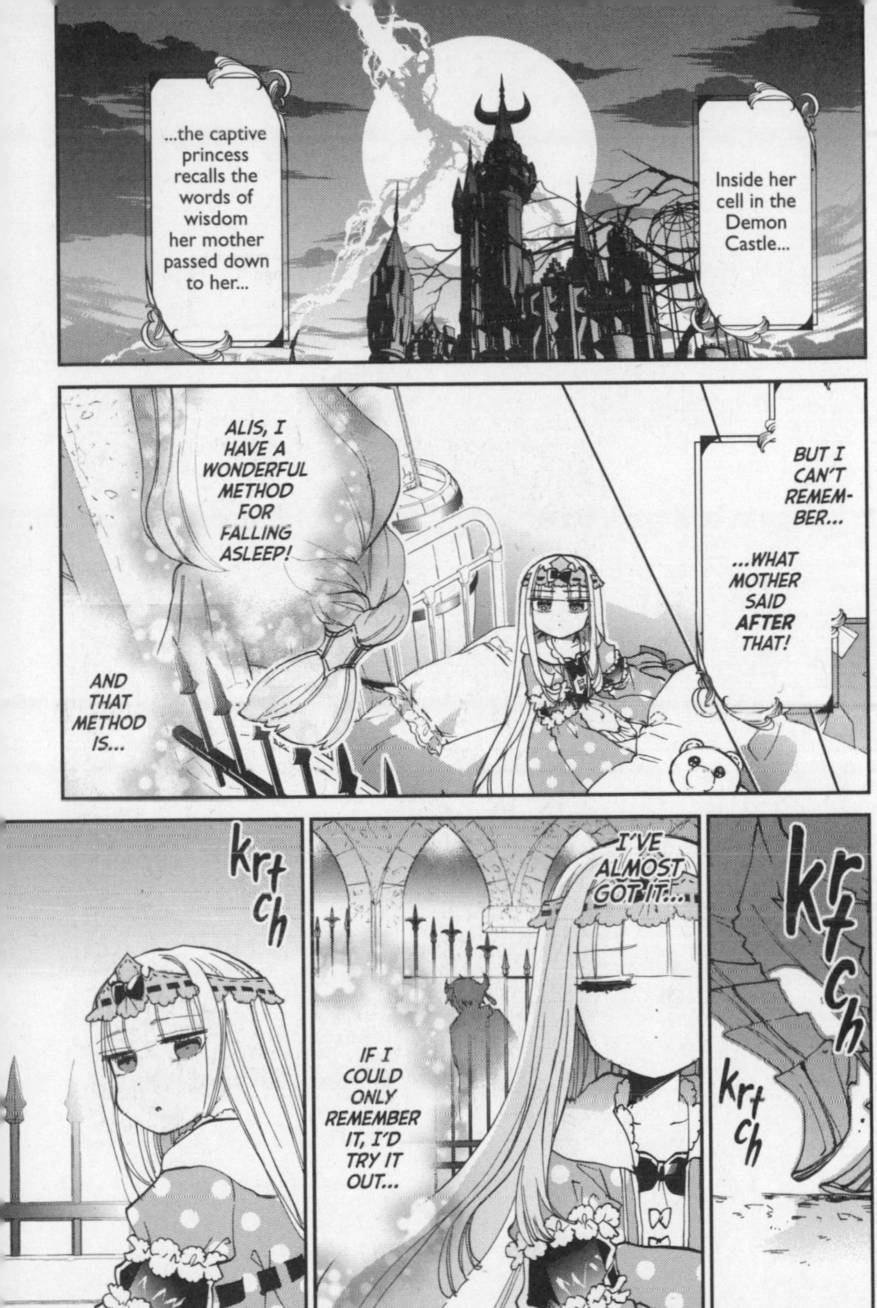
Inside her cell in the Demon Castle...
...the captive princess recalls the words of wisdom her mother passed down to her...
ALIS, I HAVE A WONDERFUL METHOD FOR FALLING ASLEEP!
AND THAT METHOD IS...
BUT I CAN'T REMEMBER...
...WHAT MOTHER SAID AFTER THAT!
krtch
krtch
I'VE ALMOST GOT IT...
IF I COULD ONLY REMEMBER IT, I'D TRY IT OUT...
krtch

38th Night: Demon King—Sleep or Die

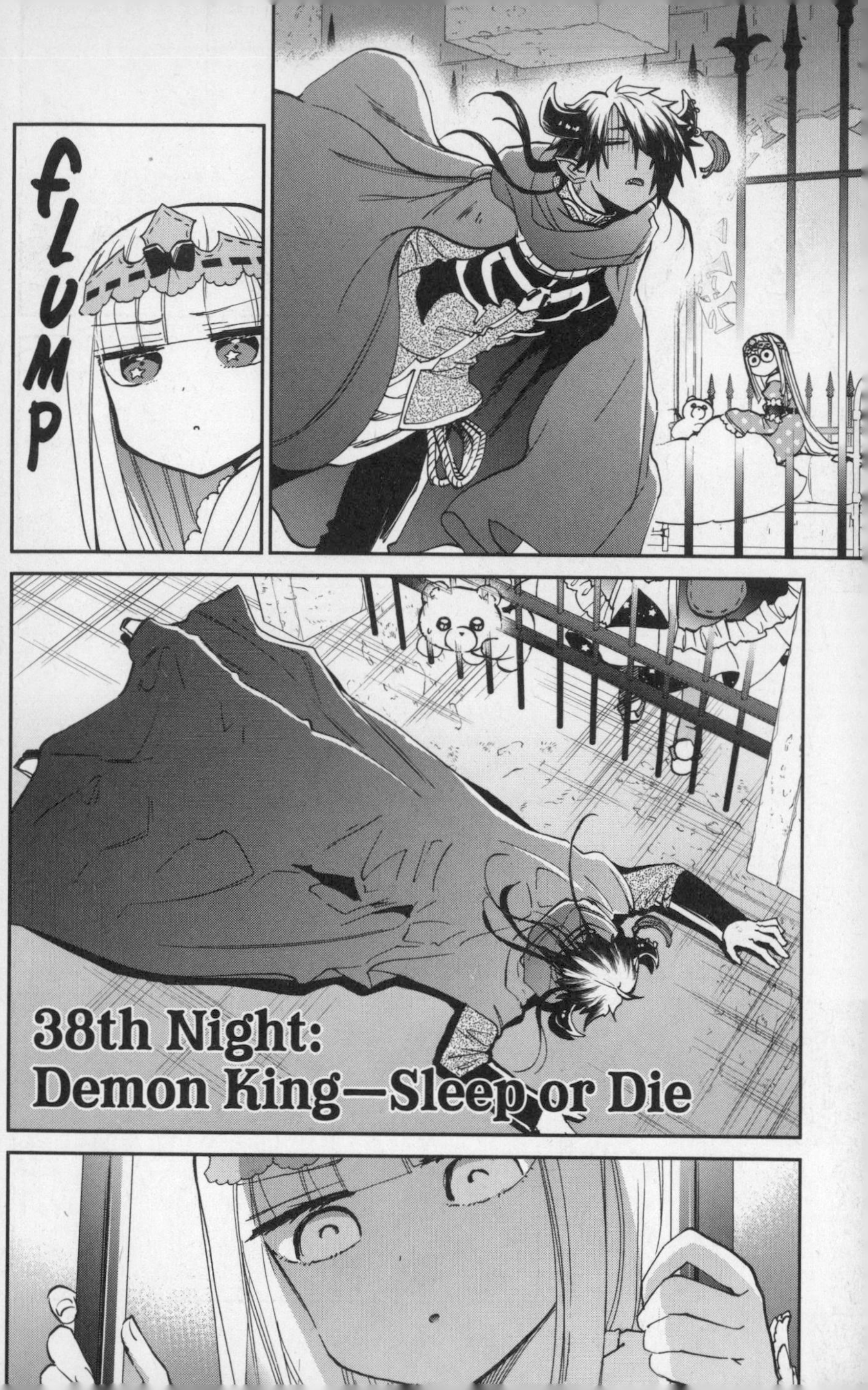
FLUMP
38th Night:
Demon King—Sleep or Die

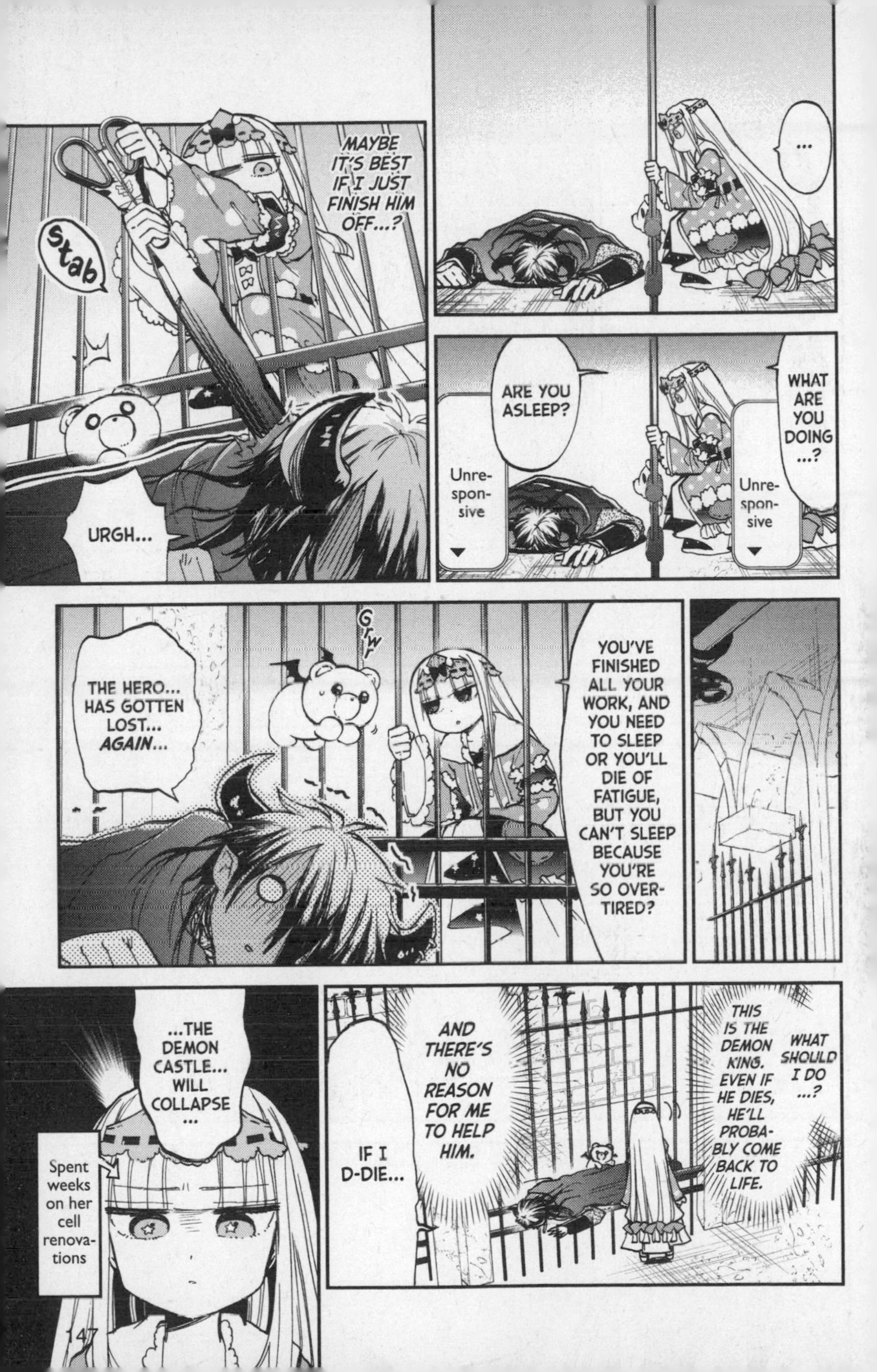
...
WHAT ARE YOU DOING ...?
Unre-spon-sive
ARE YOU ASLEEP?
Unre-spon-sive
MAYBE IT'S BEST IF I JUST FINISH HIM OFF...?
Stab
URGH...
YOU'VE FINISHED ALL YOUR WORK, AND YOU NEED TO SLEEP OR YOU'LL DIE OF FATIGUE, BUT YOU CAN'T SLEEP BECAUSE YOU'RE SO OVER-TIRED?
Grwr
THE HERO... HAS GOTTEN LOST... *AGAIN*...
WHAT SHOULD I DO ...?
THIS IS THE DEMON KING. EVEN IF HE DIES, HE'LL PROBABLY COME BACK TO LIFE.
AND THERE'S NO REASON FOR ME TO HELP HIM.
IF I D-DIE...
...THE DEMON CASTLE... WILL COLLAPSE ...
Spent weeks on her cell renovations

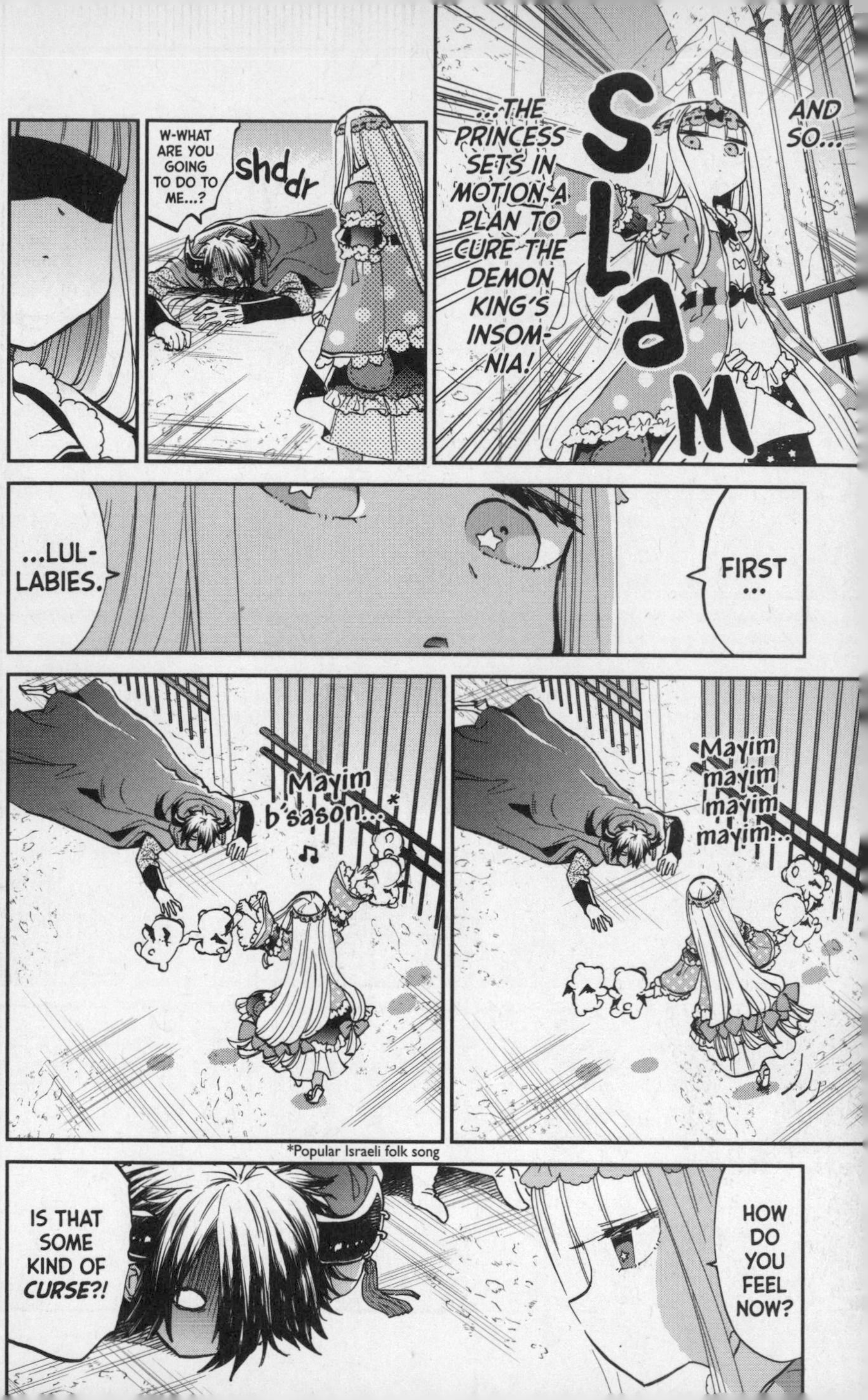
AND SO...
...THE PRINCESS SETS IN MOTION A PLAN TO CURE THE DEMON KING'S INSOMNIA!
SLAM
W-WHAT ARE YOU GOING TO DO TO ME...?
shddr
FIRST...
...LULLABIES.
Mayim mayim mayim mayim...
Mayim b'sason...*
IS THAT SOME KIND OF *CURSE*?!
HOW DO YOU FEEL NOW?

*Popular Israeli folk song

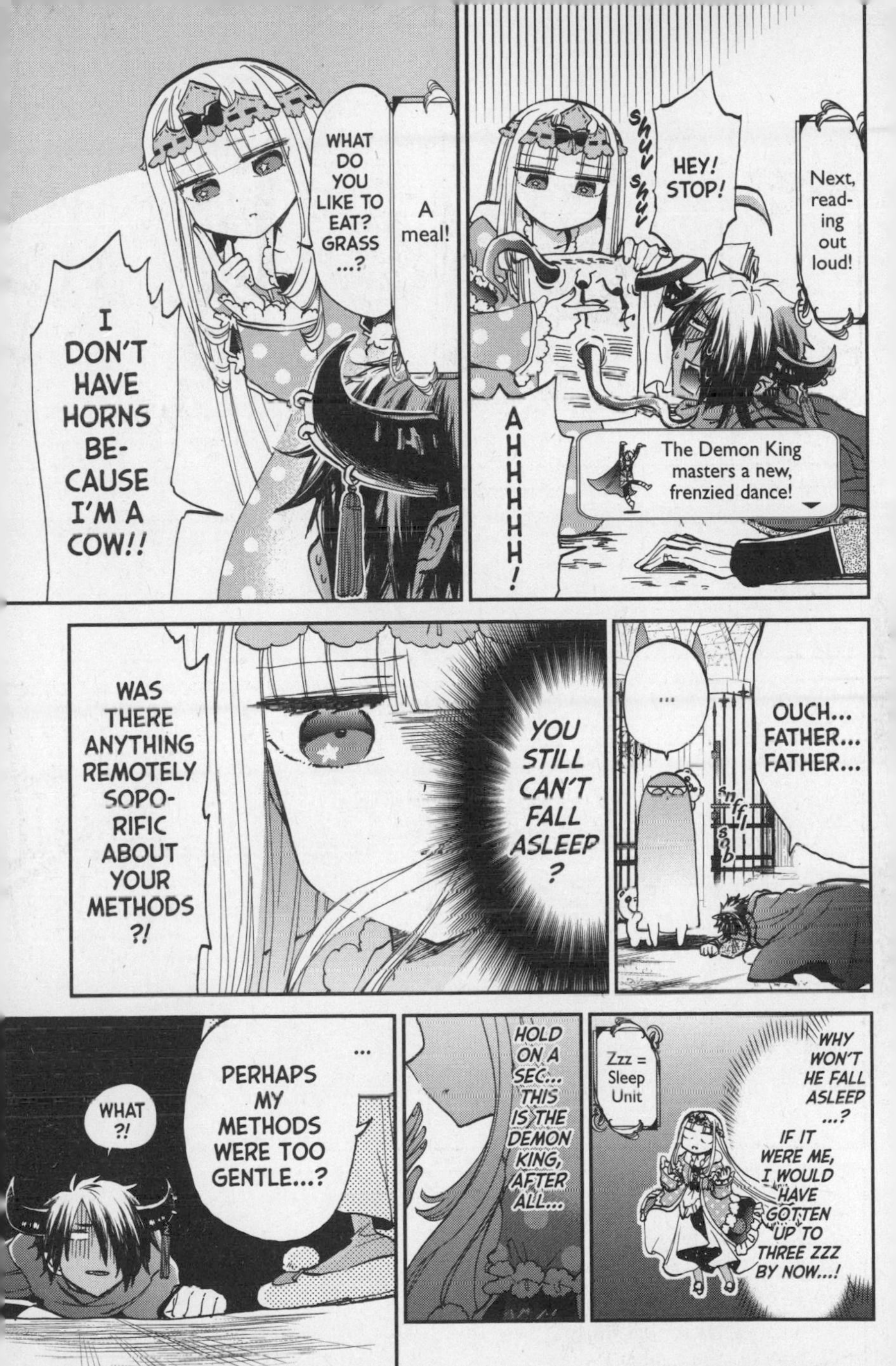
Next, reading out loud!
HEY! STOP!
SHUV SHUV
AHHHHH!
The Demon King masters a new, frenzied dance!
A meal!
WHAT DO YOU LIKE TO EAT? GRASS ...?
I DON'T HAVE HORNS BECAUSE I'M A COW!!
OUCH... FATHER... FATHER...
SNFFL SOB
...
YOU STILL CAN'T FALL ASLEEP?
WAS THERE ANYTHING REMOTELY SOPORIFIC ABOUT YOUR METHODS?!
Zzz = Sleep Unit
WHY WON'T HE FALL ASLEEP...?
IF IT WERE ME, I WOULD HAVE GOTTEN UP TO THREE ZZZ BY NOW...!
HOLD ON A SEC... THIS IS THE DEMON KING, AFTER ALL...
...
PERHAPS MY METHODS WERE TOO GENTLE...?
WHAT?!

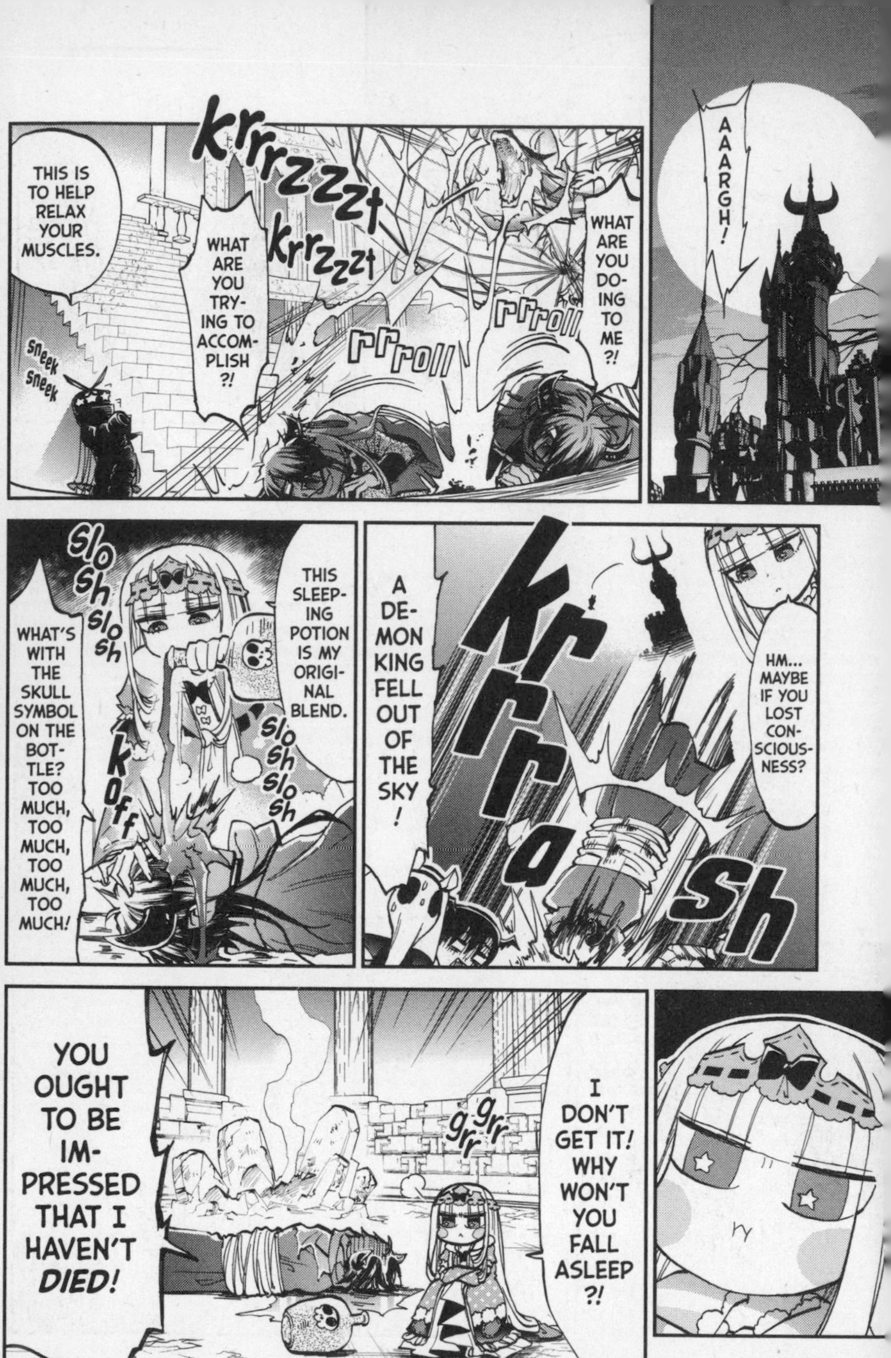
AAAARGH!
WHAT ARE YOU DOING TO ME?!
rrroll
rrroll
krrrzzzzt
krrzzzt
WHAT ARE YOU TRYING TO ACCOMPLISH?!
THIS IS TO HELP RELAX YOUR MUSCLES.
sneek sneek
HM... MAYBE IF YOU LOST CONSCIOUSNESS?
krrrrash
A DEMON KING FELL OUT OF THE SKY!
THIS SLEEPING POTION IS MY ORIGINAL BLEND.
slosh slosh
slosh slosh
WHAT'S WITH THE SKULL SYMBOL ON THE BOTTLE? TOO MUCH, TOO MUCH, TOO MUCH, TOO MUCH!
koff
I DON'T GET IT! WHY WON'T YOU FALL ASLEEP?!
grr grr
YOU OUGHT TO BE IMPRESSED THAT I HAVEN'T *DIED*!

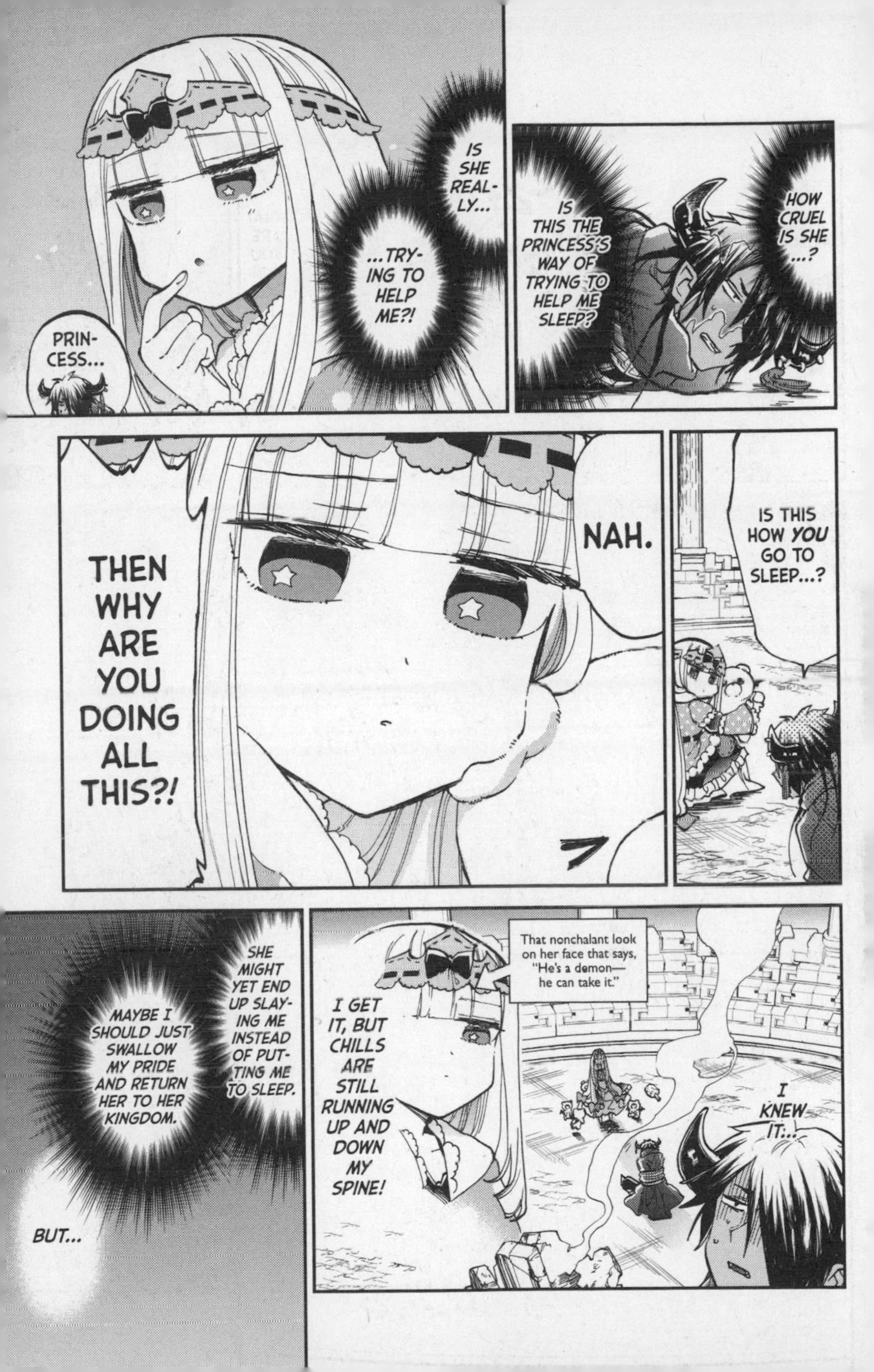
HOW CRUEL IS SHE ...?
IS THIS THE PRINCESS'S WAY OF TRYING TO HELP ME SLEEP?
IS SHE REALLY...
...TRYING TO HELP ME?!
PRINCESS...
IS THIS HOW *YOU* GO TO SLEEP...?
NAH.
THEN WHY ARE YOU DOING ALL THIS?!
I KNEW IT...
That nonchalant look on her face that says, "He's a demon— he can take it."
I GET IT, BUT CHILLS ARE STILL RUNNING UP AND DOWN MY SPINE!
SHE MIGHT YET END UP SLAYING ME INSTEAD OF PUTTING ME TO SLEEP.
MAYBE I SHOULD JUST SWALLOW MY PRIDE AND RETURN HER TO HER KINGDOM.
BUT...

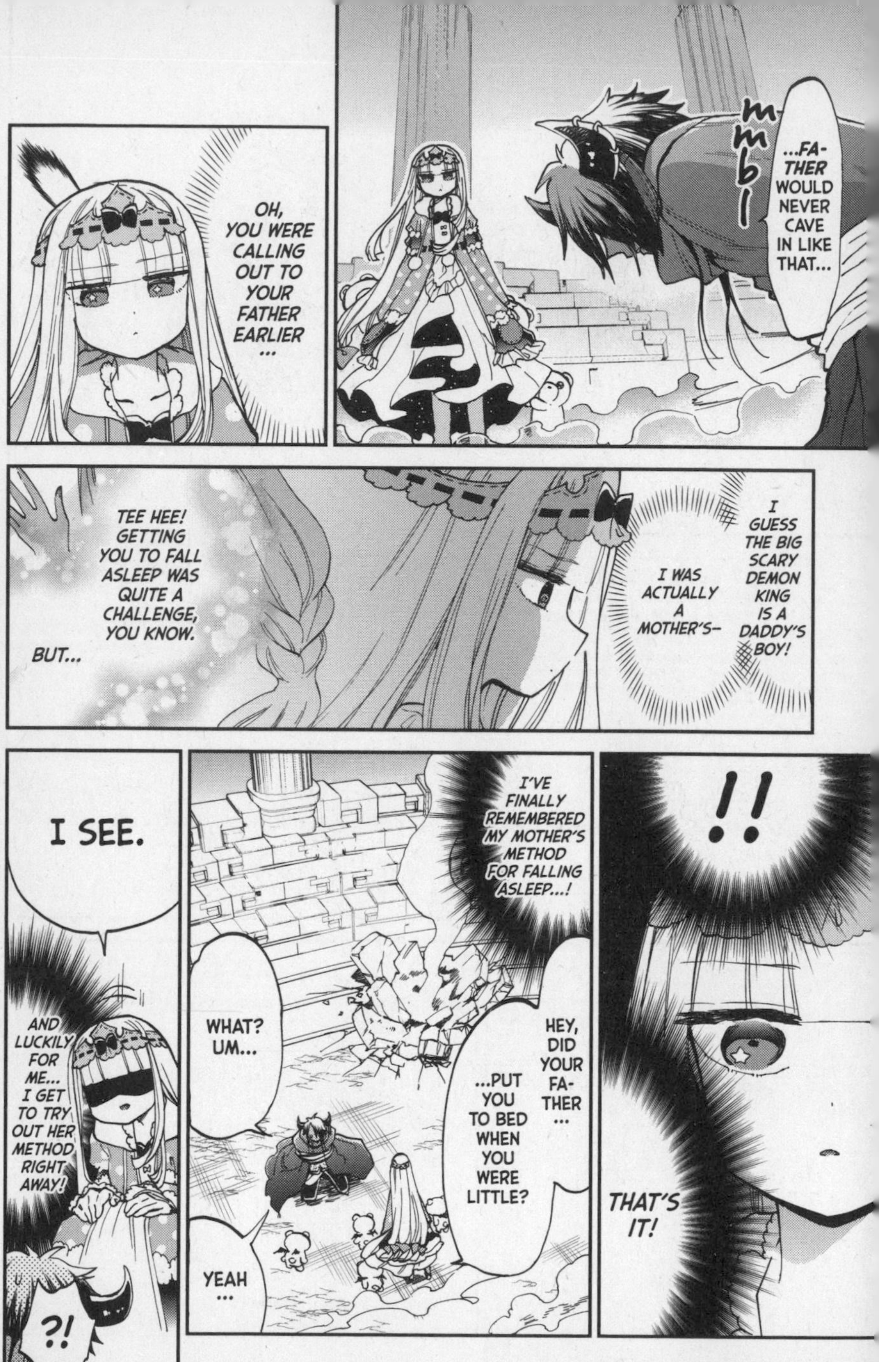
mmbl
...FA-THER WOULD NEVER CAVE IN LIKE THAT...
OH, YOU WERE CALLING OUT TO YOUR FATHER EARLIER...
I GUESS THE BIG SCARY DEMON KING IS A DADDY'S BOY!
I WAS ACTUALLY A MOTHER'S—
TEE HEE! GETTING YOU TO FALL ASLEEP WAS QUITE A CHALLENGE, YOU KNOW.
BUT...
!!
THAT'S IT!
I'VE FINALLY REMEMBERED MY MOTHER'S METHOD FOR FALLING ASLEEP...!
HEY, DID YOUR FA-THER...
...PUT YOU TO BED WHEN YOU WERE LITTLE?
WHAT? UM...
YEAH...
I SEE.
AND LUCKILY FOR ME... I GET TO TRY OUT HER METHOD RIGHT AWAY!
?!

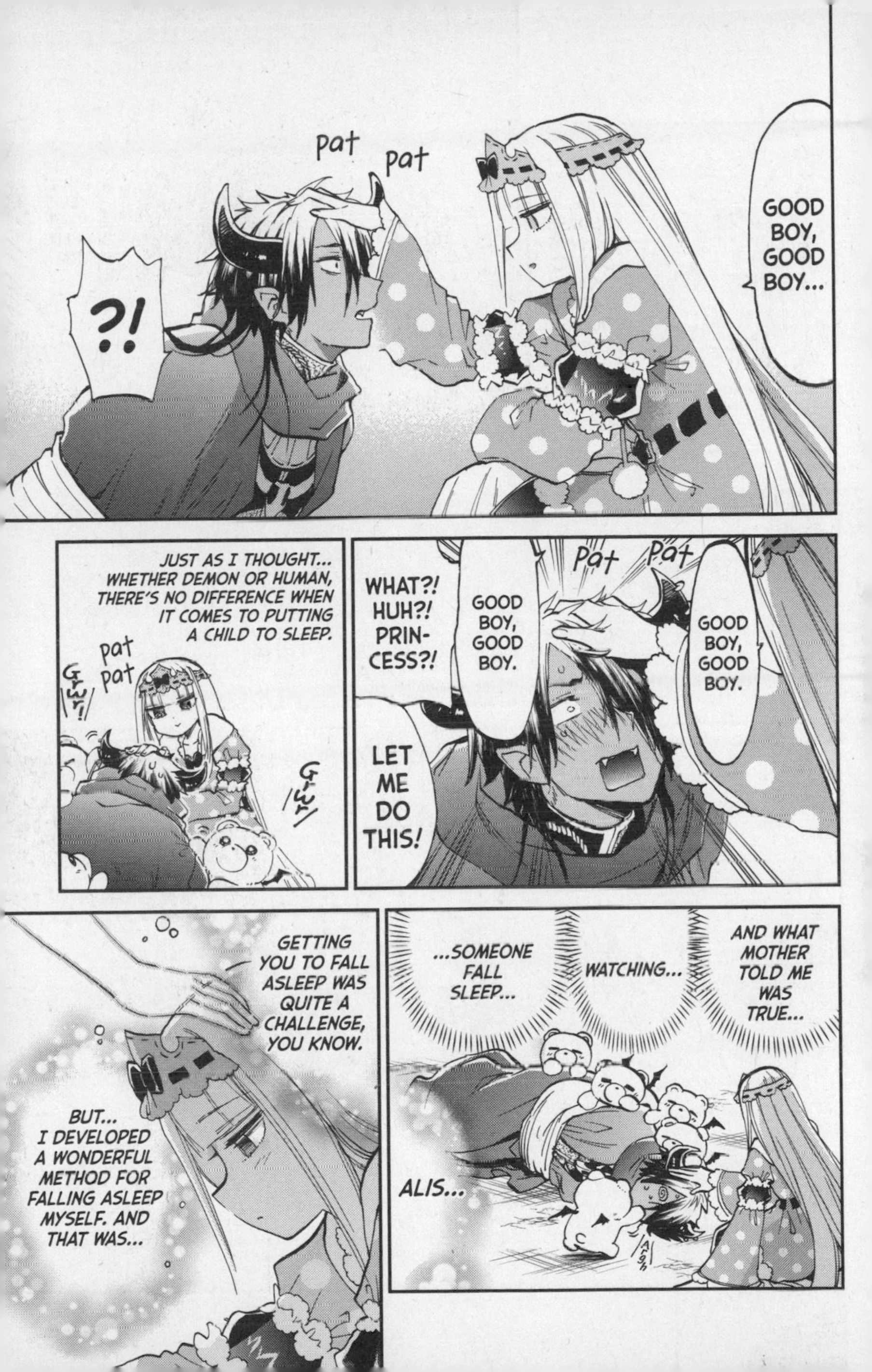
GOOD BOY, GOOD BOY...
pat
pat
?!
GOOD BOY, GOOD BOY.
Pat
Pat
GOOD BOY, GOOD BOY.
WHAT?! HUH?! PRIN-CESS?!
LET ME DO THIS!
JUST AS I THOUGHT... WHETHER DEMON OR HUMAN, THERE'S NO DIFFERENCE WHEN IT COMES TO PUTTING A CHILD TO SLEEP.
pat pat
Grwr!
Grwr
AND WHAT MOTHER TOLD ME WAS TRUE...
WATCHING...
...SOMEONE FALL SLEEP...
ALIS...
GETTING YOU TO FALL ASLEEP WAS QUITE A CHALLENGE, YOU KNOW.
BUT... I DEVELOPED A WONDERFUL METHOD FOR FALLING ASLEEP MYSELF. AND THAT WAS...

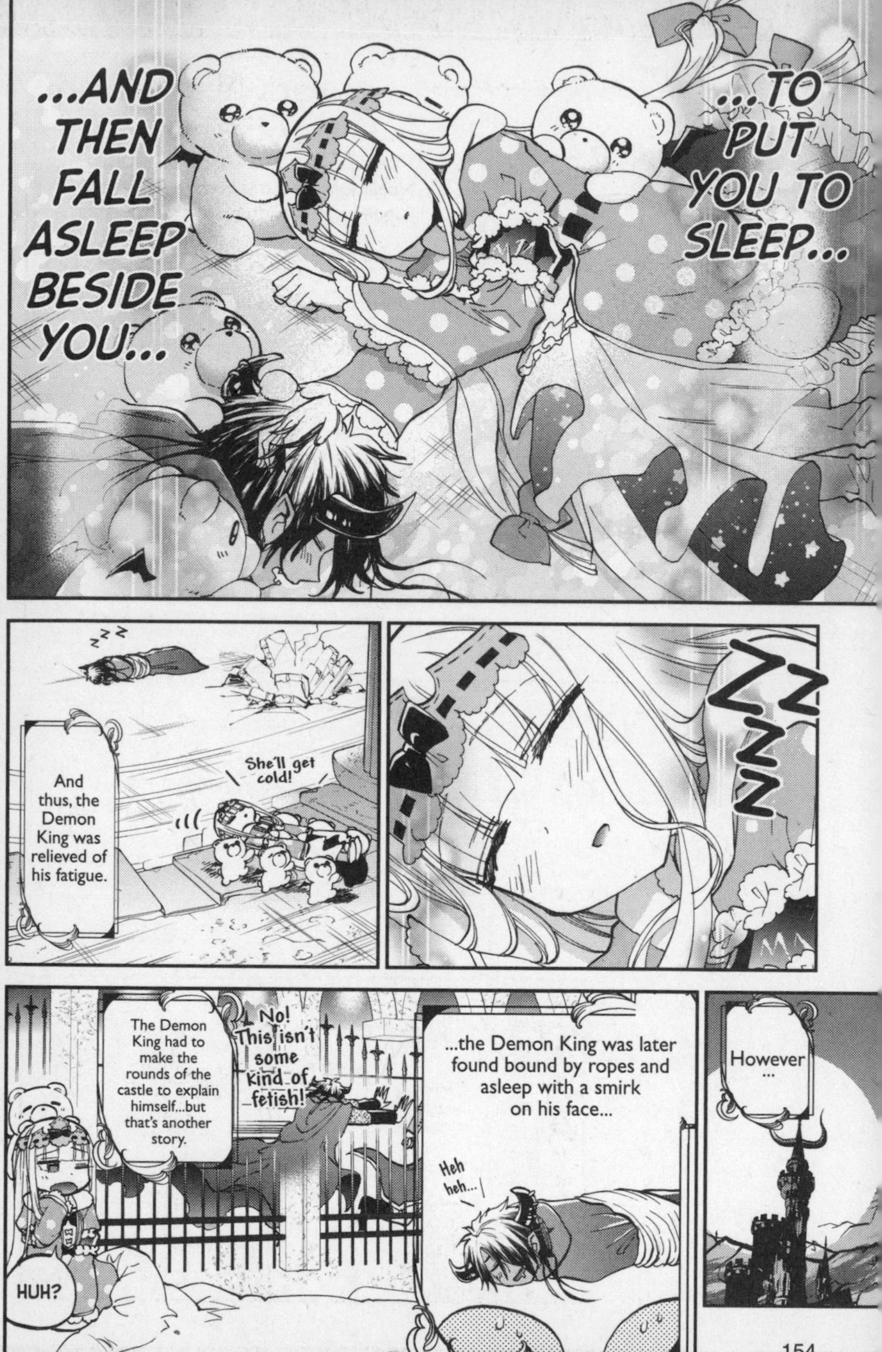
...TO PUT YOU TO SLEEP...
...AND THEN FALL ASLEEP BESIDE YOU...
ZZZ
And thus, the Demon King was relieved of his fatigue.
She'll get cold!
However...
...the Demon King was later found bound by ropes and asleep with a smirk on his face...
Heh heh...
No! This isn't some kind of fetish!
The Demon King had to make the rounds of the castle to explain himself...but that's another story.
HUH?

Aurora Nem Lis Goodereste

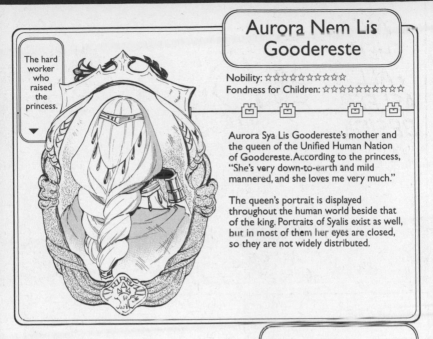

The hard worker who raised the princess.

Nobility: ☆☆☆☆☆☆☆☆☆☆
Fondness for Children: ☆☆☆☆☆☆☆☆☆☆

Aurora Sya Lis Goodereste's mother and the queen of the Unified Human Nation of Goodereste. According to the princess, "She's very down-to-earth and mild mannered, and she loves me very much."

The queen's portrait is displayed throughout the human world beside that of the king. Portraits of Syalis exist as well, but in most of them her eyes are closed, so they are not widely distributed.

Former problem:
"She says she doesn't have any."

Current problem:
"She says she doesn't have any."

The Demon King's Mwahaha Sleep
...
First discovered by Neo Alraune
She was so horrified she ran away.
ZOOM
Argh!
tmp tmp

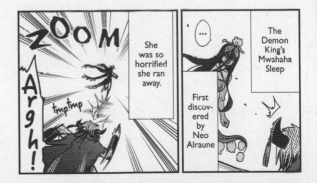

Would you like to change your class?

0 changes remaining

Executioner

"Line up, please."

▼

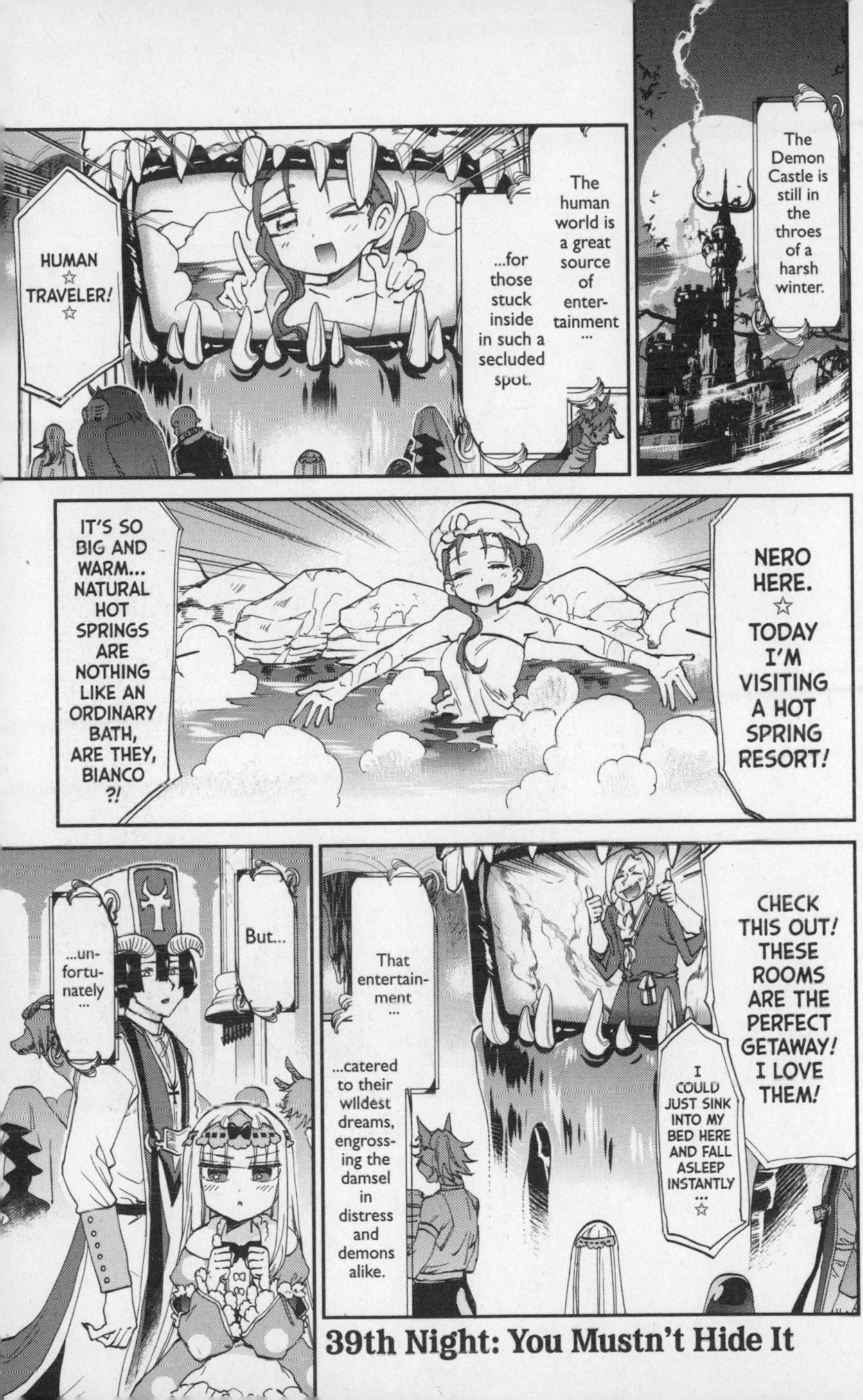
The Demon Castle is still in the throes of a harsh winter.
The human world is a great source of entertainment...
...for those stuck inside in such a secluded spot.
HUMAN ☆ TRAVELER! ☆
NERO HERE. ☆ TODAY I'M VISITING A HOT SPRING RESORT!
IT'S SO BIG AND WARM... NATURAL HOT SPRINGS ARE NOTHING LIKE AN ORDINARY BATH, ARE THEY, BIANCO?!
CHECK THIS OUT! THESE ROOMS ARE THE PERFECT GETAWAY! I LOVE THEM!
I COULD JUST SINK INTO MY BED HERE AND FALL ASLEEP INSTANTLY... ☆
That entertainment...
...catered to their wildest dreams, engrossing the damsel in distress and demons alike.
But...
...unfortunately...

39th Night: You Mustn't Hide It

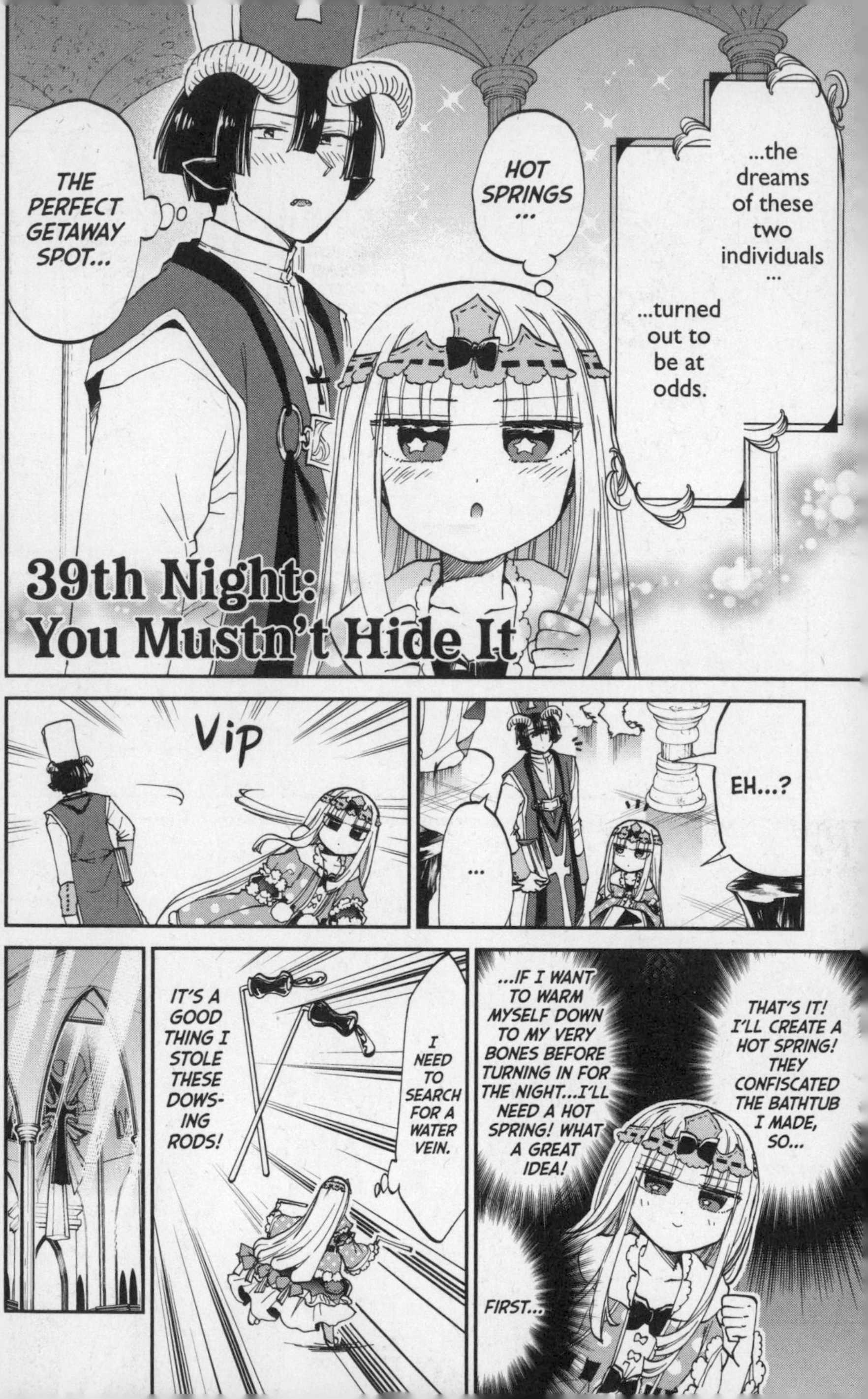
...the dreams of these two individuals ...
...turned out to be at odds.
HOT SPRINGS ...
THE PERFECT GETAWAY SPOT...
39th Night: You Mustn't Hide It
EH...?
...
Vip
THAT'S IT! I'LL CREATE A HOT SPRING! THEY CONFISCATED THE BATHTUB I MADE, SO...
...IF I WANT TO WARM MYSELF DOWN TO MY VERY BONES BEFORE TURNING IN FOR THE NIGHT...I'LL NEED A HOT SPRING! WHAT A GREAT IDEA!
FIRST...
I NEED TO SEARCH FOR A WATER VEIN.
IT'S A GOOD THING I STOLE THESE DOWS-ING RODS!

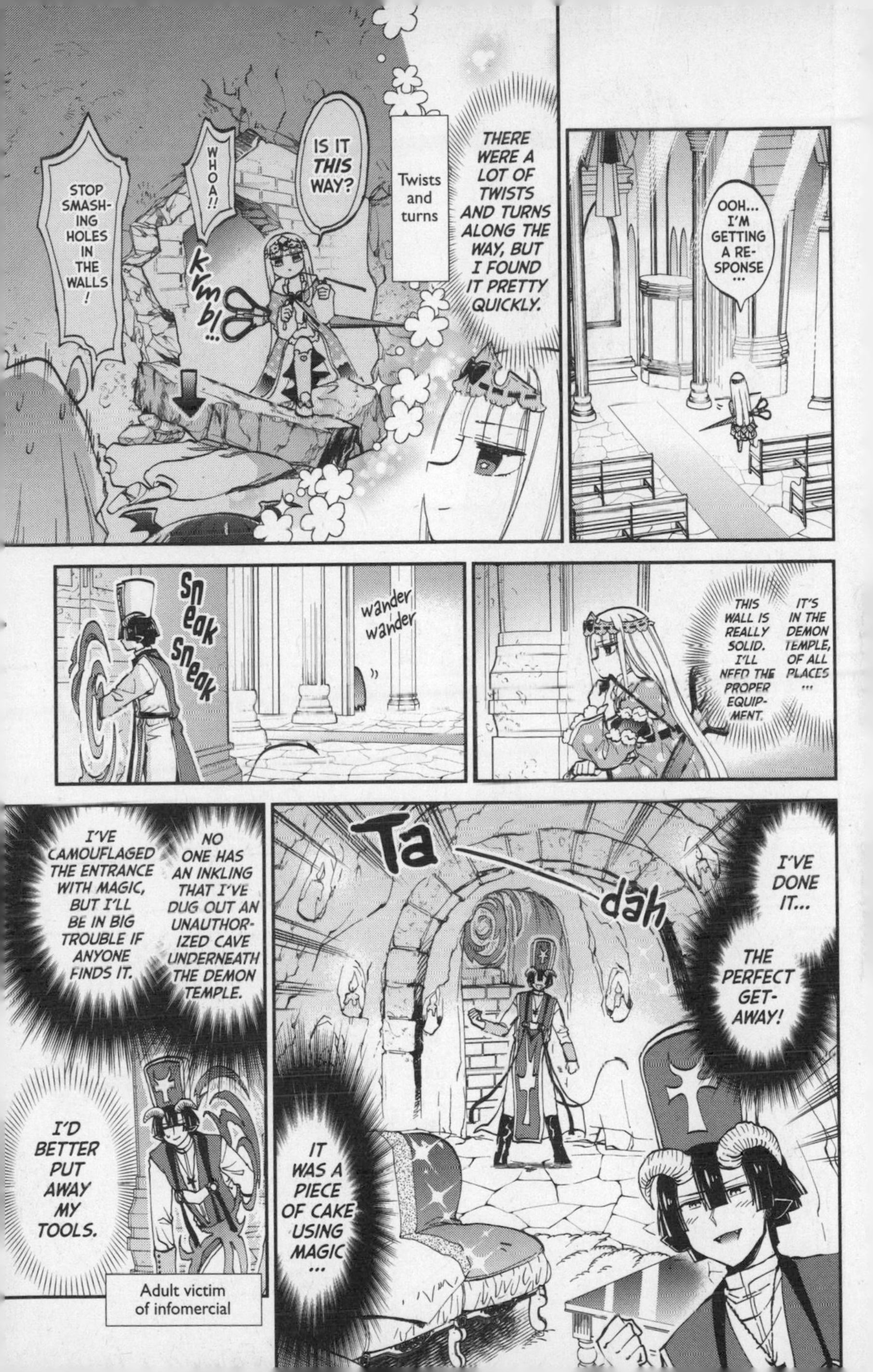
OOH... I'M GETTING A RESPONSE...
THERE WERE A LOT OF TWISTS AND TURNS ALONG THE WAY, BUT I FOUND IT PRETTY QUICKLY.
Twists and turns
IS IT THIS WAY?
WHOA!!
STOP SMASHING HOLES IN THE WALLS!
krmbl...
IT'S IN THE DEMON TEMPLE, OF ALL PLACES...
THIS WALL IS REALLY SOLID. I'LL NEED THE PROPER EQUIPMENT.
wander wander
sneak sneak
Ta dah
I'VE DONE IT...
THE PERFECT GETAWAY!
IT WAS A PIECE OF CAKE USING MAGIC...
NO ONE HAS AN INKLING THAT I'VE DUG OUT AN UNAUTHORIZED CAVE UNDERNEATH THE DEMON TEMPLE.
I'VE CAMOUFLAGED THE ENTRANCE WITH MAGIC, BUT I'LL BE IN BIG TROUBLE IF ANYONE FINDS IT.
I'D BETTER PUT AWAY MY TOOLS.
Adult victim of infomercial

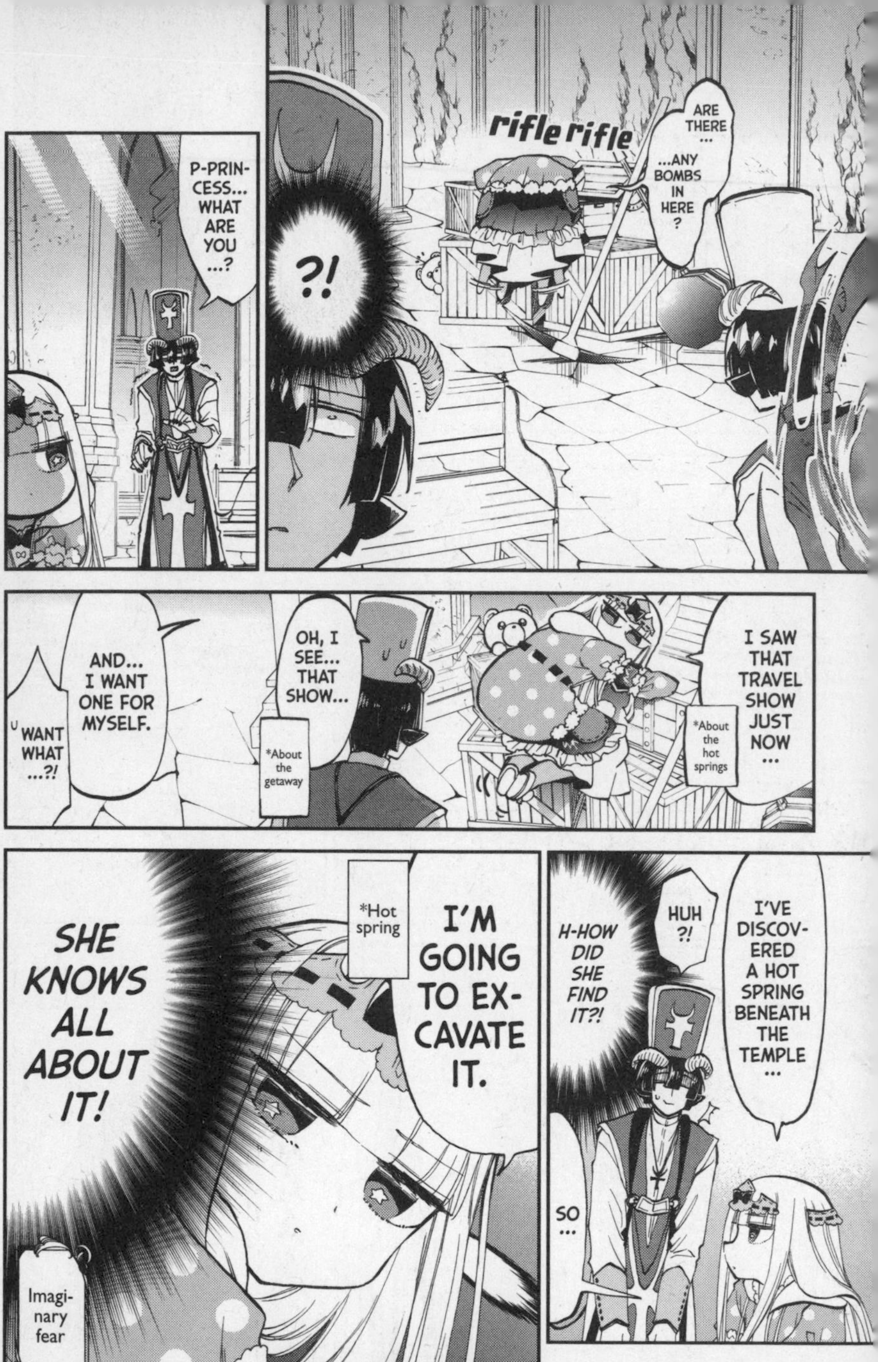
rifle rifle
ARE THERE... ...ANY BOMBS IN HERE?
?!
P-PRINCESS... WHAT ARE YOU...?
I SAW THAT TRAVEL SHOW JUST NOW...
*About the hot springs
OH, I SEE... THAT SHOW...
*About the getaway
AND... I WANT ONE FOR MYSELF.
WANT WHAT...?!
I'VE DISCOVERED A HOT SPRING BENEATH THE TEMPLE...
HUH?!
H-HOW DID SHE FIND IT?!
SO...
I'M GOING TO EXCAVATE IT.
*Hot spring
SHE KNOWS ALL ABOUT IT!
Imaginary fear

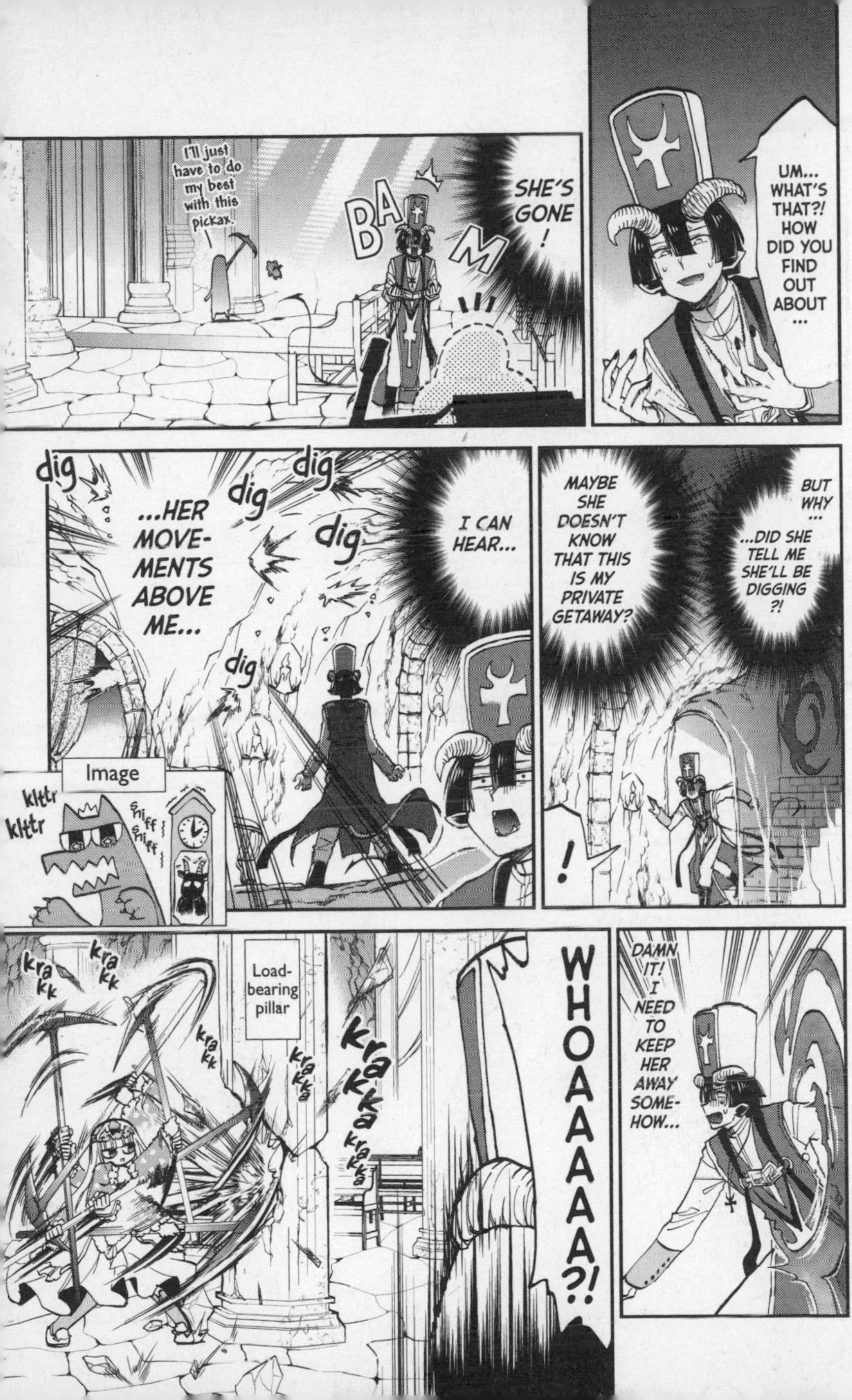
UM... WHAT'S THAT?! HOW DID YOU FIND OUT ABOUT ...
SHE'S GONE!
BAM
I'll just have to do my best with this pickax.
BUT WHY ...
...DID SHE TELL ME SHE'LL BE DIGGING ?!
MAYBE SHE DOESN'T KNOW THAT THIS IS MY PRIVATE GETAWAY?
!
I CAN HEAR...
...HER MOVEMENTS ABOVE ME...
dig
dig
dig
dig
dig
Image
klttr klttr
sniff sniff
DAMN IT! I NEED TO KEEP HER AWAY SOME-HOW...
WHOAAAAAA?!
krakkakakka
krakka
krakk
Load-bearing pillar
krakk
krakk

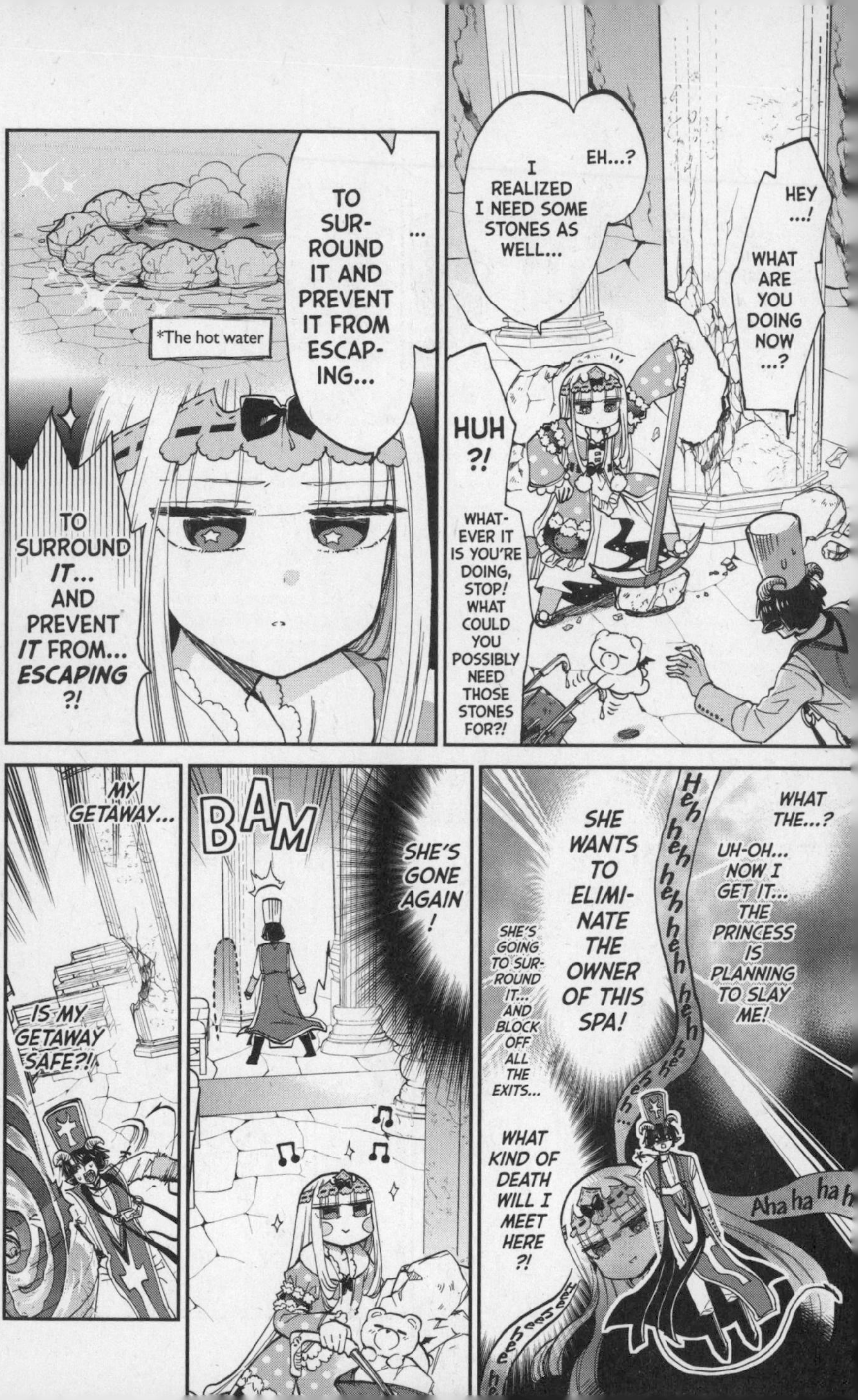
HEY...! WHAT ARE YOU DOING NOW...?
EH...?
I REALIZED I NEED SOME STONES AS WELL...
HUH?!
WHATEVER IT IS YOU'RE DOING, STOP! WHAT COULD YOU POSSIBLY NEED THOSE STONES FOR?!
TO SURROUND IT AND PREVENT IT FROM ESCAPING...
...
*The hot water
TO SURROUND IT... AND PREVENT IT FROM... ESCAPING?!
WHAT THE...?
UH-OH... NOW I GET IT... THE PRINCESS IS PLANNING TO SLAY ME!
SHE WANTS TO ELIMINATE THE OWNER OF THIS SPA!
SHE'S GOING TO SURROUND IT... AND BLOCK OFF ALL THE EXITS...
WHAT KIND OF DEATH WILL I MEET HERE?!
Aha ha ha h
BAM
SHE'S GONE AGAIN!
MY GETAWAY...
IS MY GETAWAY SAFE?!

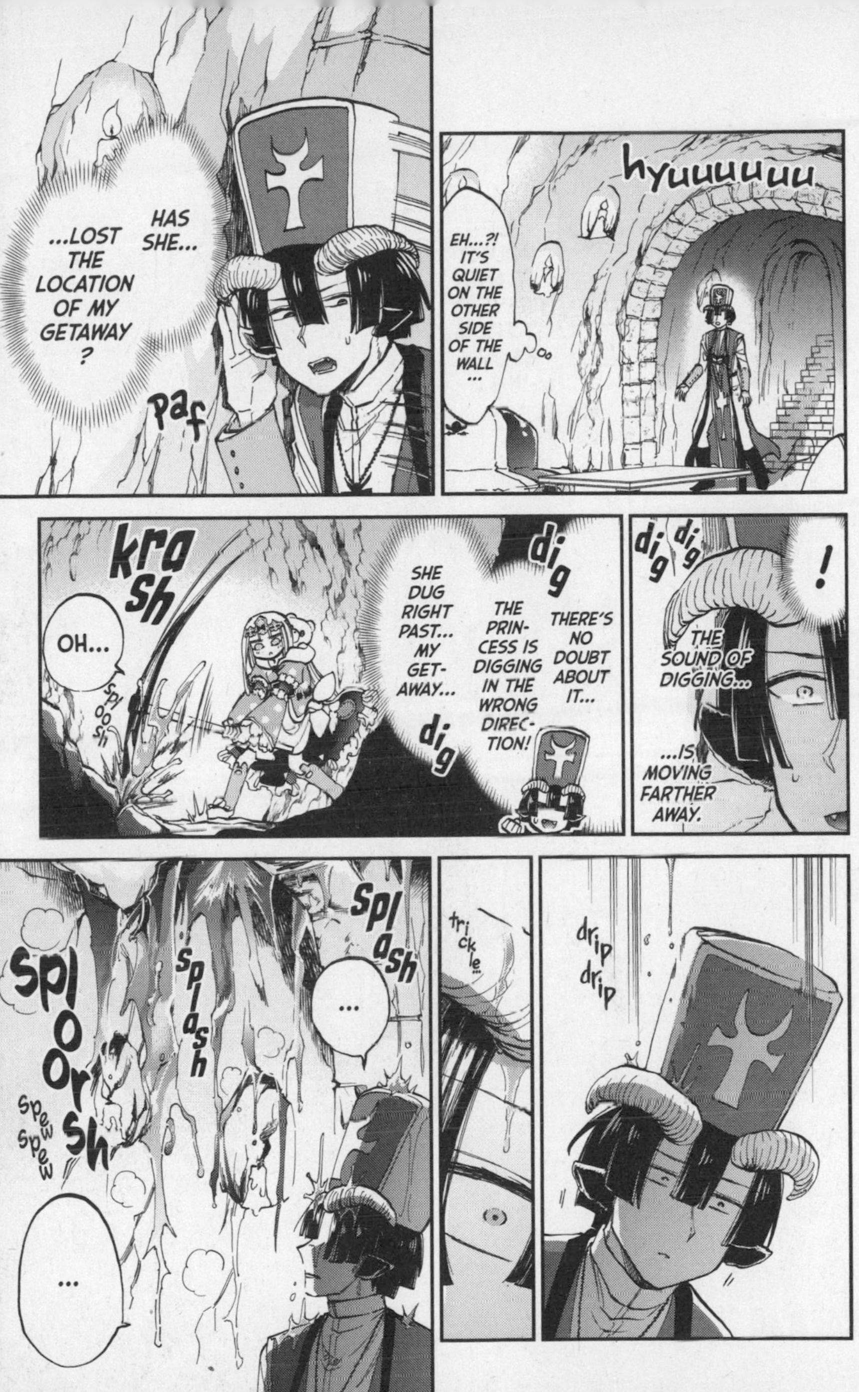
hyuuuuuu
EH...?! IT'S QUIET ON THE OTHER SIDE OF THE WALL...
HAS SHE...
...LOST THE LOCATION OF MY GETAWAY?
paf
dig dig
!
THE SOUND OF DIGGING...
...IS MOVING FARTHER AWAY.
dig
THERE'S NO DOUBT ABOUT IT...
THE PRINCESS IS DIGGING IN THE WRONG DIRECTION!
SHE DUG RIGHT PAST... MY GETAWAY...
dig
krash
OH...
splooosh
drip drip
trickle...
splash
...
splash
sploorsh
spew spew
...

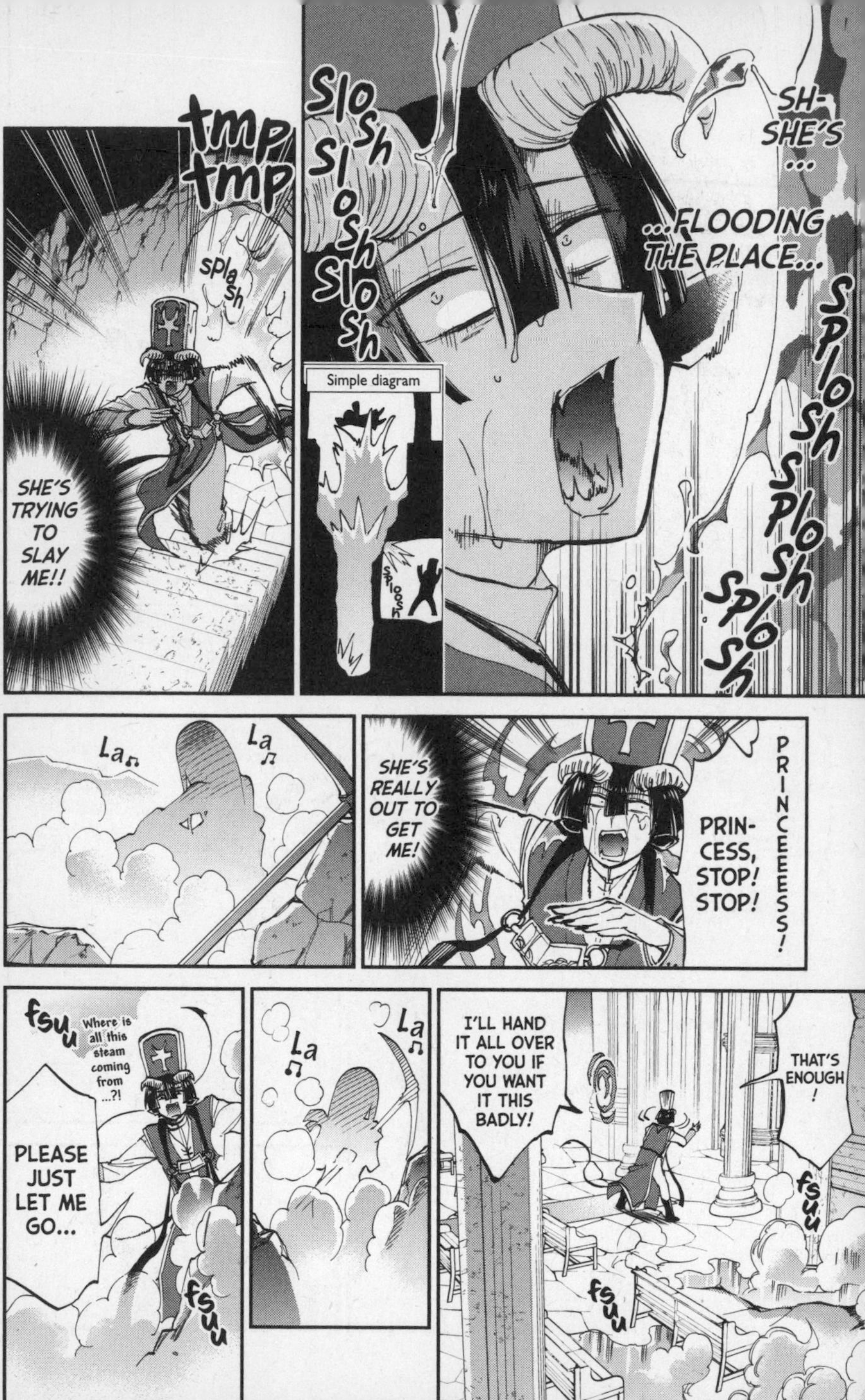
SH-SHE'S ...
...FLOODING THE PLACE...
SPLOSH SPLOSH SPLOSH
slosh slosh slosh
Simple diagram
sploosh
tmp tmp
splash
SHE'S TRYING TO SLAY ME!!
PRINCEEESS!
PRIN-CESS, STOP! STOP!
SHE'S REALLY OUT TO GET ME!
La♫
La♫
THAT'S ENOUGH!
I'LL HAND IT ALL OVER TO YOU IF YOU WANT IT THIS BADLY!
fsuu
fsuu
La♫
La♫
fsuu
Where is all this steam coming from ...?!
PLEASE JUST LET ME GO...
fsuu

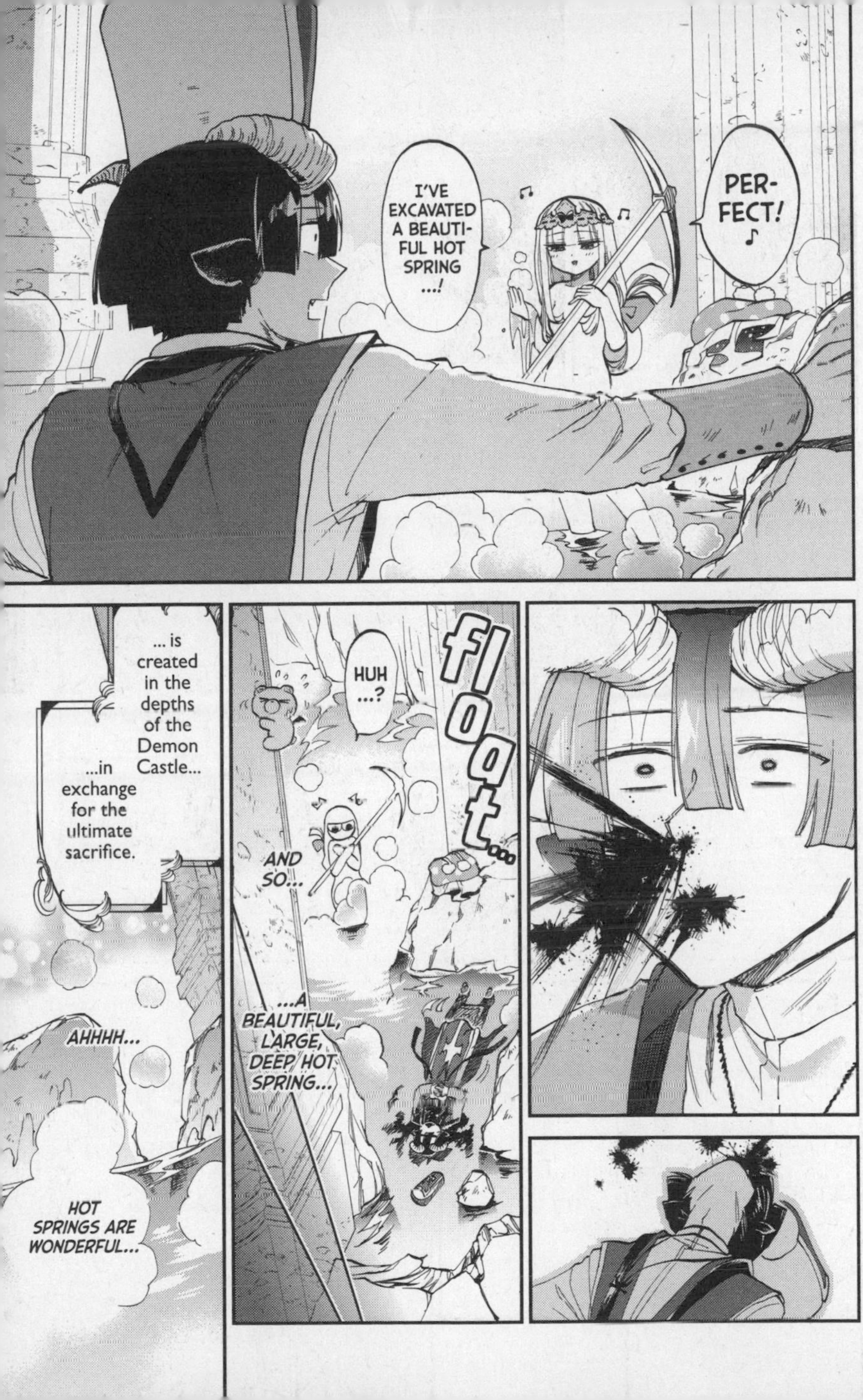
PER-FECT! ♪
I'VE EXCAVATED A BEAUTI-FUL HOT SPRING ...!
float...
HUH ...?
AND SO...
...A BEAUTIFUL, LARGE, DEEP HOT SPRING...
... is created in the depths of the Demon Castle...
...in exchange for the ultimate sacrifice.
AHHHH...
HOT SPRINGS ARE WONDERFUL...

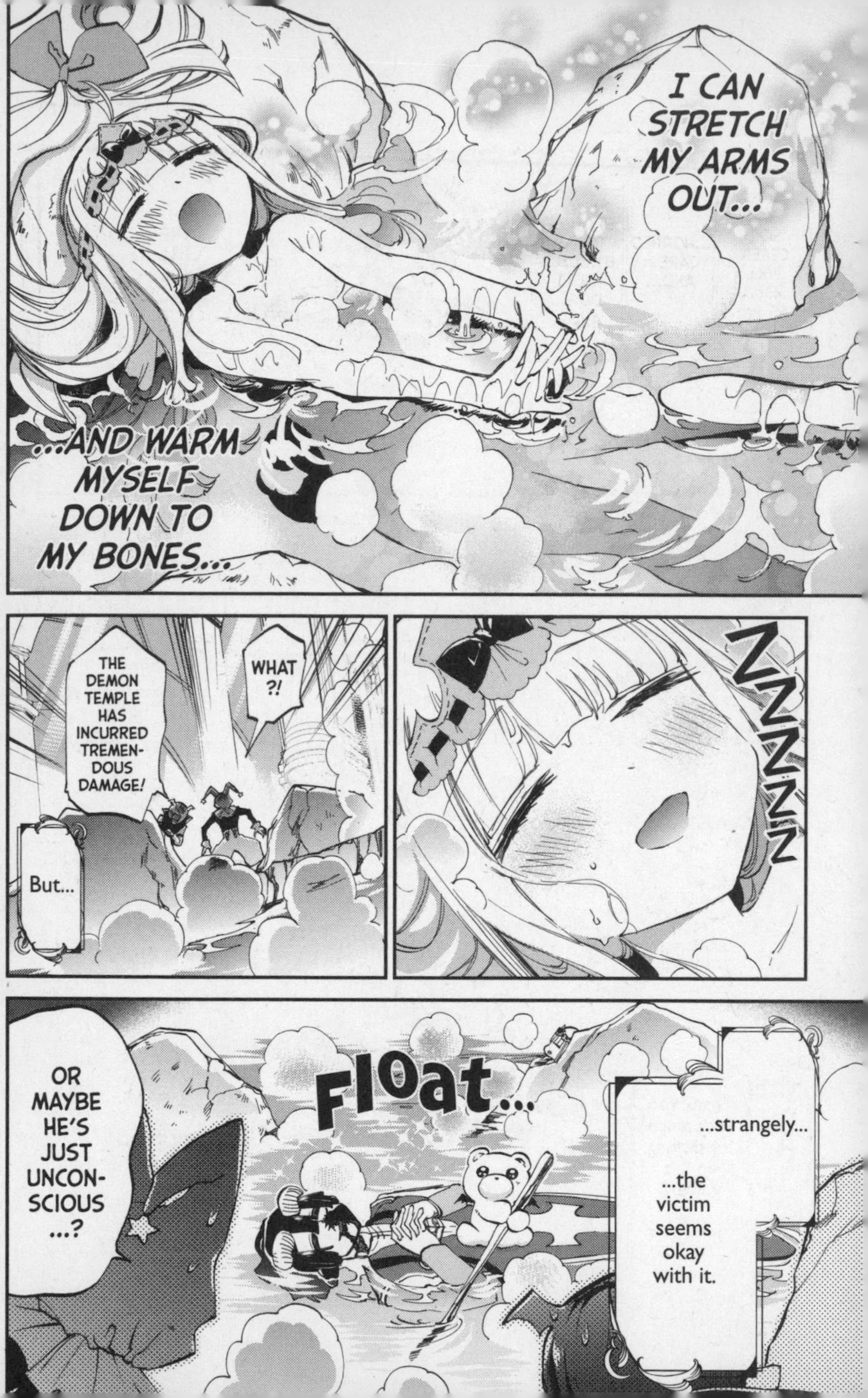
I CAN STRETCH MY ARMS OUT...
...AND WARM MYSELF DOWN TO MY BONES...
ZZZZZ
WHAT?!
THE DEMON TEMPLE HAS INCURRED TREMENDOUS DAMAGE!
But...
...strangely...
...the victim seems okay with it.
Float...
OR MAYBE HE'S JUST UNCONSCIOUS...?

Demon Castle Mini Game

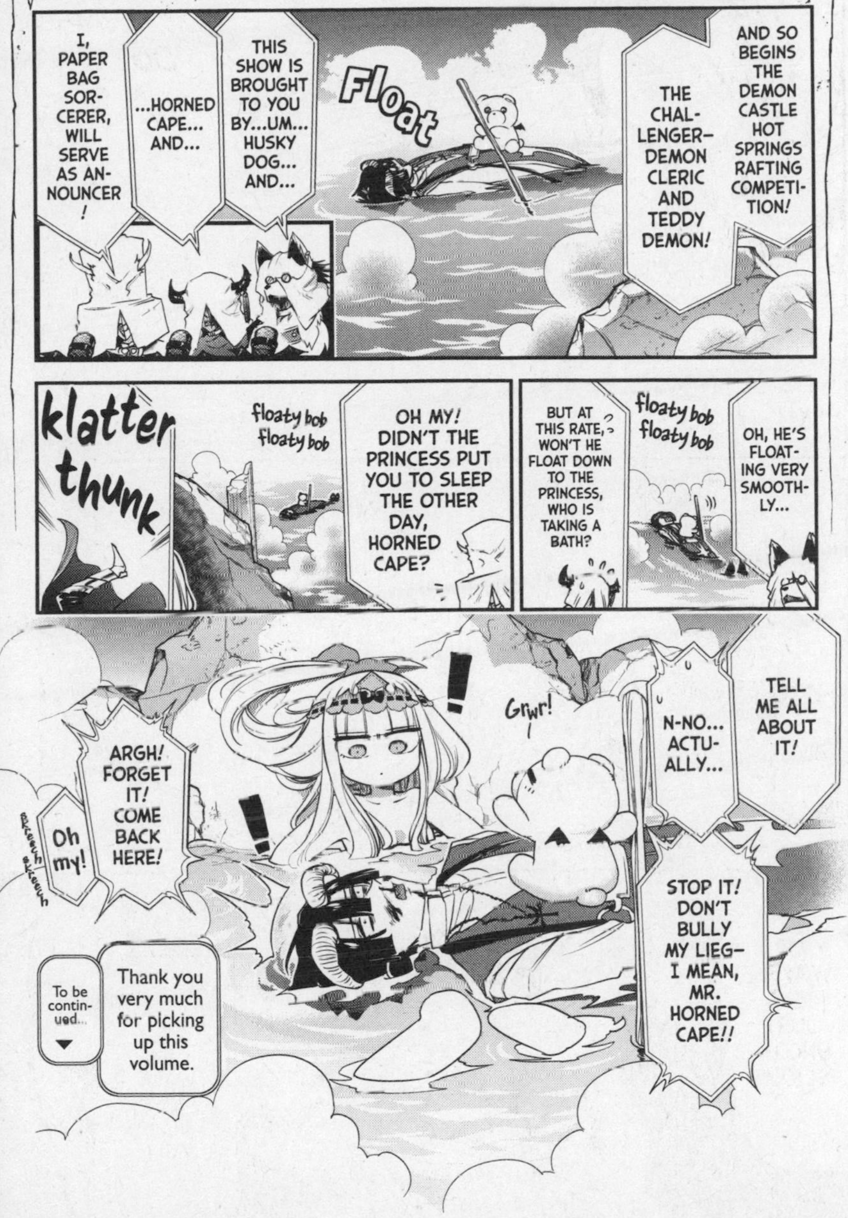

AND SO BEGINS THE DEMON CASTLE HOT SPRINGS RAFTING COMPETITION!
THE CHALLENGER—DEMON CLERIC AND TEDDY DEMON!
Float
THIS SHOW IS BROUGHT TO YOU BY...UM... HUSKY DOG... AND...
...HORNED CAPE... AND...
I, PAPER BAG SORCERER, WILL SERVE AS ANNOUNCER!
OH, HE'S FLOATING VERY SMOOTHLY...
floaty bob floaty bob
BUT AT THIS RATE, WON'T HE FLOAT DOWN TO THE PRINCESS, WHO IS TAKING A BATH?
OH MY! DIDN'T THE PRINCESS PUT YOU TO SLEEP THE OTHER DAY, HORNED CAPE?
floaty bob floaty bob
klatter thunk
TELL ME ALL ABOUT IT!
N-NO... ACTUALLY...
Grwr!
STOP IT! DON'T BULLY MY LIEG— I MEAN, MR. HORNED CAPE!!
ARGH! FORGET IT! COME BACK HERE!
Oh my!
skreech skreech
Thank you very much for picking up this volume.
To be continued...

The fact that the story doesn't end in volume 3 means that there will be a volume 4! Oooh!

— KAGIJI KUMANOMATA

Ko-tatsu
Magical Device of Indolence

MATERIALS

Security Guard Weapon Set
Heat Source Powered by
Volcano Snakeskin
Ghost Shroud

▼

Those who lurk beneath the cover...

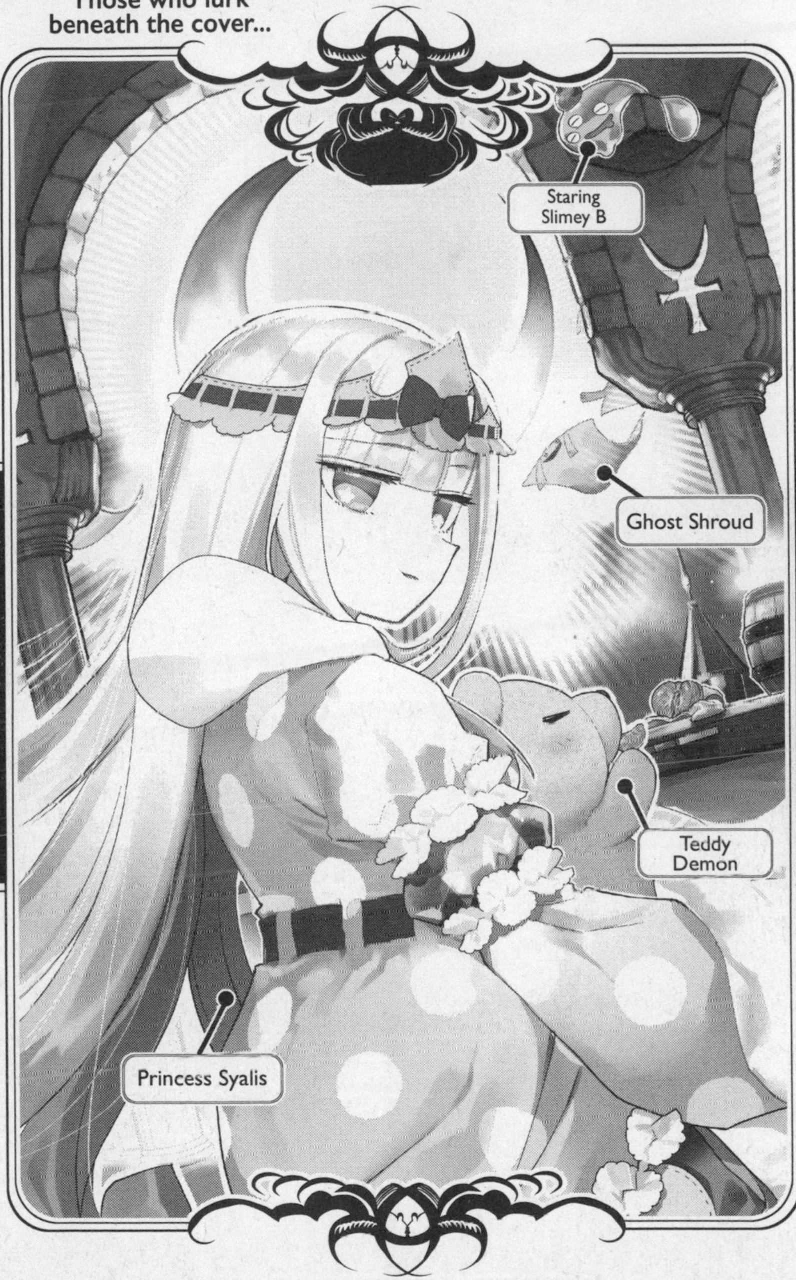
Staring Slimey B
Ghost Shroud
Teddy Demon
Princess Syalis

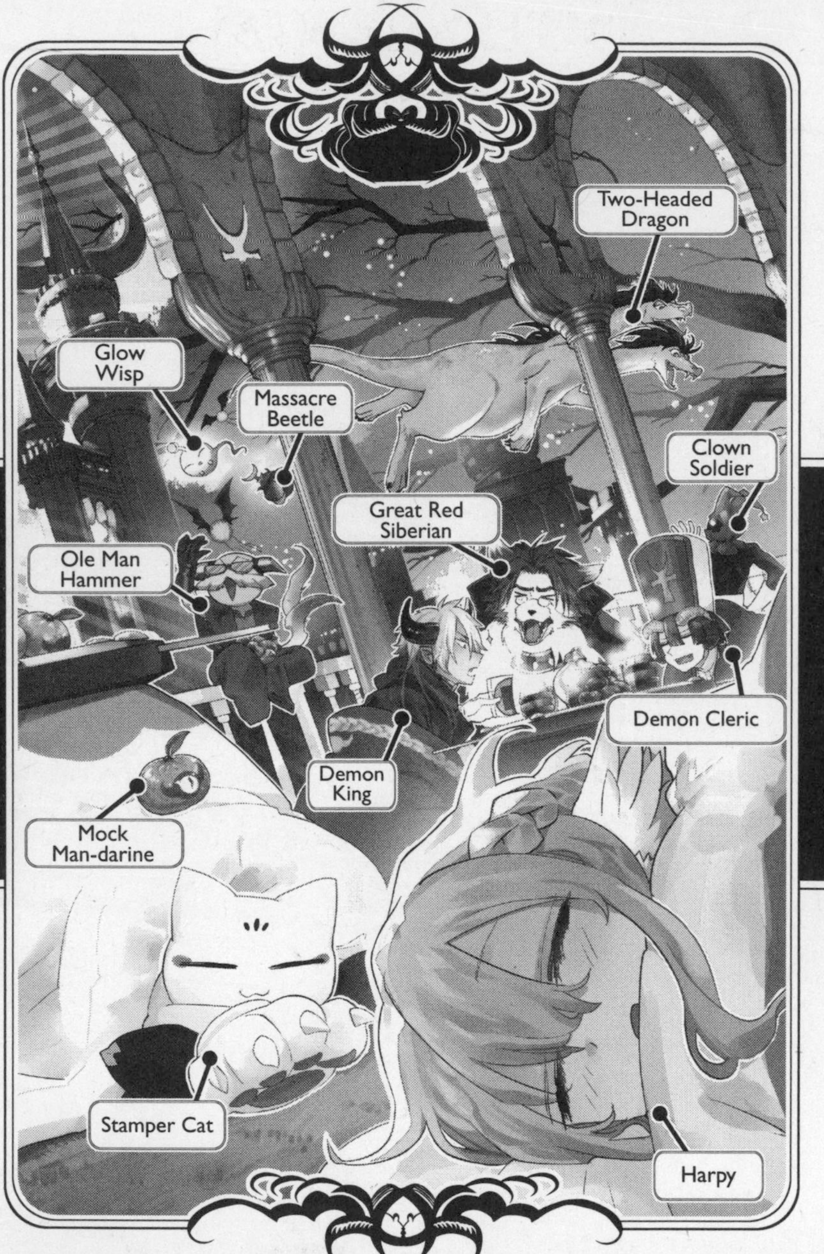
Two-Headed Dragon
Glow Wisp
Massacre Beetle
Clown Soldier
Great Red Siberian
Ole Man Hammer
Demon Cleric
Demon King
Mock Man-darine
Stamper Cat
Harpy

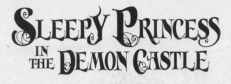

SLEEPY PRINCESS IN THE DEMON CASTLE

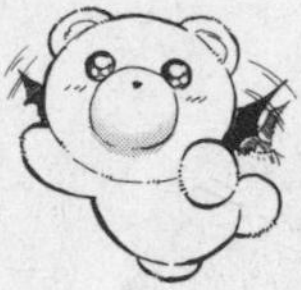

3

Shonen Sunday Edition

STORY AND ART BY

KAGIJI KUMANOMATA

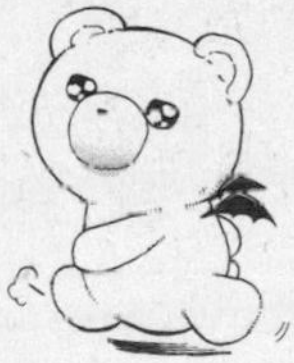

TRANSLATION **TETSUICHIRO MIYAKI**
ENGLISH ADAPTATION **ANNETTE ROMAN**
TOUCH-UP ART & LETTERING **SUSAN DAIGLE-LEACH**
COVER & INTERIOR DESIGN **ALICE LEWIS**
EDITOR **ANNETTE ROMAN**

Printed in Canada

Published by VIZ Media, LLC
P.O. Box 77010
San Francisco, CA 94107

10 9 8 7 6 5 4 3 2 1
First printing, October 2018

ratings.viz.com RATED T TEEN

PARENTAL ADVISORY
SLEEPY PRINCESS IN THE DEMON CASTLE is rated T for Teen and is recommended for ages 13 and up. This volume contains fantasy violence.

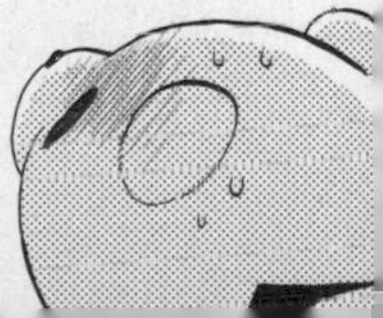

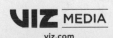

VIZ MEDIA
viz.com

SHONEN SUNDAY
shonensunday.com

VOLUME

4

Valentine's Day arrives, and Princess Syalis is hard put to get the haul of chocolate she's accustomed to receiving back home in her kingdom. Her latest plots to get a better night's rest include learning to hibernate, becoming a ghost and getting an annoying earworm out of her head. Now how can she put a stop to the Teddy Demons summoning her every time they get into a kerfuffle...? *Then*, the princess gets kidnapped from her kidnappers!

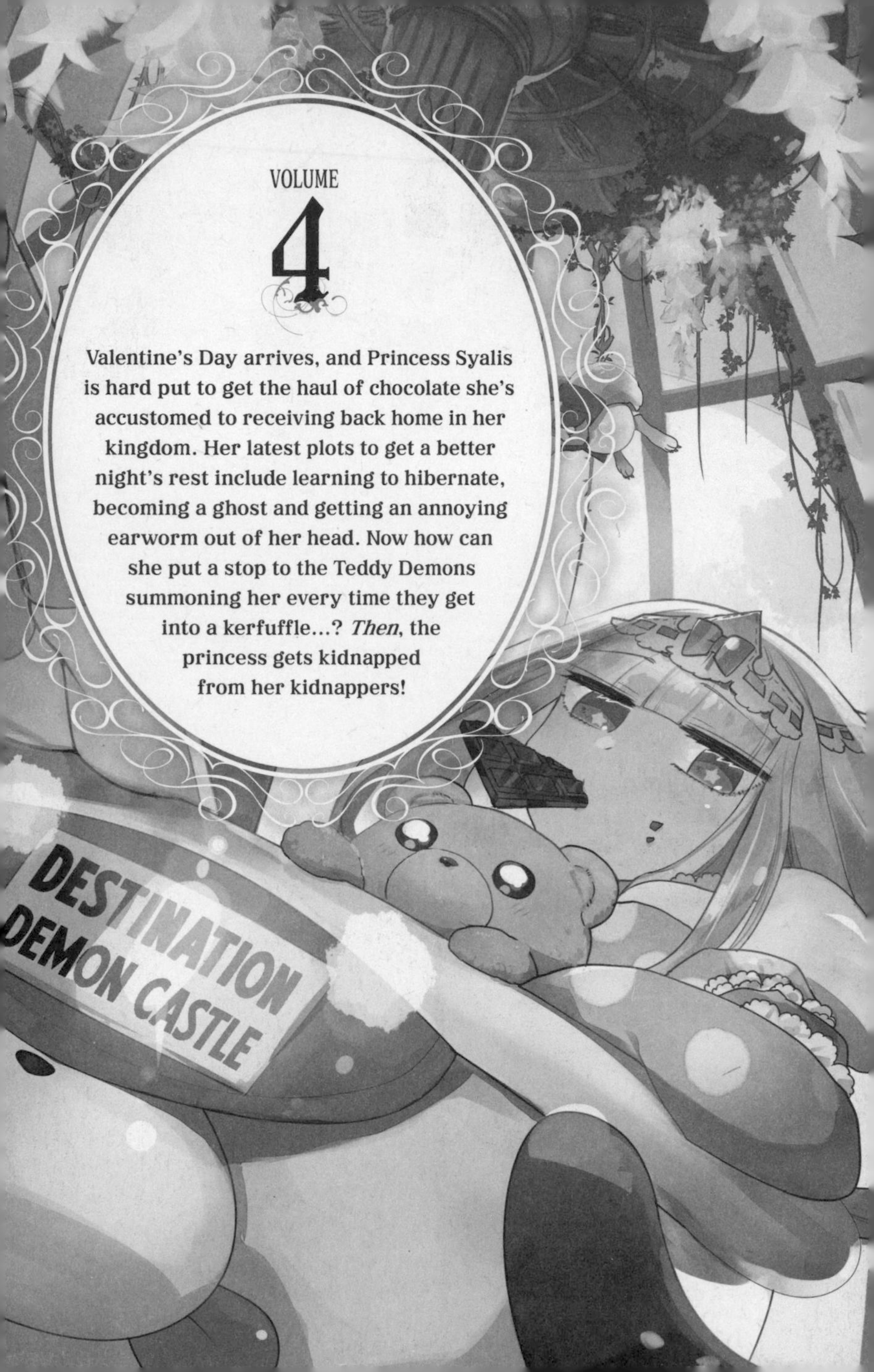

DESTINATION DEMON CASTLE